Heinerman's Encyclopedia of Fruits, Vegetables and Herbs

The Healing Power *of* Fruits, Vegetables *and* Herbs

Dr. John Heinerman

MAGNI

The Magni Group, Inc.
P. O. Box 849
McKinney, Texas 75070
www.magnico.com
info@magnico.com

This book is a reference work based on research by the author. The opinions expressed herein are not necessarily those of or endorsed by the publisher. The directions stated in this book are in no way to be considered as a substitute for consultation with a duly licensed doctor.

ISBN: 978-1-882330-98-0

Printed in the United States of America

Fondly dedicated to
Briant Stringham Stevens
and my father and brother, Jacob and Joseph Heinerman

"Home remedies probably always will have a place in the treatment of mankind's aches and pains. Physicians do not expect, and do not desire, that patients shall dash to the doctor with every minor discomfort, every trifling injury, every small ache or pain. It is sensible to care for such things by simple, safe home means."

—Vincent Askey, M.D., Past President of The American Medical Association (as quoted in Euell Gibbon's *Stalking the Healthful Herbs*).

"An herb in time can save nine."

—John H. Talbot, M.D., Past editor of the *Journal of the American Medical Association* (*JAMA*). His commentary appeared in *JAMA* 188:156 (May 25, 1964).

"The kitchen is the *first* line of defense in dealing with most ailments."

—Michael Tierra, C.A., N.D. (*The Way of Herbs*).

Other Books by the Author

The Science of Herbal Medicine
The Treatment of Cancer with Herbs
The Complete Book of Spices
Herbal Research Manual for Professional Therapeutics
Herbal Dynamics
Aloe Vera, Jojoba and Yucca
Herbal First Aid
Understanding Herbal Medicine and Natural Childbirth
(Co-authored with E. P. Donatelle, M.D.)
Basic Natural Nutrition
(Edited with other co-contributors)
Mormon Corporate Empire
(Co-authored with Anson Shupe, Ph.D.)

Foreword

I think all of us have been exposed to natural remedies at one time or another in our lives. The mustard plaster, the chicken soup, June bug juice for warts and the various cough remedies that your grandmother or auntie put together from some kitchen magic. Back in the '20s and '30s my father, a pediatrician, had a list of remedies for the variety of infections and conditions he was called upon to treat. One of his favorites was the corn starch enema. I can still hear him telling mothers over the phone how to cook up the corn starch . . . "until it clears. Then let it cool, and then let it run in and out of the child." It was to give fluid to the dehydrated, reduce the temperature in the feverish and soothe the lower bowel hit by the intestinal flu. I'm sure it gave the parents something to do, so they felt useful. As the '30s and '40s advanced, he was attracted, really fascinated, with the new pharmaceutical "science."

The promise of medicine—actually of the pharmaceutical industry—was that there would soon be a drug for every disease. The doctor was to be the diagnostic expert; once the condition was named, the remedy was easily found by looking in the index. The detective work was fun, the results were usually predictable and the patients were gratified because they got well so rapidly.

But no one even considered, or remembered to consider, those time-honored, natural, herbal, diet ways of getting well until people began to notice the nasty side effects and uncomfortable allergies from these "miracle" drugs.

A few of the parents of my patients and many of the grandmothers began to ask—really tell—me about some alternate ways of controlling coughs, cuts, sores, eczema, sore throats, minor burns, aches, pains, earaches, insomnia and hyperactivity. I was fascinated and even got some parents to try these things. Especially in the middle of the night when the drugstores were closed. A garlic enema was used for pinworms and equal parts of gin, lemon juice and honey almost always stopped the tickly or barky middle-of-the-night cough.

One day a mother called to say that three days before, while she was cooking hamburgers, two identical drops of grease flew out of the pan and landed on her forearm. As she had some sliced, raw onions nearby, she quickly grabbed a section and held the raw side to just one of the painful, throbbing, red spots on her skin. She was going to do the controlled experiment. She held it there for a while until the pain subsided and then bandaged it on for a few hours. The untreated one remained painful and blistered in the usual fashion; it finally healed in a week. The onion-treated one was just a spot of brown, wrinkled skin in two days. It works.

Of course, you say, these are interesting anecdotes, but you would prefer a few double-blind, cross-over studies. Well, here is the book that will help show that good food and herbs *are* what they are cracked up to be.

John Heinerman has brought together case histories, his own extensive research from years of combined study and travel and a complete literature review. Many pharmaceutical companies in an effort to find "safe" drugs have looked to the plants, herbs and seeds. They have extracted the essence from these plants and have come up with something they could patent, but they did not realize that these various elements in the plants work in concert. The reason for the therapeutic response is in these combinations of elements in the plants, herbs and seeds. The drug companies have been frustrated as these natural teas, syrups and powders cannot be patented—no patent, no income.

All the research has found is that we animals are bags of water with vitamins, minerals, enzymes, hormones, proteins, fats and sugar floating about therein. Over the centuries of experimenting, humans have found which of nature's flora (and some fauna) do *what.* Now with sophisticated biochemical analysis we are able to understand the *why.* Tests can determine what vitamins and minerals and oils are in the plants and in what proportions. Sure, we know about carrots and vitamin A and night blindness. Yes, we know about the calming effect of calcium and magnesium-bearing foods. Okay, so magnesium will help insomnia (magnesium is necessary to build chlorophyll, the green in plants), and relieve jumpiness, control muscle cramps, reduce craving for chocolate and raise one's threshold to noise. When an herb has been found to do these things, then we know it, at least, has magnesium in it. But just taking magnesium may not be enough. It is as if nature knew what other elements were necessary to be incorporated in the plant to make it tastier or more absorbable. There are reasons for everything.

That is the beauty of this latest of Heinerman's output. You can easily look up what your symptoms are, find the remedy (ies) and why it works. There is a lot of "Aha, so that's why," in this book.

If something does not work for you, you might have made the wrong diagnosis. But you may have fixed the remedy with the wrong proportions, or you got your supplies from the wrong supplier. But if you have appendicitis and think your own herbal therapy is going to keep you from the surgeon's knife, you have a fool for a doctor. Don't throw out all of modern medicine. We need the best of East and West and the best of the old and the new.

Thank you, John Heinerman, for opening up a whole new world of health to us, the uninitiated and naive.

Lendon H. Smith, M.D.

A Word from the Author

Some prominent medical doctors that I know of are of the opinion that taking care of your own health problems may, in the long run, be a lot better for you than to use the services offered by modern medicine.

One such physician, who practiced medicine in Chicago for over 25 years, was Chairman of the Medical Licensing Committee for the State of Illinois for nearly six years, and was Associate Professor of Preventative Medicine and Community Health in the School of Medicine at the University of Illinois, is Robert S. Mendelsohn, M.D.

Dr. Mendelsohn wrote a controversial bestseller entitled *Confessions of a Medical Heretic*. In his book, which surprisingly enough was read by many of his medical doctor friends throughout the country with many of them privately agreeing with his sentiments, Dr. Mendelsohn expressed some pretty strong views against the practice of medicine as we now know it to be.

> I no longer believe in Modern Medicine. The greatest danger to your health is the doctor who practices Modern Medicine. I believe that Modern Medicine's treatments for disease are seldom effective, and that they're often more dangerous than the diseases they're designed to treat.
>
> You can liberate yourself from Modern Medicine—and it doesn't mean you'll have to take chances with your health. In fact, you'll be taking less of a chance with your health, because there's no more dangerous activity than walking into a doctor's office, clinic or hospital!

But if the reader should think that Dr. Mendelsohn's comments are a mite too harsh and an exception to the rule, then consider the loudly voiced opinions of other medical doctors who are encouraging their patients to seek more help from home remedies and alternative care therapies instead.

A growing number of physicians who write health-oriented books are suggesting to their readers and patients to go outside the realm of modern medicine to get safer and less expensive remedies for their individual health problems. Nowhere is this more evident than with my friend,

Lendon Smith, M.D. Lendon has practiced pediatrics for well over 30 years and recently retired from his position as Clinical Professor of Pediatrics at the University of Oregon Medical School in Portland. In his bestseller, *Feed Yourself Right,* Lendon tells Americans that they should be looking in other places for solutions to their health problems, besides just modern medicine.

> You might also want to search elsewhere. A health professional with a degree other than the M.D. may be worthwhile. A chiropractor usually can find something out of place and get it back in place. A clergyman may help with guilt. A naturopath could discover a food/nutrition/biochemical malfunction and suggest nutritional approaches that may help the body correct itself. You *do* have some choices. (Italics added for emphasis.)

Further along Lendon recommends certain vegetables and spices for particular health problems such as high blood pressure. Among those he cites are garlic and onions, two remedies suggested in this book for hypertension as well. Thus you, the reader, can see by now that the very concept of this book, if not some of its actual remedies, have been publicly endorsed by a growing number of medical doctors.

More and more M.D.s across the country are recommending that their patients try other methods of health care and seek professional help from those who are not necessarily licensed, practicing physicians. This is where the value of such a book as this comes in handy. You are provided with fairly reliable remedies that are safe and relatively inexpensive, which can be used in the privacy and convenience of your own home with a minimal amount of knowledge and instruction.

For legal purposes, however, I must say that all of the remedies mentioned herein are based on my own intensive research among many different cultures and years of experience in working with folk healers worldwide. Hence, I alone am responsible for their selection and recommendation, *and not my publisher.* Thus, having absolved my publisher of all responsibility connected with their uses and effectiveness, I kindly commend you for having the courage and the determination to take health matters more into your own hands. Hopefully this work will be of some valuable assistance to you in achieving better care over your single most important possession in life, namely your own body! With you *solely* in charge, there's bound to be improvements of some kind in overall health care.

John Heinerman

Table of Symptoms Contents

Heinerman's Encyclopedia of Fruits, Vegetables and Herbs

A

ALFALFA (*Medicago sativa*)

Brief Description

Alfalfa is a perennial herb commonly found on the edges of fields, in low valleys and is widely cultivated by farmers for livestock feed. An erect, smooth stem grows from an elongated taproot to a height of a foot or more. Flowers are blue-to-purple during the summer months, finally producing the characteristic spirally coiled seed pods.

Alfalfa or lucerne was used by the Persians to feed their horses to make them look sleeker and feel stronger. The Arabs designated this common hay feed for livestock, "The Father of All Foods." Some modern herbalists have gone even further than this, characterizing alfalfa as being "the Big Daddy of 'em all" in terms of nutritional value, considering that the plant is so rich in calcium that the ashes of its leaves are almost 99% pure calcium.

Prevents Hardening of the Arteries

This has been a discovery of late by scientists rather than traditional herbalists, surprisingly enough. Clinical nutritionists have clearly demonstrated that alfalfa meal, when fed to caged monkeys whose diets included high levels of cholesterol helped to prevent them from getting atherosclerosis and also reduced the serum cholesterol levels.

Based on such medical findings, it's therefore strongly recommended that you take 2 capsules of good quality alfalfa powder with every meal when too much cholesterol might be a problem. Your local health food store carries alfalfa under the Nature's Way label or similar quality brand.

An Infection Fighter

A medical doctor, Henry G. Bieler, who for years treated many of the great film stars of Hollywood, recounted an episode with alfalfa in his bestseller, *Food Is Your Best Medicine.*

It seems while he was practicing in the rural areas of Idaho many years ago, he travelled a great distance to visit a farmer who was suffering from a very bad leg ulcer. The open sore was discharging pus just above the ankle and the entire limb appeared to be dangerously close to having gangrene set in.

Dr. Bieler inquired of the farmer and his wife if they had any alkaline vegetables around the house, but unfortunately none were available. The only plant available that he could think of was alfalfa, of which they had plenty on hand.

He persuaded the astonished wife to pick the tender young alfalfa shoots, chop them up very fine and combine them with equal parts of water and canned grapefruit juice.

The patient was also given canned vegetables, whole grain bread and raw milk in the correct amounts. Eventually, the leg condition completely healed up with the farmer strictly adhering to this dietary regimen.

The rich chlorophyll content found in alfalfa, and other green plants like it, was used by some doctors in major hospitals in the 1940s for treating infections resulting from surgical incisions, bed sores and inner ear problems. In such cases, capsules of Nature's Way Alfa-Max from your local health food store may be of great benefit. Better still, though, would be fresh juice made from raw alfalfa sprouts whipped up in a blender or else run through a juicer. About 4–6 oz. of the juice taken at one time and also applied externally on any surface infection will be of considerable help.

Making Your Own Sprouts

To make your own sprouts, soak a teaspoon of alfalfa seeds in a quart of tepid water overnight. Next morning, rinse the seeds thoroughly with tepid water and drain. Place them in a jar tightly covered with damp cheesecloth. Store in a dark place. Twice a day, rinse the sprouting seeds and drain them well, returning them to the dark after each rinse. After 4–5 days, place the sprouts in the sunlight for a few hours to green them, then store in the refrigerator. Use alfalfa sprouts instead of lettuce, since they are far more nutritious.

Control Aid in Diabetes

According to an August, 1984 report in the *Journal of Nutrition,* scientists at the University of California at Davis found that alfalfa extracts with a lot of manganese definitely improved the condition of a diabetic who failed to respond to insulin. It is thought that 2 capsules twice or three times daily might be worth trying in instances such as this.

Highly Nutritional

Powdered alfalfa contains vitamins A, B-1, B-6, B-12, C, E and K-1, niacin, pantothenic acid, biotin, folic acid, etc., as well as many essential and nonessential amino acids. Additionally, it contains 15–25% proteins, major minerals and trace elements like calcium, phosphorus, manganese, iron, zinc and copper, together with many naturally occurring sugars (sucrose, fructose, etc.).

% Recommended Daily Allowances

Nutrient	*Alfalfa* (*1 oz.*)	*Parsley* (*1 oz.*)	*Kelp* (*.1 oz.*)	*Molasses* (3 tbs.)	*Milk Powder* (*1 oz.*)
Protein	10%	10%	0%	0%	14%
Calcium	75%	43%	5%	51%	38%
Iodine	0%	0%	3300%	0%	0%
Iron	85%	100%	0%	96%	2%
Magnesium	45%	20%	7%	45%	9%
Phosphorus	14%	13%	1%	6%	29%
Potassium	25%	41%	5%	59%	13%
Sodium	0%	3%	4%	2%	4%

(*Bestways*, 11/81)

ALOE (*Aloe vera*)

Brief Description

Aloe is a perennial succulent native to East and South Africa, but also cultivated in the West Indies and other tropical countries. The strong, fibrous root produces a rosette of fleshy basal leaves. The tissue in the center of the leaf contains a mucilaginous gel which yields aloe gel or aloe vera gel. When Columbus set sail for America, he wrote in his diary, "All is well, aloe is on board!" Aloe was the material used to embalm Pharaoh Ramses II and to preserve the body of Jesus Christ.

Aloe Gel Gets Rid of Warts

A lady from Lubbock, Texas had a wart on her arm the size of a pencil eraser. Each morning she soaked a small piece of cotton in aloe gel and taped it over the wart. Every 3 hours more gel was added with an eyedropper. Next day, fresh cotton was used and the process repeated. By the fourth day, the wart was beginning to dry up. Two weeks later when the cotton was removed, what remained of the wart came off clean. There was no scar to ever indicate a wart had once been there.

The Medicine Doctors Rave About

Probably no other single herb in modern times has been so well spoken of in regard to its many marvelous healing virtues by members of the medical and dental professions as has been that of aloe vera.

Modern doctors have used aloe successfully for X-ray burns, sunburn, chemical burns, first degree burns, traumatized tissue (after normal and regular cleansing), decubitus ulcers or bedsores, primary candidal dermatitis (skin inflammation caused by infection of the yeast *Candida albicans*), stomal ulcers (intestinal ulcers between the stomach and that portion of the small intestine called the jejunum), herpes simplex, periodontal surgery, insect bites and stings, irritating plant stings (such as from stinging nettle) and other minor dermatological (skin) manifestations.

An oral surgeon from Dallas, Texas reported amazing results in treating facial edema (swelling), immediate denture placement, lockjaw (mouth rinse) and cold sores (mouth rinse).

How to Use Aloe

Aloe vera comes in various forms: the natural gel; prepared ointment, salve or lotion; liquid drink concentrate and encapsulated powder. For a number of minor burns, swellings and inflammations (both internal and external), some of the natural gel from a broken or cut leaf rubbed on or in these afflicted areas will promote rapid healing. For larger inflammations (sunburn), more severe burns (chemical) or sores (herpes), a good ointment, salve or lotion with a high concentration of purified aloe gel may be the best thing to use. In these instances, a simple dressing may be called for. One of the more reliable aloe ointments for heavy duty use may be obtained from AVA of Dallas, Texas (see Appendix).

Internal use falls into several categories. Oral problems can be solved with the natural gel from a broken or cut leaf. For laxative purposes,

Nature's Way capsulated aloe vera, found in your local health food store, is good to use. And for all other internal uses, the most healing aloe liquid I know of is an aloe juice concentrate mix (1 oz. = 1 qt.; 4 oz. = 1 gal.) available only by mail-order from Great American in St. Petersburg, Florida (see Appendix).

Nutritional Properties

Aloe vera contains 96% water, which provides water to injured tissue without closing off the air necessary for tissue repair. "The remaining 4% of the pulp," states *Runner's World* magazine for Dec. 1981, "contains complex carbohydrate molecules, believed essential to aloe's natural value as a moisturizer. Substances present include . . . enzymes, trace sugars, a protein containing 18 amino acids; vitamins; minerals like sulphur, silicon, iron, calcium, copper, sodium, potassium, manganese and more. The mixture of active ingredients in aloe is called aloin, and is obtained from the gel in the leaf. It's responsible for the plant's healing properties."

AMARANTH (*Amaranthus hypochondriacus, A. cruentus*)

Brief Description

Not a true cereal, but rather a fruit, it belongs to the same family (chenopodium) as the edible weed, lamb's-quarter. Looking like a sesame seed, it has a pleasant, nutty flavor and can be popped like corn or steamed and flattened into a flake. It requires very little water and fertilizer, growing almost anywhere the common weeds do. It is thought that amaranth was brought to this hemishpere by those first migrants from the Tower of Babel, who travelled eastward across China and launched their barges on the Pacific, eventually reaching what is now western Mexico around 2000 B.C.

Food of the Future

Amaranth seed has been described as the "perfect protein food of the past for meals of the future," by *U.S. News & World Report* for Nov. 25, 1985. Robert Rodale, publisher of *Prevention* and *Organic Gardening* magazines, first reintroduced amaranth to this country in the early 1970s after the U.S. Dept. of Agriculture showed a lack of interest in it. Right now, though, it's only available from one or two specialty companies, such as Nu-World Amaranth, Inc. of Napersville, Illinois (see Appendix), but is expected to be in supermarkets by 1990.

Diarrhea and Bleeding

Amaranth seed and leaves have been used effectively as an astringent for stopping diarrhea, bloody stools and urine, and excessive menstruation. It also makes a good wash for skin problems ranging from acne and eczema to psoriasis and hives. It's an excellent douche for vaginal discharges of purulent matter, a nice gargle for sore mouths, gums, teeth and throats, and a fantastic enema for colon inflammations and rectal sores.

To make an amaranth tea for all these purposes, simply bring 3 cups of water to a rolling boil. Then add 2 tsp. of seeds, cover and simmer on a very low heat for about 5 minutes. Remove from heat and add 1 tsp. of leaves (if available) or else just let steep for 30 minutes. Drink 2 cups daily for internal problems.

ANGELICA (*Angelica archangelica*)

Brief Description

This stout biennial or perennial herb prefers cold and moist places, and is, therefore, quite common to countries such as Great Britain, Scotland, Lapland and Iceland. In the folklore of all North European countries, it's held in the highest esteem as "a protection against contagion, for purifying the blood and for curing every conceivable malady possible."

According to legends, angelica was revealed in a dream by an angel to cure the deadly bubonic plague.

China's Famous "Women's Remedy"

In China, angelica has been used for several thousand years to treat many kinds of female problems. The 10 different angelica species, collectively known by the name of dang-qui (also dong-quei or dong-quai or tang-kuei), are second in China only to ginseng.

Richard Lucas, in his book, *Secrets of the Chinese Herbalists,* described angelica as having "an affinity for the female constitution," being good for treating anemia and weak glands, regulating monthly periods, correcting hot flashes and vaginal spasms (common premenstrual symptoms) and assisting women through the difficult transition of menopause.

Lucas recommended 2 capsules of dong-quai twice or three times daily for severe female problems, with less than this for more moderate conditions. He also mentioned that "since its taste somewhat resembles that of celery, the capsules may be broken open and the contents added to hot soups or broth" without detracting from their flavor.

It has been reported that angelica helped relieve PMS (Premenstrual Syndrome) and was used successfully instead of estrogen.

A middle-aged woman from San Rafael, California wrote to me a couple of years ago concerning the remarkable transition to menopause she was able to make with this herb.

> During most of my adult life I've never been bothered with the usual PMS (Premenstrual Syndrome) problems that other women generally suffer from. So when I entered menopause I thought it would be a snap! Boy, was I ever wrong!
>
> All my internal female organs ached like the devil. I couldn't sleep decently, because I'd wake up in the middle of the night with terrific cramps.
>
> A friend referred me to a Chinese herbalist she knew in downtown San Francisco. Because of the difficulty of my case, he suggested I take 2 capsules 3 times a day until all my spasms stopped and my organs no longer hurt. Then keep on taking only 1 capsule twice a day throughout the menopause phase until it was finished.
>
> The dong-quai worked like a charm and my miserable feelings disappeared in a little over a week.

Contains Coumarins

The rootstock of this herb has a sweet, spicy, agreeable odor to it. This is due mostly to the rich presence of many coumarins—white crystalline compounds with a vanilla-like odor to them. These coumarins are valuable in reducing high-protein edemas, especially swelling of the lymph nodes (lymphedema), as well as in treating the psoriasis often accompanying arthritis. The constituent bergapten accounts for its antipsoriac properties, while other compounds such as linalool and borneol help to explain its antibacterial and antifungal activities. Other constituents include resin, starch and a number of naturally occurring sugars like sucrose, fructose and glucose.

ANISE (*Pimpinella anisum*)

Brief Description

Anise has been popular in the ancient Chinese and Ayurvedic (Indian) medical systems for many centuries. There are several varieties of aniseed, the most common of all being the ash-colored kind from Spain. Anise belongs to the same botanical family (*Umbelliferae*) as parsley and carrots.

A Multi-Purpose Healing Tea

Imagine having a tea that will get rid of oily skin, improve your memory, calm a nagging cough, produce breast milk for nursing mothers and serve as a natural antacid in place of either Tums or Rolaids for heartburn and indigestion.

Well, all of these wonderful things can be accomplished simply by bringing 1 quart of water to a boil. Then add about 7 tsp. of aniseed, reduce heat to a lower setting and simmer contents down to 1-1/2 pints. Then strain, and while still warm, add 4 tsp. each of honey and glycerine (obtained from a drugstore to preserve syrup tea).

Take 2 tsp. of this syrup every few hours to relieve hacking coughs, or 2 tbsps. three times daily to strengthen the memory. If using as a tea, omit and drink 2 cups once or twice daily for skin problems, milk needs or to relieve stomach problems.

APPLE (*Pyrus malus*)

Brief Description

The wild apple or crab apple grows throughout Europe and as far as Central Asia, where it seems to have originated. The people of Asia Minor took no notice of it for a long time, but the Greeks had already cultivated it. In Rome at the time of the Emperor Augustus there were no less than 30 different varieties recorded. Today there are more than 1,400 varieties of apples worldwide. Although tradition holds that the forbidden fruit in the Garden of Eden was supposed to have been the apple, apocryphal literature strongly suggests that it was the grape instead.

An Apple a Day Keeps the Doctor Away

This very old rhyme had become a polite way universally of explaining that apples are an ideal preventative of both constipation *and* diarrhea. The July, 1978 number of *The American Journal of Clinical Nutrition* reported that apples helped to decrease the time it took to have a bowel movement, by increasing the stool weight, which in turn increased the number of trips to the bathroom during a 24-hour period.

In her book on herbs, Mary Quelch recommends "a baked apple at night to be followed by another at breakfast [as] one of the most efficacious remedies" known for constipation. So the next time you begin to reach for the Ex-Lax, think instead in terms of munching a Rome Beauty, Delicious, Jonathan or Winesap.

Conversely, apples are also very good for treating acute diarrhea or "Montezuma's Revenge," the bane of so many tourists traveling to foreign countries where cleanliness is definitely a low priority item. Take one ripe apple and grate it, allowing the pulp to stand at room temperature for several hours until considerably darkened before eating. The oxidized pectin present in the fruit is the same basic ingredient in Upjohn Pharmaceutical's Kaopectate brand diarrheal medicine.

An Infection Fighter

You probably never imagined that an apple could possess some penicillin-like properties. Well, Canadian scientists in the Dec. 1978 *Applied & Environmental Microbiology* demonstrated that fresh apple juice or fresh apple sauce can knock the heck out of stomach flu and polio viruses.

And how about those nasty little germs that can cause tooth decay? Two British doctors gave a group of kids a thin slice or two of raw apple after each meal or snack and discovered in a while that they had a substantial decrease in cavities as a result.

Cider Vinegar Eliminates Gallstones

A woman from Napanee, Indiana who had been bothered with gallstones for a number of years went to a clinic for a total physical. The X-rays showed a lot of stones of varying sizes. A naturopathic physician advised her to drink nothing but apple cider vinegar for four days straight, in 1/2 cup amounts five times a day. And on the second, third, and fourth days, she drank equal parts (1 /4 cup each) of apple cider vinegar and pure virgin olive oil mixed together. The stones passed on the fifth day, never to come back again.

This shouldn't come as much of a surprise. According to Volume 31 (1987) of *Annals of Nutritional Metabolism,* "Apple fiber extracts containing a high level of pectins decreased the level of cholesterol in hamsters." Therefore by eating more apples, cholesterol-induced gallstones can be prevented from forming.

Other Uses for Cider Vinegar

Apple cider vinegar has still a wider range of applications as the following list shows:

- Helps heal burns when soaked gauze is applied to injured areas.
- Relieves pain and itchiness when rubbed on insect bites and stings.
- Removes dandruff when used as a hair rinse after washing hair.
- Eliminates body odor when used in place of an underarm deodorant.
- Cures athlete's foot when sore feet are soaked daily in strong solution.

Unique Baked Apple Recipes

The first recipe below is adapted with the permission of La Rene Gaunt and the publishers of her book, *Recipes to Lower Your Fat Thermostat* (see Appendix), while the second is of my own creation when I was in the restaurant business years ago.

Baked Apples with Date Stuffing

Needed: 6 washed, cored and halved Rome Beauties; 6 tbsp. chopped, pitted dates; 1/3 cup cranberry juice; dash each of cinnamon and nutmeg. Put apples in glass baking dish. Stuff them with 1 tbsp. chopped dates and sprinkle with cranberry juice. Sprinkle them with cinnamon and nutmeg next. Cook, covered, in an oven at 400° F. until they're tender, 45–60 min. Serve lukewarm, topped with a little plain yogurt and a smidgen of pure maple syrup.

Baked Beans with Apples

Golden Delicious apples add a juicy note to this rich-flavored bean bake. Core and slice one Golden Delicious apple. Layer slices on bottom of a 1-1/2 quart casserole greased with lecithin, reserving several slices to put on top. To 1 quart of baked beans, stir in 1/4 cup packed brown sugar, 1 tbsp. each orange juice and apple cider vinegar and 2 tbsp. prepared mustard. Mix these ingredients thoroughly and pour into the casserole dish. Arrange apples on top. Cover and bake at 350° F. for about 1 hour. Uncover and bake 30 min. longer. Yields 4–6 servings.

APRICOT (*Prunus armeniaca*)

Brief Description

Botanists have characterized this sweet-sour fruit as more of a plum, although it does belong to the same family as peaches and almond nuts.

This brass- or copper-colored fruit originated anciently in Central Asia. It is said that when the first body of emigrants to leave the Tower of Babel in central Iraq crossed over the Caucasus Mountains then turned westward towards the Caspian Sea, they brought with them young apricot tree seedlings, some of which were planted along the way.

Luxurious Beauty Agent

A two-step program I've recently introduced to selected audiences around the country has been drawing praise from many of the people who've tried it themselves, reporting back how much softer and wrinkle-free their skin was afterwards. The method originated with my Hungarian grandmother, Barbara Liebhardt Heinerman, whose skin was as soft and unlined as a baby's behind when she passed away in her eighties.

First Step: In a blender put enough chopped fresh apricots with a smidgen of water to equal 1 cup; or else pour in a cup of concentrate, without the water.

Next, coarsely chop or slice a peeled, halved avocado (without the pit) into the blender. Thoroughly blend until the mixture is a smooth, even consistency. Add a tad of pure virgin olive oil, and blend again for a minute or two.

Apply this mask in a thin, uniform layer all over your face, neck and throat, leaving it on for 45 minutes. Rinse off with water. The ideal time for doing this is several hours before retiring to bed.

Second Step: Put a little heavy dairy cream or half-and-half into a dish and add the juice of half a lemon; blend well. Use only enough to cover those areas you deep-cleansed with the fruit-vegetable mask. With fingertips or cotton balls, gently massage in with a rotating action. This may take a while to do, but be sure the get all the areas previously covered with the mask. Then retire for the night.

In the morning gently bathe the face with a barley or oatmeal soap bar, which can be obtained at local health food stores or specialty cosmetic outlets. I don't recommend the use of rouge or other cosmetics while on this program.

The apricot-avocado mask can be used two to three times per week, but the heavy cream-lemon juice combination should be applied every single night before retiring. Within a matter of weeks, it will look and feel more luxurious and should elicit comments from those around you who are wondering where you got your "face lift" from.

A Delicious Recipe

This fantastic fruit salad has been adapted from Better Homes & Gardens' *Eating Healthy Cook Book.*

Apricot Fruit Salad

Chill the unopened can of apricots several hours before serving so they'll be refreshingly cold. Needed are: one 16-oz. can unpeeled apricot halves (juice pack), chilled; 1/2 cup halved seedless green grapes; 4 Romaine lettuce leaves; 2 oz. Neufchatel cheese (softened); 1/4 tsp. ground ginger and ground nutmeg.

Drain apricots, reserving 1 tbsp. of the juice. Cut apricot halves in half to form quarters. Arrange apricots and grapes on 4 individual lettuce-lined salad plates. Stir together Neufchatel cheese and ginger. Gradually stir in reserved apricot juice to make of drizzling consistency. Drizzle over fruit. Sprinkle with nutmeg. Makes 4 servings.

ARTICHOKE (*Cynara scolymus*)

Maurice Messegue, Europe's greatest herbalist, says that the part of the artichoke we are in the habit of eating is the least active, while all the rest of it, which is unbelievably bitter, is actually the most nutritious and therapeutic for you. "For myself," he states quite emphatically, "I use every bit of the artichoke and encourage others to do the same!"

Two vegetables are called artichokes, but have absolutely no relation to each other. We distinguish them as the globe artichoke and the Jerusalem artichoke. The former is a green vegetable somewhat like a tiny cabbage, except that its leaves are smaller and thicker. While the latter isn't even an artichoke, nor has anything to do with Jerusalem. It came here from South America, and first was called "girasole" from its likeness to the sunflower. Later this was corrupted into "Jerusalem." The tubers are pleasant enough to consume, but have no medical value.

A Terrific Cholesterol Manager

To make your own special leaf tincture for better managing the problems of too much cholesterol, slightly crush and soak about 5-1/4 cups of artichoke leaves in 2 pints of alcohol for 10 days. Strain, and take 1 tbsp. twice daily in between meals. This should help keep cholesterol from accumulating in fatty globs within the body.

Volume 5 of *Experimental Medicine & Surgery* for 1947 confirmed artichoke's cholesterol fighting properties very well. Laying hens and human subjects manifesting early signs of atherosclerosis had their blood cholesterol contents lowered by administration of artichoke powder. Cynarin is the compound within artichokes that protects man and beast alike from hardening of the arteries and keeps serum triglyceride levels very low.

Brain Food to Make You More Alert

To increase your mental powers, pull an artichoke to pieces, leaf by leaf, and put into a jar with barely enough water to cover. Set a saucer on the jar and stand it in a pan of boiling water for 2 hours, adding more water to that in the pan as it boils away. Remove the jar from the pan and strain the contents, squeezing the leaves well. 3–4 tbsp. of this infusion should be taken 3 times a day.

Artichoke leaves also seem to be pharmacologically active in the brain and portions of the central nervous system. According to *Nutrition Reviews* for April, 1978, the leaves contain "several active compounds similar to caffein" in some ways. A new kind of herbal combination called Artichoke/Garlic may be obtained through the mail from Old Amish Herbs out of St. Petersburg, Florida (see Appendix). Recommended intake has been 2–4 capsules per day with meals as necessary.

Remedy for Liver Problems

Certain acids in artichokes definitely help to activate liver function. Scientific literature indicates a definite improvement in liver problems when artichoke is regularly used.

A Quick Three-Minute Salad

Ever in a hurry and don't have much time to fix yourself something to eat? How about whipping up an instant artichoke salad? Prior to this, when you have more time on your hands, cook some artichoke hearts until tender; drain, then marinate in apple cider vinegar in the refrigerator until needed. Cut a plump, ripe tomato in quarters or slices. Arrange around marinated artichoke hearts on pieces of chilled Romaine lettuce. Spoon some cold yogurt over them, sprinkle with a dash of kelp and eat with delight.

ASPARAGUS (*Asparagus officinalis*)

Brief Description

Asparagus was cultivated in ancient times by the Romans. The vegetable is a member of the lily family, and grows like weeds on the seacoasts of England and in the southern parts of the USSR and Poland, where the tundra steppes are literally covered like a carpet with this garden delicacy. Cattle and horses graze on it with delight.

Blemish Remover

For those bothered with blackheads, pimples and general facial and lip sores, this simple preparation might do the trick in getting rid of these problems. Tie 24 large spears into two separate bundles of 12 each. Trim even. Stand butts down in preheated boiling water up to about 1-1/2 inch below the tips. Simmer for half an hour uncovered until tender. Store cooked spears in refrigerator and use in the recipe below. Save the asparagus water, however, and cleanse the face morning and night with it.

Remedies Kidney Problems

Cooked asparagus and its watery juice are very good for helping to dissolve uric acid deposits in the extremities, as well as inducing urination where such a function might be lacking or only done on an infrequent basis. Asparagus is especially useful in cases of hypertension where the amount of sodium in the blood far exceeds the potassium present. Cooked asparagus also increases bowel evacuations.

Handy Casserole

This has been adapted from *Recipes to Lower Your Fat Thermostat* (see Appendix) with permission of the publisher.

Luscious-Layered Casserole

Needed: 1 cup sliced onion; 1 cup chopped green pepper; 1 cup sliced mushrooms; 1/2 lb. sliced potatoes; 1 cup thinly sliced carrots; 1/3 cup raw brown rice; 1-3/4 cups short parboiled asparagus spears (use those in remedy above); 3-1/2 cups stewed, mashed tomatoes (you can replace the tomatoes with onion soup and turn this into a different casserole).

Sauté the onion, pepper and mushrooms in a lightly oiled frying pan set on medium heat. Use either olive oil or lecithin from your local health food store to oil pan and baking dish. Next place sliced spuds in a 2-1/2 qt. baking dish. Then alternate layers of carrots, rice, onion mixture and asparagus. Finally stir kelp into mashed tomatoes and pour over the vegetables. Cover and bake in preheated oven at 350° F. for 2 hours. Serves about 8 people.

AVOCADO (*Persea americana*)

Brief Description

The avocado tree, which is related to the laurel, grows in semitropical climates. Orchards occur from Santa Barbara, California all the way to Lima, Peru. Today, southern California harvests about 600 million avocados each year. Giant prehistoric ground sloths feasted on ripe avocados, rapidly packing masses of oily flesh into their mouths, and later defecating seeds with hardly a sense of their passing. The famous Amazon plant specialist, Richard Spruce, wrote that he was acquainted with wild jaguars deep in the rain forest, that would sometimes gather around an avocado tree, "gnawing the fallen fruit and snarling over them as so many cats might do."

Lowers Blood Cholesterol

Patients at the V.A. Hopsital in Coral Gables, Florida ranging in age from 27 to 72 were given 1/2 to 1-1/4 avocados per day. Twice a week blood samples were taken. 50% of them showed a definite decrease in serum cholesterol from 8.7–42.8%. Eating half an avocado every other day would probably help your own cholesterol drop some.

Avocado-Chamomile for Psoriasis

A rather remarkable twofold approach towards relieving the itchy misery of psoriasis is by eating half of an avocado daily and applying an extra-rich cream of chamomile flowers extract to the skin. The oils in the avocado will work internally towards the surface of the skin, soothing deep muscle inflammation. The oils in CamoCare Soothing Cream help the skin to literally repair itself from the damage done by psoriasis. CamoCare is distributed in the U.S. by Abkit, Inc. out of New York (see Appendix) and is available at most local health food stores nationwide.

An Ancient Mayan Beauty Secret

While working at an archaeological site several years ago near the Honduran-Guatemalan border, I noticed that all of the Chorti women (descendants of the ancient Maya) rubbed their hair and bodies with an oil to keep them soft and resilient.

Through our interpreter, I learned that they were using avocado oil to keep their skin from getting burned by the hot, glaring sun and the rough elements of wind and rain. They even rubbed some on their lips to keep them nice and moist.

Some of the Chorti women seemed to be in their late 20s or early 30s. Imagine my utter astonishment when my interpreter told me that most of them were in their mid-to-late *fifties!* Now I'm a pretty good judge of age because of my training in anthropology, but their constant use of avocado oil sure fooled me about how old I *thought* they were.

You too, can experience near ageless beauty again simply by using avocado oil in place of other lotions and creams.

A Quick Laxative Recipe

My father, Jacob Heinerman, uses ripe avocados regularly as a fast-acting laxative. He'll peel two of them and mash the meat up good in a dish, adding a little kelp, 3 tbsp. apple cider vinegar, and 1 tsp. lemon juice. After mixing them together, he'll spread the mixture on some sprouted cracked wheat or pumpernickel bread and eat it.

Not only does it make incredibly delicious sandwiches, but usually within just a couple of hours or less it will promote a pretty vigorous bowel movement. He seldom ever has constipation as a result of this in spite of being 74.

Another Avocado Recipe

The Ultimate Guacamole Dip

Needed: 4 large peeled, pitted avocados; 7 tsp. peeled, grated onion; 1/8 tsp. cayenne (optional); 1/2 tsp kelp; two 8 oz. cans of peeled tomatoes; 4 tbsp. plain yogurt; 1/2 tsp. lemon juice; 1/2 tsp. Worcestershire sauce. Mash all the ingredients together in a large mixing bowl and whip until well-blended and smooth. Chill before serving. Use natural corn chips from your local health food store for dipping.

B

BANANA (*Musa sapientum*)

Brief Description

Banana is an herb that grows up to 20 feet or more in height. It has a stout, cylindrical, succulent pseudostem arising from a large, fleshy corm. This corm sends up a series of suckers, forming clumps. Bananas are native, in various forms, from India and Burma through the Malay Archipelago to New Guinea, Australia, Samoa and tropical Africa. It's universally cultivated in tropical regions.

Curious Uses for Banana Peel

A familiar trick used in silent screen comedies was for someone to slip on the proverbial banana peel.

But more sober and serious uses for banana peels appear in folk medical literature throughout the world. Green banana peels are grated and dried or else burned to ash in Curacao and then applied to cancerous sores, herpes lesions and diabetic leg ulcers with some good effects. In Trinidad a poultice of ripe banana peel is applied to the forehead and back of the neck to relieve excruciating migraines. In the Bahamas a decoction of fresh green peel is taken as a remedy for hypertension. Also the inner surface of the ripe banana skin may be applied directly to burns, rash and boils for healing relief. Curiously enough, the inside of the peel also makes a dandy shoe polish for scuff marks.

M.D. Cures Over 200 Wart Cases with Ripe Peel

One of the most remarkable folk treatments I've ever encountered has to do with the successful removal of plantar warts.

Matthew Midcap, M.D. shared with me some of his firsthand experiences with ripe banana peel, which he uses in his clinical practice in Morgantown, West Virginia.

Dr. Midcap says this cure will work on all kinds of warts and "has always been 100% effective thus far."

> I first read about this banana treatment in the Dec. 1981 issue of the *Journal of Plastic Reconstrutive Surgery.* A short article by an Israeli physician from the city of Safad related how he treated a single patient—a 16-year-old girl with painful plantar warts—with just ripe banana peels. The doctor in Wheeling with whom I was working in a clerkship capacity while still a medical student then, decided to join me in conducting further experiments based on this one recorded episode. His name is Dr. Phillip Polack.
>
> One of our very first patients was a male Caucasian, 48 years old. He's a prominent banker in Wheeling and loves to play golf. But a cluster of plantar warts on the bottom of one foot, about 2 inches in diameter, prevented him from enjoying his favorite sport. By the time he came to us, he had tried all the standard medical therapies available: acid therapy, cryotherapy where they freeze it off, surgery and even radiation. But nothing seemed to work, they just kept coming back. I cut a piece of ripe banana skin and applied the inside white mushy part against the warts, taping it down good with some adhesive tape.
>
> I instructed him to keep it on, removing only when bathing or showering. After which, he was to dry his foot well and apply another ripe peel. He came in each week to have us scrape away the old, dead wart tissue. Within less than a month we could see his warts were definitely getting smaller. In six months he was not only completely cured, but has never experienced another recurrence of them since then. He has been golfing a lot since then without any pain.

A Healing Fruit

In parts of Central America, cooked banana pulp is given as a remedy for diarrhea. In other places the mashed fruit pulp is bound around the neck to relieve sore throat and to reduce swelling of the adenoids. It's helpful in some cases of stomach ulcers, diverticulitis and colitis, but not in every instance. The oil in banana makes it a very difficult food to digest for some adults, especially the elderly. It needs to be *well* chewed and consumed slowly in small portions in order to digest properly.

A diet of bananas, according to an early 1959–1960 issue of *Postgraduate Medicine,* is ideal for treating celiac disease, an allergic sensitivity to the gluten in some grains and usually found in young children. Physicians at the Vanderbilt School of Medicine fed as many as 10 bananas a day to some of their young patients with remarkably good results. When treating a young child with this disease, be sure to consult with a proper medical or health authority regarding his or her entire diet, since things like candy and sugar are also restricted as a rule.

Healthy Snack Food for Adults

Several health benefits for older adults from banana consumption have been reported in the medical literature. In one study when a banana was given as a snack, either alone or with milk during the daily rest period, reported illness among industrial female workers decreased. The fruit was an ideal mid-morning pickup for them. In a second report, improvement in morale and decreased absenteeism among clerical workers were observed when employees were given supplements of bananas. Workers who were given these natural fruit snacks were more cheerful and attentive and less tired on the job than those who didn't receive any bananas. The last experiment was conducted at a retirement home. 117 residents received a ripe banana each day for periods of 16–30 days. After awhile these residents no longer suffered any digestive disorders. Banana is also good to offset insulin shock in diabetics.

Building Incredible Strength and Size

Bananas are good for putting on extra pounds in order to acquire more muscle and strength for very physical types of competitive sports such as football or wrestling. Sports medical doctors who work with athletes usually prescribe foods like bananas, potatoes and rice along with the usual weight lifting and other muscle-building exercises in order that the extra weight is added as usable muscle rather than turned to mere flab. Japanese Sumo wrestlers eat tremendous amounts of rice and bananas in order to maintain their incredible girths (which is *all* muscle, by the way)!

For those needing to put on an extra 40 pounds or so, it's recommended that a couple of bananas each day either in a liquid drink or pudding or just plain straight, will help towards building additional muscle protein when accompanied with the usual exercises.

Scrumptious Banana Bread

A delicious banana-date bread recipe has been modified from one appearing in the Better Homes & Gardens' *Eating Healthy Cook Book,* which I recommend getting.

Banana Date Bread

Needed: 1-1/2 cups all-purpose flour; 1/2 tsp. baking soda; 1/2 tsp. ground cinnamon; 1/4 tsp. baking powder; 1/4 tsp. ground nutmeg; 2 egg whites; 3/4 cup dark honey; 1/4 cup blackstrap molasses; 1 cup mashed ripe bananas; 1/4 cup olive oil; 1/2 cup chopped, pitted dates and some liquid lecithin from any health food store.

Stir together all dry ingredients. Next blend well the egg whites, honey, molasses and bananas; add oil and keep stirring. Then turn flour mixture into it. Add the dates. Lightly oil an 8 x 4 x 2 loaf pan with lecithin. Put batter into pan. Bake at 350° F. for 55 min. Cool in pan 10 min. then remove and cool on a wire rack.

BARLEY (See GRAINS)

BASIL (*Ocimum basilicum*)

Brief Description

Cultivated worldwide as an annual plant. Many varieties have different compositions and flavoring characteristics. The herb is strongly affected by environmental factors like temperature, geographic location, soil and amount of rainfall. Its thin branching root produces bushy stems growing from 1–2 feet high and bearing leaves of a purple hue, and two-lipped flowers, varying in color from white to red, sometimes with a purple tinge.

A Multi-Purpose Health Tea

Maurice Mességué, a world-renowned French herbal folk healer, swears by basil as an excellent nightcap tea for restlessness and migraines. He also recommends the tea to promote more milk in nursing mothers, and as a useful gargle for *Candida albicans* or yeast infection of the mouth and throat. It's also very, very good for women to take before and after childbirth to promote blood circulation.

The steaming tea is also good for a patient with fever to hold his head over and inhale while covered with a blanket. Cool basil tea is good for all kinds of eye problems, both as an eyewash and internal tea.

Obviously fresh basil leaves and unground seeds are the best to use when making a tea. If such is obtainable in your immediate area, then bring 2 pints of water to a boil and add 15 basil seeds. Cover and reduce the heat, slowly simmering them for about 45 minutes. After which, remove from heat and add 1-1/2 handfuls of fresh or half-dried basil and steep for another 25 minutes or so. Drink or gargle with this tea on the average of 2 cups per day as needed. When lukewarm, the strained tea can also be used to bathe the eyes.

If ground basil is all that's available, another form of tea can be made and used for most of the previously described problems *except* as an eyewash. Bring 3-1/2 cups of water to a boil; remove from heat and add 1-1/4 level tsp. ground basil. Cover and steep for half an hour. Sweeten with a touch of pure maple syrup and drink on the average 1 cup twice daily.

Magical Headache Reliever

Ever had a headache and needed a simple remedy for relieving it? It's easy to prepare. Just take a level teaspoon of dried, ground basil and put into 1 cup hot water for 10 minutes, then strain. When the liquid is cool, add 2 tbsp. Tincture of Witch Hazel that's been previously refrigerated for awhile. You can get the Witch Hazel Tincture at your local drugstore or supermarket pharmacy section. Apply the solution as a compress to the forehead and temples, for relief you wouldn't believe possible!

BAY LAUREL (*Laurus nobilis*)

Brief Description

Bay laurel or sweet bay is a small evergreen shurb or tree native to the Mediterranean region and Asia Minor. It has been admired for its beauty and aromatic leaves since the Greek and Roman times. The leaves are leathery, lanceolate, pointed and experience maximum oil content increases during early and mid-summer only. Several botanicals are known by the name of "bay"—i.e., West Indian bay (*Pimenta racemosa*) and California bay (*Umbellularia californica*). Hence, the term "bay" in the existing herb literature can mean any one of these botanicals, among others.

Anti-Dandruff Rinse

Bay makes a terrific anti-dandruff rinse. Simply bring a quart of water to a boil. Remove from heat and add approximately 3 level tsp.

of crumbled bay leaves. Cover and let steep for 25 minutes. Strain and refrigerate tea. When washing your hair, first rinse all soap out with ordinary water. Then pour some liquid bay tea on your head and massage well into the scalp. Follow with a few more ounces of the same cool tea, working it in good with your fingertips. Leave in the hair for about an hour or so, then rinse out. Should keep dandruff from occurring if faithfully used each day.

Bronchitis and Cough Remedy

Use boiled bay leaves as a poultice applied directly on the chest and covered with a cloth of some kind to relieve bronchitis and hacking cough.

Benefit to Arthritic Pain

Oil of bay may be rubbed on arthritic aches and pains, muscle sprains and tendon swellings for relief. To make the oil, simply heat some of the leaves in a little olive oil over very low heat for about 20 minutes without actually cooking the oil too much or causing it to burn and smoke. Set aside and allow the leaves to further simmer for awhile. Strain and use the oil as needed for these conditions and others like lower backache, varicose veins and so forth.

BAYBERRY BARK (*Myrica cerifera*)

Brief Description

Wax myrtle or bayberry is an evergreen shrub native to the eastern U.S. from New Jersey to Southern Florida and west to Texas. It also grows in the Bahamas, West Indies and Bermuda. The fruit is a grayish-white, round drupe-like nut covered with a waxy crust. The medicinal properties are similar to those of wild Oregon grape root or barberry (*Berberis vulgaris*).

Cures, Prevents Varicose Veins

Mike Tierra, a practicing herbalist in California recommends bayberry for "relieving, curing and preventing varicose veins" as a fomentation. It is made by dipping a moisture-absorbent towel or cloth into some bayberry tea and applying the towel over the affected legs as hot as can be tolerated without burning. The towel is covered by dry flannel cloth and a heating pad or a hot water bottle is placed on top of this. A plastic covering can be used to protect bedding if applied overnight.

Reduces Fever, Expels Parasites

To make a potent tea for using externally for varicose veins, and internally for raging fevers, intestinal parasites and liver and kidney problems, simply bring 1 quart of water to a boil, then add 2–3 tbsp. of chopped bark, cover and simmer on low heat for 5 minutes. Remove and let steep for an additional 40 minutes. Strain, sweeten with honey or pure maple syrup and drink. Take about 2–3 cups per day as needed.

An Aid in Women's Complaints

Two to three cups of tea per day, consumed orally or used as a douche, are of value in stopping bleeding of the lungs, bowels and uterus, in treating prolapsed uterus, excessive menstruation and vaginal discharge. Also it's a darned good laxative, either in capsules (3 at a time) or tea (1–2 cups daily).

BEANS (*Phaseolus* genus)
(See also under GREEN BEANS)

Brief Description

BLACK BEANS. These are small, oval beans with a tender texture and a mushroom-flavored, somewhat earthy taste to them.

BLACK-EYED PEAS. These oval, medium-sized beans have a nutty crunchiness to them and possess a fine-flavored taste remiscent of a meatless vegetable stew.

CHICKPEAS. These round beans have a distinctive nutty flavor and chewy firmness to them.

FAVA BEANS. Such beans are large, flat and oval with a firm texture and a dainty taste. They are very popular in Europe, especially in Great Britain.

KIDNEY BEANS (Dark Red, Light Red and White). All three colors of beans are oval-shaped with a somewhat soft, bland taste to them. The dark red ones are mostly sold in cans and used in salads, while the light red are sold dry and made into chili, refried beans and creole dishes.

LENTILS. These small, disk-shaped beans have a subtle mildness characterized with a distinctive flavor and rather firm texture.

LIMA BEANS. These large, white oval beans date from 7000–5000 B.C. in Peru and yield a mild taste and a soft texture when cooked. Quite often, though, they are dried, canned and marketed under the names of wax or butter beans.

MUNG BEANS. Also known as green or golden gram in India, they are highly esteemed for their tiny seeds, which become rather sticky on cooking, but are accounted both wholesome and nourishing. These are dried and boiled whole or split, or else parched and ground into flour. In China they are added to green noodles and used for bean sprouts, a use to which they are also put here in America.

NAVY, WHITE and GREAT NORTHERN BEANS. All three of them are firm, mild beans in varying sizes, ranging from small to medium and large.

PINTO BEANS. These are small, oval beans with a mild flavor and texture to them.

SPLIT and WHOLE PEAS (Yellow and Green). Both varieties are small and possess a soft, grainy texture marked with a certain distinctive flavor.

SOYBEANS (*Glycine* or *Soja max*). These firm, round, bland-tasting beans are not of the genus *Phaseolus* as the others happen to be.

Food to Make You Healthier Looking

Very few of us these days possess what might be correctly termed "a radiant glow of health." In a large part, its absence in many of our countenances is due to our poor dietary and social habits, and unwise ways of living. But by consuming varieties of beans more often, we can regain a healthier and more fuller look in the course of time.

The best direct evidence for this comes from the opening chapter in the Book of Daniel. We are told that "Daniel purposed in his heart that he would not defile himself with the portion of the king's meat, nor with the wine he drank." But instead asked Melzar, the prince of the eunuchs, "Give us pulse to eat, and water to drink." At the end of nearly a week and a half, Daniel and his three friends' "countenances appeared fairer and fatter in flesh than all the children which did eat the portion of the king's meat." "Pulse" is believed to have been either lentils or beans.

If you want to maintain a vibrant look of radiant health, then beans and lentils should be a frequent part of your diet.

Legumes Promote Vigor and Vitality

In ancient times beans and lentils were often associated with men and women of strength, or considered to be the standard fare of consumption in activities requiring great feats of strength and vigor. The Bible provides us with several remarkable accounts to this effect. Esau's "mess of pottage" made for him by Jacob is one example and is believed to have been lentil soup. II Samuel 23:11–12 is another instance in which lentils were associated with valor and courage.

Some clinical evidence exists to back up the vigor and vitality claims which have been assigned to various legumes. Chickpea (garbanzo bean) is a very important food staple in India where it goes by the common name of Bengal gram. According to Vol. 7 of the *Journal of Ethnopharmacology* for 1983, the sprouted seeds of chickpea are "extremely nourishing and constitute a regular item of diet for athletes and professional wrestlers in India" and "is used as a food for horses which gives them an untiring stamina." This is due to the high content of pangamic acid or vitamin B-15, which has been sold in health food stores nationwide as a stamina-builder of sorts. Additional studies concerning the strength-giving properties of B-15 in other legumes and vegetables have appeared in Soviet, Hungarian and Indian medical journals in the past.

Bean Juice for Constipation and Hyperactivity

When I was at a recent scientific symposium held at the University of Rhode Island in Kingston during July, 1987, a chemist from Japan whom I was introduced to, explained to me how black bean juice is used in his country to correct constipation caused by eating too much white bread and refined foods and to calm hyperactive children. According to him, 2 tbsp. of cleaned black soybeans are boiled in 2 qts. of water for 10 minutes, then simmered until just 1 qt. of water remains. Some kelp is added to season before the broth is strained. One cup of juice three times per day is recommended.

Possible Cancer Preventative

Certain enzymes called proteases break down proteins and also play multiple roles in the production and development of various cancer tumors. Beans and grains contain protease inhibitors (PIs), a variety of substances which block protease activity. When ingested as part of the diet, PIs interfere with these cancer-producing enzymes. These same PIs also prevent the growth of tumor cells. Additionally, they prevent the release of deadly oxygen radicals, thereby protecting against possible DNA damage and subsequent cancer. Finally, PIs prevent radiation-induced cancer and enhance tissue resistance to invasion by tumor cells. If people consume adequate amounts of PIs in the form of beans and grains, they can then be protected against cancer at a variety of sites.

Lowers Cholesterol and Triglycerides

The American Journal of Clinical Nutrition for October 1983 cited a number of recent studies that all varieties of bean can definitely lower serum cholesterol and triglyceride levels in the body substantially. Enough so, in fact, to suggest they be reintroduced into our diets again on a more frequent basis in order to keep too much fat from accumulating in the circulating blood.

A possible dietary pattern to follow to bring this about, would be to have a bowl of oatmeal for breakfast three times a week and bean soup (without ham or sausage) several times at lunch. This combination of both is an ideal grain-legume mixture to fight cholesterol buildup. Variations to this theme might be oatmeal cookies or muffins for breakfast or snacks and baked beans or bean casserole for dinner.

A Diabetic's Delight

Published dietary studies show that beans can be a diabetic's delight. The *Indian Journal of Medicinal Research* for February, 1987 reported that three types of legumes had a very significant effect on lowering blood sugar levels in diabetic patients. These reductions were directly related to the dietary fiber content of each legume. Because of this legumes ought to be included in the diet at least twice a week.

Help for Hypertensives

Dr. Louis Tobian, chief of the hypertension section of the University of Minnesota Hospitals, has been a busy man the last few years. You see, he's been conducting some very important studies concerning the role of potassium in treating high blood pressure.

Using stroke-prone rats that were bred to have dangerously high blood pressure, he fed half a regular diet and half a diet with potassium supplements. Only 2% of the rats on the high potassium diet died from strokes, compared to 83% on the regular diet. His findings led him to speculate that potassium actually protects against strokes and kidney disease, and that his rat studies suggest the way a high potassium diet may act in humans.

The October 1986 issue of *Sports Fitness,* which reported Dr. Tobian's work, recommended navy beans (1 cup = 750 mg.) or lima beans (1 cup = 1163 mg.), among other foods, as giving the body the potassium power it needs to prevent and reduce hypertension.

Potassium estimates for other varieties of cooked beans in 1-cup portions are as follows: red kidney, 629 mg.; pinto, 670 mg.; black-eyed peas, 573 mg.; chickpeas or garbanzos, 570–590 mg.; lentils, 500 mg. and soybeans, 972 mg.

"Meat" Protein Without the Meat

For those who are quite health-minded and wish to reduce their intake of red meat somewhat without experiencing any loss of energy or strength, they might want to consider increasing their intake of beans instead. A registered dietician with the Stanford Heart Disease Prevention Program described beans as being "a power-packed, nutritious food." Elsewhere chickpeas, lentils and other legumes have been described as "ideal meat substitutes" and "unexcelled meat stretchers."

Boston Baked Beans Classic

Needed: 2 cups Great Northern or navy beans, soaked for 10 hours in 7 cups water; some ham hocks; 1 chopped Bermuda (white) onion; 1 tbsp. lemon juice; 3/4 tsp. kelp (powdered seaweed from health food stores); 1 tbsp. dark honey; 2/3 cup blackstrap molasses; 1 tsp. pure vanilla; 1/2 tsp. pure maple syrup; 1-1/2 tbsp. catsup; 1/ 8 tsp. dry mustard; 1 chopped garlic clove.

Preboil ham hocks until tender. Remove meat from bones, adding it with a little of the juice to a large pan. While the ham hocks are cooking, simmer the soaked beans for 1-1/2 hours until tender but not broken. Skim off any foam on the beans prior to cooking. Put beans and half the juice into the large pan with the deboned ham pieces and their juice. Add the diced garlic and onion.

Mix together in a separate bowl the kelp, honey, molasses, vanilla, maple syrup, catsup and dry mustard, adding 1-1/2 cups boiling water. Stir well and pour over the beans. Cover and bake at 275° F. for about 7 hours, adding additional water if necessary. Stir with a wooden ladle every couple of hours. Uncover during the last 45 min. to brown beans and meat a little. Be careful not to burn them. Serve warm with pumpernickel bread.

To get rid of the gas effect which beans produce, just soak them for at least 24 hours prior to cooking, adding 1/2 tsp. ginger root for every 2 cups of beans. Another alternative is to take an anti-gas herb product called Ginger-up (2 capsuled) with any meal that includes beans or may cause heartburn. It's available from Great American in St. Petersburg, Florida (see Appendix). Drinking acidophilus or buttermilk also helps to disperse gas.

Homemade Tofu

Tofu resembles a soft cheese and is a custardlike food made from soybeans in much the same way that cottage cheese is made from milk. It's quite mild tasting, and has been called the "food of 10,000 flavors" because it tends to borrow the flavor of the foods, sauces and marinades it's prepared with. Tofu is now widely available in most supermarkets, having been popularized by the Japanese.

I am grateful to Mishio Kushi and his publisher (St. Martin's Press) for their generous use of his instructions for making homemade tofu as found in his excellent treatise.

Diet for a Strong Heart

Needed: 3 cups organic yellow soybeans; 6 quarts spring water; 4-1/2 tsps. natural nigari. Soak beans overnight, strain and grind in an electric blender. Place ground beans in pot with 6 qts. of water and bring to a boil. Reduce flame to low and simmer for 5 mins., stirring constantly to avoid burning. Sprinkle cold water on beans to stop bubbling. Gently boil again and sprinkle with cold water. Repeat a third time. Place a cotton cloth or several layers of cheesecloth in a strainer and pour this liquid into a bowl. This is soy milk. Fold corners of the cloth to form a sack or place cloth in a strainer and squeeze out remaining liquid. Pulp in sack is called *okara* and may be saved for other recipes. In a blender, grind the nigari, which is a special salt made from sea water and available in many natural or health food stores nationwide.

Sprinkle powdered nigari over soy milk in a bowl. With a wooden spoon carefully make a large, X-shaped cut with two deep strokes in this mixture and allow to sit 10–15 minutes. During this time it will begin to curdle. The next step calls for a wooden or stainless-steel tofu box (available in many natural food stores) or a bamboo steamer. Line box or steamer with cheesecloth and gently spoon in soy milk. Cover top with layer of cheesecloth and place lid on top of box or steamer so it rests on cheesecloth and curdling tofu. Place a brick or weight on the lid and let stand for an hour or until tofu cake is formed. Then gently place tofu in a dish of cold water for half an hour to solidify. Keep the tofu covered in water and refrigerate until used. Tofu will stay fresh for several days in the refrigerator. However, it's best to change the water daily.

Tofu is extremely versatile and has a variety of textures depending upon how it's cooked. It can be sliced, diced, cubed, pressed or mashed and boiled in soups, sautéed with vegetables or grains or baked in casseroles. It may also be used in dips, sauces, dressings and desserts. The *okara* or pulp mentioned earlier can be added to soups or cooked with vegetables. A simple salad dressing can be made by mixing together in a food blender some tofu, sesame seed oil, lemon juice, kelp and tarragon. You've got a creamy dressing that's less expensive than commercial dressings made from dairy products, and has *only one-third* their calories. Tofu also makes a wonderful medicinal plaster for concussions as mentioned elsewhere in this chapter.

BEETS AND SWISS CHARD (*Beta vulgaris, B. vulg. cicla*)

Brief Description

Edible beet roots are related to the sugar beets (*Beta vulgaris saccharifera*), grown for the making of sugar, the extraction of which began in the 18th century. The edible roots of beets are of two basic colors, red and yellow. The English pioneered the red variety, but elsewhere in Europe the yellow-rooted kind was once much preferred because of its sweeter taste and greater suitability for pickling.

There is also a white-rooted beet which is cultivated chiefly for its leaves and stalks. The tops are used in place of spinach and the ribs are like asparagus in some ways. In the Middle Ages, no meal was considered complete without a soup made from the leaves of this Swiss chard, as it is often called.

Hospital Beet Therapy for Cancer

One of the most remarkable and tremendously successful programs for treating many different kinds of cancer tumors was commenced in the late 1950s by Alexander Ferenczi, M.D., at the Dept. for Internal Diseases at the district hospital at Csoma, Hungary, using nothing but raw, red beets. Portions of his intriguing medical success were recently translated from Hungarian and reprinted in the Australian *International Clinical Nutrition Review* for July 1986.

Dr. Ferenczi's clinical report included methods of administering the beets and several very important case studies:

> In D.S., a man of 50 years of age, a lung tumor was diagnosed by me, and subsequently confirmed in a Budapest hospital and also in a country hospital, which corresponded clinically to lung cancer . . . I started the treatment with beetroot in the described manner. After 6 weeks of treatment the tumor had disappeared . . . After 4 months of treatment he gained 10 kg. (22 lbs.) in weight, the erythrocyte (mature red blood cell) sediment rate (e.s.r.) was reduced from 87 millimeters/h to 77 mm/h. Thus he represented the symptoms of a clinical recovery.

A side-by-side comparison of two cancer patients, one on beet therapy and the other not, further demonstrates the efficacy of this marvelous treatment.

> We received simultaneously two patients for treatment. One suffered from cancer of the prostate and the other from cancer of the uterus. The body weight of both was the same. The patient with cancer of the prostate was treated with beetroot. The patient with cancer of the uterus could not take it, but remained in our ward. The condition of the man started to improve. When admitted, he was bedridden with a permanent catheter. After one month the catheter was removed. The patient walked around and put on weight, whereas the female patient lost weight. After 3 months, there was a difference in weight of 10.5 kg. (23.15 lbs.) between the two.
>
> Experience gained up to now points to the fact that beetroot contains a tumor inhibiting (anti-cancerous) active ingredient. However for the present no clue has been found as to the nature of this active substance. One thing is certain, that it is not very unstable because it also acts when taken orally; therefore digestion does not harm it. The very apparent red color may suggest that the active substance is the coloring matter. Treatment with beetroot presents several advantages over the rest of the medication used in the treatment of cancer. Firstly, because it is non-toxic and one can administer red beetroot in unlimited quantities. Also there are unlimited supplies of beetroot at our disposal. We have therefore endeavored to administer to the patient this active substance in the most concentrated form and in the largest quantities possible, because the beetroot or rather the juice could not be given in larger quantities.

Now beet root is available to consumers several different ways. One Lawrence, Kansas firm, Pines Int'l, makes a very nice organic red beet root concentrate. This beet powder is available at most local health food stores.

One, however, has to be careful with the amount of beets consumed at any given time. Certainly not because they're harmful, but rather due to their incredibly strong ability to quickly break up cancer in the body. A woman in her thirties who was treated with beetroot for breast cancer contracted a fever of 104° F due to the rapid breakdown of the tumors. In instances such as this, beets clean up the cancer faster than the liver is capable of processing all of the wastes dumped into it at any one time. Consequently, the internal administration of beetroot needs to be staggered out somewhat, and closer attention given to detoxifying the liver and colon at the same time the beetroot therapy is commenced.

Dr. Ferenczi concluded his medical report with this undeniable fact: "The results achieved with beetroot are no worse than those with well-known chemical preparations, such as those with Tetramin (an experimental anti-neoplastic)." He attributed the anti-cancer strength in beets to their natural red coloring agent, betaine.

Iron Fortification for Women

Several very good sources of iron for women, besides dessicated liver tablets, egg yolks, legumes and iron-fortified cereals, are red beetroot and Swiss chard. One to 2 level teaspoons of Pines' beet powder added to an 8-oz. glass of water or juice supplies a lot of iron. The balance may come from a variety of other foods, including cooked Swiss chard, dark Romaine lettuce, parsley, poultry and fish. Beets, along with carrots and parsnips, are also good for hypoglycemia.

Anti-Cancer 'Quack Salad'

I'm indebted to Dr. James Duke, head of the USDA's Germplasm Resources Laboratory in Beltsville, Maryland, for letting me feature here a slightly revised version of the cancer preventative salad that he calls Quack Salad. You'll need the following ingredients: 1 cup washed, unpeeled, raw, grated red beet; handful of chopped walnuts (unpackaged, unsalted); 3/4 cup coarsely diced celery; 1/2 cup washed, snipped endive; 1 medium-to-large washed, unpeeled and sliced cucumber; 1/4 tsp. cumin; 1 tbsp. flaxseed; 1 peeled, chopped garlic clove; pinch of powdered cayenne pepper; 1/2 peeled, chopped white onion; handful of shelled, chopped peanuts (not canned, salted or fried); 1/2 tsp. sage; 2 medium-sized, washed, quartered, ripe tomatoes.

Lightly toss everything together in a large wooden salad bowl until thoroughly mixed. To make the dressing, add 1/4 tsp. kelp and 1 finely minced garlic clove to 2-1/2 cups of lemon juice. Mix well and pour over the salad.

Russian Beet Soup

During my visit to the Soviet Union in the summer of 1979, I was fortunate enough to meet an old gentleman in Leningrad whose father had been the personal chef to the last of the great Russian czars, Nicholas Romanov. Through an interpreter I learned of a marvelous beet-cabbage soup (called borscht in Russian) that his father prepared for the Romanovs.

Palace Borscht

Needed: 3/4 celery; 1-1/4 cups raw beets; 3/4 cup carrots; 3/4 cup finely chopped green onions; 1 cup shredded cabbage; 3 tsp. grated ginger root; 12 oz. of roast duck (or chicken or turkey) carcass; 2-1/2 cups beef stock; 1/4 tsp. kelp; 3 tsp. caraway; 3/4 tsp finely shredded orange peel; 3/4 tsp. basil; 3/4 tsp. thyme; 1/2 cup tomato purée; 1-1/2 cups apple cider; 1/2 cup vodka.

Place poultry carcass in oven and brown for a while. Bring beef stock to a boil. Add the poultry carcass. Reduce to low heat and simmer for one hour before draining. Cut the celery, beets and carrots julienne style, that is into strips about 2-in. long and 1/4-in. square, and add to the stock, with the chopped green onions, spices and tomato purée. Stir together well with a wooden ladle, then simmer for another 30 min. Add the finely shredded cabbage, apple cider and vodka. Simmer another 15 min. Serves about 6.

BERRIES

Brief Description

The following is a selected list of berries known for both their nutritional as well as medicinal values.

BLACKBERRY (*Rubus villousu*). Known by their deep purple-black fruits.

BLUEBERRY (*Vaccinium gaylussacia, V. corymbosum*). The cultivated kind of a blue-black color used principally for its food value.

BOYSENBERRY (*Rubus* species). A huge blackberrylike fruit with a raspberrylike flavor. Named after Rudolph Boysen, their originator.

CRANBERRY (*Vaccinium macrocarpum).* A low, creeping shrub common to New England states and boggy areas. Distinguished by its bright red berry. Most commonly used around holidays like Thanksgiving and Christmas.

CURRANTS (Black, Red) (*Ribes nigrum, R. rubrum*). Small red, black and even white berries closely related to gooseberries, with a tart flavor.

DEWBERRIES (*Rubus canadensis*). Part of the blackberry family and regarded as one of the tastiest of the entire *Rubus* species. The hybrid youngberry was developed from it.

ELDERBERRY (Sweet, Black, Red) (*Sambucus canadensis, S. nigrum, S. racemosa*). A small shrub or tree yielding red-brown to shiny black berries.

GOOSEBERRY (Garden) (*Ribes grossularia*). The small fruit looks like a little green basketball with a stem because its skin has striated lines that appear to divide the berry into uneven sections. Has a tartness to it.

HAWTHORN BERRY (*Crataegus oxyacantha*). Many species found around the world. Some are tastier than others. Berries can be red, purple or nearly black, depending on the species, and are found on either trees or large bushes.

HUCKLEBERRY (*Vaccinium myrtillus*). Same as the blueberry, only more noted for its medicinal uses. Fruit can be either blue-black or red. Both kinds of blueberries are more closely related to the cranberry.

JUNIPER BERRY (*Juniperus connumis*). An evergreen shrub found in dry, rocky soil throughout North America, Europe, Asia and even the Arctic Circle. Fruit is a berrylike cone which is green the first year and ripens to a bluish-black or dark purple color in the second year.

LOGANBERRY (*Rubus loganobaccus*). Developed in California by a Scotsman. A hybrid from raspberry and blackberry. The fruit is large, long, dark red in color with a strong tart flavor to it.

OLLALLIEBERRY (*Rubus species*). Originally from Oregon but grown extensively in California, it's a cross between the black loganberry and youngberry, and is bright black, medium size, firm and sweeter than loganberry is.

MULBERRY (*Morus alba, M. rubra, M. microphila*). The white mulberry occurs throughout New England, the red in the Appalachias and the Texas variety in that state, with many hybrids as well. Tart, but juicy and tasty.

RASPBERRY (Red, Black) (*Rubus idaeus, R. crataegifolius, R. occidentalis*). Red raspberry produces a spring and fall crop, with the latter being sweeter on account of the cooler weather (unless the spring is cool, too). The red raspberry has less seeds and is juicier than the black variety. The black is darker and its shape is more odd, being that of a skull cap rather than the ball shape of the red kind. Its season is only 4 weeks (June–July).

ROSE HIPS (*Rosa* species). Over 100 kinds in the world. Fruit resembles a berry, but is actually a ripened hypanthium (an enlargement of the torus below the calyx). Noted for its strong vitamin C content.

SALMONBERRY (*Rubus spetabilis*). Its name comes from its yellow color. Common to the northwestern U.S. Has a strong, sour taste. Better cooked than raw.

STRAWBERRY (Cultivated, Wild) (*Frangaria ananassa, F. vesca*). Well-known enough that it needs little or no description to speak of.

THIMBLEBERRY (*Rubus parviflorus* or *R. nutkanus*). Common throughout the Pacific Northwest, its raspberry-red berries are shaped like a thimble, hence the name. It has an especially soft texture like juicy velvet that almost seems to literally melt in your mouth.

General Health Benefits

One thing nearly all berries are good for are as tonics for rejuvenating both the heart and blood. A major medical journal noted that an extra serving of fresh fruit, such as berries, each day may decrease the risk of stroke by as much as 40%, regardless of other known risk factors due to their high potassium content.

For another, they are remarkable cleansing agents serving as effective stimulants for the bladder and colon. Then too they apparently seem to make ideal accompaniments to heavy meals consisting of fatty meats.

Finally, it can be said that most berries have varying degrees of antiviral activity to them. Vol. 41 of the *J. of Food Science* for 1976 carried an interesting article, "Antiviral Activity of Fruit Extracts," in which it showed that poliovirus was inactivated by strawberry extract. Several other fruits such as raspberries, blueberries and wild cranberries helped to inactivate other intestinal viruses, including herpes simplex virus. Berries are also very purifying for the blood, cleansing for the skin and increase the beauty of your complexion. Following are some entries for most of the berries listed here and several health benefits to be expected from each, although some of them may contain a dozen or more uses.

Blackberry for Bowel Regulation

Blackberry is one of those remedies which seems to work both ways in correcting bowel disorders. A lady from Costa Mesa, California related her personal experience with blackberry:

> When my youngest daughter was about 6 months old she had diarrhea. I took her to a doctor and he prescribed a medication for her which didn't help. Grandmother came to visit and she told me to put about 1 tsp. of allspice in a cheesecloth bag, and simmer it in unsweetened blackberry juice for a few minutes. When cool, I gave

> my daughter a teaspoonful about every 4 hours. Within 24 hours the complaint was checked and in 48 hours she was completely over it. I've used this same remedy on the rest of the family whenever they have diarrhea, only in larger doses, and have found it works miracles.

Blueberry for Non-Insulin Diabetes

There is a substance in blueberries called myrtillin which reduces blood sugar as insulin would. To make an anti-diabetes tea for the non-user of insulin, steep 1 tsp. of the cut, dried leaves in a cup of hot water until lukewarm. Drink 1 cupful four times daily. Clinical evidence shows that several *Rubus* species (blackberry, blueberry, raspberry, etc.) have produced a noticeable decrease in blood sugar levels in diabetic rabbits and humans. But the tea made from the berries' leaves needs to be used two to three times daily on a regular basis or else glucose levels soar. This hypoglycemic effect may be due to an increase in the liberation of insulin in the beta cells of the pancreas. Blueberries and the leaves also exhibit anti-diarrheal properties as blackberries do.

Cranberry for Kidneys

If you have any kind of kidney problems, then you should be drinking cranberry juice every single day! At least this is what a number of major medical journals and some doctors have to say about the subject. One report noted that 60 patients with acute urinary tract infection were given 2 cups or 16 fl. oz. of cranberry juice per day for 3 weeks with over 70% of them showing moderate-to-excellent improvement in their conditions. *The Journal of Urology* for 1984 revealed "that cranberry juice is a potent inhibitor of bacterial adherence" in the urinary tract.

Cranberry juice is also good for dissolving kidney stones. So said a U.S. Navy doctor in the Jan. 3, 1963 *New England Journal of Medicine*. He wrote then, "I have found that an 8 oz. glass four times daily for several days followed by 1 such glassful twice daily is valuable therapy in stone-forming patients." A personal testimony to this effect comes from a friend of mine, Charles Eady of Harahan, Louisiana (a suburb outside of New Orleans).

> Four years ago (1981) in carrying a heavy display case in an awkward position, I managed somehow to dislodge a kidney stone I'd apparently had for a long time. I began urinating blood and having severe pains as a result of this. I began drinking cranberry juice from the health food store and in 3 days the problem was completely cured—no more blood, burning or pain.

Recently there has come onto the market a heavily concentrated cranberry formula for cleansing the kidneys. The powdered, encapsulated product is based in part, on an old Pennsylvania Dutch remedy from the Amish country around Lancaster, Pennsylvania. It may be obtained by mail-order from Old Amish Herbs in St. Petersburg, Florida. Or an equally nice dried cranberry juice product under the Nature's Way label is available from your local health food store. Three capsules of either on an empty stomach twice daily is recommended.

Currants Work Health Miracles

Black, red and white currants all manifest strong antiseptic properties—enough so, in fact, that they can be used in the treatment of Candida yeast infection, some forms of cancer, whooping cough, multiple sclerosis and various skin diseases. They're also an excellent antidote for any kind of ptomaine food poisoning, especially from meat.

Black currant fruit and the berry seeds both contain the rare and badly needed Gamma Linolenic Acid (GLA), which only occurs in mother's milk and evening primrose. Black currant constitutes one of the richest natural sources of GLA yet discovered.

What kind of health benefits then can we expect from it? Well, stronger immune and central nervous systems for one. And, for women, a relief from possible premenstrual syndromes, which include migraines and menstrual cramps. Also for both sexes, stronger hearts and improved circulations, with considerably less bad cholesterol in the blood that would clog major arteries. Probably this is why Eskimos eat a lot of berries such as currants with their varieties of fatty meats. Hypertension and arthritic inflammations also receive definite improvements when GLA-rich currants (either fresh or frozen) or currant juice are consumed on a more frequent basis.

Elderberries for Inflammation and Coughing

Fresh elderberry juice evaporated into a syrup (on low heat) and mixed with lard or a creamy base, makes a good ointment for burns. A tea made by lightly cooking the berries is a soothing lotion for sore eyes. An extract is available from health food stores under the Nature's Way label as well.

To make a good tonic for the throat, bring to a boil 1 qt. of elderberry juice with 1 tbsp each of cloves, nutmeg and cinnamon. Replace the evaporation loss with water. 30 minutes later, strain, then add 1/2 cup each dark honey and blackstrap molasses, boil and skim, cool and refrigerate. Can be diluted or used straight for coughs, sore throats and lung irritations.

Gooseberry Remedies from Pioneer Days

Pioneer women in the old American West made a tea from gooseberry fruit and leaves to help cure any uterine difficulties incurred from too many childbirths. Some pioneer women's answer to a cold was to add a little red current jelly to a glass of whiskey and to give this to the patient just before sleep. The berry juice from either black currants or gooseberries mixed in with a little honey was regarded on the frontier as an almost infallible remedy for throat irritation. Rocky Mountain Indian squaws had a hankering for gooseberries during early stages of their pregnancy, much as modern women might experience unusual cravings for pickles and ice cream. Any kind of acute skin inflammation, ranging from erysipelas to poison ivy rash could be treated in those days by making an infusion from the ripe gooseberries, straining them well and then rubbing that lotion on for immediate relief.

Hawthorn Is Good Heart Medicine

Hawthorn is a valuable drug for the treatment of various heart ailments and circulatory disorders, including angina. You can get hawthorn berries from your local health food store under the Nature's Way label. About 2–3 capsules per day is sufficient for adequate maintenance of the heart. A tea can also be made by soaking 1 tbsp. of crushed berries in 1-1/2 cups cold, distilled water for 8 hours, then quickly boiling and straining. Sweeten with honey and drink when lukewarm. As always with serious ailments of this sort, seek and follow the advice of a trusted health care professional of your choice.

Nothing Like Juniper for Wounds and Sores

Juniper berries are used to flavor gin and alcoholic bitters. A strong tea made of the berries (8 tbsp. berries in 1 qt. boiling water steeped 1 hour) makes a great remedy for scalds, burns, sores and all kinds of infected wounds when they're washed thoroughly with the tea several times a day.

A few years back on our farm in the wilderness desert of southern Utah, I accidentally cut my hand badly on some rusty barbed wire. While meditating upon the situation momentarily, the thought flashed quick as lightning into my mind to have one of our ranch hands pick some juniper berries from a nearby tree, pound them into a poultice, and apply it to my wound. This was done and my hand bound up with a clean, wet hanky. By that night, the throbbing pain had ceased—and come the next morning, the laceration was on its way to healing very nicely.

The same tea mentioned above is good to inhale when lukewarm to relieve nose, throat and lung congestion. Just drape a heavy towel over your head and sit with your face held about 8 inches above the pot the tea is in.

Raspberry Leaves for Easy Births

A Utah Mormon mother took raspberry leaf tea to make her deliveries a lot easier. Prior to this, a great deal of pain had attended her labors. But when she switched to using the tea throughout her pregnancy, little or no pain attended her. She relates that in the recovery room with her "were several other young women who had just given birth also, moaning and groaning," but she felt just fine.

She took a cup each day during her 9-month pregnancy, and about 4 cups of strong, *hot* tea prior to entering the hospital. Contractions started in just a couple of hours and her delivery was a snap and virtually pain-free. To make a tea, bring 4 cups of water to a boil. Remove from heat and add 6 tbsp. to dried raspberry leaves. Steep 40 min. Drink cool twice daily to help curb morning sickness and very hot just prior to entering labor. This tea is also excellent for curbing nausea and morning sickness.

Rosehips for Pneumonia

Most of us recognize that the vitamin C from rosehips is good for fighting colds and flu. But it's outstanding for pneumonia, bronchitis and other respiratory problems as well.

If fresh rosehips aren't readily available to you, then make your own tea with dried hips from any health food store. Keep in mind, however, that a lot of the vitamin C has disappeared during the drying process and more escapes during the tea-making. One company which has been apparently able to retain a goodly portion of ascorbic acid in their Old Fashioned Rosehips capsulated product is Old Amish Herbs out of St. Petersburg, Florida (see Appendix).

But hips still have quite a bit of minerals in them and other antibiotic principles to knock out a cold with, which aren't affected by heat. Heat a quart of water to lukewarm. Remove from heat and add 6 tbsp. of rosehips. Steep for 20 minutes or so. After straining, add some honey, stir well, then drink right away. Or you can take 3–4 rosehip capsules (Nature's Way) from any health food store several times a day with some warm juice or water.

Strawberries for Clean Teeth and Beautiful Skin

Nothing else quite cleans the skin so well as strawberries do. A California herbalist I know, Kathi Keville, shared with me her strawberry facial cream:

Kathi's Strawberry Facial Cream

Needed: 1/2 cup fresh strawberry juice; 1 cup almond oil; 1/2 oz. beeswax; 1 tbsp. lanolin. Melt the beeswax and lanolin into the oil. Cool to body temperature or just a little warmer. Warm the juice to the same temperature and whip the two together until cool. Pour into a jar and let set. The strawberry scent is easily lost under the lanolin, so a few drops of essential oil may be desired to fragrance the cream.

Both strawberries and raspberries make excellent dentifrices—an almost perfect means of preventing tartar from settling on the teeth. When either berry is cut in half, the fruit is then rubbed over the tartar-covered teeth or mashed to a pulp and gently applied with a wet, soft-bristled toothbrush. For best results, the juice should stay on the teeth for as long as possible and then only be rinsed with a little warm water.

To make a good berry mouthwash, simply add 1/4 cup honey to a cup of berry juice and bring to a boil for a few seconds. Cool then add 1-1/2 cups distilled water and 1/2 cup of thyme tea and 4 drops of peppermint oil. Gargle and rinse the mouth with this. Kills all kinds of infection and leaves a nice, sweet taste and odor.

BIRCH (*Betula alba, B. lenta*)

Brief Description

White birch grows to about 70 feet in height and is found mainly in the northern U.S., Canada and northern Europe. It has white bark and bright green leaves that are minutely hairy. Black birch averages 60–85 feet in height and occurs from Maine to Georgia and west to Michigan. The bark is brown when the tree is young, dark gray later and is horizontally striped. On older trees the bark is more irregularly broken. The leaves are ovate, pointed and alternate in pairs on the tree.

An Unbeatable Remedy for Wounds and Sores

Birch is practically unexcelled in the tree bark remedies for successfully treating psoriasis, eczema, herpes, acne and similar chronic skin diseases. A tea was once made by boiling the bark which eastern U.S. Indians used on the skin either as a poultice or ash to treat burns, wounds, bruises, eczema and sores. A similar tea can be made by bringing 1 quart of water to a boil, reducing the heat, adding 3 tbsp. dried bark, covering and simmering for about 10 minutes. Remove from heat and steep for an additional hour. Clean muslin cloth soaked in the strained solution, lightly wrung out and then laid on the afflicted skin makes a good poultice.

In the Nov. 1979 issue of the Soviet medical Journal *Vestnik Khirurgii Imeni* was a report of superficial, deep and cavity wounds being successfully treated in 108 patients with a 20% tincture of birch buds in a 70% alcohol solution. To make your own tincture, combine 4 oz. (approx. 8 tbsp.) of powdered or cut birch or fresh birch buds (if available in your area) with 1 pt. of vodka. Shake daily, allowing the bark or buds to extract for about 2 weeks. Let the materials settle and pour off the tincture, straining through a fine cloth or filter. Apply as often as needed to wounds and sores alike, Birch bark can be obtained from Indiana Botanic Gardens in Hammond by mail-order (see Appendix).

BLACKBERRY (*See under BERRIES*)

BLACK COHOSH (*Cimicifuga racemosa*)

Brief Description

Black cohosh is a perennial plant native to North America. It occurs frequently on hillsides and in woods at higher elevations. Its range is from Maine and Ontario over to Wisconsin and down as far as Georgia and Missouri. The plant has a large, creeping, knotty rootstock that's often scarred with the remains of old growth. It produces a stem up to 9 feet in height and has flowers yielding an offensive, stinking smell.

Hypertension in Women

Women in the most common subgroup, Premenstrual Tension Syndrome-A (PMT-A), were anxious, irritable, moody and nervous 1–2 weeks before their period. Such women were also inclined to eat five times more dairy products and three times more refined sugar than women without the disorder.

Because black cohosh is able to reduce hypertension somewhat and exert a slight sedative action on the nerves, it may be good for women suffering from PMT-A. Recommended dosage is about 2 capsules twice daily. Black cohosh is available from health food stores under the Nature's Way label and blue cohosh by mail-order from Indiana Botanic Gardens in Hammond (see Appendix).

BLACK (WHITE) PEPPER (*Piper nigrum*)

Brief Description

Black pepper is the dried full-grown but unripe fruit, while the white kind is the dried ripe fruit with the outer part of the pericarp removed by soaking in water and then rubbing it off. It's less aromatic than black, but has a more delicate flavor. Major producers of both kinds include India, Indonesia, Malaysia and mainland China. They should not be confused with red or cayenne pepper which comes from the *Capsicum* species.

Nifty Frostbite Remedy

During my 1979 sojourn to mainland China, I happened to get up into the cold parts of Inner Mongolia. There I picked up a nifty remedy for treating frostbitten fingers, toes, ears and nose I'd like to pass on to you.

Well in advance of the coming of winter, soak 2 tbsp. of whole black peppercorns and 1 tbsp. each of coarsely grated horseradish and ginger roots in 1-1/4 cups of white wine for a week. Then filter and strain, storing away in a tightly stoppered bottle in a cool, dark place until needed. At which time, using either a basing or artist's brush, paint afflicted body parts generously with this solution to bring immediate comfort and relief from stinging pain.

Great Insecticide

Black pepper has been proven toxic against a number of agricultural and household pests, including ants, potato bugs, silverfish, some roaches and moths. Sprinkle ground pepper in those areas where such insects frequent. A strong tea makes a good spray for keeping aphids and cutworms off tomato and cabbage plants. In 2 quarts boiling water, put 5 tbsp. peppercorns and 2 tbsp. chopped garlic cloves. Simmer down to 1 quart for 2 hours. Cool, then use on plants.

Remedy for Montezuma's Revenge

When traveling abroad in foreign countries where the purity of the water is somewhat questionable, chronic diarrhea and abdominal cramps often result when such unpurified water is drunk by unsuspecting visitors. A handy remedy for this is to carry along with you some black pepper and kelp. Then whenever such intestinal discomforts suddenly hit you, just mix 3 tsps. of black pepper and 1-1/2 tsp. of kelp in 2 cups of *boiled* water that has been allowed to cool first. Repeat as often as necessary.

BLACK (GREEN) TEA (*Camellia sinensis*)

Brief Description

Tea drinking in some Asian countries has evolved into quite a delicate art, much as wine sampling or tasting has done in France. There are connoisseurs of finely brewed tea, who can tell what type of water was used, what kind of utensils were involved and the approximate conditions under which a particular tea is made. In mainland China, some teas are so incredibly strong to the palate that they're served in (literally) thimble-sized cups.

Relieves Migraines

Black and green teas both contain caffeine (1–5%). Since caffeine constricts the blood vessel in the head, it's able to calm the pain caused when they throb and swell. During my 1980 visit to the People's Republic of China, I noticed a number of traditional medical hospitals administer black tea to their patients suffering from migraine headaches.

In the Soochow Chinese Traditional Medical Hospital in Soochow, there was a remarkable 92% recovery rate for migraines. To 1 cup of hot water, simply add 2 teabags of black tea and steep for 20 minutes until very strong. Then drink while still very warm, but not so hot as to burn the tongue or injure the inside of the mouth. "Works every time!" I was told by my hosts in China.

Great Infection Fighter

Throughout mainland China I found black tea being used in numerous hospitals and clinics to successfully treat all kinds of infection and inflammation of the stomach, lower intestines, colon and the liver with recovery rates averaging between 83–100% for the majority of patients treated. A strong cup of warm tea was given four to five times daily for these various infectious diseases.

Reduced Atherosclerosis

University of California scientists have discovered that tea drinkers experience a lot less hardening of the arteries than coffee drinkers do. It seems that the caffeine in coffee is bound with some heavy oils, which tend to elevate serum cholesterol levels quite a bit. But not so with either dark or green teas. In fact, it's believed that the caffeine content in both teas may actually help to cut cholesterol somewhat. Besides this, the tea's polyphenols act in concert with the vitamins C and P present to help strengthen the blood vessel walls of the heart more.

Tea Removes Dental Plaque

During 1983–84 dental scientists at Washington University in St. Louis conducted a series of experiments proving that black tea definitely inhibits the growth of decay-causing bacteria common to plaque buildup on the teeth. This is probably due to the high natural fluoride content found in both teas.

A 1977 dental study conducted in Taiwan showed that 50 weaning rats given cavity-producing foods like white bread, white sugar and carbonated soft drinks, but also given green or black teas, had anywhere from half to three-fourths *less* cavities than those rodents which didn't receive any tea. Brew a Lipton Brisk Tea bag in a cup of hot water for at least 6 minutes in order to get the maximum removal of fluoride. Also squeezing the tea bag before discarding helps. Use either tea as a good mouth wash and dental rinse after every meal of sweets. The April 1986 issue of *Dentistry* encouraged people to drink more tea in order to reduce cavities and plaque buildup.

BLESSED THISTLE (*Cnicus benedictus*)

Brief Description

Blessed thistle was widely used during medieval times. Frequent mention of its uses were made in some of the great herbals of that era

(Gerard's *Herbal* in 1597 and Turner's *Herbal* in 1568). This particular herb had religious connotations surrounding it, hence other common names for it like holy thistle or Holy Ghost herb. Blessed Thistle apparently helped to relieve pain and inflammation of the heart in the 16th and 17th centuries. William Shakespeare recommends "laying it to your heart" because it "helpeth that doth hurt and annoye the hart," in his play, *Much Ado About Nothing*. The herb is found in moist areas, waste places, meadows and pastures.

Best Thing for Nursing Mothers

Blessed thistle is one of the best medicines for promoting breast milk in nursing mothers. To make a tea for this and also improve the heart, just bring 1 pint of water to a boil. Remove from heat and add 1-1/2 level tbsp. of cut, dried herb. Let steep for 45 minutes. Strain and drink warm, 1 cup at a time about half an hour before nursing an infant. Or for convenience, a mother may wish to take the herb in the powdered form 2 capsules three times daily during the nursing period. Powdered herb for the tea may be purchased by mail-order from Indiana Botanic Gardens in Hammond (see Appendix) or in capsule form under the Nature's Way label from any local health food store. A good blend of this and other herbs for increasing milk flow is available from Old Amish Herbs under the name of Thistle Milk (see Appendix).

BLUEBERRY (See under BERRIES)

BOYSENBERRY (See under BERRIES)

BRANS
WHEAT BRAN (*Triticum aestivum*)
SORGHUM BRAN (*Sorghum vulgarie*)

Brief Description

Bran is a relatively inexpensive and abundant source of dietary fiber, being the coarse outer coat or hull of the grain of wheat, separated from the meal or flour by sifting or bolting.

Sorghum bran, on the other hand, comes from sorghum, a major cereal crop in many third world and developing nations. In fact, it's the world's third largest cereal food grain. Sorghum is a coarse kind of grass with a stalk very similar to that of corn.

A Bran the Celiac Patient Can Tolerate

Celiac disease is an acute sensitivity to certain fractions of wheat gluten that may be expressed in such symptoms as chronic diarrhea, constant intestinal problems, possible anemia and the like. Patients with celiac disease are placed on a totally wheat-free or gluten-free diet.

An interesting study reports that sorghum is able to increase defecation and stool softness as much as wheat does, yet lacks the gluten that's harmful to those suffering from celiac disease. It could serve as an ideal laxative bran for them in place of wheat. It's also of value in colitis or other chronic gastrointestinal inflammations which might be aggravated by the increased harshness of bran particles. Sorghum bran may be obtained from some larger health food stores or specialty outlets that import particular food items from other countries.

Free from Western Diseases

In the early 1970s South African rural blacks eating more than 50 grams of dietary fiber per day were relatively free from appendicitis, colon diseases like diverticulosis, polyps, hemorrhoids or cancer, coronary artery disease, diabetes and hiatus hernia. But when they moved to the big cities and adopted Western eating preferences for more refined foods, then they began to suffer from these same Western diseases. Bran is a valuable addition to your diet to help keep you from getting many of these ailments.

How Bran Works as a Laxative

Here is a rather novel way of describing bran's effects in the colon in nonscientific jargon for lay people to easily comprehend. Fiber passing through the intestines is somewhat like a wet sponge, absorbing and holding not only water and toxicants but such compounds as bile acids, which in turn might modify cholesterol metabolism. The sponge, due to its great bulk, also increases the size of the stool and decreases the emptying time of the colon.

Bran Prevents, Heals Ulcers

Wheat bran eaten by healthy volunteers on a regular basis has a greater buffering effect on gastric acid juices in the gut than refined carbohydrate foods do. Which suggests some protection against the development of duodenal ulceration.

In another experiment, 21 patients aged 15–70 years diagnosed with solitary rectal ulcers consumed at least 6 tbsp. of coarse wheat bran on a daily basis for an average of nearly a year (10.5 months). Fifteen patients were completely healed, indicating a 71% effectiveness for bran in regard to this type of ailment.

Curbing Hunger with Bran

Have a problem with the munchies? Always nibbling and getting fatter as a consequence? How about trying a little bran every day to reduce your appetite for those sinfully delicious but naughty no-no's? A 1983 Swedish experiment tested bran on 135 members of a weight loss club in Stockholm, discovering that if they took an extra helping of bran just before mealtime, it greatly reduced their hunger feelings.

You might try this either with a slice or two of stone-ground whole wheat toast (lightly buttered) or with 1 tbsp. of bran stirred into a glass of some kind of juice, taken before your next meal. You'll find out that you'll be eating *a lot less* as a result. And *less* fatty, sugary foods means *less* pounds put on.

A Good Cancer Preventative

No less authority than Dr. Varro Tyler, head of the Schools of Pharmacy, Nursing and Health Services at Purdue University, believes that bran can help prevent certain kinds of cancer. In his book, *Honest Herbal,* he explains how it probably works: "(1) Bran dilutes, in the large amount of water held by the fiber, any carcinogens which might be present and (2) decreases the contact time with potentially damaging substances, since the larger stool is expelled more rapidly."

Bran Good for Diabetes

Both adult and juvenile-onset diabetes mellitus can be helped by the frequent consumption of either wheat or sorghum brans. One clinical study noted that wheat bran can exert a mild reduction in the insulin needs of young, insulin-dependent diabetic subjects. An improvement of glucose tolerance was noted in diabetic patients after ingestion of bran, according to another report.

Based on the evidence just given, it's recommended that diabetics take about 1-1/2 tbsp. of bran per day, either mixed in with something like plain yogurt or vegetable juices such as V-8 or carrot-and-mixed greens. Over an extended period of time, a definite improvement of some kind should become noticeable.

Best Tonic for Irregularity

There's no two ways about it—bran *is* the best tonic you could ever use for correcting the problem of irregular bowel movements. In one fascinating medical study, "before and after" results were given of stool weights in those who ate refined food, then added about 1 tbsp. of bran twice a day to their diets a week later. Below is a simple table illustrating the dramatic changes in the stool weights of eight healthy male doctors and medical students between the ages of 25–43 without and with bran in their weekly diets.

	Experiment A		**Experiment B**	
	Without Bran	*With Bran*	*Without Bran*	*With Bran*
Wet weight	107 ± 44	174 ± 51	126 ± 47	215 ± 22
Dry weight	26 ± 9	41 ± 9	31 ± 10	47 ± 6

The physicians and surgeons from Western General Hospital in Edinburg, Scotland who compiled this report, estimated that without bran intake, a 176 lb. man passing only 3-1/2 oz. of stool per day would excrete fecal material equivalent to his body weight about every 2 years. But by the ingestion of about 2 tbsp. of bran daily this output would be achieved in only 12 months. And the coarser the bran particles are, the more water-holding capacity or laxative properties it's going to have.

A superb FarmLax used by some horse-and-buggy Amish in Ohio contains a unique bran blend and is available through Old Amish Herbs (see Appendix).

Two Guaranteed Laxative Cereals

There are many prepared cereals on the market today claiming to be high in fiber and so forth. But why take the manufacturer's word for it? Be on the safe side and know what you're getting. Go ahead and make your own! Here are two recipes to choose from.

Fruit/Nut Granolax

Needed: 2 cups rolled oats; 3 cups wheat germ; 1/2 cup shredded wheat; 1/2 cup bran; 1/2 cup chopped dates; 1/2 cup raisins; 1 cup chopped dried apples; 1/2 cup shelled cashews; 3 cups dry milk; 1/2 cup sunflower seeds; 1/2 cup pumpkin seeds; 3/4 cup chopped dried papaya. Get a good cutting board and either a Chinese vegetable cleaver or a sharp French knife and start chopping and slicing everything up into tidbit portions (the size depends on your own preference).

Needed: 1/2 cup honey; 1/8 cup pure maple syrup; 1/8 cup blackstrap molasses; 1 tbsp. pure vanilla; 1 tsp. cinnamon; 2 tsp. cardamom. Mix well together by hand with a wooden ladle in a large bowl.

Combine the dry ingredients together with the liquid. Stir until uniformly mixed. Rub a shallow pan with some lecithin (from health food store), then spoon out mixture in an even layer. Bake for 1-1/2 to 2 hours at 225° F. Bake a little longer if a dry, crunchy consistency is desired. Makes approximately 13 cups. Have a bowl of this every morning for breakfast and for a midnight snack.

Basic Granola

Needed: 8 cups rolled oats; 2 cups wheat germ; 1 cup shredded coconut; 1/2 cup dark honey; 1 cup water and 2 tbsp. pure vanilla.

Stir the dry oats, wheat germ and coconut together in a large mixing bowl with a wooden ladle. Next mix together in a separate bowl the honey, water and vanilla. Then add it to the dry ingredients and mix well. Pour contents into a large, greased cake pan. Bake at 275° F. for about 1 hour and 15 minutes, depending on how crisp you like it. You can add raisins and chopped, pitted dates to the hot granola after taking it out of the oven if you wish.

BREAD
(See also GRAINS)

Brief Description

One slice of either pumpernickel, rye or wheat bread would be about equal to 8 slices of white bread for increasing stool output. "The best way to increase intake of fiber-rich food," writes Denis Burkitt, M.D., a prominent British physician, "is to increase bread consumption, making sure that white bread is replaced by bread made from flour that is as near as possible to wholemeal. Whole wheat bread has three times the amount of dietary fiber compared to white bread."

Satisfying the "Munchies" with Bread

Ever get the hungries and feel like snacking on foods that put on more weight? Well, two slices of whole wheat bread will fill you up for several hours over a lot of other refined foods. White flour products are virtually worthless. This can be illustrated by the fact that it takes eight loaves of white bread to have the same laxative effect on the colon as does just one loaf of whole wheat bread. So having a peanut butter sandwich on two pieces of whole wheat or two slices of whole wheat toast lightly buttered with some cinnamon and cardamom sprinkled across them can be a nice way of satisfying a growling stomach without adding too many extra calories.

Bread Poultice Checks Tetany

A case I recall some years ago in Lander, Wyoming involved a young girl who got bit on her ankle by a pit bull terrier. An old gent down the street happened to hear of the incident and called on the distraught parents. He asked them for permission to treat her leg. They knew of his reputation as a local healer of sorts and agreed to it, not fully convinced themselves that they should subject their young girl to the further trauma of a hospital or doctor's office.

He immediately went to work and made a unique poultice by soaking some slices of slightly moldy bread in condensed milk and applying the same to their daughter's ankle with some strips of clean gauze taped on the ends with adhesive tape. The next morning he changed the dressing, and later that night all redness and inflammation had disappeared for good.

The Healing Aroma of Freshly Baked Bread

A therapeutic aspect seldom or never discussed in any self-care book that I'm aware of concerns the psychological and emotional benefits to be derived just from the aroma of freshly baked bread. While Freud or your favorite analyst may not have recommended this for mental problems, I do simply because I've witnessed the success of it on several occasions for myself.

Some cultures actually believe that the smell of fresh bread has medicinal importance. The January 1983 issue of *Natural History,* for instance, notes that "freshly baked bread, piled high on the body of a malaria sufferer, is believed to have the power to relieve malaria attacks," on the Italian isle of Sardinia. And in the Sardinian village of Esporlatu, people on the street will swear to the fact that "the smell of fresh bread is so potent it can keep sickness and death far away."

Some years ago I had an opportunity to spend some time interviewing several psychologists and therapists at the Utah State Hospital in Provo. One case, in particular, which was called to my attention then, compelled me to investigate this matter further in later years to my own satisfaction. In the case described to me, a middle-aged woman who had been committed for severe reactive depression wasn't responding at all to any of their given therapies. And the medication she was getting each day didn't really help that much either. She finally began to come out of her basement doldrums when they assigned her to work in the hospital kitchen with the baker, helping to make bread of all things. When asked to report to her therapists what was making her feel better, she responded by telling them that the aroma of the freshly baked loaves gave her an indescribable exhilaration of sorts—so much so in fact, that she began to feel and think there was hope for herself after all. About 2-1/2 months later she was discharged, apparently helped by the smell she was exposed to for several hours each day, as well as working her frustrations out in the kneading and punching of the dough. After this she never required further therapy again.

Making a Good Loaf of Bread

The following recipe appeared in the Dec.–Jan. 1978 issue of *Quest* magazine.

Rye Bread

Needed: 2 packages active dry yeast; 1/2 cup warm water 115°–125°); 1 tbsp. honey; 1-1/2 cups dark malt beer; 2 tbsp. butter; 1 tbsp. salt; 1/4 cup plain yogurt; 2-1/2 cups dark rye flour; 1 cup pumpernickel flour (or 1/2 cup rye and 1/2 cup whole wheat); 1 cup gluten flour; 1 cup all-purpose white flour; 1 tbsp. egg white mixed with 1 tbsp. water; cornmeal.

In a large bowl dissolve yeast in warm water and stir in honey. Heat beer until warm enough to melt the butter in it; add salt and yogurt. Cool to lukewarm, then mix with yeast liquid. Add all the flours, except for about 1/2 cup of the white. Mix well, then turn out on a floured surface and knead, adding the reserved flour as necessary, for 5–10 minutes.

When dough is smooth, although it may still be slightly sticky, put it in a buttered bowl, turn it once, cover it, put it in an 85° place (inside a cool oven with a pan of steaming water underneath works well) and let it rise until double in size (about 2-1/2 hours). Shape into 2 oval or round loaves and place on a baking sheet sprinkled with cornmeal. Rise again, lightly covered, until double in size, about 1-1/2 hours. Preheat oven to 375° F.; bake for 45–50 min. It will sound hollow if hit with a knuckle. Cool on a rack. Makes 2 loaves.

BROCCOLI (See under CABBAGE AND ITS KIND)
BRUSSEL SPROUTS (See under CABBAGES AND ITS KIND)

BUCKWHEAT (See under GRAINS)

BULGHUR (See under GRAINS)

BURDOCK (*Arctium lappa*)

Brief Description

There are basically two kinds of burdock. Common burdock (*A. minus*) is the kind more commonly found intercropped with corn and wheat in the midwest. On the other hand, greater burdock is the one primarily harvested for its root as an important source of food for the Japanese. They use it there as we use carrots here. This variety of burdock has the big, round, brown bristly burrs, hence the common name of cocklebur.

Unsurpassed Blood Purifier

Burdock root is perhaps the most widely used of all blood purifiers, among the best the herbal kingdom has to offer for this, and *the* most important herb for treating chronic skin problems. It's one of the few that can effectively treat eczema, acne, psoriasis, boils, herpes and syphilitic sores, styes, carbuncles, cankers and the like.

To make an effective tea, bring 1 quart of water to a boil. Reduce heat to simmer, adding 4 tsp. cut, dried root. Cover and let simmer for 7 minutes, then remove from heat and let steep for 2 hours longer. Drink a minimum of 2 cups per day on an empty stomach (more if chronic skin problems persist). A larger quantity can be made and used to wash the skin with often. Or capsules (4 per day) from your local health food store under the Nature's Way label may be taken instead.

Eliminating Stones

A great remedy for getting rid of some stubborn kidney and gallstones is to make a burdock-catnip tea. Bring 4 cups of water to a boil and add 2 tbsp. of chopped, fresh or cut dried root. Reduce to simmer for about 10 minutes, covered. After which, remove from heat and add 3 tsp. chopped or cut fresh or dried catnip herb.

Let steep for 1-1/2 hours. Then strain and to each cup add 1 tsp. lemon juice and 1/2 tsp. pure maple syrup or blackstrap molasses to sweeten. Drink slowly. Exactly 10 minutes later, take orally 1 tbsp. of pure virgin olive oil.

Repeat this regimen 3 times each day. The tea soothes irritated tissues and helps to break up or partially dissolve the stones, while the oil acts as a lubricant to remove them from the body more easily. It's *very important* that *no* greasy, fried foods, soft drinks, refined carbohydrates like white flour or white sugar products or red meat and poultry be consumed during this treatment; otherwise, absolute and complete success cannot be fully guaranteed.

After taking the last cup of tea and spoonful of oil at night just before retiring, be sure to sleep on your right side with a pillow underneath your armpit. This resting posture, some claim, seems to expedite the removal of stones from the body more quickly.

A Wild Vegetable Dessert

Who would ever think that vegetables would serve as delicious desserts in place of more standard fare like pie and ice cream? Well, in the case of burdock root, you have such a tummy pleaser fit for a king.

Burdock Roots, Hawaiian Style

Needed: 2 tbsp. sweet butter, 1/4 cup packed brown sugar; 1 tsp. lemon juice; 1 cup canned, drained pineapple chunks (save juice); 1/2 cup pineapple syrup drained from chunks; 2 tbsp. cornstarch; 2 cups burdock roots, cut into rounds and precooked until tender.

Melt butter in skillet over low heat, add brown sugar and lemon juice, stir. Mix pineapple syrup with the cornstarch, stir well and add to the butter and sugar mixture. Stir constantly over low heat until the mixture is a thick sauce, about 20 min. Add the burdock roots and pineapple chunks to the sauce and heat through. Serve warm.

A Nourishing Herb-Fish Soup

An alternative-care medical doctor from Tokyo, Japan told me what he prescribed to many of his patients recuperating from recent illness or surgery, or who just needed extra vim, vigor and vitality, at a recent conference in Rhode Island.

First secure a fresh-water fish of some kind from your local fish market or supermarket meat counter. Carp, salmon and trout are the best. About a pound of fish is necessary, along with 1-1/2 lbs. of fresh burdock root, 1 tbsp. of sesame seed oil, 2/3 cup of uncooked barley pearls, 1 tsp. fresh, grated ginger root, several unused green tea bags, 1/2 cup chopped chives, 2 tbsps. lime juice and some kelp.

Nothing of the fish should be removed; head, fins, scales and bones all kept intact. Chop the entire fish into 1-1/4-in. chunks (appx. a dozen pieces), then cut the head into several more pieces, removing the eyes. Next cut the burdock root into *exceedingly thin* slices. Sautée this herb root for half an hour in sesame seed oil. After this place the pieces of fish on the bed of sautéed burdock. Cover with just enough water to maintain a nearly 3-in. level over the fish.

Next scatter the barley over the fish and roots, along with the chives and kelp. Then place several unused tea bags in opposite corners of the pot *and on top* of the fish. Cover and bring to a boil, then reduce the heat to a lower setting and slowly cook for at least 5-1/2 hours. At the end of this period of time, uncover the pot and remove the tea bags. Then add the grated ginger and lime juice, cover and simmer again for an additional 15–20 minutes. The entire preparation can be consumed over several days time.

BUTTERNUT (See under NUTS)

C

CABBAGE AND ITS KIND (*Brassica* species)

BROCCOLI	(***Brassica oleracea italica***)
BRUSSELS SPROUTS	(***Brassica oleracea gemmifera***)
CABBAGE (Green, Red, Savoy)	(***Brassica oleracea***)
CAULIFLOWER	(***Brassica oleracea botrytis***)
COLLARDS AND KALE	(***Brassica oleracea acephala***)
KOHLRABI	(***Brassica oleracea***)
MUSTARD GREENS	(***Brassica*** **species**)
MUSTARD SEED (Yellow)	(***Brassica alba***)

Brief Descriptions

BROCCOLI—Originally an Italian ethnic dish until 1920 when the D'Arrigo brothers from San Jose, California popularized it in Boston. Shoots have a milder taste than cabbage. California produces 96% of all broccoli sold in the U.S.

BRUSSELS SPROUTS—Cute little cabbage developed in Belgium in the 16th century. About 75% of our nation's supply comes from California.

CABBAGE (Green, Red and Savoy)—Domestic green is often used in cooking and for making sauerkraut; the red or purple kind is used in pickling and the savoy has a loose head, crinkly leaves and a milder flavor than the others.

CAULIFLOWER—The head isn't a cluster of flower buds, but the tips of a mass of closely compacted stems. 75% of our cauliflower comes from California.

COLLARDS AND KALE—Kale has curly leaves, while collards have broad, smooth ones.

KOHLRABI—A vegetable from outer space, some say, due to its pale-green bulb with gangly tentacle-like stems sprouting from all sides.

MUSTARD GREENS—A popular food in the South, especially among the poorer classes, such as collards and kale are, but quite nutritious.

MUSTARD SEED—Seeds of the white mustard are used a lot in prepared mustards, where it's combined with vinegar and spices like turmeric for the yellow color.

Strong Cancer Preventative

An overwhelming abundance of medical and scientific evidence has been published in the last decade to show that cabbage and its kind can help to prevent cancer if used in the diet properly.

Prestigious journals such as *Federation Proceedings* (May 1976), *Cancer Research* (May 1978), *J. of the National Cancer Institute* (Sept. 1978), *Mutation Research* (Vol. 77, 1980) and *Science News* (April 13, 1985) have reported significant research showing that the sulphur and histidine in broccoli, Brussels sprouts, cabbage, cauliflower, kale, kohlrabi and mustard greens inhibit the growth of tumors, prevent cancer of the colon and rectum, detoxify the system of harmful chemical additives and increase our body's cancer-fighting compounds.

The bottom line to all this, then, is that you should be consuming lots of these vegetables if you ever expect to substantially reduce your risks of getting cancer.

Lowers Serum Cholesterol

Cabbage and its kind, especially items like Brussel sprouts, can dramatically lower what is often called "bad" cholesterol (low-density lipoproteins). This "bad" cholesterol usually causes hardening of the arteries in the course of time. At least two scientific publications have reported these findings. By including cabbage and its other members in your diet more often, you stand a very good chance of not developing coronary heart disease later on in life.

Increases Elimination

Cabbage promotes increased bowel movements. A 1936 medical journal noted that for every gram of powdered cabbage leaves fed to three healthy male medical students, their respective stool weights increased by 18 grams each. A more recent study showed that when 19 healthy male hospital staff volunteers consumed finely powdered cabbage supplements with their regular diets over a three-week period, their stool weights increased by 20%. This can be attributed to the water-holding capacity of cabbage fiber. About 5 cups of shredded cabbage, raw or cooked, is suggested twice a week in the diet for improved colon function.

Fights Yeast Infection

Some native folk healers in various American ethnic groups such as Hispanics and Blacks, have prescribed raw cabbage juice for yeast infections covering the head, skin, hands and feet, as well as for treating Premenstrual Syndrome (PMS). In giving women relief from PMS, the cabbage juice has been taken internally or else used as a vaginal douche or both in some cases with relatively good success. Luc De Schepper, M.D., a Los Angeles physician experienced in Candida research, lists cabbage, Brussel sprouts, broccoli, watercress, chives and spinach as mandatory sulphur foods for suppressing yeast infection.

A Fantastic Ulcer Healer

Different medical journals have separately confirmed that *raw* cabbage and raw cabbage juice is just the ticket for relieving *and healing* any kind of gastrointestinal ulcer, be it duodenal, peptic or what have you. Half a cup, morning and night, of raw juice is a terrific antacid remedy plus a great ulcer healer.

A relatively new anti-ulcer product which some Florida practitioners have been prescribing to their patients of late comes from herbs used for stomach problems by the horse-and-buggy Amish of Ohio. It may be obtained by mail-order from Old Amish Herbs under the name of Cabbage Compound (See Appendix).

Radiation Protection

Two important medical studies published nearly 20 years apart, showed that rabbits and guinea pigs previously exposed to lethal doses of uranium and X-rays were afforded considerable protection against their harmful effects when cabbage leaves were added to their basic diets. Considering the excessive radiation to which we're constantly exposed today, ranging from home computers and microwave ovens to color TVs and high-tension power lines running through the neighborhood, it may be a good idea to add more cabbage to your weekly diet for extra protection.

Grandma's Old-Fashioned Mustard Plaster

Mustard plaster is one of those reliable "old timey" remedies held over from grandma's era, due to its considerable value in treating a wide variety of disorders—asthma, bronchitis, pneumonia, fever and chills, sciatica, neuralgia, gout, bumps, bruises, sprains, tendonitis, common cold and flu, eruptive sores and boils.

A simple plaster still used by some farm folks in rural Indiana and by hillbillies in Kentucky, involves mashing the leaves and stems of fresh mustard plant into a pulp. The surface of the skin is then coated with Crisco lard or Vaseline before the pulp is applied and bound in place with some gauze and adhesive tape. By coating the skin with petroleum jelly, it prevents the mustard from causing serious blisters or raising welts on it. This plaster can be kept on for several hours or else left on overnight for best results.

Relieves Aches and Pains

If you're suffering from rheumatoid arthritis, lower backache, abdominal cramps and so forth, then this remedy, however unusual, is for you. After cutting out the midribs from several large green cabbage leaves, just iron them with a steam iron until they're soft as velvet. Then rub a little olive oil on one side and put them on the areas of pain, covering them with a heavy towel. Leave for a while before changing again. *Guaranteed* relief, every single time!

Mouth-Watering Recipes

The following recipes involve different members of the *Brassica* family and come either from firsthand sources or else have been adapted from materials appearing in *Delicious!*, the *L.A. Times*, *Bestways* and the book, *Vegetables.*

Agent 007's Broccoli Harlequin

Albert R. Broccoli gained fame for 15 James Bond films produced over the past 25 years. In addition to that he belongs to that famous Italian family which brought the seeds of this now famous vegetable named after them, from Italy to America at the turn of the century.

Broccoli, himself, at the age of 78 offers this recipe.

Needed: 1 small head cauliflower; 2 small bunches broccoli; 4 tbsps. butter; 2-3 tbsps. plain yogurt; 2 tbsps. grated Parmesan cheese; 1/4 tsp. salt; freshly ground black pepper to taste (I recommend substituting kelp for the salt and pepper); 3/4 cup rye or pumpernickel breadcrumbs.

Break the cauliflower into flowerets and remove most of the white stalks. Steam the cauliflower for 3-4 minutes or until still firm. Steam the broccoli for about 6 minutes or until soft enough to purée. Prehend oven to 350° F. Purée broccoli with butter and yogurt. Lightly grease a 6-cup, oven-proof dish with olive oil, mound the cauliflower in it and sprinkle with the cheese, salt and pepper (or kelp). Season the broccoli purée with salt and pepper (or kelp); then spoon it over the cauliflower and sprinkle the top with the breadcrumbs. Bake for 20 minutes. Serves 6-8.

A James Bond Breakfast

The world's most secret agent prefers breakfast to any other meal of the day, according to information scattered throughout all of the Ian Fleming and John Gardiner novels. And it seldom varies—orange juice, strong coffee without sugar, scrambled eggs, toast and frequently bacon. Occasionally though, Bond has indulged himself in a little breakfast delight consisting of steamed broccoli and soft-boiled eggs.

Steam 4 stalks of broccoli until tender, and cut into thin strips. Soft-boil 4 eggs for 4 minutes. Lay the broccoli strips on a plate. Shell the eggs and chop them in a bowl. Blend in 4-6 tbsps. of lime juice with kelp to taste. Spread this over the broccoli, then garnish with paprika and a little finely chopped parsley. Serves 4.

Real Creamy Coleslaw

Needed: 1-1/2 cups plain yogurt; 6-1/2 tbsp. brown sugar; 1 tbsp. pure maple syrup; 3-1/2 tbsp. apple cider vinegar; 3/4 cup olive oil; 1/3 tsp. each of powdered garlic, onion, mustard and celery; dash of kelp; 1-1/2 tbsp lemon juice; 3/4 cup half and half; 1/2 tsp. sea salt; 1 head each green and red cabbage, very finely shredded.

Blend together the yogurt, sugar, syrup and oil. Add spice powders, kelp, lemon juice, half-and-half and salt. Stir until smooth as silk. Pour over the coleslaw in a large bowl and toss until cabbage is well coated. If you wish, you can add just half of the dressing to a head of cabbage, saving the rest to dress fruit salad or other salads with. Keeps in a closed container in the fridge for nearly a week. Recipe makes about 1 quart of dressing.

Southern-Style Mustard Greens

Needed: 1 lb. each of collard and mustard greens; 3 strips bacon; 1/4 cup chopped onion; 3/4 cup hot water; 1 tsp. sea salt; 2 tbsp. apple cider vinegar; 1/4 tsp. kelp. Wash greens well, removing tough stems and ribs, and shred leaves. Fry bacon in large pot over medium heat until crisp. Remove bacon and drain on paper towels. In the same pot fry onion until golden brown, then add greens, water, salt and kelp. Cover and simmer for about 25 min. until tender. Drain and reserve the liquid (called "pot likker" in the South), and transfer greens to a serving dish. Sprinkle with vinegar and more kelp. Crumble bacon over top and serve. Cornbread can be served on the side for sopping up the "pot likker." Makes a real tasty dish!

CALENDULA (*Calendula officinalis*)

Brief Description

More popular in Europe than in America, calendula yields bright yellow to orange flowerheads. And is prolific in numerous waste places and gardens as a hardy weed of sorts. An old folk belief says that if its flowerheads should close up after 7:00 a.m., it will rain for sure the next day.

Its greatest value in either salve or dilute tincture form is for any kind of external skin, muscle or blood vessel problems—wounds, sores, varicose veins, pulled muscles, boils, bruises, sprains, athlete's foot, burns, frostbites, etc.

Heals Intestinal Ulcers and Colitis

Two important medical studies published side by side in Vol. 20 of the Soviet journal, *Vatreshni Bolesti* for June 1981 confirm the value of calendula in healing duodenal ulcers, inflammation of both the stomach and duodenum and intestinal colitis. In the first instance, an equal mixture of comfrey root and calendula brought healing relief to 19 patients with duodenal ulcers and 19 others suffering from gastroduodenitis. A tea made of both herbs (1 tbsp. of each herb in 1 quart boiling water, simmered 5 minutes, steeped 40 minutes) was administered to each patient (2 cups daily) with considerable success.

In the second study cited, 24 patients with chronic nonspecific colitis were treated with a combination of herbs consisting of equal parts of dandelion root, St. Johnswort, lemon balm, calendula and fennel seed, made into a strong tea (1 tsp. of each herb in 1-1/2 qts. boiling water, steeped 1 hour) and given to each of them three times a day, 1 cup at a time. According to the published medical report's brief English abstract: "As a result of the treatment, the spontaneous and palpable pains along the large intestine disappeared in 95.83% of the patients by the 15th day of their admission to the clinic." This is sufficient testimony to demonstrate the clinical validity of this wonderful herb for successfully treating all manner of inflammation.

Varicose Veins Disappeared

A West German herbalist, Maria Treben, relates the following episode:

> On a visit, the lady of the house showed me her legs covered with varicose veins. I fetched calendula from her garden and prepared the ointment [recipe listed below]. The residue I put immediately on her legs (the residue can be used four to five times). She spread the ointment, the thickness of the back of a knife, on a piece of linen and bandaged her legs with it. You will be surprised, when I tell you, that four weeks later, when she visited me at home, the varicose veins had disappeared. Both legs had nice, smooth skin.

Making a Healing Salve and Tincture

Finely chop two heaping handfuls of fresh calendula leaves, flowers and stems. Next gently melt enough lard in a heavy frying pan on low heat to equal about 2-1/2 cups. Add the chopped calendula, stir with a wooden ladle for a few minutes, then remove the pan from the stove, cover and let the contents set for an entire day. The next day warm the pan up again, filter contents through cloth and pour into clean jars. Seal tightly and rub liberally on the skin whenever necessary. A ready-made Calendula Dairy Salve from Old Amish Herbs (see Appendix) is unique from all other ointments in one respect—its base consists of pure pork lard, one of the most absorbent materials for the skin. This salve is good for man and beast alike.

To make a tincture soak a handful of flowers in 2 cups of whiskey for 14 days on a window sill in the sun. Shake several times each day. When taking internally for hepatitis, cramps and inflammation, use 12–15 drops at a time.

CANTALOUPE (See under MELONS.)

CAPSICUM (See under CAYENNE.)

CARAWAY (*Carum carvi*)

Brief Description

Caraway is a biennial or perennial cultivated and found wild in the northern and northwestern U.S., Europe and Asia. The hollow, furrowed, angular, branched stem commences to grow in the second year from a white, carrot-shaped root. The leaves are bi- or tri-pinnate and deeply incised, the upper ones on a sheath-like petiole. The small white or yellow flowers make their appearance in the late spring (usually from May to June). The seeds are dark brown, flat and oblong in shape.

Women's Tea for Tardy Menstruation

A nutritious broth or vegetable-herb tea can be made from the following ingredients and taken by women who have delayed periods in order to encourage the onset of their menstrual cycle. Bring 1 quart of water to a boil. Add 1 tsp. caraway seed, 1/2 small chopped carrot, 1/2 of 1 chopped celery stalk and 1/2 tsp. grated ginger root. Cover and simmer on low heat for 25 minutes. Uncover and remove from heat. Add 1 tsp. *each* fresh chopped parsley, fresh cut watercress, dried peppermint and yarrow. Cover again and steep an additional 20 minutes or so. Strain, sweeten and flavor with a few drops and pinches of honey and cinnamon. Drink 3 cups each day on an empty stomach until period commences.

Nature's Anti-Gas Medicine

To prevent heartburn and acid indigestion, simply bring 2 cups of water to a boil, adding 4 tsp. slightly pounded seeds. Simmer on low heat 5 minutes, then steep away from heat an additional 15 minutes. Sweeten to taste with a little honey and drink one cup with each meal for pleasant digestion of food. When taken warm, the tea will also promote the onset of menstruation, help relieve uterine cramps very nicely, promote breast milk secretion in nursing mothers and help clear away mucus from the back of the throat. Small amounts may also be given to infants suffering from intestinal gas with good results.

Culinary Value

Not only do caraway seeds add a certain pungent flavor to cabbage, turnips, potatoes and breads, but they also help to digest the starches in some of these foods. The seeds are indispensable in making rye, pumpernickel and Swedish breads. Likewise, they find added attraction in many European dishes, especially stews and soups, ranging from Hungarian Goulash to Russian Borsht. Apple sauce, pickled beets, sauerkraut, squash and pumpkin pies shouldn't be without them either.

CARDAMOM (*Elettaria cardamomum*)

Brief Description

Cardamom is a perennial found throughout southern India, but is also cultivated quite extensively in the tropics as well. The simple, erect stems reach an average height of 8 feet from a mere thumb-thick, creeping rootstock. The leaves are lanceolate, dark green and glabrous above, lighter and silky-like beneath. The small, yellowish flowers grow in loose racemes on prostrate flower stems. The fruit is a three-celled capsule holding up to 18 seeds. Cardamom is used in cooking and for flavoring wormwood and valerian.

Remedy for Celiac Disease

Celiac disease is an intolerance for the gluten in grain commonly occurring in children, and marked by frequent diarrhea and continual digestive problems. Generally a gluten-free diet is prescribed to help them. But when I was in mainland China in 1980, I discovered in some city hospitals we visited, the use of powered cardamom sprinkled on cooked cereal to correct this problem in youngsters. I've recommended it here to some of my friends whose children have the same kind of problem with relatively good results. They're able to handle grains like cooked oatmeal or whole wheat bread when sufficient cardamom has been previously included.

Culinary Advantages

Because of its mild, pleasant, ginger-like flavor, cardamom can be used in a number of bean dishes, holiday beverages such as eggnog or baked goodies like Danish sweet rolls and fruit cakes. It's especially valuable, however, in cooked cereals and whole grain breads for those unable to tolerate the gluten.

CAROB (*Ceratonial siliqua*)

Brief Description

Carob pods grow on a dome-shaped evergreen tree with dark-green compound leaves consisting of 2 to 5 pairs of large, rounded glossy leaflets. The tree can reach a towering height of nearly 50 feet and is native to southwestern Europe and western Asia, but is also widely cultivated in the Mediterranean region.

The pods are the so-called "locusts" consumed by John the Baptist during his wilderness residency, hence the other common name of "St. John's bread." Seeds were used in ancient times as weight units for gold from which the term "carat" is reportedly derived. The Prodigal Son in Jesus' famous parable subsisted on discarded carob pods, as mentioned in Luke 15:16—"And he would fain have filled his belly with the husks that the swine did eat."

Kidney Failure Reversed

In the medical journal *Nouv-Presse-Med.*, a French physician related how a clinical case of chronic kidney failure was successfully reversed with carob gum. Approx. 2 level tsp. of carob powder in cranberry juice or milk, taken four to five times daily should be of some use in stimulating inactive kidneys.

Remarkable Anti-Diarrheal

One of the very best remedies for human infant and adult and livestock diarrhea is carob powder. A back issue of *Western Dairy Journal* advocated the mixing in of carob powder with regular feed to cure and prevent scours or diarrhea in heifer calves.

An even more effective use for halting the same condition in people has been found as the following episode with a Montana sheep rancher residing near Harlowton shows:

> I am 65 and have had diarrhea for years. I was always listless and worn out. The least work would wear me out. I didn't realize that diarrhea was nearly all of my trouble.
>
> I tried carob powder and it worked wonders. In my case, it takes a highly heaping soup-spoonful to fix me up. I take it each meal . . . I have used carob and it has helped me a lot. I wish I had known about it a few years earlier.
>
> Medical doctors gave me medicine similar to Kaopectate, but I had to take it in enormous quantities to get relief. About 4 fluid ounces of Kaopectate was required per night in many cases, or a little less of the prescribed medicine for the same results. Carob works much better.

When traveling to foreign countries, always carry a can of carob powder with you to use. Carob pods are particularly rich in one class of tannins, which manifest strong anti-viral properties. Thus, it would appear that carob powder might work just as well as some kinds of antibiotic drugs usually given to treat bacterial-induced diarrhea.

And for diarrhea in infants—quite a common problem it seems—carob powder rates magnificent in its performance here. A number of related articles in back issues of the *Journal of Pediatrics* conclusively show that carob is able to completely correct this dangerous nuisance in any infants suffering from diarrhea. The powder can be given in a formula drink preparation or if the baby is old enough to eat solids, it can be mixed in apple sauce or some kind of pudding and fed that way with satisfying results.

Chocolate-Cocoa Substitute

There are many advantages to using carob in place of either chocolate or cocoa. First, it has far less calories than either cocoa or sweet chocolate. Second, it's a darned sight cheaper. Third, because it's so naturally sweet, it takes a lot less to make brownies or a shake. Fourthly, it doesn't have the addictive substance, caffeine, like the other two have, which can be potentially harmful to children. Finally, it doesn't interfere with calcium assimilation like chocolate or cocoa do. And, it doesn't cause acne either.

Indulging Recipes

Here are some recipes you can really indulge yourself in without fear of getting fat, incurring pimples or feeling guilty for eating unhealthy things.

Carob Brownies

Needed: 1/2 cup honey; 1/2 cup safflower oil; 1/2 cup carob powder; 2 beaten eggs; 2 cups whole wheat flour; 1/4 tsp. sea salt; 1/2 cup granular lecithin; 1 tsp. almond extract; 1/2 cup ground or finely chopped nuts.

Blend honey, oil and carob powder. Add beaten eggs. Stir in flower and salt. Add lecithin and almond extract, then the nuts. Pour into an oiled 8-in. square pan. Bake at 350° F. for 30 min. Cool and cut into squares.

CARROT (*Daucus sativus*)

Brief Description

Carrots around the world grow in all shapes and colors. Westerners would mistake the Asian types, with their bulbous purplish red roots, for beets. Other colors are pale and deep yellow, red and white. The roots range from spherical to cylindrical. One variety in the Far East grows up to a yard long.

Unusual Mouth Wash

French herbalist, Maurice Mességué advises that carrot tops be made into a tea for an effective mouth wash and gargle, due to their strong antiseptic action. Bring 3 cups of water to a boil, adding 1/2 cup chopped carrot tops. Simmer for 20 minutes, steeping another 30 minutes. Strain and store in refrigerator. Rinse and gargle mouth each morning with some.

Heals Burns and Scalds

Shauna Wilson of Atlanta, Georgia wrote to me several years back of a treatment she used on her 4-year-old daughter's arm, after the girl had pulled a pan of boiling hot water down on herself from the stove by accident. "I soaked her arm in ice water first, then dressed the injury with some gauze which had been dipped in carrot juice and lightly wrung out," she said. "I repeated this several times more the next day, and by the third day most of the swelling and inflammation was gone."

Lowers Cholesterol and Cancer

A diet supplemented by raw carrots each day helps to lower cholesterol in the body. It's recommended that you eat a carrot salad or munch on a carrot every time you consume greasy food.

Carrots contain high amounts of the anti-cancer nutrient, beta-carotene. Scientific documentation has shown that this root vegetable really does help to keep the incidence of cancer down in those who consume it regularly versus those who seldom ever include it in their diets. For instance, the December 1986 issue of *Epidemiology* noted that pancreatic cancer risks are substantially higher in those who consume fried and grilled meat and margarine, but significantly reduced with almost daily consumption of carrots and citrus fruits.

Energy Stimulant

Ever have a glass of carrot juice and feel a surge of energy afterwards? It's probably due to the high natural sugar content. Some of the Pennsylvanian Amish folks use a tonic called Carrot Concoction from Old Amish Herbs (See Appendix) to give them more vim and vigor when fresh carrot juice isn't always available. Equal parts of carrot and pineapple juice make a nice energy drink for those with hypoglycemia.

Infantile Diarrhea Cured

Some 3 dozen cases of infantile diarrhea were cleared up with nothing but carrot soup and carob. These Innsbruck, Austria infants all experienced chronic diarrhea lasting nearly a week or more. It was discovered that the diarrhea had been caused by the *E. coli* bacteria strain. But carrot soup containing 2% carob powder was able to successfully block the activity of this virus within the infants' upper small intestinal tract, resulting in no more diarrhea in any of them. (See the recipe on page 68 for making carrot soup.)

Vegetable Laxative

Carrots also clear up constipation as well. Carrots promote some looseness of the stool, while grains and leaves increase bowel gas. Two separate medical studies published 42 years apart cited the laxative properties of raw carrot pulp. (*Journal of Nutrition* 11:444, 1936 and *Lancet,* Jan. 7, 1978). A 1978 report observed quicker actions when cabbage and carrots were combined together in the same meal. An old 1931 nutrition review cited that for each gram of carrots consumed by three healthy male medical students, their respective stool residues increased in weight by 19 grams or 1/2 an ounce. (See the recipe on page 68 for a good carrot-cabbage raisin salad to really get the bowels moving!)

Protects Against Toxic Chemicals

There's nothing quite like carrot fiber to protect the body against certain chemical pollutants. Rats experiencing loss of weight, extensive diarrhea and an unthrifty appearance when given harmful chemicals in their diets, had a complete reversal of all of these negative symptoms when carrot root and cabbage powders were added to their daily regimens. And, interestingly enough, many Soviet doctors recommend carrots in the diets of factory workers exposed to harmful chemicals from time to time.

Kick the Smoking Habit

In the 1983 comic strip, "Wizard of Id" by Parker and Hart, two of the king's guards were chatting in the courtyard. One asks the other, "I understand you used to smoke 4 packs a day?" His companion agrees, adding, "Now I eat a carrot whenever I crave a cigarette." "How's it working out?" asks the first guard. "Fine," replies the second, as he hops away like a bunny rabbit.

But there's more truth to this than meets the eye. Over the years in my travels around the world I've heard some pretty good stories relating to the use of carrots for knocking the nicotine habit. But none quite so dramatic or simple in detail as what a lady friend of mine in Indonesia related to me in October, 1986. Her name is Josephine Hetarihon, age 35, and she works as an executive secretary in Jakarta. This is her story:

> It was on Sept. 26, 1979 that I finally managed to quit smoking. I had been smoking 2 packs a day of Dunhill before this.
>
> I started smoking when I was in junior high school at the age of 15. A friend suggested that I use carrots to help me quit.
>
> It took me about two weeks on this carrot program until I was able to quit smoking altogether. I would eat about 2-3 carrots a day. I found that the sweet taste of the carrots satisfied me enough so that I didn't crave a cigarette.

Relieves Asthma

The 88-year-old English theologian, Reverend John Wesley, who founded the Methodist church, recommended eating boiled carrots and drinking the warm broth thereof as a "seldom fail" remedy for relieving asthma. Lukewarm carrot juice also has a similar effect.

Therapeutic Recipes

Our culinary recipes should also be our household remedies. The two recipes below are, therefore, intended not only to taste good, but also to keep you in a fit state of health as well.

Miracle Carrot Soup

Needed: 5-1/2 washed, unpeeled carrots; 8 cups water; 1/2 tsp kelp; 1/2 tsp. sea salt; 1/2 tsp honey. 1/2 cup chopped onion; 6 tbsp. melted butter; 6 tbsp. flour; 2 cups hot milk.

Chop carrots up fine. Combine them with the water, kelp, sea salt and honey. Cook for 1 hour. Add the chopped onions and simmer on low heat for 10 more minutes. Melt butter in skillet on medium-to-low heat. Slowly stir in flour, but don't brown. Simmer for 10 minutes without burning, stirring frequently. Then add hot milk to skillet and whip smooth by hand with a wire whip. Add this to the soup, whipping thoroughly by hand until well mixed. Serves 6 or can be refrigerated and used for medicinal purposes whenever necessary.

Protective Carrot-Cabbage Salad

Needed: 2-1/4 finely shredded carrots; 2-1/2 cups finely shredded or chopped cabbage; 1/3 cup finely chopped green bell pepper; 2 tbsp. raisins; 3 tbsp. canned pineapple chunks; 1 tbsp. pineapple juice from can; 1 cup plain yogurt; 10 chopped dates.

Mix the carrots, cabbage and bell pepper together in a large mixing bowl. Add the raisins, pineapple chunks, juice and dates. Stir everything together again, mixing well. Finally turn in the yogurt with a wooden ladle and mix thoroughly until a smooth, somewhat tight consistency to the salad is formed. Serves six on Romaine lettuce leaves. Or refrigerate and eat some every day to protect yourself against the harmful chemicals in our environment and food and water supplies.

CASABA (See under MELONS)

CASCARA SAGRADA (*Rhamnus purshiana*)

Brief Description

The tree from which the valuable reddish-brown bark is obtained, is a small to medium-sized deciduous with hairy twigs, capable of reaching heights near 50 feet in some instances. The tree is native to the Pacific Coast states and provinces of the U.S. and Canada. The bark is removed from trees with trunk diameters of about 4 feet or more. It's then permitted to dry and aged for 1 year before use, as the fresh bark has an emetic principle which is destroyed on prolonged storage or by heating.

Guaranteed Laxative

If your colon isn't functioning like you think it should be, this is the herb for you. The Nov.-Dec. 1982 issue of the Italian medical journal *G. Clin. Medica,* reported that a preparation containing cascara was definitely an effective therapy for clearing up simple constipation in many elderly patients. Up to 3 capsules at a time should do the job nicely. For a complete "roto-rooter" cleansing effect of the bowels, one might want to try Nature's Way Naturalax 3 Formula available from any health food store.

CASHEW (See under NUTS)

CATNIP (*Nepeta cataria*)

Brief Description

Catnip is a perennial herb of the mint family. Its erect, square, branching stem is hairy and grows from 3–5 feet high. The oblong or cordate, pointed leaves have scalloped edges and gray or whitish hairs on the lower side. The flowers are white with purple spots and grow in spikes from June to September.

Sure Cure for Insomnia and Hyperactivity

A major constituent in catnip, nepelactone is quite similar in its chemical structure to the valepotriates, the sedative principles of valerian root. This helps to explain why a "cup of hot catnip tea taken at bedtime insures a good night's sleep." Mice given catnip extract experienced a reduction of overall activity and an increase in their sleeping time. And a hot water extract administered to young (9- and 27-day-old) chicks in a hatchery caused "a significant increase" in their average daily and weekly light sleep time.

To make yourself a nice nightcap that will put you into slumberland for sure, simply bring 1-1/2 cups of water to a boil. Remove from heat and add 1 tsp. of preferably the freshly cut herb or else 1 tsp. of the dried material and let steep for about 20 minutes until lukewarm before drinking. Honey may be added if desired. An Old Amish Herbs remedy called Night Nip works pretty good for insomnia too (see Appendix). Three capsules before retiring is suggested. The tea is also very good for reducing fevers, the miseries of hayfever and nausea. A small cup of warm catnip tea sweetened with honey is good for calming hyperactive kids.

Relieves Aching Tooth, Gums

Hillbilly residents in the Ozark and Appalachian Mountains employ either mashed fresh catnip leaves or the dried herb powder as a crude poultice application directly to sore gums or aching teeth, to relieve the intense pain and suffering. If the powder is to be used, the finger or a piece of cotton are moistened with water and then some of the powder applied on their surfaces, after which the same is put into the mouth and held firmly against the aching tooth or just rubbed on the gums for quick relief. The fresh leaves seem to bring nearly instant relief, while the dried powder takes a little longer to work.

Remarkable Eyewash

A strong catnip tea can be used as an effective eyewash to relieve inflammation and swelling due to certain airborne allergies, cold and flu and excess alcoholic intake ("bloodshot eye" syndrome). Bring 3 cups of water to a boil and add 5 tsp. of cut fresh leaves. Reduce to low heat and let simmer for only 3 minutes. Remove from heat and let steep an additional 50 minutes. Strain and refrigerate in a clean fruit jar. Use as an eyewash with an eye cup several times each day. Or soak a clean terry-cloth towel in a warm solution of the tea and apply over the eyes for half an hour. Used catnip tea bags, while still warm and wrung out, can also be put on the eyelids for some relief.

Marijuana Substitute

In my occasional campus lectures before college students or high school kids on the subject of herbs in general, I often get asked the familiar question, "What herbs are there that you can legally smoke to get you high?" And my answer, based upon solid clinical evidence, has invariably been catnip, even though I believe young people shouldn't be using them as such.

In a past issue of *JAMA* (*J. of the Am. Med. Assoc.* 236:473, 1976), UCLA psychologist, Dr. Ronald K. Siegel, has also mentioned catnip in this regard. But the most compelling evidence for catnip's psychedelic effects comes from the Feb. 17, 1969 issue of *JAMA*. Several cases were reported, of which one is excerpted here for the benefit of readers who may personally know young people that might benefit from a safer and more legal herbal hallucinogen, than those which are harmful to the health and definitely illegal.

> A 17-year-old white, female high school student has been undergoing psychotherapy for two years for relatively mild behavior disorders. The patient has smoked marijuana for approximately one year, usually twice a month. She has used cataria for 3 months, approximately once a week. She describes the effects of catnip as being similar to marijuana; i.e., relieving depression, elevating mood and producing euphoria . . . The subject can voluntarily reactivate this experience for up to 3 days after having smoked cataria and often does so to escape the boredom she experiences in school.

Catnip cigarettes or tea are also very good for overcoming any kind of dizziness.

CAULIFLOWER (See under CABBAGE AND ITS KIND)

CAYENNE AND BELL PEPPERS, AND PAPRIKA (*Capsicum frutescens, C. Annuum*)

Brief Description

The capsicum species are divided into two groups: The sweet or mild-flavored varieties primarily used as vegetables; and the hot peppers, often referred to as chilies, that are used for spiking sauces and seasonings.

The bell pepper is the sweetest and largest variety. It's typically sold green, but later in the season one can usually buy red, yellow and purple ones as well. The bright-colored ones have merely been allowed to ripen longer on the vine and are sweeter.

Then there's the fiery kind, often measured in BTU's (British Thermal Units) according to their individual hotness. Cayenne pepper is a perennial in its native tropical America, but is annual when cultivated outside of the tropical zones. Growing to a height of 3 feet or more, its glabrous stem is woody at the bottom and branched near the top. The leaves are ovate to lanceolate, entire and petioled. The drooping, white to yellow flowers grow alone or in pairs of three between April and September. The ripe fruit or pepper, is a many-seeded pod with a leathery outside in various shades of red or yellow. There's a host of hot chili varieties; serrano, yellow wax and jalapeno are the most common California chilies around.

Keeping Cool with Hot Chilies

The active ingredient in cayenne and other chili peppers, capsaicin, delivers the fiery kick to Mexican food, turns plain pickle juice into Tabasco sauce, makes ginger ale a real thirst quencher, lets the good times roll in Cajun cuisine and makes curry powder a more interesting spice all around.

Capsaicin, in fact, is able to first stimulate and then to desensitize the warmth detectors in the hypothalamus gland, so that a drop in body temperature is evident. This enables natives in hot southern climates like Central and South America and Africa, for instance, to tolerate the heat a lot better than we would. That's onc of thc reasons why they consume so much capsicum and other chili peppers, to keep themselves cool, believe it or not!

Really Relieves Arthritis

Incredibly amazing relief for rheumatoid arthritis sufferers can come from red pepper, as crazy as it may seem to some skeptics. It seems that the pain which arthritic victims suffer so much from takes place something like this: a unique protein called nerve growth factor (NGF) helps to produce a hormone known as substance P (SP), which transmits all pain signals throughout the body to the brain quick as lightning, producing the expected verbal response of "Ouch, that hurts!" or a facial grimace of pain. Now when cayenne is taken into the body on a regular basis, its main constituent, the fiery capsaicin does several things: (A) It blocks the supply of NGF; (B) Causes a massive release of SP from the hypothalamus, which at first increases arthritic pain but later diminishes quite a bit; (C) By producing such a depletion of SP from the hypothalamus, pain signals no longer are able to get to the brain. The first noticeable result is *NO FEELING* OF PAIN in those with arthritis. An interesting side note to all of this is that some U.S. Navy doctors have been studying capsicum's usefulness in helping to alleviate the "phantom limb pain" which war veteran amputees often experience, according to *Science Digest* for Sept. 1983.

The recommended dosage for effective pain relief from crippling arthritis is approximately 2 capsules, three to four times a day with milk or apple juice. This must be done on a regular, consistent basis in order for lasting benefits to be derived. Don't worry about the early increases in pain; it will diminish soon enough, leaving your body relatively pain-free before long.

Brings Down Blood Sugar Levels

A report in the *West Indian Medical Journal* (31:194–97) mentioned how a pack of mongrel dogs picked up off the streets in Kingston, Jamaica were given powdered cayenne pepper. The result was a dramatic plunging of their blood sugar levels for up to several hours at a time.

Which is to say, if you're diabetic that an average of 3 capsules of Nature's Way or any health food store brand of capsicum will help bring down high blood sugar levels very nicely. If you're just the opposite and hypoglycemic, you'd better avoid cayenne altogether, both in food and in most herbal formulas, too.

Lowers Cholesterol

A group of rodents were fed high fat diets, but given some cayenne pepper as well. There was an increased excretion of cholesterol in their feces and no rise in their liver cholesterol to speak of. So when you're consuming any kind of greasy food, be sure to drink an 8 oz. glass of tomato juice that has 1.8 tsp cayenne and a squeeze of lemon juice in it with these meals.

Halts Bleeding Quickly

For any sudden gash, nick or serious cut, just apply enough cayenne pepper or powdered kelp or both to the injury until the bleeding stops.

I cut my hand between the thumb and first finger several years ago while dining in a restaurant. I drew a small crowd around my table when I requested some capsicum to dress the injury with. A few "oohs and ahhs" accompanied the success of my treatment when all bleeding ceased within a matter of minutes.

Prevents Blood Clots

The New England Journal of Medicine reported that residents of Thailand have virtually no blood clot problems to speak of because of their frequent consumption of red pepper. If you use capsicum on a regular basis you won't ever have to worry about getting blood clots! About 2 capsules a day is good for general health maintenance and eating more Mexican, Indian and other spicy foods laced with red pepper will virtually guarantee keeping your blood pretty thin and moving fairly good as a rule.

An Ulcer Healer

How can something so hot help something so painfully raw and sensitive as a stomach ulcer heal up quite nicely in the course of time? The internal consumption of capsicum stimulates the gut's mucosal cells which release more slimy mucous that neatly coats the walls of the intestines, including sore, bleeding ulcers. If you've ever watched a dog lick its wounds or held a burnt finger in your mouth, you'll know about the kind of relief I'm talking about which comes to stomach ulcers covered by lots of mucous. That then is about how cayenne pepper helps to heal ulcers. Suggested intake is one capsule twice to three times daily with meals.

Knocks Out Cold and Flu Miseries

Some Jewish grandmothers in Brooklyn, New York have relied upon a pinch of cayenne pepper and a finely chopped garlic clove in a bowl of hot chicken soup as the best way to fight the aches, pains and fever accompanying colds and flus. Called "Jewish penicillin" by many, it's often recommended by medical doctors in place of antibiotics.

Cayenne also seems to work quite well with vitamin C. In fact, vitamin C doesn't perform as well unless cayenne accompanies it for some reason. An Old Amish Herbs remedy called Super C has cayenne, ginger and vitamin A in with vitamin C to make it more potent (see Appendix).

Keeping Your Toes Warm in Winter

Cayenne pepper sprinkled in your socks keeps your feet warm in winter. I know an old duck hunter from Malad, Idaho who always put some cayenne in the bottoms of his woolen socks and also into the fingertips of his mittens or gloves, when staying out in the cold behind a duck blind for long periods of time.

Antidotes for Reducing Pepper's Hotness

The stuff that gives hot peppers their fiery properties, capsaicin, dissolves in either fat or alcohol. Which probably explains why either milk or beer are so popular for helping to quench the flames when any of these species are ingested for dietary or medicinal purposes.

Salve for Sprains and Bruises

An ointment used in mainland China and Taiwan a lot for treating athletic and work-related injuries such as sprains, bruises and swollen, painful joints is made with one part ground hot pepper and five parts Vaseline. Prepare by adding the ground hot pepper to the melted Vaseline, which is then mixed well and cooled until it congeals. This ointment is applied once daily, or once every two days, directly to the injured area.

In a 1965 report from a journal of traditional medicine from Zhejiang, 7 of 12 patients thus treated were cured and 3 improved, while 2 did not respond to this treatment. In the effective cases, 4–9 applications were usually used.

Energetic Recipes

Capsicum and paprika are known to increase energy levels within the body to a certain extent. Capsicum especially is included in some herbal energy products currently found on the market, such as Nature's Way Herbal Up sold in most health food stores nationwide. When I was in the Soviet Union in 1979 doing research, Dr. Venyamene Ponomaiyov, professor of chemistry and pharmacology at the Pyatigorsk Pharmaceutical Institute in Pyatigorsk, Georgia, informed me that he and some of his colleagues had discovered that cayenne pepper dramatically increased the intensity of electrical energy auras around the volunteers who used capsicum frequently in their diets. This finding indicates just how strength-promoting cayenne can be.

The three recipes below all use one or several kinds of the peppers cited in this section. They are designed to not only satisfy hunger by filling you up, but also to give you extra energy and vitality for an active lifestyle.

Stuffed Bell Peppers

Needed: 6 medium green bell peppers; 3 cups savory Spanish rice and 1 cup tomato sauce. Wash and core peppers. But don't discard the seed cores. Instead finely dice them and mix them in with the savory Spanish rice. Steam peppers for 20 minutes. Then fill each one with 1/2 cup of this rice mixture. Place in a casserole and top with tomato sauce. Bake at 350° F. for 45 minutes, or until tender. Serves 6.

Savory Spanish Rice

Needed: 1 medium chopped onion; 1 small chopped green pepper; 1/4 lb. lean ground round; 1/2 cup raw brown rice; 1 clove minced garlic; 2 cups chopped tomatoes; 1 bay leaf; 1/8 tsp. cayenne pepper. Sauté onion and green pepper until tender. Brown beef and drain. Combine all ingredients. Bring to a boil, stir and reduce heat. Simmer 45–60 minutes or until rice is tender. Stir often to prevent sticking. Remove bay leaf before serving.

Mild Tomato Sauce

Needed: l cup canned tomato sauce; 1 tbsp. apple cider vinegar; 2 tsp. Worcestershire sauce; 1 tbsp. finely diced onion; 3/4 tbsp. paprika; 1/2 tsp. finely diced garlic clove. Combine and bring to a boil. Turn heat down and simmer about 8 minutes. Serve over bell peppers stuffed with Spanish rice.

The above three recipes have been adapted from La Rene Gaunt's *Recipes to Lower Your Fat Thermostat* (see Appendix) and used with the kind permission of the author and her publisher.

CELERY (*Apium graveolens*)

Brief Description

Celery is one of the oldest vegetables ever used in recorded history. The ancient Egyptians were known to gather wild celery from marshy seaside areas for food. It is a plant of many uses and little waste: the leaves and dried seeds make good seasoning; the outer ribs are best cooked and the inner ribs may be consumed raw as they are good for the heart.

The variety most commonly available is the light-green to medium-green Pascal celery. Stalks are firm and solid with a maximum of green leaves. They usually have a glossy surface and snap easily. As a member of the distinguished parsley family, it enjoys some of the same reputable medical claims often attributed to the former herb. The ancient Greeks on the Isthmus of Corinth around 450 B.C. regularly crowned their winning athletes with crowns of celery stems and leaves.

In 1982, the average American ate 7.8 lbs of celery, 11% more than 5 years earlier. In 1983, it was a $235 million crop in America, compared with $184.5 million for carrots and only $152 million for broccoli. California supplies the nation with more than 60% of all celery production.

Calm Frayed Nerves

The seeds and the stalks of celery both contain a sedative compound called "phthalide" (the "ph" is silent). In mainland China, celery juice was useful in reducing hypertension in 14 out of 16 patients. The juice was mixed with equal amounts of honey and about 8 tsp. was taken orally three times each day for up to a week. Make your own celery juice at home with a juicer or buy it fresh from a health food store. Mix equal parts of it and carrot juice together and drink an 8 oz. glass once a day to help strengthen frayed nerves and calm you down.

Quick Relief for Hornet Stings

Several years ago while participating as an instructor in a plant identification hike with 20 others in Provo Canyon, near Robert Redford's Sundance Ski Resort, one of our number who was barefoot, accidentally stepped on a black hornet. Intense pain and swelling commenced within minutes.

I asked everyone to look around for some plantain or yarrow, but to no avail. Another member of our small group had some celery sticks in a plastic bag. I asked for one, started chewing it vigorously until I had ground it to a pulp with my back molars. I then applied this wad of celery and saliva directly to the wounds and held it there for about 15 minutes. The throbbing ceased and she felt more comfortable thereafter. A crudely made mud pack with more chewed celery inside brought added relief for some hours later. She managed to hobble along with the rest of us, supported between two of her friends.

Helps Keep Weight Off

Robin W. Yeaton, Ph.D., who worked for the UCLA Program Development Symposia in October, 1985 told me on an airplane flight that she lost over 30 lbs. in 2-1/2 months, by nibbling on a lot of celery sticks whenever the urge to snack came over her. The sodium seemed to have a positive effect in helping her to shed additional pounds too.

Using Celery in Recipes

Be sure that the celery you use is always fresh and crisp as possible. Avoid any kinds that are wilted, brown or diseased-looking. And above all, do *not* store celery in your refrigerator for longer than 3 weeks. According to the Nov.-Dec. 1985 *Journal of Agricultural Food Chemistry,* the furocoumarins present in very small amounts in fresh celery can increase 25 times or more after about 3 weeks' storage. Old celery has caused cancer in animals.

For a simple dish on the stir-fry principle, add sliced celery to bite-size pieces of chicken and allow to simmer covered for 20–30 minutes. Or, use lamb with celery in much the same manner. Creamed celery, another wintertime Sunday dinner favorite of the '30s and '40s, can be adapted to today's cooking styles by spicing it up with either cheese or nut meats. Toasted almonds add the crunch to this interesting version.

Creamed Celery with Almonds

Needed: 8–10 celery branches with leafy tops intact; 1 tbsp. diced shallots (an onionlike plant); 3 tbsp. butter; 1/4 tsp. sea salt; 1 tbsp. whole wheat flour; 1/2 cup cream; 1/2 cup chicken broth; 1 cup toasted almonds.

Slice the celery on the diagonal, melt the butter in a heavy pan with a tight-fitting lid. Add the shallots first, then the celery. Cover the pan; cook until celery is tender, about 8 minutes. You should not have to add liquid. Shake the pan every now and then to prevent scorching. When the celery is tender, add the sea salt and sprinkle in the flour. Toss celery with a mixing spoon to distribute flour.

Place the pan over a double boiler; add cream and chicken broth. Cook until the raw flour taste is gone, and mixture thickens slightly, about 5 minutes. Add 3/4 cup of the toasted almonds and toss. Place the celery mixture in a serving dish; top with the remaining almonds. Sprinkle paprika over the top and serve. Serves 3–4.

THE CHAMOMILES
GERMAN CHAMOMILE (*Matricaria chamomilla* or *recutita*)
ROMAN CHAMOMILE (*Anthemis nobilis* or *Chamaemulum nobile*)

Brief Description

German chamomile is a fregrant, low annual herb, with lovely flower heads and can reach a height of 16 inches. The leaves are pale green and sharply incised. Roman chamomile is a strongly fragrant, hairy, half-spreading and much branched perennial with white ray-like flowerheads and can grow to a foot in height. Both chamomiles are extensively cultivated throughout Europe and the Mediterranean countries, as well as found growing in the U.S., Canada and Argentina.

Calms Headaches and Hyperactivity

If you've ever suffered from an occasional migraine headache or have hyperactive children or grandkids, then you should consider the success that the famous French herbalist, Maurice Mességué, had with chamomile. After just 14 days of intensive treatment with chamomile a man who had debilitating migraines was cured. To make a nice, relaxing tea, simply steep 2 tbsps. of fresh or dried flowers in 1 pint of boiling water for 40 minutes. Strain, sweeten with pure maple syrup and drink 1–2 cups at a time.

Fantastic Beauty Aid

European herbalists rave about the great cosmetic benefits to be derived from the use of chamomile. When the face is washed with a tea of the herb several times a week, it will show a healthier and softer glow. The same tea also makes a wonderful hair conditioner, especially for blond hair, making it more manageable and shinier.

To make a tea, simply bring 1 pint of water to a boil, then remove from heat and add 2 tsp. of dried flowers. Cover and let steep for 45 minutes. Strain and use when lukewarm to cool. The crude, dried, cut herb is available from any local health food store or from Indiana Botanic Gardens (see Appendix).

Wonderful for Skin Problems

Chamomile is especially useful on the skin, helping to treat a number of problems that range from flaky scaliness and inflammation to wrinkles and stretch marks. A remarkable chamomile cream preparation imported from Europe has been receiving rave reviews by skin care specialists and consumers here in America. Called CamoCare, it's not available at most health food stores nationwide or from Abkit, Inc. (see Appendix).

I have received a number of testimonies concerning the success which many people have received from this wonderful chamomile cream made in Frankfurt. John Sinnette, 78 years old, of Tustin, California is one of these.

> I was frankly a bit skeptical that it would do any good for the rash on my belly and legs, since it had been of long duration and the anti-fungal cream that a doctor had given me had done very little good. Much to my surprise, the red rash almost completely disappeared within about four days of application twice a day!

Reduces Inflammation and Swelling

Chamomile may be used as a compress and wash for all external conditions of inflammation and as an oil rub for muscular stiffness and temporary limb paralysis. To make an effective tea to be drunk and also as a wash, just bring 1–2 pints of water to a boil, adding 2 heaping tsp. of dried or fresh flowers. Immediately remove from heat and steep for 20 minutes or so. Drink a cup at a time 2–3 times daily and wash inflamed areas of skin with the same several times each day as well.

To make a good massage oil for limb stiffness and paralysis, including lower backaches, simply fill a small bottle loosely with some fresh chamomile flowers and then add some olive oil until it covers the flowers. Put a tight lid on the bottle and keep in the sun for two weeks, thereafter storing in the refrigerator and using as needed. Warm whatever oil is going to be used before massaging well into the skin.

And to help soothe tired, irritated eyes, just soak some chamomile tea bags in a little ice water and then apply to the eyelids for incredible relief. This is especially good to do during allergy season.

Great Relief for Allergies

One of the chief components in both chamomiles, but especially so in the German variety, is azulene. This compound has helped in the prevention of allergic seizures, even in guinea pigs for up to an hour after administration. Azulene might also possibly cure hayfever. Chamomile is good for relieving asthmatic attacks in kids and adults. An effective chamomile throat spray is marketed to most health food stores under the CamoCare label, and has been used for this purpose. An asthmatic can spray some of this chamomile concentrated in the mouth toward the back of the throat to relieve choking sensations and to better facilitate breathing.

Besides drinking 3–4 cups of warm Chamomile tea on a daily basis during allergy season for adults, and 1–2 cups per day for young children, it's also advisable to inhale the warm vapors by covering the head with a heavy bath towel and holding the face about 8–10 inches above a pan containing freshly made tea for about 12–15 minutes at a time.

Regenerates the Liver

Only a few herbs in the plant kingdom are capable of regeneration or producing brand-new liver tissue. Tomato juice is one of these and German chamomile tea is another. Two compounds, azulene and guaiazulene, initiated new growth of tissue in rats which had had a portion of their livers surgically removed prior to this, according to Vol. 15 of *Food & Cosmetics Toxicology* for 1977. For encouraging the formation of new liver tissue, it's recommended that up to 6 cups of chamomile tea be consumed every *other* day or an average of 3–4 cups per day. In this particular instance, the tea seems to work much better than powdered capsules would. This treatment would probably be especially good for those suffering from degenerative liver diseases such as infectious hepatitis or the more deadly AIDS virus.

CHAPARRAL (*Larrea divericata*)

Brief Description

Chaparral is one of the most amazing herbs ever found in the plant kingdom. It thrives on nutritionally bankrupt soil and settles in where even the hardiest of cacti fear to tread. Chaparral secretes a powerful anti-growth substance that keeps all other vegetative intruders away. *Nothing* grows around the immediate perimeter of this shrub—not even other chaparral!

This incredible plant survives in the hottest of desert hells on as little as a few tablespoons of water per year, yet somehow manages to still retain its distinctive bronze to mustard-green hue.

Ideal Dandruff Remover

In times spent with Mexican-American residents in and around Tularosa, New Mexico and with the Pima Indians in Arizona, I've learned that chaparral is a most effective remedy for helping to get rid of dandruff. In fact, it even works better than the popular shampoos that are advertised nationally.

Here's how to use it. Bring 1 quart of *cheap whiskey* or some *cheap* brand of *wine* to a boil. Add up to 6 tbsp. of dried chaparral, which you can get from any health food store or by mail-order from Indiana Botanic Gardens (see Appendix). Reduce heat and simmer for 20 minutes, then remove and steep for up to 8 hours. DO NOT use any aluminum cookware, though, but rather enamel, silverstone or stainless steel.

Strain into a fruit jar and keep in your bathroom somewhere. Every time you shower and wash your hair with soap, first be sure to rinse it well before using this chaparral alcohol mixture. Pour a cup of the stuff into your scalp and work in well with your fingertips. After this leave and DO NOT RINSE anymore with water. In less than a week, dandruff problems should be virtually eliminated. After that, use it several times a week to keep dandruff from ever recurring.

The same mixture can be used on cats and dogs suffering from lice or fleas. After bathing them, just apply it as you would to your hair for the same wonderful results.

Candida Disappears

The same solution used either as a douche or taken internally every day, 1 cup at a time, but with thc tca madc from water instead of liquor this time, will help to combat yeast infection and cause any Candida present to virtually disappear. The feet may also be soaked in the same strong alcoholic solution to fight athlete's foot.

Longevity Factor

The world's oldest living organism is *not* a bristlecone pine tree in the White Mountains north of Bishop, California. Rather it is a ring of creosote bushes in the Mojave Desert 150 miles northeast of L.A. The age scientists have assigned to these chaparral bushes after careful analysis—11,700 years old! This is due to their NDGA content.

The second most important compound in chaparral is called nordihyroguaiaretic acid or NDGA for short. It is a very strong anti-oxidant, meaning it's been used in numerous food products in the past, especially in fats and oils, to prevent rancidity from occurring. The authors of *Life Extention—A Practical, Scientific Approach* say that if you want to live a long time, you need to be taking some kind of anti-oxidants to hold your "free radicals" in check.

"The tiniest killer in your body," they say, "isn't a virus at all"—it's a type of recklessly delinquent molecular fragment with considerable irregular behavior that can cause blood clots, arthritis, senility and greatly hasten the aging process in all of us. They say that "when you cook with food containing fats and oils, it's wise to include anti-oxidants if you plan to store any leftovers."

But foods like ground hamburger, they point out, "is a particularly rich source of these dangerous free radicals." With this in mind, it seems like a good idea to take one chaparral capsule after consuming a Big Mac and french fries in order to offset some of the damage all of those free radicals you've ingested are capable of doing. And while chaparral may not hold quite the same promises expected of ginseng for longevity, it can certainly help to slow down the aging process quite a bit from the foods we eat on a daily basis.

Holds Cancer in Check

The medical doctor most involved with the limited success that chaparral has achieved with some kinds of cancer, is Charles R. Smart, M.D., an internationally known cancer specialist, who retired in early 1985 as Chief of Surgery at LDS Hospital in Salt Lake City. In an interview published in the June 1978 *Herbalist* magazine, he was quoted as saying "that chaparral tea produced regression of tumors but *not* necessarily cures" with "the possibility of reacquiring the cancer continuing to exist." Therefore, it's in this context as a control mechanism rather than as a purported cure that chaparral is being offered for the reader's serious consideration.

Dr. Smart's initial experience with this wonderful desert shrub began on Oct. 20, 1967 when an 85-year-old white man was evaluated at the University of Utah Medical Center for a rapidly growing malignant melanoma of the right cheek associated with a large tender mass just adjacent to it. The sore on his cheek was surgically removed, examined and pronounced malignant. Dr. Smart's medical report, which was subsequently published in the April 1969 issue of *Cancer Chemotherapy Reports,* mentioned that this unidentified gentleman returned to the hospital several more times for further lesion excisions and finally a wedge biopsy of the facial area and a needle biopsy of the growing neck tumor.

By this time his physical appearance looked terrible. He had lost considerable weight and had become pale, weak and fairly inactive. Major surgery was suggested, "but the patient decided to return home without treatment, feeling that his age and condition precluded surgical treatment.

According to Dr. Smart's published report, the unidentified patient "began taking 'chaparral tea' by steeping the dried leaves and stems in hot water—about 7–8 grams (approximately 1 tbsp.) of leaves per quart of water—and drank 2–3 cups of tea, only rarely missing a dose, and taking *no other* medications." Smart's patient began this home treatment for his cancer sometime in November 1967 and by February 1968 had experienced a substantial decrease in his facial lesion, with the neck tumor completely disappearing. "He looked better and had begun to gain weight and strength," Dr. Smart reported.

The patient returned again to the University of Utah Medical Center in Sept. 1968 "and was re-examined. Doctors were quite astonished to say the least—the cancer was virtually gone, their patient had gained about 25 lbs. and looked greatly improved in color and general health."

The unidentified patient was a Mormon Temple worker by the name of Ernest Farr, who then resided in Mesa, Arizona. He lived for another 9 years, passing away at the remarkable age of 96 of, believe it or not, the very same cancer which his chaparral had held in check all this time! The irony here was that some of his children and grandchildren wouldn't permit him access to any more chaparral, believing the success he had attributed to it to be merely a figment of his tired imagination.

The medical community never completely rejected chaparral, nor its main anti-cancer component, that lightweight, yellowish-white crystal powder known as NDGA. Based on the limited success of which Dr. Smart and his medical team had had with chaparral on several other cancer cases besides Mr. Farr's, Dr. Meny Bergel and a medical team in Rochester, N.Y. began a lengthy series of experiments using NDGA from chaparral on a group of 32 cancer patients with inoperable tumors or where surgery and radiation had been unsuccessful.

In an unpublished paper entitled, "The Use of NDGA in Therapeutics," Dr. Bergel recounts the success his team had in being able to at least substantially reduce the excruciating pains which many of the group experienced with their various tumors, although nothing was said about the cancers themselves regressing.

Chaparral is also useful for holding leukemia in check according to one medical publication. And several other impressive successes have been recorded with this desert shrub in *Unproven Methods of Cancer*

Management published by the American Cancer Society in 1970. Four patients responded well to treatment with tea—two with advanced melanomas, one with metastic choriocarcinoma and one with widespread lymphosarcoma. After just 2 days of treatment, the patient with lymphosarcoma experienced a 75% disappearance of his disease. The choriocarcinoma patient who hadn't responded well to other therapies, responded well to chaparral tea for several months. And of the two melanoma patients, one experienced a 95% regression and the remaining disease was excised, while the other remained in remission for up to 4 months before another lesion developed.

A final historical footnote to Dr. Smart's report on chaparral would provide a fitting climax to one of nature's most superb immune system strengtheners. About the time that his study was made public, another Arizona couple by the name of Murdock were facing a similar bout with cancer like Ernest Farr had been. Tom Murdock's wife suffered an incurable tumor which several previous operations and radiation treatment had failed to correct.

Hearing of Dr. Smart's cautious but positive optimism expressed in regard to chaparral, they decided to try the herb for themselves. Mrs. Murdock began drinking as much as 2 quarts of the tea a day. As reported in the Sunday, Oct. 16, 1983 issue of the Salt Lake City newspaper, the *Desert News,* "After drinking the chaparral tea Mrs. Murdock started getting better."

This started Tom Murdock on the road to selling herbs. His first product choice was obviously chaparral capsules. "What started out as a last-ditch effort to save Mrs. Murdock's life worked and resulted in the formation of the largest health food company in the country," the newspaper account related. That company is Nature's Way, now managed by one of the Murdock's sons, Ken, in Springville, Utah.

CHERRY (*Prunus avium*)

Brief Description

Since the caveman era, wild cherries have existed in the temperate parts of Asia, Europe and North America. The hundreds of varieties on the market today may be classified in terms of sweetness and color. Bing and Royal Ann cherries are both sweet, but Bings have deeply colored juice, whereas the juice of the other variety is colorless. Sour cherries—the ones most favored for pies, tarts and turnovers—are similarly divided: morellos have colored juice and amarelles colorless liquid. The very popular tart cherry, Montmorency, is light to dark red with red juice. Sweet cherries are available from May through August, while sour cherries go from late June to mid-August.

Great Gout Cure

Nothing works better for gout than either raw sweet cherries (15 per day), cherry juice concentrate (1 tbsp. three times daily), or else a tea made of the stems. To make the tea just bring 2 pints of water to a boil, then throw in half a handful of stems, reduce heat and simmer for 7 minutes, then remove and let steep, covered, for 20 more minutes. Drink at least 2 cups a day to keep the gout under control. All of these remedies also work well for arthritis.

Controls Hacking Coughs

The bark of a related species, wild black cherry (*P. serotina*), is frequently used in many cold and cough preparations, such as Smith Brothers' Cough Drops. To make your own terrific cold and cough syrup is relatively easy. Just combine in a stainless steel pot 3 cups of water, 1/2 cup of whiskey (any brand) and 1/2 cup blackstrap molasses and bring to a boil.

Reduce heat to the lowest setting possible, then add 16 tbsp. or 1 cup of cut, dried wild cherry bark purchased from any local health food store. Stir well with a wooden ladle, cover and let simmer for about 25 minutes until the mixture has been reduced a little in volume and is somewhat thick. Stir every so often as necessary. Then let steep for about 15 minutes, after which it should be strained through a coarse strainer into a clean fruit jar or bottle.

Store in a cool, dry place and take 2–3 tbsp. of the syrup several times a day to control hacking cough due to asthma, bronchitis, emphysema, smoking and the flu. A tea can be made with the same ingredient amounts, except the molasses and whiskey, to relieve sinus congestion and other symptoms of the common cold.

Antidote for Fish Food Poisoning

A tea made from cherry bark and other ingredients is a useful antidote to counteract the effects of bad shellfish and spoiled fish in general. Bring 1 pint of water to a boil. Then add 1 tsp. each of cherry or wild cherry bark, fresh, grated ginger root and finely chopped Bermuda onion. Cover, reduce heat and simmer for 7 minutes. Then remove from stove and steep for an additional 20 minutes or so. Drink both cups when lukewarm.

Dessert Recipe

The following recipe has been adapted from Better Homes & Garden's excellent work, *Eating Healthy Cook Book.* The kindness of the editors is greatly appreciated (see Appendix).

A Delicious Cherry Cobbler

Remember to spoon the batter onto a *hot* cherry filling. That way, the biscuit topper cooks faster and more uniformly. Needed: 1 cup flour; 1 tbsp. pure maple syrup; 1 tsp. baking powder; 1/4 cup butter; 1 slightly beaten egg; 1/4 cup canned goat milk; 4 cups fresh or frozen, unsweetened, pitted tart red cherries; 1/3 cup brown sugar; 1/3 cup water; 1 tbsp. quick-cooking tapioca.

For biscuit topper, stir together flour, maple syrup and baking powder. Cut in butter until the flour mixture resembles coarse crumbs. In a small mixing bowl stir together the egg and goat's milk. Add milk mixture all at once to the flour mixture, stirring just enough to moisten. Then set aside.

For cherry filling, in a medium stainless steel saucepan combine cherries, brown sugar, water and tapioca. Let stand for 5 minutes, stirring occasionally. Cook and stir until it begins to bubble like a hot spring or small geyser.

Turn the hot cherry filling into an 8 × 1-1/2 inch round baking dish or a 1-1/2 quart casserole. Immediately spoon biscuit topper on top of the cherry filling to form 8 mounds. Bake in a 400° F. oven about 25 minutes or until a wooden toothpick inserted in the center of the topper comes out clean as a hound's tooth. Serve warm. Should make 8 servings.

CHESTNUT (See under NUTS)

CHICKPEA (See under BEANS)

CHERVIL (*Anthricus cerefolium*)

Brief Description

Chervil comes from a Greek word meaning "leaf of rejoicing" or "cheer-leaf." The 16th century English herbalist Gerare confirmed this original meaning when he wrote: "It is good for old people—it rejoiceth and comforteth the heart and increaseth their strength."

Chervil is of East European origin and is to be found growing wild in southeast Russia and most of Iran. It found its way to England thanks to the ancient Romans. Today, however, the leaves and stems are principally used in France for seasonings, salads, soups and as a pot-herb.

This annual plant has a round, finely grooved, branched stem which grows 12 to 26 inches high from a thin, whitish root. The leaves are opposite, light green and bipinnate, the lower leaves petioled, the upper sessile on stem sheaths. The small, white flowers grow in compound umbels from May to July. The elongated, segmented seeds ripen in August and September.

Excellent for Eye Disorders

Chervil has an outstanding track record in parts of Europe (especially France) for successfully treating a variety of eye disorders, among them being severe inflammation of the deeper structures of the eye (ophthalmitis), separation of the retina from the choroid (detached retina) and loss of eye lens transparency (cataract). And when used in conjunction with other eye herb remedies such as eyebright, the results are nothing short of simply amazing.

A distinguished oculist in Paris in the last century used chervil locally in ophthalmia. He proposed applying chervil poultices to the affected eye and also washing the eye with a decoction of the same plant. This treatment has been recommended due to the good results obtained by other specialists.

The medicinal virtues of this herb are very much linked with its smell and this is quickly destroyed by heat. So it's a plant that should not be cooked, not even broiled. "The ancients used it for eye troubles," notes Maurice Mességué, a famous French folk healer, "and I have been able to confirm for myself its value in such cases. I, myself, like to use parsley and chervil against conjunctivitis and other eye inflammations. Steep the chopped leaves in boiling water, cool to body temperature and apply the solution with an eye cup. It soothes the burning sensation and acts as a disinfectant."

One of the most successful formulas for many eye disorders to ever come out of France has been attributed to Professor Leon Binet, a prolific author of medical books and a former Dean of the Faculty of Medicine in Paris. His remedy calls for equal parts (or 1 tsp. each) of freshly cut chervil, parsley, Roman chamomile (*Anthemis nobilis, not* German chamomile) and lavender flowers, all to be added to 1 pint of boiling water and permitted to steep away from any heat for about 20–30 minutes. I recommend that an equal amount (1 tbsp.) of fresh or dried eyebright herb also be added to the solution, which is later strained and applied to both eyes with an eye cup three times a day. This is good for cataracts, detached retinas and occasionally glaucoma.

CHICKWEED (*Stellaria media*)

Brief Description

This apparently feeble member of the pink group is actually a lusty annual with matted to upright green stems that take over many areas. Commencing its growth in the fall, it vigorously thrives through the sleet and snowstorms of winter, even in the far north, survives most weed killers, beginnning to bloom while the snow is often still on the ground, and many times it finishes its seed production in the springtime. It's so abundantly fruitful, however, that it flowers throughout most of the country every month of the year.

Growing to a foot high in matted to upright trailing stems, it has egg-shaped lower and median leaves and stemless and highly variable upper leaves. In the star or great chickweed (*S. pubera*), the characteristic blooms, brightly white and about 1/2 inch across, have such deeply notched petals that their 5 appear more like 10, the number of stamens. Usually gathering themselves together at night and on cloudy or foggy days, they unfurl under the brilliant sun.

Antidote for Blood Poisoning

Chickweed ranks beside herbs such as burdock root as being terrific blood cleansers! Where there exists a threat of blood poisoning or tetanus due to chemical dye or dirt getting into the bloodstream, here's what you should do. First make a poultice and apply it directly to the affected area in order to draw out as much of the poison as possible. To make the poultice, simply blend together 1 tbsp. each of the powdered ginger root, capsicum and kelp, adding just enough honey/wheat germ oil (equal parts) to form a nice, smooth paste of even consistency. Spread this on clean surgical gauze and apply to the area. Cover and leave for up to 7 hours before changing again, if necessary.

At the same time administer internally capsules of chickweed (6 at a time) or a tea (2 cups at a time) made by adding 1 tbsp. dried herb to 2 cups boiling water and steeped for 20 minutes before straining and drinking. The same steps can also be followed with great success in treating carbuncles, boils, venereal disease, herpes sores, swollen testicles and breasts and so forth. All of the herbs mentioned above can be purchased from your local health food store under the Nature's Way label.

Nice Salve Relief for Itching, Rashes

Chickweed brings great comfort to the miseries of chronic itching and severe rashes. Just make a salve using fresh chickweed, if possible; otherwise the dried powder will have to be used instead.

Needed: 1-1/2 cups coarsely cut fresh chickweed (or 1/2 cup liquid chlorophyll with 1 cup powdered chickweed); 2 cups pure virgin olive oil; 6 tbsp. beeswax. Warm up the oil and beeswax in a pan on top of the stove on medium heat. Then combine all the ingredients in a heavy cast iron skillet or small heavy roast pan and place in the oven for about two hours on just the "warm" setting. Then strain through a fine wire strainer while mixture is still hot, pour into small clean jars and seal tightly.

Herbal Weight-Reducing Program

Most of the herbal literature, past and present, recommends using chickweed in treating obesity. My friend, Mike Tierra, a licensed, practicing herbalist in Santa Cruz, California, mentioned in his *Way of Herbs* that "chickweed is particularly useful for reducing excess fat, having both mild diuretic and laxative properties."

Mike then gives his own weight-reducing program which has helped many of his heavier patients shed unwanted pounds. *Needed:* The following powdered herbs—kelp (5 parts), cascara sagrada (1 part), senna leaf (1 part), cinnamon (1 part) and licorice root (1 part). (I've omitted Mike's 1 part of poke root because I don't consider it that safe to use.) Fill some "00" gelatin capsules purchased from any drugstore with the above herb mixture and take 1-2 capsules three times daily, *before* meals, with a cup of herbal tea.

To make the herbal tea, combine equal parts of these cut, dried herbs—chickweed, cleavers or bedstraw and fennel seed—or approx. 2-1/2 tbsp. of the same in 1 pint of boiling water. Let steep for half an hour before drinking. Both methods should have the scales soon dropping in your favor and pleasing you very much.

Naturalist's Recipe

The late great Nature lover and herb forager, Euell Gibbons, devised several recipes using fresh chickweed.

Gibbons' Chickweed and Greens

"Chickweed is so tender that it cooks almost instantly," he wrote, "and it should always be short-cooked to preserve the maximum amount of its health-giving nutrients. To make Chickweed and Greens, I always use about 2 parts chickweed and 1 part stronger greens. The stronger greens are put on first, covered with boiling water and cooked about 10 minutes; then the chickweed is added, and after the water has regained a boil it's cooked about 2 minutes more. Drain, but don't throw away that cooking water. Chop the greens right in the cooking pot, using kitchen shears; season with salt, butter, a little pepper and some finely chopped raw onion. Sprinkle each serving with some crumbled crisp bacon. This makes a hearty and palatable dish that requires no apologies."

I've made the above omitting the fried bacon because I so intensely dislike pork, believing it's bad for your health, and have substituted kelp for the salt and capsicum for the black pepper. Also, I've squirted the juice of halves of lemon and lime over the cooked green and stirred just before serving. They give the dish an extra lip-smacking goodness. He suggests that the chickweed/other green cooking water be drunk for obesity problems.

CHICORY, ENDIVE AND ESCAROLE (*Cichorium intybus, C. endiva-latifolia*)

Brief Description

Chicory is a scruffy, weedy perennial that is usually cultivated and also found wild in the U.S. and Europe. The plant has many 2- or 3-foot, sticklike stems; open, widely spaced foilage and milky sap. The striking thing about chicory, however, is its bright, almost iridescent blue flowers that bloom incongruously on the stems as if stapled to the wrong plant. The rootstock is light yellow outside, white inside and contains a bitter milky juice too.

In the U.S. the name endive usually refers to the small, pale, cigar-shaped plant, while escarole refers to the broad, bushy head with waxy leaves. Endives have a slightly bitter taste. All three salad plants in this family, endive, chicory and escarole, were believed to have been some of the bitter herbs consumed by the Children of Israel during the Passover before their hasty exodus from Egypt. Chicory root is frequently used in natural coffee substitutes and added to regular coffee to give it a richer flavor and reduce its caffeine content somewhat.

Chicory Coffee for Male Birth Control

There is some clinical evidence that chicory root might be helpful in rendering male sperm temporarily infertile. Scientists in Ahmedadbad, Gujarat, India administered brewed water extracts of dried powdered chicory roots to 30 male adult Swiss mice, while a corresponding group received no chicory at all, only water to drink instead. In a week and a half, the mice were autopsied. Those which had been on the chicory root brew, registered considerable infertile sperm counts as well as decreased weight in their testicles. This information may prove helpful for men not desiring to use condoms.

Good-quality roasted chicory root, either cut or powdered, may be obtained from better health food stores or through mail-order from Indiana Botanic Gardens in Hammond (see Appendix). Brewing the roasted root with the drip method of coffee making works best, to give you a very flavorful and rich blend. Making the chicory coffee extra strong and drinking up to 6 cups per day should be enough to render the average adult male's sperm infertile for at least a week without having to resort to other means of birth control.

Effective Liver Cleanser

The same above brewing method makes an excellent drink for cleansing the liver and spleen as well as treating jaundice. An average of 2 cups per day for these purposes is sufficient it seems.

Combats Fat in the System

Lab rodents that were deliberately fed a very high fat diet containing chicory roots, experienced a remarkable decrease in their blood cholesterol levels later on. This suggests that whenever deep-fried foods or fatty meats are to be consumed, a cup or two of chicory root brew be consumed with the meal for protection against eventual hardening of the arteries.

Lowers Rapid Heartbeat

Over a dozen years ago a group of Egyptian scientists investigated the potential use of chicory root in treating tachycardia or rapid heartbeat. Their study showed the presence of a digitalis-like principle in both the dried and roasted root which actually decreased the rate and volume of heartbeat. Its effects were demonstrated in the toad heart, for instance.

While further research obviously still remains to be done before determining its full impact on human health, it would seem that a cup or two of the root brew by the drip method might just help alleviate this condition somewhat, whenever it occurs.

Neutralizes Acid Indigestion

A cup of the *cold* root brew is excellent for settling an upset stomach or correcting acid indigestion and heartburn.

Dissolves Gallstones

Chicory root and endive tea is very good for getting rid of gallstones. To 1 quart of boiling water, add 3 tbsps. cut root. Reduce heat and simmer for 20 minutes, then remove from the heat and add half a cup of finely cut, raw endive, cover and steep for 45 minutes. Drink several cups at a time twice a day in between meals, but especially so about 2 hours before retiring for the night.

A Complete Chicory Snack

To enjoy something different and slightly off the beaten path that's both healthy and exhilarating, try a snack using all three kinds of chicory species. Accompany the following "wild" salad idea with a cup of instant Country Beverage containing chicory from Old Amish Herbs (see Appendix).

Wilted Chicory Greens Salad

Needed: 1 medium-sized onion, sliced and separated into rings; 1 cup sliced, fresh mushrooms; 1 minced clove garlic; 2 tsps. butter; 1/2 tsp. dried, crushed basil; 1/2 cup loosely packed raisins and 2 cups each of endive and escarole snipped into pieces with kitchen shears or scissors.

In a large saucepan cook the onion, mushrooms and garlic in butter on low heat until tender, but don't brown. Stir in the dry basil a dash of kelp if you like. Then add both kinds of chicory greens and 2 tbsp. of apple cider vinegar. Cook and toss mixture occasionally for 2-1/2 minutes or until the greens begin to turn limp or wilty-looking. Just before removing from the pan, add the raisins and give everything a final stir.

Transfer right away to a serving dish. Should be eaten relatively soon while still warm. Two pieces of lightly buttered pumpernickel toast also make a great accompaniment to this salad and warm chicory coffee.

CHIVES (See under Garlic Onion)

CHOCOLATE (FROM CACAO BEANS) (*Theobroma cacao*)

Brief Description

Chocolate is obtained from the ground, roasted beans of the cacao tree. This evergreen with leathery, oblong leaves reaches a height of nearly 30 feet and a trunk width of about half a foot. The leaves are typically evergreen, with whitish or yellowish flowers slightly tinted with orange and pink. The berries are borne directly on the trunk and the branches may be red, yellow, purple or brown in color. Inside the thick, ridged and furrowed fruit rind, are a white or pinkish acid pulp enclosing 25–60 brown or purple, bitter and somewhat oily seeds.

It is these seeds or cacao beans which are of prime economic importance and yield cocoa powder, cocoa butter and chocolate upon curing by fermentation and drying, followed next with roasting and finally by grinding while still very hot. Chocolate was first introduced to Cortez in 1519 by Montezuma. Currently Americans now spend an average of some $3 billion to satisfy a craving for 1.8 billion pounds of the stuff.

Removes Skin Wrinkles

Cocoa or cacao butter, from which chocolate is made, can be used to help remove wrinkles on the neck in a skin condition known as ''turkey neck,'' remove wrinkles around the corners of the eyes (''crow's feet'') and also those at the corners of the mouth. Put a little cocoa butter on the ends of your middle three fingers and gently massage in a rotating motion into the wrinkled skin every morning and evening. Perform this procedure each time for about 10 minutes. Within a couple of weeks, most of the smaller wrinkles should be fainter in appearance and the remaining deeper ones not so apparent and noticeable as before.

Facial Mask for Dry Skin

Cocoa powder isn't just for drinking or making cakes with. It's a very good facial mask for softening up old, dry skin that has a slightly weathered look to it. Add enough dairy cream and a little olive oil to about 2 cups or less of cocoa powder to make a dough that's easily pliable and not runny or too stiff. It should be of a thick enough consistency so that you can apply it all over your face much as you would do with a mud pack or green clay poultice. The addition of the olive oil helps to give it greater elasticity and prevents it from drying out too soon or becoming somewhat cakey or chalky-like.

Now 2 cups of plain, dry cocoa powder yield slightly over 2 tbsp. of pure fat, of which about 10–12% is linoleic acid. Add to this approx. 3 tbsp. of olive oil, which gives an additional 12% or so of linoleic acid, and you have a facial mask containing at least 25% linoleic acid not to mention what the dairy cream is apt to provide as well. With the cream, the total linoleic acid content can be expected to be near 30% for that matter.

Why all the fuss over linoleic acid? Simply because it's one of the ingredients to healthier, more youthful-looking and lovelier skin. Dermatitis, a skin disease characterized by scaling, flaking, thickening and color change, can be treated with linoleic acid. And the main nutrient which gives baby's skin such a nice smooth, subtle, almost velvety softness, is none other than linoleic acid.

This then is why I've recommended this particular mask for dry, rough skin. In a couple of weeks or less, you should begin to notice a definite change for the better in regaining some of that youthful complexion back.

Helps Reduce Hypertension

Dry cocoa powder is used by some native practitioners in the Philippines for treating high blood pressure. They attribute this to the theobromine present, which enlarges the constricted blood vessels common in hypertensive victims.

The high potassium content shouldn't be overlooked either. Now the National Academy of Sciences has set a minimum level of daily potassium intake at 1,875 mg. Putting 2-1/4 tbsps. of cocoa powder in one cup of goat's milk and drinking the same twice a day is one way of illustrating that you'd be getting close to 80% of this minimum amount set.

The research work of Dr. Louis Tobian with the University of Minnesota School of Medicine in Minneapolis and Dr. Elizabeth B. Connor at the University of California at San Diego has proven beyond a doubt that a diet high in potassium is one of the real secrets to lowering blood pressure levels and holding them in check. Therefore, cocoa powder may be of some dietary value in helping to reduce hypertension, but neither cocoa nor chocolate are recommended for migraine headaches.

The Ultimate Mousetrap Bait

Want to get rid of mice, but don't have a cat? Or tried various kinds of bait, and nothing seems to work? Well, just bait new traps with fresh chocolate. And voilá! Your mouse troubles are over. They'll practically kill themselves to get it.

Giving Your Love Life a Boost

It's not so far-fetched as you may think to say that chocolate might be a reasonable aphrodisiac to give your love life a boost of sorts. Chocolate, you see, is loaded with the same kind of stuff called phenylethylamine (PEA) that the brain cranks out in big quantities when stimulated by the passions of love. In his fascinating book, *The Chemistry of Love,* New York City psychiatrist Michael R. Liebowitz, M.D. says that romantically depressed people tend to crave chocolates. He speculates that their PEA levels are low and chocolate gives them a big PEA boost.

Wickedly Delightful Recipe

If you're trying desperately hard to lose weight or curb that sweet tooth of yours, then I *strongly* advise you to quickly flip the page and go on to the next entry. *Don't even bother reading this!* Because if you do I'm afraid you might be tempted to try making this next recipe, which Queen Elizabeth of England and Queen Juliana of the Netherlands have indulged themselves in, in times past. It's a dessert treat fit for royalty with a divine taste that is almost out of this world. It's to the point of being sinfully delicious if you're counting calories these days.

Incredibly Rich Chocolate Hazelnut Cake

Needed: 6 oz. (approximately 31-1/2 tbsps.) semi-sweet or bitter-sweet baking chocolate; 6 oz. (approx. 31-1/2 tbsps.) creamery sweet butter; 4 large eggs; 1/4 cup brown sugar; 1/4 cup blackstrap molasses; 1/2 cup ground, toasted hazelnuts; 4 tbsps. sifted flour; 1/4 tsp. almond extract; 1/4 cup dark honey; 1/8 tsp. cream of tartar; pinch sea salt.

Preheat oven to 375°. Grease an 8x3-in. round cake pan with lecithin (purchased from your health food store), then flour the bottom and sides of it. Melt chocolate and butter over low heat in a small saucepan placed in a larger pan partly filled with water. Stir occasionally until melted and smooth, then remove from heat. Meanwhile separate eggs, placing the whites in a clean, dry mixing bowl with the salt and cream of tartar. In another bowl whisk the yolks with 1/4 cup sugar, 1/4 cup molasses and the almond extract, until the entire mixture forms a nice ribbon when the beater is raised up. Then stir in the warm chocolate mixture, nuts and flour. Set aside for the time being.

Next beat the egg whites, sea salt and cream of tartar until soft peaks form. Slowly pour in the honey until the whites are stiff but not dry. (NOTE: 1/8 cup honey and 1/8 cup brown sugar may be necessary to achieve desired stiffness.) Fold about 1/3 of the whites thoroughly into the chocolate batter to lighten it, then quickly fold in the remaining whites. Turn mixture into the prepared pan and bake for 45–50 minutes. A toothpick inserted into the center of the cake should show moist crumbs—not too dry, not too runny—just right! Cool the cake in the pan, then glaze with the chocolate cognac glaze cited below.

Chocolate Cognac Glaze

Needed: 4 oz. (approximately 21 tbsp.) creamery sweet butter cut into small morsels; 6 oz. (approx. 31-1/2 tbsp.) semi-sweet or bitter baking chocolate cut into tidbits; 1 tbsp. blackstrap molasses; 1 tsp. pure maple syrup; 2–3 tsp. cognac.

Place chocolate, butter, molasses and maple syrup in a small saucepan and warm gently in a water bath over low heat. Stir frequently until the glaze is silky smooth and completely melted. Be careful, though, that you do not get it too hot. Remove from heat immediately, stir in cognac and set aside until nearly thickened or set up. Refrigerate if you are in a rush.

After the glaze is cool, until almost set but still spreadable, you are then ready to apply it to the cake. Run a knife around the edges of the completely cooled cake to release it from the sides of the pan. Cooled cake will have settled in the center leaving a high rim around the sides. Press this rim firmly with your fingers so it's level with the center. Now reverse the cake onto a cardboard circle cut exactly to fit the cake itself. Place on a decorating turntable or on a work surface covered with wax paper.

The bottom of the cake has now become the top instead. Spread the sides and top with just enough cooled glaze to smooth out any imperfections, crevices or rough places. This is termed the "crumb coat," being an undercoating to prepare for a smooth final glaze. Gently reheat the remaining glaze over just barely warm water until it's smooth and pours easily, with a consistency of heavy dairy cream.

It should be just lukewarm by now. Strain the glaze through a very fine strainer to remove any air bubbles or crumbs that might be present. Pour all the glaze onto the center of your cake top. Use a metal spatula to coax the glaze over the edges, coating all sides. Use as few strokes as possible. When the cake is coated, lift it off the wax paper or decorating turntable and let it dry on a rack before moving it to a serving platter.

Now this cake may be presented as it is or decorated with chopped, toasted hazelnuts if you wish, which have been pressed around the sides of the cake just before the glaze hardens. Or, melted chocolate can be piped through a paper cone for a more elaborate decoration.

To toast your hazelnuts or filberts, just put them on a cookie sheet in a 375° F. oven for about 20 min. Let the nuts cool, then rub off most of their skins between your hands. After this, pulverize them, a handful at a time, in your blender or food processor, using an on-off quick action to prevent making nut butter out of them.

These recipes have been adapted and somewhat modified by me from those provided by Jinx Morgan and her husband, Jeff, who've been innkeepers on the beautiful island of Tortola in the British Virgin Islands.

CHRYSANTHEMUM (See under ORNAMENTAL FLOWERS)

CINNAMON (*Cinnamomum zeylanicum*)

Brief Description

Cassia or Chinese cinnamon comes from Burma, while true cinnamon is a native of Ceylon. Cassia is more pungent, while true cinnamon is more light and delicate; it's also more expensive than cassia is. Cassia nips the tongue and is more suited to spiced meats, pilaus (rice or cracked wheat with boiled meat and spices) and curries, while true cinnamon is more desirable in sweet dishes, pastries, breads and cakes. Cinnamon was included as a major ingredient in a "holy anointing oil" that Moses used.

Fantastic Mouth Wash

In place of Listerine try another antiseptic mouthwash that really does "kill germs on contact." Half a teaspoonful of tincture of cinnamon added to half a tumbler of warm water makes an excellent mouth wash when the breath is unpleasant and the teeth decayed.

To make a tincture, combine 10-1/2 tbsp. powdered cinnamon in 1-1/4 cups of vodka. Add enough water to make a 50% alcohol solution. Put in a bottle and let set somewhere for two weeks, shaking once in the morning and again in the evening. Then strain and pour the liquid into a bottle suitable for storage. This tincture will last a long time.

Settles Upset Stomach

One of the most delicious, if not helpful, remedies for acid indigestion, heartburn and cramps is to sprinkle a little cinnamon and cardamom on hot, buttered raisin toast and slowly eat, chewing thoroughly before swallowing.

Cold and Flu Fighter

To make an effective French folk remedy for colds and flus, combine 2 cups of water, a small stick of cinnamon and a few cloves together in a saucepan and bring to a slow boil for about 3 minutes. Remove and add 2 tsp. lemon juice, 1-1/2 tbsp. dark honey or blackstrap molasses and 2 tbsp. of good quality whiskey. Stir well, cover and let steep for 20 minutes or so. Drink 1/2 cup at a time every 3–4 hours. It's pleasant tasting and really breaks up fever and congestion accompanying either the common cold or influenza.

Reduces Yeast and Fungal Infections

An incredible experiment, *Journal of Food Science* for 1974, demonstrates the power of cinnamon over most yeasts and fungi. Slices of white, raisin, rye and whole wheat breads, manufactured without the usual mold inhibitors, were subjected to various aflatoxins, a group of toxic molds so dangerous that they can cause liver cancer and kill humans and animals alike. These toxins often occur in food.

The toxic molds grew like crazy on all of the other breads, except for the raisin bread where growth was described as being "scant or not visible at all." In trying to identify whether it was the raisins or cinnamon responsible for this, food scientists discovered that as little as 2% or 20 mg. of the spice per milliliter of a yeast-extract and sucrose broth inhibited 97–99% of these molds.

What this tells us is that cinnamon is a super remedy for reducing the incidence of *Candida albicans,* a widespread yeast infection and to clear up athlete's foot. Use either a strong vaginal douche or footbath for these problems. To make a solution, bring 4 cups of water to a boil and add 8–10 broken cinnamon sticks. Reduce heat to low setting and let simmer for about 5 minutes or less. Remove and let steep covered for 45 more minutes. Use while still lukewarm for either problem.

Can Help Prevent Cancer

Two cancer specialists with the British Columbia Cancer Research Centre in Vancouver reported that the cinnamic acid in cinnamon helps to prevent cancer induced by many chemicals in many of the foods we eat. They suggest cinnamon be used more often in food preparations as a preventative measure.

Old-Fashioned Recipe

Cinnamon-Molasses Cookies

Needed: 1/2 tsp. baking soda; 1/2 tsp sea salt; 2-1/4 tsp. ground cinnamon; 1 cup (2 sticks) soft butter; 1 cup blackstrap molasses; 1/4 cup dark honey; 1/4 cup brown sugar; 2 large eggs; 1/2 cup plain yogurt; 4 cups sifted all-purpose flour. Blend the first four ingredients together. Gradually add the molasses, honey and sugar. Beat in the eggs. Stir in the yogurt and flour next. Mix all ingredients thoroughly. Drop rounded-teaspoon portions of dough, 2 inches apart, onto cookie sheets covered with lecithin from your local health food store. Bake in a preheated hot oven at 400° F. for 12 min. or until lightly browned around the edges. Store in an airtight container. Makes 48 large cookies as a rule.

CITRUS FRUITS

GRAPEFRUIT (*Citrus paradisi*)
KUMQUAT (*Citrus japonica*)

LEMON (*Citrus limon*)
LIME (*Citrus aurantifolia*)
ORANGE (Bitter) (*Citrus aurantium*)
ORANGE (Sweet) (*Citrus sinensis*)
TANGERINE (*Citrus reticulata*)

Brief Description

Grapefruit is not a hybrid, but a distinct plant species in itself. It first appeared in the 18th century in Barbados or Jamaica as a mutant from a Southeast Asian citrus fruit, the pomelo or Shaddock, which had been brought to Barbados by a trader named Captain Shaddock in 1696.

Kumquats are the smallest of all citrus fruits and have been cultivated in China and Japan for thousands of years. They are usually eaten skin and all, their rinds being quite sweet while the pulps are tart and juicy.

Lemons and limes originate from small evergreens with sharp, stiff thorns and originated in Asia a long time ago. Lemons were known to the ancient Romans, while British seamen acquired their famous nickname "limeys" in the 19th century, after limes were added to their daily rum rations to prevent scurvy.

Both kinds of oranges (bitter and sweet) are native to China and India. The bitter orange tree is hardier and more resistant to plant infections than the sweet orange tree. Like lemons, oranges were brought to the Mediterranean lands by the Moors, where their cultivation flourished. Orange seeds or saplings were later carried to the New World by Columbus, who planted them on the island of Hispaniola.

Named after the city of Tangier in North Africa, this small, loose-skinned citrus fruit is actually a variety of Mandarin orange—the most important variety. The juicy segments, which separate readily, are dark orange, with a sweet, delicate flavor. The skin ripens to a deep orange-red and is popular in Chinese folk medicine.

Kumquats for Hypertension and Obesity

These small citrus fruits seem to help those suffering from high blood pressure, if a couple of them are consumed each evening after dinner. Since kumquats are both sweet in their rinds and quite tart in their pulps, they appear to be an ideal snack food for obese subjects, satisfying both sweet and sour cravings at the same time.

Lemon Peel for Bleeding Gums

If your gums bleed quite a bit after brushing, then cut a small section of lemon peel from the fruit. Next turn it inside out so the white part is facing you. By wrapping enough of the peel around the tip of your second finger and holding the edges firmly with your thumb, you can rub your gums for a few minutes each day with the white part. Bleeding should stop in a few days.

Lime Juice for Toothaches

One of the best remedies used in the West Indies for getting rid of a toothache is to soak a wad of cotton with some fresh lime juice and then put it directly on top of or next to the site of pain. In 5 minutes or less, the aching should cease.

Sour Citrus for White Teeth

To keep your teeth pearly white, simply brush them two to three times each week with a combination of equal parts fresh grapefruit, lemon and lime juices. This solution also helps to reduce tartar as well. NOTE: It is *not* a good idea to suck on a lemon or lime when you have a sore throat, since prolonged contact with citric acid can cause serious deterioration of the enamel in time.

Tangerine Relieves Body Pain

A tea made from tangerine peels is excellent for relieving aching bones and sore muscles due to flu and fever. Bring 1 quart of water to a boil, adding chopped or coarsely shredded peel from 3 tangerines. Steep 1 hour, then strain. Drink 1 cup of warm tea every 5 hours, sweetened with a little honey.

Beauty Tips from an Exclusive Salon

Paul Nienast is unique in the world of beauty care. His salon at 2603 Oaklawn Avenue in a very posh part of Dallas is probably one of the most exclusive of its kind in America. This is not due to the fact that it rivals salons in Paris or New York City for professional hair and skin care, nor even for society's elite who flock to it from all over the country in search of eternal youth. His salon is exceptional because it probably uses more fresh fruits, vegetables, grains, oils and dairy products on its rich and powerful clientele than any other single salon in America.

In a word, this is a beauty shop for both men and women that relies almost entirely on natural substances, many of them freshly made on the spot for individual customers' needs.

Paul's famous $250 "fruit juice" perm consisting entirely of fresh citrus juices obtained from grapefruit, lemon, lime and orange is one example. "I find that these fruit acids leave the hair a lot softer, freer and without the chemical odors commonly associated with regular permanents," he said in a taped interview for this book. "We've had many people who having tried our 'fruit juice' perm, have said they never intended having any other kind of perm ever again. A perm like ours will last up to six months, whereas a regular perm is required about every two months. And while our cost to clients is pretty high for this, yet they only need two of these a year in comparison to six or eight regular permanents," he observed.

Paul's special perm involves many different steps that are normally associated with a regular permanent. But in the parts requiring chemical solutions to set the hair with, citrus juices are used instead. You too can experience one of Neinast Salon's expensive $250 "fruit juice" perms, but at a fraction of the cost and in the privacy and convenience of your own home or with your local hair dresser.

After the initial cleansing procedures have been followed, a combination consisting of the freshly squeezed juices from 6–9 oranges, 1-1/2 grapefruits and 1/2 each of a lemon and lime, well mixed together, is then applied to the hair where chemical solutions would ordinarily be used. This juice mix forms the initial perm and doesn't leave any kind of smell to speak of.

Paul also consented to share for the very first time with the public in a book such as this, some of his other remarkable "secret" techniques for incredibly beautiful skin that could fool many people into thinking you're 15–20 years younger. His wrinkle-remover formula is one of the most popular and sought after by the thousands who flock to his salon every month.

Take 2 slices of a lemon and put them in a wooden bowl (never metal or plastic). Add just enough half-and-half to cover which has been previously heated to lightly above warm. Cover the bowl and let set for about 3 hours, after which the solution is strained and gently massaged directly into the skin in a rotating fashion with the tips of the middle three fingers. Allow it to dry on the skin, then remove with a wet wash cloth and a little olive oil.

By doing this morning and evening, wrinkles should begin to disappear within a matter of just a few weeks or even less, depending, of course, on just how deep and old the skin lines are. If the skin is very oily, use 4 slices of lemon instead. On the other hand, if the skin is somewhat dry, use only 1 slice of lemon and double the amount of half-and-half.

"My wrinkle-removing formula is also terrific for rough, chapped 'dishpan' hands," Paul added. "From personal experience, I can tell you that there's probably not another application around that is so perfect for whitening and softening the hands with. I suggest that a couple of orange slices be added as well to the two lemon slices before the warm half-and-half is poured over them."

Paul finds a lemon juice compress to the skin is great for clearing up discoloration problems. "Just soak a wash cloth or small hand towel in a solution of the juice from 3–4 lemons and 1 lime diluted with a little hot water," he said, "then apply directly to the skin for up to half an hour. It really gets rid of any blotches quite nicely and sort of evens the color out more."

"I make another blotch-remover by applying a banana purée with the juice of 1 or 2 lemons mixed in. It's also very effective evening out those areas that may be light and dark colors in the same place."

He briefly ranked the different citrus fruits according to their usefulness on the skin. "Only fresh fruit juice must be used in all instances," he warns. "Anything less than this simply won't do. Lemon is a good astringent for closing the pores and helping to tighten things up a bit. Because it's very acidic, I recommend diluting it with a little water. Orange juice is the best skin softener I know of in the fruit juices. Like lemon, it's good for normal to oily skin. Orange really seems to perk up dull, lifeless skin. While grapefruit isn't as dramatic an astringent as lemon, the juice is good for neutralizing fatty acids on the skin and doesn't require any diluting."

At Paul's salon in Dallas, a black fig purée with a little tangerine juice is used as a facial for half an hour to help tighten skin and close loose pores. After which it's removed with cool water. For blemishes, a paste is made by soaking a slice of white bread in 1/4 cup of warm milk along with 1 packet or cube of yeast. This is then applied to the skin for about 40 minutes and later removed with water.

A two-step treatment recommended for vibrant-looking skin is this. First take some cotton balls and completely saturate them in a solution of equal parts of apple cider vinegar and hot water. Then carefully cleanse the skin with them. After which some fresh orange juice is then applied and left to dry. A moist wash cloth can then be used to lightly wipe the face after this for fabulous looking skin!

Heavenly Foot Care

Practically everyone suffers from sore, aching feet or foot problems of some kind at one time or another. Well, there's nothing quite like a nice lemon or lime juice-chamomile cream foot rub to help ease those pains away. The feeling to be derived from something so special as this is nothing short of pure ecstacy so far as hot, tired feet and sweaty toes are concerned.

Simply squeeze a little CamoCare Soothing Cream (see Appendix) into the palm of one hand with a little lemon or lime juice. Mix well by rubbing around in your palm with two fingers. Then rub the same on the bottoms of your soles and work well in between the toes. The sensation created is something akin to standing in ice-cold, minty water. CamoCare is distributed by Abkit, Inc. out of New York to most local health food stores. Lemons and limes are available from any produce stand or local supermarket.

Lowers Cholesterol

At a local Chinese restaurant here on Main Street in Salt Lake City near our Research Center where I frequently lunch, I've noticed they always include fresh, unpeeled orange segments with their delicious buffet. I usually help myself to 10–15 of these segments to accompany large servings of their Mongolian beef with broccoli and sweet-and-sour pork. I find that these fatty foods digest a lot easier with oranges than without them. I highly recommend eating an orange after consuming meals high in fat and grease. This reduces your risk of incurring hardening of the arteries and a heart attack later on in life.

Remedies for Sore Throat

Nothing helps to clear up a sore throat like gargling with a little warm lemon juice or lemonade several times each day. Following each gargle, spray the mouth and back of the throat with some CamoCare Throat Spray (see Appendix) available from any local health food store. The combination of citrus juices and chamomile seems to work better than if either are used alone for throat and skin problems.

Corrects Indigestion

A lady from Clearwater, Florida shared with me her method for relieving an upset stomach a few years ago when I was lecturing in that city. "I just grate the outer skin from an entire grapefruit right down to the white part,'' she told me. ''Then I carefully spread these grated bits on a clean cloth to dry. When they get kind of crinkly-dry, I store them in a zip-lock plastic bag. And whenever I get an upset stomach or heartburn, I just put 3/4 tsp. of these peel gratings in my mouth and slowly suck them before chewing. Eventually my stomach is back to normal,'' she beamed with delight.

A professor from the National Naturopathic College in Portland, Oregon once told me that taking 2 tbsp. of olive oil every morning before breakfast, followed with 1/2 cup of grapefruit juice would help expel gallstones as well as stop any gallbladder pains.

In Samoa, a few tablespoons of fresh lime juice is taken to relieve feelings of nausea and to stop vomiting.

A tea made of any citrus peel gratings is great for overcoming intestinal gas problems, especially when eating beans, for example. Just grate about 4 tbsp. of fresh citrus peel, then steep in 2 cups of boiling water for 30 min. When lukewarm, drink 1 cup at a time.

Eating whole oranges helps clear up diverticulitis. And fresh lime juice added to a little hot water will quickly stop diarrhea in infants, young children and even the elderly.

It is claimed by some health food enthusiasts and so-called ''nutritional experts'' that a grapefruit diet will help a person to lose weight; but there's no scientific validation for this whatsoever. At best, half a grapefruit every day may help curb hunger a little in some who are obese, but that's it.

Lemon and Migraines

Elana Russo of New York City wrote about a remedy which her grandmother used for getting rid of migraine headaches. A peeled lemon skin was turned white side down and placed on a handkerchief. Then the handkerchief was put against the forehead with the yellow side of the peel against the skin. When a burning sensation became evident, it was removed and generally, the headache would be gone by then.

Another remedy recommended to me by my Indonesian friend, Dr. Auzay Hamid, is good for headaches. When women in Jakarta are bothered by migraines, they just go and wash the dishes or some clothes by hand to bring quick relief. A couple of lemons are cut and the juice squeezed into the hot, soapy water as well. The hot lemon water seems to transfer excess blood from the head down to their hands, besides reducing the swollen blood vessels in the top of the head. For severe migraines that don't seem to go away, standing barefoot in two pans of hot lemon water by the sink while washing dishes in hot lemon water is sure to work just fine. An upright, standing position is necessary, though, for guaranteed success.

Insect Remedy

If you just squeeze some lemon juice on a mosquito or centipede bite or a bee or wasp sting, within a matter of minutes the itching and pain will completely stop! This remedy was recommended by Thor Heyerdahl in his book *Fatu-Hiva.* And to keep ants out of your kitchen, just squeeze a little lemon juice along the base boards and window and door sills and watch them head for the hills.

COCONUT (see under NUTS)

CLEAVERS OR BEDSTRAW (*Galium aparine, G. verum*)

Brief Description

Cleavers is an annual plant found in moist or grassy places and along river banks and fences in Canada, the eastern half of the U.S., and the Pacific Coast. A slender taproot produces the weak, square, procumbent or climbing, prickly stem that grows 2–6 feet in length. The rough, oblong-lanceolate to almost linear leaves occur in whorls of six to eight around the stem. The small, white or greenish-white flowers appear from May to September. The plant exudes a strong, honey-like odor and is best gathered in July.

Helps Tighten Loose Skin

Cleavers makes an excellent wash for the face as it tightens the skin. For those with the customary wrinkles and sags that come with old age, this might be an herb to give serious consideration to.

Bring 1 quart of water to a boil. Remove from heat and add 3-1/2 tbsp. of dried herb. Cover and steep for 40 min. Wash the face and neck often with this. Packs consisting of a wash cloth or small terry-cloth hand towel soaked in the tea, lightly wrung out and then applied to the entire facial area for up to 10 minutes several times a day, should help to tighten up loose skin folds. Gradual results should become evident within 2 weeks. One of the first things to look for is a new kind of life feeling in formerly tired, worn-out skin.

Calms Epileptic Seizures

The late naturopathic physician, John Lust, recommended cleavers for epileptic seizures. A tincture probably is the most effective. Use 10–15 drops once a day as a rule or twice a day if seizures are too frequent and close together. A tincture is available from Eclectic Institute of Portland, Oregon (see Appendix). And the cut, dried herb for tea is available from health food stores or Indiana Botanic (see Appendix).

CLOVE (*Caryophyllus aromaticus* or *Syzygium aromaticum*)

Brief Description

Cloves are one of the most famous of all spices. The 30-foot trees stand like neat evergreen sentinels with their clusters of crimson flowers and seem to flourish best near the sea. That's probably why the island of Zanzibar today is the most renowned clove-growing country of all. "On a hot, muggy evening when the light breezes filter through the trees," describes Tom Stobart in his *Herbs, Spices ànd Flavorings,* "if one approaches the island from downwind, one can smell cloves even before the land comes in sight."

Stops Toothaches and Bad Breath

Rubbing oil of cloves on sore gums or generously applied on a cotton wad then placed on an aching tooth, will, in both instances, bring rapid relief for several hours. Clove is a powerful, penetrating antiseptic which makes it ideal for an effective mouth wash. In 2 cups of hot water, put 3 whole cloves or 1/4 tsp. ground cloves, and steep for 20 minutes, stirring occasionally. Then pour through a fine strainer and use as a mouth rinse and gargle twice a day for bad breath.

Curbs Cravings for Alcohol

Reformed alcoholics who continue to get the yen every now and then for a taste of hard liquor, should just put 2 whole cloves in their mouth for a while, slowly sucking on them but being careful not to chew or swallow them. By doing this their cravings are somehow effectively curbed for the time being.

COFFEE (*Coffea arabica, C. canephora*)

Brief Description

Different types of coffee are preferred in various parts of the world. Arabica coffee is produced mostly in South and Central America, particularly Brazil, Colombia, Mexico and Guatemala, while robusta coffee is produced mainly by African countries such as the Ivory Coast, Uganda, Angola and so forth. In the U.S., Colombian and Central American coffees are preferred over Brazilian and African coffees. The March, 1981 *National Geographic* concluded that the world's annual bean production could make 3,644,000,000 cubic feet of liquid coffee, a volume equal to the Mississippi's outflow for an hour and a half. And although internal consumption can possibly cause a variety of health problems, ranging from pancreatic cancer and genetic birth defects to elevated serum cholesterol levels and hypoglycemia, it does have several therapeutic benefits.

Grounds Make a Brisk Body Rub

Some health authorities have recommended rubbing the skin with a dry luffa brush in order to enliven the skin more. But in Japan, people are buried up to their necks in roasted coffee grounds and rub the grounds all over their bodies to shed old dead skin and stimulate circulation. You may try the same thing on a more limited scale with the warm ground rubbed on your face and neck in a rotating fashion. You'll find your skin will feel like new in a short time!

Coffee Enema for Really Good Clean-Out

Robert Downs, D.C., an Albuquerque chiropractor, claims that an occasional enema several times a year is good for getting rid of hidden toxins that might lurk somewhere in the colon. And the *J. of the Am. Med. Assoc.* for Oct. 3, 1980 mentioned that coffee enemas, in particular, have become very popular throughout the country for treating chronic, degenerative diseases.

Fill a hot water bottle two-thirds full of lukewarm, *freshly brewed* coffee. The coffee should be as strong as possible. Next add one-third lukewarm water to which has been added 2 tbsp. of olive oil. Spread some newspapers on the bathroom floor. Affix the hot water bottle somewhere towards the top half of the door, making sure you have attached the long hose and closed the end of the syringe beforehand so water doesn't run out.

Then lay down on your back, bending both legs at the knees and spreading them apart some distance. Lubricate the syringe with a little petroleum jelly or some saliva from spitting on it to make insertion easier and less painful. Gently work the syringe into your rectum with one hand, while at the same time using the other hand to pull one cheek of your gluteus maximus aside.

Once the syringe is all the way in, you may then bring your upraised knees and legs together a little and release the control stem just above the syringe on the hose. Water will commence to flow into your bowels, but you should keep your fingers on top of the control stem in case the water needs to be quickly shut off for some reason. It's a good idea to permit the water to enter in short spurts, rather than in longer moments, by pressing down and then releasing the control stem every 10 seconds or so.

This way more water can safely enter the colon without causing undue discomfort. *Only take in that amount of water which your bowels can adequately handle with minimum pain!* To attempt more than what can be contained is only asking for trouble—not only in the mess created on the floor, but also the potential damage that could be done internally as well if one doesn't use good judgement.

Neither the coffee nor the olive oil is going to hurt you. In fact, they are probably the best combination of enema ingredients I know of to really tackle impacted fecal material in a quick and direct way! Unfortunately, some overzealous health enthusiasts and cancer quacks working in substandard Mexican border town clinics tend to overdo a good thing and administer several such coffee enemas in a single 24-hour period, day after day and sometimes week after week. Common sense says this is excessive and harmful, to say the least. Soap suds enemas ought to be avoided, says Volume 83 of *Postgraduate Medicine* because they may be harmful to the delicate membrane linings in the colon and rectum.

COLLARDS AND KALE (See under CABBAGE AND ITS KIND)

COLTSFOOT (*Tussilago Farfara*)

Brief Description

Coltsfoot is one of those quirky creations of nature which involves putting the cart before the horse. Or, in this instance, "the son before the father" as its old Latin name of *Filius ante patrem,* implies. Very early in the Spring, coltsfoot develops flat orange flower heads, but only after they eventually wither do the broad, hoof-shaped, sea-green leaves develop. Coltsfoot is fairly common and isn't picky about the soil it grows in.

Relieves Respiratory Congestion

In the Soviet city of Donetsk, 151 men and 60 women metal construction workers exposed to fumes from welding and metal varnish and paints were given herbal inhalation therapy to improve their breathing capacities. Factory workers were given a tea consisting of equal parts of coltsfoot, yarrow and plantain leaves and flowers to inhale as well as drink afterwards.

Bring 4-1/4 cups of water to boil. Remove from the heat and add the above 3 herbs. Steep them for 1 hour. Then lean over the pot, covering your head with a heavy bath towel, holding your face about 5 inches above it. Remove the lid and slowly begin inhaling. Do this for 5 minutes, then strain the tea and drink 1-1/2 cups. Repeat this routine several times each day, always making a fresh brew the next day. Follow this treatment for two weeks in severe cases of congestion like asthma, bronchitis and hay fever.

A Good Chew for Inflammation

A new kind of smokeless product containing absolutely no tobacco whatsoever but strictly natural herbs, has been developed by Coltsfoot, Inc. of Grants Pass, Oregon (see Appendix). Two of the main constitutents are coltsfoot herb and cinnamon, along with orange peel, angelica, hawthorn, tang kuei and bee pollen. A pinch of this can be placed in the mouth, mixed with a little saliva by the tongue and then removed and applied directly on any burn, bee sting, mosquito bite or general sore for immediate relief.

COMFREY (*Symphytum officinale*)

Brief Description

Comfrey is a perennial plant common in moist meadows and other moist places in the U.S. and Europe. The rootstock is black outside, fleshy and whitish inside and contains a glutinous juice. The angular, hairy stem bears bristly, oblong lanceolate leaves, some petioled, some sessile. There are also tongue-shaped basal leaves that generally lie on the ground. The whitish or pale purple flowers have a tubular corolla resembling the finger of a glove and grow in forked racemes that look scorpionlike.

Comfrey Rapidly Heals Wounds and Ulcers

The Soviet medical journal, *Vutreshi Bolesti* for June 1981 contained a report of 170 patients hospitalized for severe gastrointestinal ulcers, and of 90% of them being healed with a combination of comfrey root and calendula (equal parts) made into a warm tea and taken (2 cups) twice a day. Comfrey, the article noted, is also an effective antacid. A brief testimony from Christine Hays of Culver City, California published in the Nov. 1977 *Prevention* magazine related how her own stomach ulcers disappeared by drinking comfrey tea for a while. Comfrey's success with this and external wounds and sores may be attributed in part to the silicon, potassium, phosphorus and nitrogen found in the allantoin.

Comfrey for Cancer

At least three major medical journals in the past have given positive support for comfrey's remarkable ability to reduce certain types of tumors. These include *The British Medical Journal* for Jan. 6, 1912, Vol. 114 of the *Proceedings of the Society for Experimental Biology & Medicine* for 1963, and Vol. 16 of *Chemical & Pharmaceutical Bulletin* for 1968. An incredible recovery from jaw bone cancer with the use of comfrey by a retired American Air Force colonel was recorded in the Feb. 1979 issue of *Let's Live* health magazine. This astonishing success with various forms of cancer may be attributed in part to germanium and cobalt present in root and leaf alike.

By the same token, unfortunately, some species of comfrey, especially the closely related Russian comfrey (*S. x uplanicum*) contain a group of compounds called pyrrolizidine alkaloids which, in large amounts, can have a deleterious effect on the liver over a lengthy period of time. The herb may be used with relative safety provided one doesn't overdo a good thing.

Heals Bumps and Bruises

A contributor to Rodale's *Natural Home Remedies* book related how her young son, who fell from a grocery cart and sustained severe bruises to his face, was cured the next morning by her application of ice packs first, followed by a cloth soaked in comfrey root tea. This also works well for getting rid of black-and-blue marks and taking some of the dark blue or purple out of varicose veins, including reducing their size substantially if applied frequently enough.

To make a tea for this and all of the other preceding uses, just bring 1 quart of water to a boil. Reduce heat and add 2 tbsp. dried, cut leaves and steep for 1 hour. Use tea internally and externally as needed. And for a terrific paste for burns, sprains and setting fractures, combine 3 parts of powdered comfrey root or leaves and 1 part powdered lobelia herb with 1/2 part of wheat germ oil and 1/2 part of honey. Store in a cool place until needed. Works great for the above problems.

CORIANDER (*Coriandrum sativum*)

Brief Description

Coriander is a small annual plant that has been cultivated for several millenniums and is still grown in North and South America, Europe and the Mediterranean countries. The round, finely grooved stem grows almost 2 feet tall from a thin, spindly-shaped root. The leaves are pinnately decompound while the flowers appear in flat, compound umbels that may be either white or red in appearance. The brownish, globose seeds have a disagreeable smell until they ripen, at which time they acquire a distinctly spicy aroma.

Eliminates Genital Odors and Bad Breath

In the southeastern mainland China city of Canton, coriander leaves and seeds are used to help remove unpleasant odors occurring in the genital areas of men and women. And also to get rid of halitosis or bad breath. Bring 2 quarts of water to a rolling boil. Reduce heat and add 3-1/2 tbsp. of seed. Simmer for 1-1/2 hours until the amount has been reduced to slightly less than a quart of liquid. At this point, add 2 tsp. fresh, finely grated orange peel and one pitted, finely chopped date. Simmer for an additional 15 minutes, at which time remove from heat entirely. Add 1 tsp. each of dried coriander leaf (if available) and finely chopped fresh parsley, with a drop or two of peppermint oil or wintergreen oil (if available, but not necessary).

Steep mixture for about half an hour, stirring occasionally. Strain through a fine sieve or filter paper and store in a pint fruit jar with a good lid to seal it. Store in refrigerator until needed. When using for genital problems, warm up whatever is needed and rub all around genital area. Let the air dry it. Or gargle and rinse mouth with 1/2 cup of it while cool, but not heated. Also very good to hold in the mouth or soak cotton with and insert to relieve toothache.

CORN AND CORNSILK (See under GRAINS)

CRANBERRY (See under BERRIES)

CUCUMBER (*Cucumis sativus*)

Brief Description

This ancient plant is a native of southwestern Asia, where cultivated seeds almost 12,000 years old have been discovered. The Egyptian pharoahs fed them to their Hebrew slaves, which caused these people later on to grumble against Moses in the Wilderness of Sin for not having any more "cucumbers and melons which we did eat in Egypt freely of."

The cucumber is related to melons and, like them, has a high water content, which keeps its interior flesh cool in the hottest weather; hence, the expression "cool as a cucumber." Cukes are divided into three classes: the standard field-grown slicing kind; the smaller pickling kind, also field grown and the newer greenhouse varieties, some of which are seedless. A warm tea or cool vegetable drink made of peeled cukes is wonderful for eliminating excess fluid accumulations in body tissues, especially in chronic cases of gout and edema.

Relieves Tired, Inflamed Eyes

Putting a slice of cucumber over each eye after a long day does wonders to soothe tired, inflamed eyes. This also works well for bloodshot eyes if a mashed poultice of cucumbers in cheesecloth is applied directly on the lids for half an hour or so. It works also for itching and inflammation due to hayfever and related allergies during the summer time.

Perfect Remedy for Wasp Stings

The following was related to me several years ago on an airplane flight by Joy Adkins, then with the Department of Criminal Justice at Marshall University in Huntington, West Virginia:

> When my boy was seven, we went 'seng (ginseng) hunting together. I turned over a branch and disturbed a nest of yellow jackets. They came charging out at us like World War II dive-bombers. My son headed for the creek, swatting and swinging wildly at them every step of the way. I got stung hitting them, too.
>
> Well, we managed to get back to our house but in very painful condition. I went out and got some cukes from the garden and cut them into thin slices and put them right on top of all our stings. And you know what? So help me, you could actually feel the drawing power of these cukes as they drew the sting poison right through the skin. In fact, it kind of hurt a little, like when a person pulls the hairs on your arm. Well, the swelling went down in just a matter of minutes it seemed.

Soothes Aching Feet

Want to give your feet the ultimate treat after so many hours crammed into socks and shoes with little or no air? Cut up several large, unpeeled cucumbers into your blender. Whip them up into a somewhat thick mush of sorts. Refrigerate until cold. Get two pans large enough to accommodate your feet and pour equal parts of this cold cucumber mush in each. Then put your bare feet in them, squishing the mush around between your toes and so forth. And just lay back in an easy chair or chaise lounge and enjoy what some have called ''sheer delight'' for sore feet.

Nature's Own "Chap Stick"

Have you ever felt the outside of a cucumber? Notice the slightly greasy or oily feeling to the skin. Cucumbers have moderate amounts of fat in their skins. When your lips are chapped and dry, take an unpeeled cucumber, wipe it off good, pucker up your lips as if to put on lipstick, then just run the skin surface slowly across them in a back-

and-forth motion. This does a fairly nice job of lubricating them, I've found.

Cleopatra's Wrinkle-Remover Secret

Back in the late summer of 1980 on my return home from mainland China, I made a brief stop in Cairo, Egypt. While there, I was introduced to an Egyptologist by the name of Mostafa Abdel El-Selim, who was an expert in deciphering ancient hieroglyphic writings. He took me into an adjacent room of his small museum in the city of Nazlet El-Simman and proceeded to show me some very old-looking and highly brittle fragments of papyri estimated to be almost 2,000 years old and written in the time of Cleopatra, one of the great Queens of Egypt.

Knowing of my deep interest in herbs and folk remedies, he handed me an English transliteration of several columns of hieroglyphics which he had recently deciphered after considerable effort (part of the manuscript fragment was missing). But what I was able to read thoroughly excited me. He told me that I was holding in my hands one of the oldest beauty secrets, which according to legend, kept Cleopatra virtually wrinkle-free most of her life.

Herewith for the very first time in book form has this been reproduced with the kind consent of my friends in Egypt. I've made a few slight changes to accommodate our own 20th century technology and convenience, such as substituting the protein from fresh oxen blood to protein from fresh dairy cream, and replacing smooth stones for pounding the cucumbers with a blender to whip them up. Otherwise everything else pretty much remains the same.

Slice 2 unpeeled cucumbers lengthwise and widthwise. Put them into your blender with just enough dairy whipping cream to make a nice, thick, smooth mixture that "flows as evenly as the Nile," or, to my way of thinking, has the consistency of cooked cream-'o-wheat cereal. Then add 1 tbsp. of olive oil and blend again. Follow this with 1 tbsp. of honey and repeat the blending process again. Finally, add a little mud (I substituted cornstarch instead) and blend for a few more seconds. Set in the refrigerator for half an hour to cool more.

Scrub your face, forehead, neck and throat with several lime or lemon halves, but don't wipe dry. Immediately lay in a reclining position and slowly apply this cucumber cream mixture as you would do with shaving cream to the face or legs. Leave this mask on for about 1-1/4 hours before removing. Afterwards, when the face is thoroughly clean, dip your fingers into a cup half full of some more dairy whipping cream (*un*whipped, however). Rub in well in a rotating fashion. Let dry in the air. *Under no circumstances apply anything else.* Within a short period of time, you should begin to experience less wrinkles and if you do this often enough, who's to say that you might not be as beautiful as Cleopatra was? I should also point out that the juice obtained from liquefying a *peeled* cucumber in a food blender is most excellent for teenagers to use for reducing their acne problems caused by a steady diet of hamburgers, French fries, milkshakes and soft drinks.

A Wild Salad Dressing

Would you like to try something different on your salads for a change, and turn those "vegetable blahs" into exciting "green hurrahs"? Well then just top 'em with this wild idea of a dressing that you're going to find is unbelievably tasty when you and your guests try it.

Cucumber-Yogurt-Goat Milk Dressing

Needed: One 8-oz. carton of plain yogurt; 1/4 cup crumbled gorgonzola cheese (specialty shop or deli for this); 1/4 cup crumbled limburger cheese; 1 tbsp. apple cider vinegar; dash of kelp (health food store for this); 3 tbsp. pure maple syrup; 3/4 of a large unpeeled and shredded cucumber; 1 tbsp. canned goat's milk (goat cheese may be substituted for the above cheeses if you like a milder dressing).

In a bowl combine yogurt, two cheeses, maple syrup, cider vinegar and kelp. Stir in the cucumber. Cover and chill. Then add goat milk to thin a little. Should make 1-2/3 cups or about 10 good servings.

CUMIN (*Cumin cyminum*)

Brief Description

The stem of this small, annual herbaceous plant is slender and branched, rarely exceeding 1 foot in height and somewhat angular. The leaves are divided into long, narrow segments like fennel, but much smaller and are of a deep green color, generally turned back at the ends. The upper leaves are nearly stalkless, but the lower ones have longer leaf-stalks. The flowers are small, rose-colored or white, in stalked umbels with only 4–6 rays, each of which are only about 1/2 inch in length. These bloom in the summer then eventually turn to the so-called seeds, which are oblong in shape, thicker in the middle and compressed laterally about 1/5th inch long. In some ways they resemble caraway seeds, but are lighter in color and bristly instead of smooth, and almost straight instead of being curved. Their odor and taste is likewise reminiscent of caraway, but less agreeable to the senses than caraway is.

Poultice for Abdominal Pains

Soak 2-1/2 tbsp. of cumin seeds in some hot water for about 2 hours. Strain and dry thoroughly before crushing them with a heavy object (clean stone or hammer or rolling pin). Then mix them in with a little white flour and hot water—just enough to form a nice, thin paste. Add several drops of peppermint oil to the hot water before mixing the other ingredients in.

Spread this mixture on a piece of muslin cloth and apply over the abdomen to relieve liver, stomach and gall bladder pains. A tea made by steeping 1 tsp. of cumin seeds in 1 pint of water for an hour helps relieve muscle spasms.

Marinated Delicacy

Cumin brings out the flavor in game fowl like cornish hens and pheasants.

Cumin-Flavored Game Hen

Needed: 2-1/2–3 lbs. of uncooked Cornish game hen; 2 tsp. sea salt; 1 tsp. brown sugar; 1/2 tsp. anise seed; 1/4 tsp. ground ginger; 2 medium bay leaves; 2 tbsp. soy sauce; 2 tbsp. olive oil; 1 tbsp. apple cider vinegar; 3/4 cup flour; 4 tbsp. olive oil; 1-1/2 cups hot *distilled* or spring water; 1 tsp. ground cumin; 4 cups hot cooked wild rice.

Wash game hens and cut into serving pieces. Combine the next 8 ingredients and bring to a boil before pouring over them. Cool, then cover and refrigerate overnight. When ready to cook, remove the hens from marinade, reserving the marinade. Roll cut-up pieces of hen in flour. Brown over low heat in olive oil. Add water to marinade and pour over game hens. Cover and simmer 25 minutes. Last of all add the cumin 7 minutes before cooking time is up. Serve hot over wild rice. Serves 6.

CURRANTS (See under BERRIES)

D

DAFFODIL AND DAISY (See under ORNAMENTAL PLANTS)

DANDELION (*Taraxacum officinale*)

Brief Description

The name dandelion is sometimes loosely applied to other milky-sapped weeds with fluffy yellow flowers. But true dandelion is that ubiquitous weed growing prolifically in millions of lawns, backyards and pastures throughout America. This perennial herb has deeply cut leaves forming a basal rosette in the spring and flower heads born on long stalks. All leaves and the hollow flower stems grow directly from the rootstock. The creator of the comic strip "Marvin" once had his adorable diapered hero surveying a clump of dandelions and then thinking to himself, "Dandelions are Nature's way of giving dignity to weeds!"

Grandpa Walton's Wart and Liver Spot Remover

I recall almost a decade ago of being part of a studio audience on a late-night television talk show which featured the late screen actor Will Greer, who portrayed Grandpa Walton on "The Waltons." Greer was discussing the practical uses for the milky sap contained in the stems of dandelions.

"You just take some of them, break them open and rub that juice on any wart you have," he told his host, while at the same time illustrating it by a circular motion of his fingers on the back of his hand. "You just do that two or three times a day and I'll guarantee that you won't be plagued with warts anymore."

He also confirmed that this same milky sap was excellent for reducing dark "liver spots" which generally appear on the backs of the hands of elderly people. "I just do the same thing with them that I'd do with warts," he said, "only I use more of the juice and rub it in more thoroughly." He then held up both his hands in front of the camera for a close-up view. From the TV monitors located in the studio, we the audience were able to clearly see just how well this remedy had worked for him. Most of his liver spots had become so faded that one almost had to strain his or her eyes in order to detect any faint signs of them that might have still been barely visible.

Good for Hypertension

In the spring dandelion leaves and roots produce mannitol, a substance used in the treatment of hypertension and weak heart throughout Europe. A tea made of the roots and leaves is good to take during this period, from about mid-March to mid-May. Bring 1 quart of water to a boil, reduce heat and add 2 tbsp. cleaned and chopped fresh roots. Simmer for 1 min., covered, then remove from heat and add 2 tbsp. chopped, freshly picked leaves. Steep for 40 min. Strain and drink 2 cups per day.

Wonderful Liver Medicine

The late naturopathic physician, John Lust, stated in his *Herb Book* that dandelion root is good for all kinds of liver problems, including hepatitis, cirrhosis, jaundice and toxicity in general, as well as getting rid of gallstones. Bring 1 quart of water to a boil, reduce heat to low and add about 20 tbsp. of fresh dandelion leaves, stems and clean, chopped root. Simmer as long as it takes for the liquid to be reduced to just a pint, then strain. Take 3 tbsp. six times daily, Dr. Lust recommended.

For those desiring something more convenient in capsule form, there is the nice AKN Formula from Nature's Way, which contains considerable dandelion root and other cleansing herbs. It can be obtained from any local health food store.

Remedy for Diabetes

Dr. David Potterton, a licensed, practicing medical herbalist in Great Britain, once wrote that the high insulin content of the root may be regarded as "a sugar substitute to prescribe for people with diabetes mellitus." Three capsules of the dried root each day is recommended for this. The Nature's Way brand from your local health food store is often purchased with this in mind.

Flowers Improve Night Blindness

For those with a problem of being able to see clearly in the dark, the substance called helenin found in dandelion flowers may be just the ticket. According to the *Journal of the American Medical Association* for June 23, 1951, which carried this report, the blossoms also contain vitamins A and B-2 (riboflavin). Steep a handful of freshly picked flowers in a pint of hot water for about 20 minutes. Drink 1 cup twice a day.

Reduces Fever of Childhood Infections

If your child or grandchild comes down with measles, mumps or chickenpox, three common infectious diseases of childhood years, then dandelion tea is the thing to give him. Bring 1 quart of water to a boil. Reduce the heat and add 2-1/2 tbsp. dried, cut root and simmer, covered, for 12 minutes. Remove from heat and add 3 tsp. dried, cut leaves. Steep for half an hour. Strain, sweeten with 1 tsp. pure maple syrup or 1 tsp. blackstrap molasses per cup of tea and give to a child, lukewarm, every 5 hours or so until fever breaks and lung congestion clears up. This tea is also excellent for all types of upper respiratory infections, ranging from pneumonia to chronic bronchitis.

Homemade Wine

Delicious dandelion wine is fun and easy to make at home.

Dandelion Wine

Needed: 2 quarts dandelion flowers (make sure they're not sprayed); 1/2 gallon water; 1 orange; 1/2 lemon; 1-1/4 lbs. brown sugar; 1/2 cake yeast. Carefully remove all traces of stems. Place flowers in some kind of crockware. Add the sugar, sliced orange and lemon, then pour boiling water over everything. Let set 2 days, stirring occasionally. On the third day, strain into another crock and add yeast. Let ferment 2 weeks in a warm place.

DATES (*Phoenix dactylifera*)

Brief Description

David the Psalmist is quoted in the Old Testament as saying that "the righteous shall flourish like the (date) palm tree." Modern Arabs claim that there are as many uses for dates as there are days in the year.

These sugary fruits are a boon to desert dwellers, growing in hot, dry regions where most food plants cannot—yet they have their own rather temperamental requirements. Date palms must have a source of underground water, but any moisture in the air will keep the fruit from setting, and temperatures below 70° F. will keep it from ripening. The trees themselves can survive in cooler, wetter areas, but their nutritious fruits cannot.

Sun-ripened dates are plump and shiny, with lighter, smoother skins than the dried ones. The latter may contain added sweeteners and preservatives. Fresh dates are often described as either "soft," "semi-dry" or "dry," depending of the softness of the ripe fruit. Covered and refrigerated, they usually keep indefinitely.

Folk Remedy for Some Cancers

My friend and colleague, Jim Duke, thinks dates hold some limited merits in the treatment of various kinds of cancer. Jim is with the United States Department of Agriculture Germplasm Resource Laboratory in Beltsville, Maryland and knows a lot about herbs.

In his recent work, *Medicinal Plants of the Bible,* he devotes a couple of inches of space to their potential with cancer. For instance, he says that a poultice made from crushed date pits and date meat may help testicular tumors. And the fresh fruit, "prepared in various manners," he asserts, may "remedy cancer of the stomach and uterus, abdominal tumors, hardness of the liver and spleen and ulcerated and nonulcerated cancers." A drink made of the fresh, pitted fruit in any kind of juice (orange, carrot or pineapple) would be the most logical way to take it internally, while a handful of pitted dates made into a purée could be spread on external eruptions with apparently satisfying results. Of course, in anything this serious, competent medical treatment should also be sought, besides relying on useful folk remedies like these.

Dynamic Laxative

Ben Harris, a popular health writer, once proposed that six dates be boiled in a pint of hot water for several minutes, and then the resultant liquid drunk warm, morning and night; or six dates eaten raw followed with a glass of warm water twice a day, in order to promote active, frequent bowel movements.

Good Digestive Aid

Close to 20% of the total amino acid content of dates is the nonessential glutamic acid. The sourness of its properties is helpful in diluting excess gastric acid in the gut and relieving heartburn. So whenever your stomach feels upset, just eat a few dates or soak several in a cup of hot water for a couple of minutes and then drink the liquid.

Ingenious Ways to Use Dates

A nourishing drink for a perfect midafternoon pickup can be made using dates, milk and powdered coconut. Take about half a dozen pitted dates, 1/2 cup canned goat's milk, 1/2 cup unsweetened pineapple juice, 1 tsp. powdered coconut and an even 1/4 tsp. of pure maple syrup, and blend together for a tasty, refreshing drink when your get-up-and-go got up and went!

A spicy, lip-smacking fruit spread could be made by blending together 1 cup pitted dates, 1/2 cup chopped nuts, 1/4 cup plain yogurt, 1/2 cup powdered milk and 1/2 tsp. ground cinnamon. Refrigerate until ready for use.

Incredible Date/Fig-Nut Bread

Needed: 1/4 cup warm water; 1 tbsp. granular yeast; 1 cup warm goat's milk (canned); 1 tbsp. blackstrap molasses; 1 tsp. sea salt; 1/2 tsp. ground cinnamon; 1/2 tsp. ground cardamom; 2 tbsp. olive oil; 1/2 cup whole wheat flour; 2-1/2 cups white flour; 1/4 cup pitted, chopped dates; 1/4 cup chopped figs; 1/2 cup coarsely chopped pine nuts.

Sprinkle yeast over water; let stand 2–3 minutes and stir until dissolved. Add goat's milk, molasses, sea salt, cinnamon, cardamom and olive oil. Stir in whole wheat flour and 1 cup of white flour. Beat well. Add dates, figs and pine nuts and enough additional white flour to make a dough that will clean the sides of the bowl and can be gathered into a ball. Turn out onto a lightly floured board and knead 10 minutes. Cover dough with a cloth and let rest 20 minutes; punch dough down and divide in half. Form into 2 loaves and place in greased 7-3/8 x 3-5/8 x 2-1/4 in. loaf pans (or pans close to these dimensions). Cover with a cloth and let rise in warm place until double in bulk or until dough reaches top of pan. Bake in a preheated, 375° F. oven for about 30 minutes or until bread sounds hollow when tapped. Brush with remaining oil and remove to a rack to cool. Makes 2 loaves. (This recipe has been considerably modified from Eileen Gaten's *Biblical Garden Cookery,* courtesy of the publisher.)

DAY LILY (See ORNAMENTAL FLOWERS)

DEWBERRY (See BERRIES)

DILL (*Anetheum graveolens*)

Brief Description

Dill is aromatic, somewhat like caraway is, but much milder and sweeter. The taste of dill resembles fennel in some ways, but is slightly more pungent and aggressive in flavor.

The plant grows ordinarily from 2 to 2-1/2 feet high and looks a lot like fennel, although smaller but having the same feathery leaves, which stand on sheathing foot-stalks, with linear and pointed leaflets. But unlike fennel, it has seldom more than one stalk and its long, spindle-shaped root is only annual. It's of very upright growth, its stem smooth, shiny and hollow, and in midsummer bears flat terminal umbels with numerous yellow flowers, whose small petals are rolled inwards.

The flat fruits or so-called seeds are produced in great quantities—an ounce containing over 25,000 seeds. Pickled cucumbers and beets wouldn't be complete without dill seed. Nor would green apple pies, certain fish hors d'oeuvres, soups, beans, cabbage, cauliflower, peas, cottage cheese and some nut butters.

Get Your Beauty Sleep

If you have trouble sleeping at night, consider this remedy instead of over-the-counter and prescription drugs. Bring 1 pint of white wine *almost* to a boil (but don't boil). Remove from heat and add 4 tsp. dill seeds. Cover and steep for 30 min. Drink 1-1/2 cups lukewarm 30–45 minutes before retiring.

Increases Milk Flow in Nursing Moms

A tea made according to the above directions but using instead 1 tsp. each of anise, coriander, caraway and dill seeds is excellent for stimulating the flow of breast milk in nursing mothers, when taken daily lukewarm, 1 cup about an hour before feeding an infant.

Gets Rid of Bad Breath

Try chewing some dill seeds the next time you experience halitosis. You'll be pleasantly surprised to see how quickly they sweeten and freshen your breath.

An Interesting Salad

Dilled Green Bean Salad

Needed: 1-1/2 lbs. green beans; 1/2 cup olive oil; 1/4 cup tarragon vinegar; 1 tbsp. each chopped fresh parsley, fresh chives and dill weed; kelp to taste; small bunch of watercress. Wash and trim green beans. Boil until tender. Rinse under cold water. Drain well, patting dry with paper towel. Whisk together oil, tarragon vinegar and herbs. Season to taste with kelp. Pour over the beans and stir well. Correct seasonings, if necessary. Chill. Before serving, break watercress into small pieces and toss with green beans. Arrange on a platter. Serves half a dozen. Adapted from *Country Journal* for April 1987.

E

ECHINACEA (*Echinacea augustifolia*)

Brief Description

This is about the only herb I'm aware of that has several other very popular common names, which some might judge to be decidedly racist in tone—"Kansas niggerhead" (the midwest) and "Black Sampson root" (the south).

Echinacea is a native perennial growing from the prairie states northward to Pennsylvania, but also occurs in the cooler northern regions of some southern states as well. The stout, bristly stems bear hairy, linear-lanceolate leaves, tapering at both ends. Each of the distinctive rich purple flowers feature 12–20 large, spreading, dull-purple rays and a conical disk made up of numerous tubular florets that are in bloom from June–October. A weaker species (*E. purpurea*) is often substituted for *E. augustifolia* whenever the latter becomes scarce or too expensive for the herb industry's use.

The plant has a faint aromatic smell with a nice, sweetish taste to it, leaving a tingling sensation in the mouth not unlike that of aconite or monkshood, but without the latter's lasting numbness or dangerous poison. Tasting echinacea powder is one way of determining just how fresh or old it might be. I once found some in a Gainesville, Florida health food store that was about as lifeless and dull as any herb could be. It apparently must have sat on the shelf for a very long time and was virtually worthless as a medicinal herb.

Tremendous Immune System Booster

Medical doctors have praised the tremendous power which echinacea seems to exert upon the entire immune system. Finley Ellingwood, M.D., a Chicago physician, some years ago (1915) published a special issue of his health magazine (*Ellingwood's Therapeutist*) devoted entirely to this herb. "For 25 years," he wrote, "echinacea has been passing through critical experimentation under the observation of several thousand physicians, and its remarkable properties are receiving positive confirmation."

He noted that this herb dramatically increases the production of white killer cells in the body to help eliminate infectious diseases of all kinds. He claimed that echinacea "endows them with a certain amount of recuperative power or formative force," even going so far as to compare its effects in the body to that of the standard vaccines of the day! Various cases from tuberculosis and tonsillitis to spinal meningitis and syphilis, have been successfully treated with this remarkable herb!

German scientists over the years have demonstrated echinacea's uncanny ability to reduce malignant tumors. They found that echinacea can even mimic the actions of the body's own interferon—powerful little proteins that throw up an incredibly strong wall of resistance to superinfections like the AIDS virus, for instance.

Health writer Ed Mayer explained how he cured himself of serious hospital-induced staph infection. External treatment consisted of making a potent tea by boiling for 20 minutes in 2 cups of water, 1 tsp. powdered myrrh, 1 tsp. powdered golden seal and 1/2 tsp. cayenne. He soaked his badly infected foot for about 15 minutes daily, keeping the tea as hot as he could stand it. He then applied a paste of golden seal, echinacea and water before bandaging it.

Internal treatment consisted of high doses of vitamin C, light food and plenty of fresh fruit and vegetable juices. He also drank 3 cups a day of the following tea until the infection completely cleared up: 2 tsp. echinacea, 2 tsp. burdock root and 1 tsp. sassafras simmered on low heat in 4 cups of boiling water for about 20 minutes.

Two particularly effective herbal formulas that some doctors have recommended to their patients in San Francisco as fairly good protection against getting the AIDS virus are Resist-All and Herpes, manufactured by Great American Natural Products out of St. Petersburg, Florida (see Appendix). Both products, these doctors informed me, had heavy concentrations of echinacea in them, besides other powerful antibiotic herbs like chaparral, thyme, myrrh, pau d'arco and sarsaparilla. They had their clientele take an average of three capsules each per day for maximum protection.

Protects Against Fire

In Virgil J. Vogel's classic masterpiece, *American Indian Medicine*, is mentioned the use of echinacea for an incredible feat of endurance in the early and mid-19th century. Winnebago medicine men would sometimes chew up the raw herb in order to numb their mouths enough so that they could insert burning pieces of hot coals as if by magic to the utter astonishment of their tribes. This amazing act without sustaining serious injury made tribal members fear their supposedly great power. The echinacea juice acted as a preventative against lengthy inflammation.

EGGPLANT (*Solanum melongena*)

Brief Description

This dark, satiny fruit was first imported from India by Arab merchant caravans centuries ago. The eggplant eventually was introduced to the U.S. by Thomas Jefferson, who experimented with seeds and cuttings of many foreign plants. Eggplants can be red, yellow or even white, but the most common kind is purple and pear-shaped. Other varieties include long, oval ones which the Japanese refer to as nasubi, and small egg-shaped varieties that may help to explain how this vegetable got its name.

Relieves Abdominal Pains

The April 1982 issue of *Tropical Doctor* reported an effective native folk remedy used by Nigerian healers to stop abdominal pains. Equal parts of chopped, dried eggplant and ripe tamarind fruits were simmered in 1 quart of hot water for half an hour, strained and then drunk, 2 cups at a time, to relieve any kind of abdominal pains which women might be experiencing.

Calix Tea for Alcoholism

The calix part of the eggplant that is attached to the stem thereof, makes a dandy infusion to mellow the effects of alcohol in the bloodstream, to neutralize the side effects of certain berry and mushroom poisonings and to stop smokers' hacking coughs. Simmer 2-1/2 tbsps. of chopped eggplant calix in 2 cups of water for 20 minutes. Drink when warm.

Lowers Serum Cholesterol

Eggplant, along with onions, apples and yogurt, to name just a few, are foods which can really help lower excessive cholesterol in your blood. Eggplant, in fact, contains substances which actually bind up cholesterol in the intestines and carry it out of the body so it can't be absorbed. Adding more eggplant to your diet seems to be a good way of preventing fatty buildup in your heart.

Powdered Eggplant for Dental Health

A special dental preparation can be made from the calix or top part by which the eggplant is attached to its stem. The top parts are spread out on a cookie sheet and *slowly* roasted at 175° F. for 24–30 hours or until they can be easily reduced to a powder by either grinding them up or crushing them with a wooden mallet or hammer.

Next 1/4 cup of sea salt and 2 tbsps. of powdered kelp should be mixed together thoroughly and then evenly spread out on another clean cookie sheet, and also slowly roasted at the same temperature for about half the time. When sufficiently cooled, the sea salt and kelp should be mixed in with the powdered eggplant calixes.

Toothaches can be relieved by rubbing some of this mixture into the gums near the painful tooth for a couple of minutes. The purulent gum disease, pyorrhea, which afflicts several million Americans can be successfully treated by lightly brushing the teeth and gums with some of this eggplant-salt-kelp mixture before retiring for the night. After brushing rinse the mouth with cold water, and, then, with a moistened forefinger dipped into some of this mixture, rub some more of it on the outside of the gums. Leave it on for awhile before rinsing away.

Stops Nosebleeds and Bleeding Ulcers

This same eggplant-salt-kelp powdered blend is very useful for stopping bleeding. In case of a nosebleed, wet the corner of a clean cloth, handkerchief or paper towel with water, squeeze out the excess, then dip it into the mixture and insert the same in the nose. And for internal bleeding, just mix 2/3 tsp. of the blend with 1/2 cup of water and drink at once. Repeat this, as needed, to stop ulcers from bleeding. It should be emphasized here that those with hypertension should not take this internally!

What a Way to Go

This is probably one of the few, if not the only place, in this book that you'll find a pizza recipe. But this one beats 'em all for tasty excitement while still remaining a healthy dish that's good nourishment for your body.

Eggplant Pizza

The preparation time on this is 20 minutes and baking time 10–15 minutes. *Needed:* 1/4 cup olive oil; 2/3 cup warm water; 2 cups multi-grain biscuit mix (from any health food store); 2 tbsp. stone-ground cornmeal (health food store); 1 cup natural spaghetti sauce; 1 tsp. oregano; 1-1/2 tsp. dried basil; 1 finely minced garlic clove; 1/4 cup shredded mozzarella cheese; 1/4 cup shredded goat cheese (from a local deli); 1/4 cup grated Parmesan cheese; 1 cup thinly sliced eggplant.

Preheat oven to 500° F. Place oil and water in large mixing bowl and stir in biscuit mix. Scrape dough onto a pastry board or other flat surface that has been sprinkled with additional biscuit mix. Knead for about 2 minutes, gradually adding the cornmeal until the dough is smooth and elastic. If the dough seems dry, add a few drops of olive oil.

If using a cookie sheet, rub it with olive oil before rolling out the dough into a circle or any shape you desire. Prior to adding the topping, spread thinly sliced eggplant on another cookie sheet, lightly brush them with olive oil and broil in the oven for just a couple of minutes. Then remove and place them immediately on top of the pizza dough. Next spread on the spaghetti sauce and sprinkle with oregano, basil and garlic. Distribute the cheeses evenly over the entire surface. Bake for 10–15 minutes until the sides and bottom of the crust are golden brown and the cheese has pretty well melted.

ELDERBERRY (See under BERRIES)

ELM (SLIPPERY) (*Ulmus fulva*)

Brief Description

This deciduous beauty reaches heights of 65–70 feet and may be found planted along streets and growing in forests from Quebec to Florida, the Dakotas and Texas. The tree is covered with a reddish, dark brown, rough, furrowed outer bark, with the inner bark being whitish, slightly sweet and somewhat aromatic. The twigs are hairy, the buds dark brown, blunt and coated at the ends with long, rusty hairs. The leaves are very rough to the touch, thick and stiff, with both surfaces being hairy.

Incredible Hip Joint-and-Socket Replacement

One of the most amazing accounts I've ever read concerning what an herb can do is found in the rare, out-of-print book, *The Women of Mormondom* by Edward W. Tullidge. In there is related in great detail how a woman named Amanda Smith was inspired with a divine cure, which kept her young son from being permanently crippled for life.

On Tuesday, October 30, 1838, the small Mormon settlement of Haun's Mill in Caldwell County, Missouri was unmercifully attacked by a heavily armed band of religious hooligans. Close to two dozen young boys and teenage to adult men were murdered in cold blood and their bodies later dumped down a deep well for concealment.

Amanda Smith's youngest son had his one entire hip joint completely blasted away when one cruel attacker put the muzzle of his gun against the lad's waist and deliberately fired. The mother recovered from her initial shock and prayed to God for inspiration. She was told by an unseen voice to make a lye out of the ashes of shagbark hickory and carefully wash out all dirt and debris from the ugly, gaping wound.

Next she proceeded to get some roots and inner bark from nearby slippery elm trees and pounded them with rocks until they were quite pulpy. This mucilage poultice was then put directly into the wound until it was full and finally dressed with clean linen. The boy's mother changed the poultice every few days. In about 5 weeks her son had completely recovered—a flexible gristle having grown in place of the missing joint and socket which amazed physicians for years to come. The family later migrated to Utah where the boy enjoyed a full, active adult life without any physical hindrance whatsoever from his terrible childhood ordeal. A tea made of the bark is also good for appendicitis.

Ideal Remedy for Sores and Eczema

Certain 19th century Native Americans like the Menoiminee and Potawatomi would mix water with some powdered slippery elm bark and put it on sores and boils with good results.

And a rather remarkable remedy for eczema using slippery elm bark was contributed by a Minnesota couple. The husband's teenage sister had once been severely afflicted with eczema on both arms. The parents had exhausted their funds on the medical profession trying to find a cure for her miserable condition, but without any success. Someone recommended an application of boiled jimsonweed (a poisonous herb) and slippery elm bark, which cleared it up in no time at all.

I recommend substituting chaparral in place of this dangerous herb. Bring 2 quarts of water to a boil, adding approximately 4 heaping tbsp. cut, dried chaparral. Reduce heat to low and simmer an hour and a half until the liquid has been reduced to just 1 quart or so. Strain liquid into a clean jar and store unused amount in refrigerator until needed. Pour a cup of the warm liquid into a small saucepan. In a cup, combine enough cold water and powdered slippery elm until thoroughly mixed. Turn this into the hot chaparral liquid on the stove and heat up, stirring constantly until a thick type of paste is formed. You'll need to do a little experimenting perhaps in order to achieve the right consistency (close to cooked cream-'o-wheat).

Spread this mixture on several strips of clean surgical gauze with a wooden ladle. A tbsp. of olive oil may be added to the mixture in the pan before spreading to keep it from drying out so fast. Apply this to any rash, eczema, dermatitis, or in smaller amounts to any venereal sores, herpes lesions, leg ulcers, wounds that will not heal and so forth. Leave for several hours at a time. Repeat process a couple of times each day. Healing should be imminent before you realize it.

Recipes to Get Well by

This *is* the best herb of nourishment to administer to those recuperating from any kind of mild or serious illness, be they infant or elderly.

We are indebted to the late Euell Gibbons for these recipes found in his *Stalking the Healthful Herbs*.

Elm Lemonade for Recuperation

Gibbons informs us to pour 1 pint of boiling water over 5-1/4 tbsp. (1 oz.) of cut, dried elm bark and let steep until cool. Then add juice of 1/2 lemon and enough honey to sweeten to taste. "This same elm lemonade is highly recommended for feverish patients; allow them to drink all they take, for this drink will quench their thirst and help relieve their illness by giving them strengthening, easily digested food at the same time," he wrote in his chapter on this herb.

Homemade Anti-Smoking Lozenges

For being a great lover of the outdoors and a true believer in Nature, Euell Gibbons wasn't very health-minded in many other ways. He believed in the excessive use of white sugar, and like the late health food faddist, Adelle Davis, he was a compulsive chain-smoker. But he found that slippery elm bark really helped him to cope with the constant craving for another cigarette.

Put some finely powdered slippery elm bark into a bowl. Make a little nest in it, pour in some dark honey and carefully work the powder into the honey with the back of a wooden ladle or strong metal tablespoon. Do this until the dough is somewhat stiff. Place on a board and cut into small squares. Roll these squares again in powdered slippery elm, then store in your refrigerator. I recommend adding a dash of nutmeg or cinnamon to the powdered bark the squares are to be rolled in, for added flavor. Said Gibbons, "They make very effective lozenges, soothing my throat, dispelling my hoarseness, and allaying my cough, and I find that sucking on these lozenges satisfies my infantile oral cravings, so that I'm not constantly taking another cigarette that I don't really want."

ENDIVE AND ESCAROLE (See under CHICORY)

EVENING PRIMROSE (*Oenothera biennis*)

Brief Description

Evening primrose is a coarse, annual or biennial plant found in dry meadows and waste places and along roadsides east of the Rockies to the Atlantic. The stem is erect, stout and soft-hairy, with alternate, rough-hairy, lanceolate, taper-pointed leaves about 3–6 inches long. The yellow, lemon-scented flowers, 1 to 2-1/2 inches across, open at dusk and grow in spikes from June to October. The fruit is an oblong, hairy capsule.

New Hope for Schizophrenia and PMS

Sufferers who experience the socially crippling consequences of either schizophrenia or premenstrual syndrome (PMS) now have hope for a much better and brighter future thanks to oil of evening primrose. Kenneth Vaddadi, a psychiatrist at the University of Leeds in England, has achieved successful results in clinical trials on a small number of schizophrenic patients. It appears that about seven 500 mg. capsules daily in conjunction with vitamins B-3, B-6, C and zinc achieve remarkable results.

Thirty women who had severe PMS were put on 3 grams of oil of evening primrose daily from the 15th cycle day until menstruation during 2 cycles and placebo capsules for 2 cycles. PMS symptom severities, especially depression, were relieved a lot more with the oil than with the placebo. Improvement was noted during 62% of oil-treated cycles, but only 40% of the time with placebo. Up to six capsules per day appear to give significant therapeutic benefits.

Primrose Lowers Blood Pressure

In two separate Canadian studies, the main constituent in evening primrose, gamma-linolenic acid (GLA) and the plant oil (EVO) itself, significantly reduced blood pressure. In the first study, the GLA greatly strengthened the heart's response to chronic stress, while in the second a general lowering of blood pressure in the first 18 weeks of life became evident in hypertensively bred rats. About 4 capsules of primrose oil per day is recommended for hypertension, along with increased potassium intake (750 mg.) as well.

Relief for Chronic Disorders

While no single herb can be said to be an answer for every health problem that comes along, certain scientific research apparently justifies the use of oil of evening primrose for a host of chronic disorders. Some South African physiologist writing in the Sept. 1985 issue of *Medical Hypotheses* cited very credible evidence to support the idea that coronary artery disease, hypertension, hypercholesterolemia, allergic eczema and other atopic conditions, cancer, premature aging, and chronic inflammatory and auto-immune disorders are related to an imbalance of fatty acids in the body.

Deficiencies of GLA and another important fatty acid found in fish oils may result in the metabolic blockage of a key enzyme. This vital enzyme activity can also be inhibited by too much saturated fat, excess sugar, alcohol, high dietary cholesterol content, high levels of stress, exposure to low levels of radiation and chronic deficiencies of zinc or magnesium.

These physiologists conclude their report by suggesting that supplementation with oil of evening primrose is one good means of getting around this blockage and possibly preventing and treating many chronic disorders as well. Recommended intake is 2 capsules twice daily, in the morning and again in the midafternoon for optimal health.

I recommend the Efamol brand of Evening Primrose Oil distributed exclusively to all U.S. and Canadian health food stores under the Nature's Way label (see Appendix).

Medicinal Edibles

The following recipe is a reverse of that old adage about "food also being our best medicine." In this instance, a reliable medicinal really enlivens veal cutlets. My gratitude goes to Kathryn G. and Andrew L. March for letting me borrow this from their wonderful book, *The Wild Plant Companion* (see Appendix).

Evening Primrose and Veal with Madeira Wine

Needed: 8 very thin veal cutlets, trimmed of all fat and tenderized with a mallet or dull side of a knife; some flour; 2 tbsp. butter; 16 very small evening primrose plants, roots with tops, washed (the roots about 1/8-in. diameter, or use bigger plants and parboil them); 1/4 tsp. sea salt; 1/2 cup Madeira wine; 1/2 cup water; lemon slices.

Dredge the cutlets in flour and shake off the excess. In a 10- to 12-inch skillet, over moderate heat, melt the butter. When the foam subsides, quickly brown the veal on both sides, a few cutlets at a time. Remove those browned to a plate while doing the rest. Place the evening primrose in the pan, add the salt, Madeira, water and veal with any juices that have accumulated. Turn the heat to low and simmer, covered, for 10 minutes until the evening primrose is tender and the sauce is boiled down. Remove to a serving platter, pour the remaining sauce over the top and garnish with lemon slices. Serves 4.

F

FENNEL SEED (*Foeniculum vulgare*)

Brief Description

Fennel is a wild or cultivated biennial or perennial growing in the U.S., Europe, the Mediterranean and Asia Minor. It has a rather stiff, erect, branching stem, which bears deeply cut greyish-green flowers, followed by odd, toothed seed-vessels, filled with small somewhat compressed seeds, usually three-cornered, with two sides flat and one convex. These black or brown seeds yield a strong, agreeable, aromatic odor somewhat reminiscent of nutmegs and have a spicy, pungent taste.

Breath Sweetener

If you suffer from halitosis, just chew some fennel seeds for a while and you'll have breath fresh enough for someone to kiss who may love you a lot!

Medicinal Tea

First cook some barley in plenty of water. Strain the water and save. To 1 pint of boiling barley water, add 1-1/2 tsp. fennel seed. Reduce heat to simmer for 5 minutes; steep an extra 20 minutes. One cup taken by nursing mothers will stimulate milk flow soon; 1/2 cup before a meal stimulates appetite; the eyes washed with the same strained liquid will get rid of irritation and eye strain. This same tea made with an equal amount of peppermint and given in 1-cup amounts when cool, will help to calm hyperactive children.

Culinary Aspects

At the time of the Norman Conquest in England, fennel seed was used with all kinds of fish dishes and still is today. A real treat is to grill trout or salmon, then flame them in brandy on a bed of fennel seed which burns and imparts a truly unique flavor I can't even begin to describe to you. The spice also goes well with pork, veal, in soups, vinaigrette sauces and salads.

FENUGREEK (*Trigonella foenum-graecum*)

Brief Description

The name comes from foenum-graecum meaning "Greek Hay," the plant being used in times past to scent inferior hay. The name of the genus, Trigonella, is derived from the old Greek name denoting "three-angled," from the form of the plant's corolla. Fenugreek is an erect annual, growing about 2 feet high, similar in habit to lucerne hay. The seeds are brownish, about 1/2 inch long, oblong, with a deep furrow dividing them into unequal lobes. They are contained, 10–20 together, in long, narrow, sickle-like pods.

Reduces Cholesterol

Mongrel dogs from a nearby pound in the French city of Villemoisson-sur-Orge were fed a standard diet supplemented with fenugreek seed meal for 8 weeks. Blood test results showed that these herb seeds really reduced their serum cholesterol levels quite a bit. Based on this data, it's suggested that you might benefit from taking an average of 2 capsules of fenugreek-thyme formula each day, especially when eating meals high in fat. The product is available at most health food stores from Nature's Way.

Great for Hay Fever

A California woman mentioned having tried everything for her allergy, but nothing seemed to work. She then decided to make a tea of fenugreek seed—8 tsp. seed presoaked in 4 cups cold water for 5 hours, then boiled for 2 minutes before straining and drinking—and consumed 1 cup per day 2 months before the hay fever season began. To her utter amazement, she didn't have any serious attacks as in previous years!

Stops Ringing in the Ear

Leota Lane of Eugene, Oregon has the perfect remedy for stopping "cricket" noises and ringing in the ear. In fact, it's the only remedy that ever seems to have helped her.

She puts about 2-1/2 full soup spoons of fenugreek seeds in 3 cups of cold water and lets it set overnight. The next morning the mixture is stirred up a little and poured off as needed. When she takes her morning cup of cold tea, she replaces it with another cup of water on top of the seeds.

In the evening she has another cup of the same tea. She follows that routine for several days until the seeds have lost most of their strength, at which time they're discarded and the process starts over again with new seeds.

She states that if the seeds are boiled, the tea becomes so bitter she can't stand it. If this is a problem, then honey may be added to sweeten to taste.

Culinary Virtues

The whole seeds may be sprouted to include in salads for a really improved flavor. Or the powdered seeds may be added to any kind of Far Eastern foods, especially Indian and Pakistani dishes, for extra tartness. When making curried rice, add some powdered fenugreek to this delicious vegetable sauce which goes over the rice.

Golden Fenugreek Sauce

Needed: 3/4 cup cooked potatoes; 1 medium-cooked carrot; 1-1/3 cup water; 2 tbsp. chopped cashews; 1/2 tsp. sea salt; 1 tbsp. lemon juice; 1 tbsp. lime juice; 1/2 tsp. chopped dill weed; powdered contents of 4 gelatin capsules of fenugreek seed from any health food store.

Combine everything together in a food processor or blender until smooth and creamy. Heat and serve over hot rice or cooked vegetables of any kind.

FIG (*Ficus carica*)

Brief Description

Fresh figs have been a prized delicacy for at least 5,000 years. They were grown in King Nebuchadnezzar's famous Hanging Gardens of Babylon, mentioned frequently throughout the Bible, and exported by the ancient seafaring Greeks and Phoenicians, who may have introduced them to Italy. In the 18th century, Jesuit priests planted figs at the first Catholic mission in San Diego, California. This so-called black Mission fig is still an important variety in that state, which grows 99% of the entire U.S. fig crop. Fresh figs are usually pear-shaped, with either greenish-yellow, purple or black skins. When ripe, they are usually soft but not mushy. The ancient Roman gladiators ate a lot of figs prior to combat in the amphitheaters to give them extra physical strength and an advantage over their opponents.

Relieves Sore Throat and Lungs

Bring 2 cups of water to a boil, adding 5-1/4 tbsp. chopped figs. Simmer on low heat for 5 minutes. Cover and steep until cool. Sip half cupfuls every 4 hours or so to relieve sore throat and lungs.

Nice Fruit Laxative

In 4 cups of boiling water, put 10-1/2 tbsp. each of figs, raisins and uncooked barley. Simmer on low heat for 15 minutes, then add 2-1/4 tbsp. cut, dried licorice root and remove from heat, permitting to steep for 30 minutes or so. When cold, stir and strain. Take 1 cup at night and again in the morning as a laxative. In Egypt a few raw figs are consumed to relieve digestive problems caused by eating too much red meat, fish, eggs, cheese or milk.

Poultice for Sores and Boils

Put three to four figs in a pie tin with enough milk to cover them. Cover with another inverted pie tin and place in an oven set on a very low temperature for an hour. By that time the figs should have absorbed all the milk. Cut the figs open and lay them directly on the sore or boil. They soon draw out all purulent infection.

Some country folks used powdered figs in a paste to apply to old wounds and sores so they heal much faster. Old Amish Herbs makes such a Fig Paste for livestock and human use, both internally as well as externally (see Appendix).

Helps Clean Teeth

In parts of Africa and Central America, ripe figs cut in half are used to clean the teeth by rubbing the cut side against the enamel for several minutes.

Figs for Cancer

Scientist Jonathan L. Hartwell listed figs as a useful treatment for different kinds of cancer in his five-year survey, "Plants Used Against Cancer," which was published in the scientific journal, *Lloydia* from 1967–1971. In the July 1978 issue of *Agricultural & Biological Chemistry*, a team of Japanese scientists identified the anti-cancer component in a steam distillation of figs which reduced tumors by 39% as being benzaldehyde. A subsequent followup study with 57 cancer patients showed a 50% regression of tumors with the administration of benzaldehyde from figs, according to *Cancer Treatment Reports* for January 1980. Benzaldehyde also occurs in large amounts in edible mushrooms such as *Agaricus bisporus* and Japanese shiitake mushrooms, as well as in sweet almond oil.

This is not to suggest that figs in and of themselves are going to cure cancer. But when used with regular medical care and alternative therapies, it seems to be a very useful food in the treatment of cancer, based upon the data just presented.

Removes Arthritic Pain

Figs, like pineapple (bromelain) and papaya (papain), have an important sulphur compound called ficin, which is valuable in the treatment of chronic joint inflammation and swelling of soft tissues common to rheumatoid arthritis and traumatic injuries, such as a twisted ankle or pulled muscle ligaments.

Soak about 6 figs in 2-1/2 cups of boiling water for a few minutes to soften them up a bit; then mash into a poultice and apply directly to any area of stiffness and soreness on the body. Cover with a heavy towel or warm flannel cloth and keep on for half an hour or so. Or apply a thin cloth over them and then a heating pad, set on low heat. It will really bring incredible relief, even to lower backaches—a type of pain that is sometimes hard to get rid of.

Hot Fruit Appetizer

Here's something to really please your palate as a pre-meal warmup item.

Broiled Fresh Figs and Dates

Needed: 9 slices bacon; 12 fresh figs; 12 unpitted dates; some Roquefort cheese, cream cheese and slices of ham. Cut bacon into pieces long enough to wrap one time around the figs and dates.

Remove hard stem end of figs and make a gash on sides with a sharp paring knife. Mix together equal quantities of roquefort and cream cheeses and fill the figs; wrap in bacon, securing with a wooden pick. Pit dates and fill with equal quantities of cream cheese and ham; wrap in bacon, too. Thread the figs and dates on a long skewer and broil, turning several times, until the bacon is crisp. Serve hot from the skewer or keep hot in a small covered dish. This recipe comes from Eileen Gaden's *Biblical Garden Cookery* with the kindness of the publisher.

FLAXSEED (*Linus usitatissimum*)

Brief Description

The cultivation of flaxseed reaches back to the remotest periods of history. Both the seeds as well as the cloth woven from this plant fabric have been found in ancient Egyptian tombs. In fact, the first linen mentioned in the Bible has been proven by historians and archaeologists to have been spun from flax.

The flax is a graceful little plant with turquoise blue blossoms, a tall, erect annual 1–2 feet in height. The stems are usually solitary, quite smooth, with alternate, linear, sessile leaves nearly an inch long. The seed vessels with their five-celled capsules are referred to in the Bible as bolls, with the expression in Exodus 9:31—"the flax was bolled"—meaning that it had arrived to a state of maturity. When the bolls are ripe, then the flax is pulled and tied in bundles. In order to help in the separation of the fiber from the stalks, the bundles are placed in water for several weeks, and then spread out to dry.

From the crushed or milled seeds comes linseed oil and meal. The oil is applied to wood surfaces in thin layers to form a hard, transparent varnish. Internally the oil is used by some veterinarians as a purgative for sheep and horses or a jelly from the boiled seeds is fed to young calves.

Remarkably Effective Laxative

According to Dr. Hans Fluck, a Swiss professor of pharmacology, if 2 tsp. of flaxseed are put into half a cup of hot water and allowed to swell for up to 4 hours and the mucilage and seeds swallowed together, it will produce a swelling bulk within the intestines which will provide a substantial bowel movement a few hours later.

Best Hand Lotion Around

An Oregon woman, who has suffered from dried, chapped hands for years had tried just about every kind of hand lotion there was on the market, but with no success. Then she stumbled onto flaxseed and now makes her own lotion which she finds incredibly effective.

Her recipe calls first for whole or cracked flaxseed, about 3 round tbsp. to be soaked in 2 cups lukewarm water overnight. The next morning the mixture is boiled and strained to remove as much of the mucilage jell as possible; then the seeds are thrown away. A pint of apple cider vinegar is then added to the jell, along with 5 tbsp. of glycerine (purchased from any drugstore). The mixture is then heated again to the boiling point and immediately removed from the heat. Take an eggbeater and beat the mixture for a minute or so to keep the glycerin from separating. Bottle. Dampen hands with solution morning and evening, thoroughly rubbing into the skin and letting the air dry them. You will experience a greaseless, silky feeling on your hands. Soon they will be as smooth as satin.

FILBERT or HAZELNUT (See under NUTS)

G

GARLIC AND ONIONS
CHIVES (*Allium schoenoprasum*)
GARLIC (*Allium sativum*)
GREEN ONION (A SCALLION) (*Allium fistulosum*)
LEEK (A SCALLION) (*Allium porrum*)
ONION (*Allium cepa*)
SHALLOT (A SCALLION) (*Allium ascalonicum*)

Brief Description

Chives (usually referred to in the plural) are the smallest, though one of the finest-flavored of the onion tribe. It belongs to the same *Allium* species that garlic and onions do. Seldom found in the wild anymore, this hardy perennial is cultivated all over the world, from Corsica, Greece and Sweden to Siberia and throughout North America. The bulbs grow quite close together in dense clusters and are of an elongated form, with white, rather firm sheaths. Chives are used to season omelets, cottage cheese, baked or mashed potatoes, sour cream sauces or dips, salad greens and salad dressings.

Garlic is a close kin to onion and was widely used throughout antiquity as an aphrodisiac of sorts, a plague repellant, an antidote to ward off demons and vampires with and an embalming agent, not to mention being a popular culinary spice as well. The leaves are long, narrow and flat like lawn grass. The bulb is of a compound nature, consisting of numerous bulblets or cloves, grouped together between the membranous scales and enclosed within a whitish skin, which holds them as in a sac.

Believe it or not, the elegant and beautiful Easter lily and the dry, old smelly onion are close cousins, both coming from the lily family. This is almost like saying that the lovely Princess Grace of Monaco was the twin sister of the elderly and somewhat haggard-looking comedian, Phyllis Diller. This is the largest branch of the onion family, consisting of a mind-boggling number of varieties ranging from mild to sweet. Their skins may be pearly white, bronze or red. The interiors can be either yellow or white. The globe-shaped onions or American variety are the most pungent and may be white, yellow or red in color. Bermudas or Spanish onions are much milder in flavor, kind of large and flat and either white or yellow in appearance. A curious custom in ancient Egypt was for people about to take an oath to raise one hand and put the other on an onion, much as we do on a Bible in courts of law today.

The last three members of the onion family are also thought of as scallions. Green onions have bright green tops and very small bulbs, and can be mild or slightly sweet in flavor. Leeks are to French cuisine what beer and hot dogs are to American ball games. These big onions have flat ribbon-like leaves and resemble their diminutive cousins, green onions, in appearance, but not flavor. This was one of several vegetables that the Hebrews moaned and groaned to Moses about missing when they left Egypt for the Promised Land (see Numbers 11). Finally, shallots are definitely for the true gourmet, who prefers a delicate and distinctive flavor that's sweet yet bitey. The small bulbs resemble garlic in appearance.

A closing genealogical tidbit for those who like unusual facts is that asparagus is also a close cousin to all of these onion relatives, but without their noxious odors.

Relieves Headaches Due to Colds

A simple remedy for relieving headaches due to the sinus congestion caused by colds and flu is a tea made from chives and ginger. In 1 cup of boiling water put 1-1/2 tbsps. finely chopped chives and 1/2 tsp. finely shredded ginger root. Cover with a flat plate and steep for half an hour. Strain, then drink lukewarm. Headache usually goes away in 20 minutes or less. Repeat as often as needed.

Garlic Acts as a Natural Antibiotic

The medical world is gradually accepting the long-held view of many traditional folk healers from around the world that garlic is Nature's own antibiotic penicillin of sorts. The journal, *Medical Hypotheses* (12:227–37) noted in 1983 that "there appears to be sufficient data to indicate that garlic is indeed a natural antibiotic," and speculated that "garlic may play a role in preventive medicine and holds a promising position as a broad-spectrum therapeutic agent."

As an antibiotic, garlic has helped cure 82% of spinal meningitis cases compared with only 15% for the drug, Amphetericin (*BEPHA Bulletin,* July 1986); or, along with leeks has reduced the incidence of poliomyelitis by better than 30% compared with an untreated control group (*Antibiotics Annual, 1958–59).*

But it's in the area of cancer that garlic seems to have racked up the greatest medical successes achieved thus far. The following four selected references are but a mere handful of the many published reports implicating garlic extract in the reduction of tumors and other types of malignancies:

- *American Journal of Chinese Medicine* 11:69–73.
- *Science* 126:1112–14.
- *Journal of Urology* 136:701–705; 137:359–62.

Now one of the foremost leaders in current cancer research employing garlic therapy is Benjamin Lau, M.D., Ph.D., a professor with the Dept. of Microbiology at the Loma Linda University School of Medicine in Loma Linda, California. In one study which appeared in *Current Microbiology* (13:73–76) for 1986, Dr. Lau reported that an extract of garlic completely inhibited the activity and further progress of a parasitic fungus (*Coccidioides immitis*) which has recently become associated with some AIDS victims and is known to produce fever, pneumonia-like symptoms and inflamed skin lesions.

Some of Dr. Lau's more dramatic work of late has been with the effects of odorless garlic extract by itself and in conjunction with a certain killed vaccine (*Corynebacterium parvum*) in controlling transitional cell carcinoma and bladder cancer. Dr. Lau observed, "*Allium sativum* was shown to elicit macrophages (large scavenger cells) and lymphocytes (white blood cells) leading to cytotoxic destruction of tumor cells."

In a personal letter written to me in the early part of July 1987, Dr. Lau said, "We think most highly of garlic as a natural remedy for various ailments. We further believe garlic to be a valuable supplement to one's diet in terms of overall good health. I am currently working on a project in which we will attempt to isolate and identify anti-tumor and immune-stimulating components of garlic." There are many odorless garlic products available with varying degrees of purported benefits. One that some doctors and nutritionists have confidence in, although not the subject of Dr. Lau's experiments, is Garlicin, which can be found at any local health food store under the Nature's Way logo.

Good Salt Substitute

For those on a sodium-restricted diet due to their hypertension, a green onion or two with your meals may be just the ticket to satisfy your taste buds for salty things. For storage, trim and wash a bunch of green onions, then wrap loosely in a damp paper towel to retain moisture. Refrigerate for up to a week, changing moist paper towel every other day to retain as much freshness as possible. A green onion goes especially well with a chunk of good crusty bread.

Therapy for Burns, Insect Stings

A favorite French recipe is also a favorite French remedy as well. Vichyssoise, the cold leek and potato soup, created by a famous French chef has also been used by several renowned French herbalists as a near perfect remedy for serious burns and bee, wasp and hornet stings, and red ant and centipede bites.

To make a good vichyssoise for healing rather than eating purposes, only the following items in their given amounts are necessary: 2/3 cup each of thinly sliced leeks (green onion may be substituted if true leeks are unavailable) and thinly sliced white onion; 1/2 tbsp. olive oil; 2/3 cup very thinly sliced, peeled potatoes and 1/2 cup each of water and half-and-half.

First slowly brown the leeks and onions in the oil on medium heat without burning or smoking until they are a light straw color. Add thinly sliced potatoes and 1/2 cup water. Cover and simmer for about 1/2 hr. While still warm, force contents through a coarse sieve so that the potatoes acquire a purée consistency. After this add the other 1/2 cup of half-and-half, stir well, then cool first before refrigerating.

The consistency of the vichyssoise when used externally, should be somewhat thick without being too runny. There is sufficient quantity to cover a burn area approximately 1-1/2 ft. in length and about 1 ft. in width. Light strips of gauze may be applied afterwards and taped down to hold this vichyssoise poultice in place. Not only is this one of the most cooling remedies I know of for burns, but also one of the most effective to speed the healing process. For insect stings and bites, a small amount may be put on the afflicted site and held in place with a little gauze and tape.

Variations on this theme include adding the juice of pressed onion along with the half-and-half, or wrapping one slice of peeled onion around an insect sting or bite and leaving it on for 3 hrs. or so before removing. When this raw onion poultice is taken off, the stinger will usually accompany it, having been drawn out in the meantime. Or instead of going to all the effort to make the vichyssoise poultice (which is the best for burns), a shorter alternative may be resorted to by mixing 1/2 cup pressed onion juice with 1 cup of plain yogurt and applying it to the burn instead.

Also some white onions run through a grinder and applied directly to a twisted ankle, banged-up knee, dislocated shoulder, fractured arm or similar injuries often encountered in sports or hard labor, will soon remove the pain and swelling.

Say "Good-Bye" to Earache and Toothache

A Queensland, Australia grandmother (now deceased) by the name of Edith Evans, who invented a world-famous herbal hair restorative, shared a tried-and true earache remedy with the Canadian press during an October 1981 visit there. "Bake an onion in the oven," she said, "then cut it into slightly thick slices afterwards. Lay one of these while still quite warm on the outside of your sore ear and cover with warm flannel. Keep the other slices in the oven on a "warm" setting until needed. When the first slice becomes cold, discard and replace with another warm one. Do this until the earache disappears completely. The hot onion actually draws out pain."

Or make a garlic-onion oil by soaking 1/2 peeled, chopped onion and 3 peeled, minced garlic cloves in 1 cup olive oil for 10 days, then with an eye-dropper put between 5–7 drops of warm oil in the ear. Another alternative is to use a commercial herb oil made from green onions, white onions and garlic available from Great American (see Appendix).

Several drops placed in a hot tablespoon that's been previously heated over a flame, will warm the oil just enough to gently pour in an aching ear. After that the head should be put in a reclining position for awhile and the ear covered with a flannel or soft knap hand towel for a time. The pain should cease very shortly.

And for relieving an excruciating toothache, just soak a small wad of cotton thoroughly with some of this special oil before placing next to or on top of the bad tooth. If this oil isn't readily available, just peel and crush a clove of garlic and place it on the tooth instead. Pretty soon the hurt and pain will go away.

Super Hair Conditioner

If you want to try a super conditioner that will leave your hair incredibly soft and further enhance its present shade, then you should try making this solution out of plain onion skins, of all things!

The part you want to use is the clean, dry, brown or golden onion skin, and not the moist, inner one. Store them in a brown paper bag each time you use an onion for culinary purposes. When you have about 2-1/2 cups of lightly packed onion skins, put them into a pan and add 1 qt. of boiling water. Cover and steep them for 50 minutes, then strain through a sieve.

After shampooing your hair, towel-dry it briefly. Then rinse several times with the onion skin rinse, before finally rinsing again with clear water. This particular rinse not only conditions your hair by giving it a much softer texture, but actually provides a lovely color to your own present shade. In fact, it has even softened some of the gray in older people's hair with occasional weekly use.

Getting Rid of Cold Shivers

An assistant professor of medicinal chemistry from the University of Puerto Rico in San Juan related an interesting little remedy he had discovered for hypothermia, when we met each other at a scientific conference during July 1987 at the University of Rhode Island in Kingston. He found that by grating a couple of garlic cloves, then mixing them with a pinch of cayenne pepper before wrapping the material in a layer of cheesecloth and applying it to the base of each heel for awhile, was effective in reducing cold shivers or the sensation of coldness in elderly people. The plaster is to be removed when the heels feel hot.

Stops Hacking Coughs

An old Basque remedy common to the Pyrenees mountain range which runs along the French-Spanish border, quiets any kind of cough, from little nagging ones to the more serious hacking kinds such as whooping, smoker's and asthmatic coughs.

Take two large Spanish onions, peel them and then slice very thin. Place in a wooden bowl and nearly cover with two cups of dark honey. Next put a flat dish or board over the bowl and let set overnight. In the late morning, strain off the syrup and add to it a jigger of brandy. Bottle and refrigerate, taking 1 tsp. of the syrup every 2–3 hrs. or as needed to stop tickling of the throat and lungs as well as coughing.

Breaking Up Chest Congestion

Smokers, asthmatics and those allergic to pollen or who may be suffering from a cold or flu should find ample benefits from this simple salve. Peel and finely mince about 7 garlic cloves. Put them into a wide-mouthed, pint-size fruit jar and add just enough melted Crisco shortening to cover. Then stand the open jar in a pan of boiling water for about 3 hrs. Permit it to cool after stirring well, then pour into smaller baby food jars, screw on lids and store for use. Do not strain.

Rub some of this ointment on the throat, chest, abdomen and upper portion of the back between the shoulder blades and cover with a large, heavy bath towel for awhile. This treatment is very effective for breaking loose, accumulated phlegm and allowing greater ease in breathing.

An optional ingredient might be 1/8 tsp. of eucalyptus oil, added to the melted shortening, which will only enhance the effectiveness of the ointment, but isn't really necessary.

"Miracle" Medicines for a Multitude of Problems

Garlic and onion are very good for a wide range of other health problems, often duplicating their benefits for the same illnesses. The following table lists uses for both and explains how either may be applied for the conditions cited. In all instances, they have been proven quite effective, either through clinical verification or folk usage.

Uses	*Methods of Application*
Prevents blood clots	Both onions and garlic prevent proteins from massing to form harmful clots. They should always accompany meal intakes of greasy or fatty foods.
Reduces hypertension Controls insomnia	Prostaglandin A is the anti-hypertensive factor in onions. 2–3 capsules of Nature's Way Garlicin or 5 drops of Great American's green onion-garlic oil (see Appendix) per day are helpful for controlling high blood pressure. Eating cooked onions can relax you. And strangely enough, putting a cut raw onion beneath your pillow should correct insomnia.
Increases longevity	A prominent sociologist from the National Institute of Aging surveyed over 8,500 centenarians a decade ago and found that two preferred

Uses	*Methods of Application*
Increases longevity (continued)	foods stood out in a majority of their diets—garlic and onion.
Eliminates worms	An old Amish remedy from Lancaster County, Pennsylvania calls for using garlic and onion to help expel intestinal parasites from man and beast alike. Slices of these raw herbs or prepared oils of the same are generally consumed.
Helpful in diabetes	The medical journal, *Lancet,* for Sept. 11, 1976, noted that both garlic and onion are very hypoglycemic. Meaning they are quite useful for lowering blood sugar levels in diabetics. Up to 4 capsules of Nature's Way Garlicin or about 7 drops of Great American's green onion-garlic oil (see Appendix) is suggested for diabetics on a daily basis; but those with low blood sugar levels already should avoid these two herbs as much as possible.
Lowers serum cholesterol	Garlic and onion raise blood levels of "good cholesterol," which in turn clean out the arteries of "bad cholesterol" that can clog them up, choking off the flow of blood through the heart. Be sure to eat lots of garlic and onion when consuming fatty meats and greasy foods. 2 capsules of garlic or 5 drops of green onion-garlic oil per day is adequate for protection against atherosclerosis.
Plague preventative Infection Fighter Resists bacteria-induced diarrhea Relieves earache	The U.S. Surgeon General has declared AIDS to be "a national epidemic of plague-like proportions." Some doctors think 4 capsules of garlic or 10 drops of onion-garlic oil per day affords reasonable protection against this virus. A vaginal douche made of 4 chopped garlic cloves steeped in 3 cups of hot water for 30 mins. is good for treating yeast infection. Travellers in foreign countries experiencing diarrhea can be helped by chewing some raw garlic or take up to 10 garlic oil capsules daily to kill bacteria. Warm garlic oil also relieves an excruciating earache. A recent poster session presented by Bronwyn C. Hughes of Nature's Way Products at the 28th Annual Meeting of the American

Uses	Methods of Application
Plague preventative Infection Fighter Resists bacteria-induced diarrhea Relieves earache (continued)	Society of Pharmacognosy indicated that most garlic extracts currently sold in the health food marketplace failed to inhibit the growth of ordinary bacteria even at 400–800 times that of fresh garlic. The researcher from Nature's Way then presented convincing evidence to show that her company's new product, Garlicin, truly manifests the strong antibacterial activity which garlic is supposed to have (see Appendix).
Insect repellant	Rubbing your arms, legs, hands, face and neck with garlic oil will keep gnats, mosquitoes and other bugs away from you during the Summer and Fall. Peel and chop 10 garlic cloves, adding them to 1 pint of olive oil. Let set for 10 days before using. Also works well on household pets to help them get rid of fleas and ticks.
	Garlic makes a terrific insecticide as well as a repellant. A senior-citizen horticulture class in Reedley, California, experimented with a garlic oil spray concocted as follows: Lots of finely minced garlic was soaked in mineral oil for at least 24 hours. About 2 tsps. of the oil were added to 1 pint of water in which 2-1/4 tbsps. of Palmolive soap had been dissolved. This was thoroughly stirred, then strained into a glass container for storage. When used as a spray, 1–2 tbsps. of oil mix was blended into 1 pint of water.
	The results reported by the Reedley class were astonishing! Cabbage moths, cabbage loopers, earwigs, potato bugs, grasshoppers, mosquitoes (including larvae), whiteflies and some aphids were killed *on contact!* Houseflies, June bugs and squash bugs died within minutes after being sprayed. Cockroaches, lygus bugs, slugs and hornworms died more slowly.

An "Onion Family" Delight

A real gourmet treat you're not likely to forget are found in the two recipes below, which constitute a complete meal together.

Lusty Spanish Rice

Needed: 2 large Spanish onions, sliced very thin; 2 cloves minced garlic; 1 finely diced leek; 1 finely minced shallot bulb; 4 tbsp. olive oil; 2 cups brown rice; 1 cup chopped, shelled, unsalted walnuts; 4-1/2 cups boiling water; 2 sweet green bell peppers, sliced with center seed cores finely diced; 2 tsp. turmeric; 3 tbsps. freshly chopped parsley.

Sauté the onions, garlic, leek and shallot in olive oil until nice and brown. Then add the rice and chopped walnuts. Stir well and cook until all of the oil is absorbed. Next add the water, bringing to a boil. Cover and reduce heat to medium, cooking until all the liquid has been absorbed. In the meantime, sauté peppers and their diced centers. Remove rice from pan, adding turmeric, parsley and peppers. Serve while still hot. This makes a very tasty dish for 6 when topped with the sauce below.

Zesty Leek-Chives Sauce

Needed: 4 cups peeled and diced Pontiac (red) potatoes; 3-1/2 cups thinly sliced leeks; 1/2 cup each of finely chopped chives and green onion; 3-1/4 cups water; 1 tbsp. kelp; 1/2 cup half-and-half; some sour cream; a little chopped parsley.

Simmer potatoes, leeks, chives, green onion, water and kelp in a large heavy saucepan for 45 mins., or until contents are tender. Mash the vegetables with a fork or potato masher ad then purée in a blender. Return to pan and reheat a bit. Then remove from stove and stir in half-and-half, sour cream and parsley. Should be of the consistency of gravy. Use as a sauce to pour over helpings of Spanish rice.

GERANIUM (See ORNAMENTAL FLOWERS)

GINGER (*Zingiber officinale*)

Brief Description

Ginger is an erect perennial herb with an aromatic, knotty rootstock that's thick, fibrous and whitish or buff-colored in appearance. The plant reaches a height of 3–4 ft., the leaving growing 6–12 inches long. It is extensively cultivated in the tropics (i.e., India, China, Haiti and Nigeria), especially in Jamaica.

Anti-Nausea Remedy

A fellow colleague I've known for some years, Dr. Daniel B. Mowry of the Department of Psychology at Brigham Young University in Provo, Utah, conducted an amazing experiment to show that powdered ginger root is the best thing for nausea and vomiting, surpassing even Dramamine, the medication usually recommended for motion sickness.

36 undergraduate students were asked to take either 100 mg. of Dramamine, 2 capsules of powdered ginger root or 2 capsules of a placebo (powdered chickweed). Then each one was individually blindfolded and led to a special tilted chair that rotated when the motor was turned on.

Slightly less than half an hour was allowed to elapse after each volunteer swallowed one of the above substances, before motion sickness was induced by the rotating chair. None of those who had taken either the Dramamine or placebo were able to last the full six minutes in the chair; whereas, 50% of those who swallowed the ginger capsules remained in the chair for the full time.

The ginger root group experienced no vomiting, which suggests that the herb is good to take when traveling on an airplane, train or by ship. A product made by Great American Natural Products called Ginger-Up (see Appendix) has become very popular of late for travelers and pregnant mothers experiencing morning sickness, to use, often 2 capsules at a time.

Natural Blood Thinner

People frequently subject to blood clots are generally prescribed oral anti-coagulants to help keep their blood relatively thin. One of the most commonly used drugs for this is warfarin sodium (better known as coumadin). Unfortunately it's also used as a potent rat poison and can lead to serious internal hemorrhaging over an extended period of time. Ginger root is an ideal replacement for such synthetic blood thinners. An average of 2 capsules twice daily in between meals appears to have helped a small number of those with such problems.

Incredible Relief for Aches and Pains

Nothing seems to work quite like a hot ginger compress on muscular aches and pains, joint stiffness, abdominal cramps, kidney stone attacks, stiff neck, neuralgia, toothache, bladder inflammation, prostatitis and extreme body tension. But keep in mind that as wonderful a remedy as it is, time, considerable effort, patience and a certain change in lifestyle are all required in order to make it totally successful.

Dr. Koji Yamoda, an M.D. from Tokyo, shares this cure with me.

Bring a gallon of distilled or spring water to a boil in a large enamel pot with a lid on top. Meanwhile wash 1-1/2 fresh ginger roots, but *don't* peel them. Then proceed to grate these roots by hand, using a rotating, clockwise motion instead of the usual back-and-forth movements. This keeps those tough fibers from building up on the grater, Dr. Yamoda said.

Next put this grated ginger root in the center of a clean muslin cloth that has been cut to form an 8-inch square and slightly moistened. Then draw the corners together to form a nice, little bag and tie the top with string, thread or fish line. Be sure to leave plenty of room inside the bag for air and water to circulate.

Before putting this ginger bag in the hot water, make absolutely certain that the heat has been turned down and that the water is no longer boiling. Now uncover the pot and gently squeeze the juice from the bag into the water, before dropping it into the pot. Cover and permit the contents to simmer an additional 7 minutes. Dr. Yamoda informed me that the resulting liquid would acquire the hue of gold and yield a distinctive ginger aroma. The bag may be pressed against the sides of the pot with a wooden ladle to turn the water yellow, if the process seems to be a little slow in happening. Remove the pot from the stove when ready and set aside.

In order to be effective, ginger compresses must be applied relatively hot, he insisted, but not so much as to seriously scald the skin of the patient. Besides being used for compresses this ginger broth can also be added to bath water to soak an aching back or sore muscles in or for soaking tired, aching feet in as well. The patient should be laying flat on the floor to receive the full benefits of these compresses front or back.

A terry cloth hand towel is dipped into the pot, while holding both ends. The towel is lifted out and excess water is gently squeezed back into the pot. The steaming towel is then refolded to the desired width and applied directly to the site of pain. A second such compress can be placed immediately over or next to the first one, after which a large and fluffy, dry bath towel is placed over both compresses in order to retain as much heat as possible for the greatest length of time. The bath towel should be folded in half at least once before covering the compresses. Under these conditions, the compresses should remain fairly warm for up to 15–20 minutes. Dr. Yamoda recommended that another set of compresses be applied after this for a total treatment time of 45 minutes or so, and repeated again about 4–6 hours later or as needed.

He explained that in all of his years of clinical practice, nothing seems to have relieved most kinds of physical aches and pains as well as this remedy has. He has even used such ginger compresses on the chests of patients suffering from extreme asthma and bronchitis, with their mucus congestions breaking up in no time at all. Smaller wash-cloth-size compresses can be applied against the side of the neck, throat or jaw to relieve neuralgia, stiffness, swollen glands and toothache.

Relief for Hypertensive Headaches

Mix enough powdered ginger and cold water together in a small bowl to make a thin, smooth paste with. Then apply to the forehead and temples with the back of a large tablespoon and lay down for awhile. Will help to relieve the excruciating pressure building up inside and take away that "exploding" sensation.

Breaks Fever, Eliminates Phlegm

One of the best ways to help break a high fever and get rid of mucus buildup in the sinuses, throat and lungs, is to drink some warm ginger tea. Grate enough fresh ginger root to equal about 2 level tbsps., then add them to 2 cups of boiling water and cover, steeping for 30 mins. Drink 1 cup while still warm every 2-1/2 hrs.

GINKGO (See YOHIMBINE)

THE GINSENGS
WILD AMERICAN GINSENG (*Panax quinquifolius*)
CHINESE or KOREAN GINSENG (*Panax ginseng*)
TIENCHI GINSENG (*Panax notoginseng*)
SIBERIAN or RUSSIAN GINSENG (*Eleutherococcus senticosus, Acanthopanax senticosus*)

Brief Description

Ginseng can refer to any of 22 different plants. Some of these are members of the same family (Araliaceae) or even genus (*Panax*). Still others are completely unrelated to ginseng either botanically or chemically and are often passed off as frauds trading on the good reputation and high price of the original root.

To the untrained eye, ginseng looks pretty much like any other root: brown, gnarled and about as large as a little finger. But the root sometimes resembles part of a human body, hence its other common name of manroot.

An exception to this is Siberian ginseng, which isn't even a species of *Panax* although it is a tall, prickly shrub of the same family, Araliaceae. Siberian and Chinese ginsengs are relatively inexpensive compared to the wild American kind, which the *Wall Street Journal* said in 1983 was bought from 'seng hunters at $156.63 a pound and then resold by ginseng brokers in Hong Kong for as much as $25,000 *per root!*

Endurance Capabilities

Ginseng is best known for its anti-fatigue, energy-giving properties. But very few people know that it must be taken for awhile in order to gradually build such physical endurance, rather than expecting anything sudden to happen from only short-term use.

Soviet athletes swear by the plant to increase stamina and endurance for them during athletic performance. Professor A. V. Korobokov of the Lesgraft Institute of Physical Culture and Sport in Moscow has conducted experiments with eleutherococcus or Siberian ginseng which show indications in athletes of increased endurance, reflexes and coordination.

Soviet scientists attribute the restorative powers of Siberian ginseng to the plant's glycoside content—naturally occurring chemicals which initiate the body's stress response. A minimum of 2 capsules daily with meals for several months is suggested to increase your own personal levels of physical endurance.

Protects Against Stress-Induced Problems

Siberian ginseng has achieved renown throughout Soviet bloc countries as an effective antidote to stress-related illnesses. In a remarkable interview I had with a Soviet physician during a visit to the USSR, I learned some fantastic things about this herb.

Dr. Nikolai Gurovsky was then head of the Board of Space Medicine in the Soviet Public Health Ministry. He had personally prescribed Siberian ginseng for the two Salyut 6 cosmonauts who stayed in space 96 days the year before. Through our interpreter, he related this:

> Prior to this flight, we had closely examined other cosmonauts who had returned from previous missions in space. We found that in every case, their immune systems were depleted. Some of their internal organs had been seriously weakened by constant exposure to radiation while in space. And when they came back to earth again, it took them awhile to regain their complete sense of balance.
>
> But we decided to have our Salyut 6 team drink a special tonic of eleutherococcus we devised in the laboratory. Each day while they were orbiting in space, they took an amount equivalent to about 1 cup.
>
> Upon their arrival back, we submitted them to very intensive medical testing. And found that their immunity levels were still moderately strong. Their major glands and organs also were not as adversely affected by radiation as other cosmonauts had been. And gravity didn't seem to affect their balances quite as badly either.
>
> We attributed these differences to the herbal tonic. We intend to use it more often with other space missions in the future.

An average of 3 capsules per day of Nature's Way Siberian Ginseng in between meals or on an empty stomach is recommended for the proper management of stress and prevention of stress-induced ailments.

Improves Mating Habits

Ginseng is considered by millions to be the world's number one, ultimate aphrodisiac. Some clinical research in this direction seems to verify this activity to a certain extent. For instance, Japanese scientists have already identified sex hormone activity in ginseng preparations given to *both* male and female rodents alike. And when I was in mainland China in 1980, I discovered a lot of women taking different kinds of ginseng to improve sexual relations with their respective spouses.

Male albino rats under the influence of ginseng began ejaculation earlier, mounted their female companions more often in a 45-minute observation period and performed more acts of intercourse in a 10-day period, than did a control group of males without the benefits of ginseng.

The best preparation of ginseng to use for these purposes is any liquid tonic which has the root in the bottle with it. Several brands are available from larger, full-service health food stores or local herb shops in any metropolitan Chinatown district. Drink 4 fluid ounces of the same twice a day for at least a week in advance prior to the next sexual encounter with your companion.

GOLDENSEAL (*Hydrastis canadensis*)

Brief Description

Goldenseal is a small, perennial plant, usually cultivated for the mass herb product, but also occurring wild in rich, shady woods and damp meadows from Connecticut to Minnesota and southward. A thick, knotty, yellow rootstock sends up a hairy stem, almost a foot high, with a pair of five-lobed, serrated leaves near the top terminated by a single greenish white flower.

Magnificent for Eye Inflammations

In 1974 a Mill Valley, California physician named Jeff L. Anderson, M.D., frequently used a solution of goldenseal root in his practice to treat numerous eye ailments with, especially conjunctivitis. He mixed 1/8 tsp. each of powdered goldenseal, comfrey and chamomile together, then added the mixture to 1 cup of boiled water and steeped it for 15 mins. before carefully straining through a sterile cheesecloth. He had his patients use the strained solution at room temperature, 2–3 drops three times daily from a sterile eye dropper.

The yellow color of the root is due to the alkaloid, berberine. The *Indian Journal of Ophthalmology* for March 1983 reported that the berberine found in goldenseal root is excellent for treating inflammations of the cornea and iris brought on by the herpes simplex virus. A solution similar to the one previously mentioned can be made for these problems, except that 1/4 tsp. of goldenseal root would be used with the other two herbs. The same directions would be followed.

Suppresses Candida, Heals Mouth Sores

A douche of goldenseal is excellent for reducing yeast infection. In an electric blender combine 3 cups of water and 1-1/2 tsps. of powdered root, then douche several times each day with it until the problem is cleared up.

A simple mouth wash made of pinches of goldenseal powder and baking soda in a little water is perfect for healing any kind of sores in the mouth or on the gums and tongue.

A Good Drug Withdrawal Program

During a series of trips made by me in 1987 to Los Angeles, San Francisco, Chicago, Boston, New York City and Dallas on an assortment of speaking engagements and numerous media interviews, I had the opportunity to interview various alternative care doctors and holistic healers who have taken the natural approach towards helping addicts kick their expensive and debilitating drug habits. What follows is a distillation of all their combined wisdom in a simple program for those who may know friends and loved ones on drugs who might benefit from the procedures being offered.

My friend, Lendon Smith, M.D., in his best-seller, *Feed Yourself Right,* points out that addiction can also involve other substances we normally use on a regular basis. He then proceeds to tell the true story of what happened to a manager of a small country store in Ohio during the terrible winter of 1977/78. None of his customers ever complained as he gradually ran out of basic foods like milk, bread, fruits and vegetables. But boy did they ever get rankled and cussed him good when he ran out of Pepsi-Cola. "People can get hooked on *anything!*" Dr. Smith warns. And this includes prescription drugs as well for many of the respectable middle and upper classes of society who might never otherwise think of shooting up with heroin, snorting coke or smoking a joint.

All of those health professionals with whom I conferred were unanimous in their agreement that cleansing the system of drug residues is the *first and most important* step to follow.

Step I: Cleansing

Capsules: Goldenseal Root (4 per day for first month; reduced to 2 per day thereafter).
Chapparral Twigs (2 per day for first month; reduced to 1 per day thereafter).

Tea:

1/2 tsp. grated raw orange peel	3 tsp. dried mullein leaves
3 tsp. dried juniper berries	2 tsp. dried lemon grass
1 tsp. dried thyme herb	4 tsp. dried dandelion root

Bring 1 qt. spring or distilled water to a boil. Add orange peel, juniper berries and dandelion root. Cover, reduce heat and simmer for 5 minutes. Remove from heat, uncover and add rest of herbs. Cover and steep an additional 40 minutes. Strain, sweeten with honey and drink 1 cup when taking 2 capsules goldenseal and 1 capsule chaparral on an empty stomach. Repeat procedure again later same day. A strong coffee enema 2–3 times per week for the first month is also encouraged. (See under COFFEE for more information on preparing and giving coffee enemas.)

The next step involves giving herbal and nutritional support to the central nervous system in an effort to control the usual withdrawal symptoms (hysteria, delirium tremens and insomnia) experienced by most addicts.

Step II: Relaxing

Capsules: Valerian Root (4 per day) Skullcap Herb (4 per day)

Tea: 3 tsp. dried catnip herb; 2 tsp. dried peppermint leaves; 3 tsp. dried chamomile herb; 4 tsp. dried lemon balm leaves

Bring 1 qt. spring or distilled water to boil. Remove from heat and add all of the above ingredients. Cover and steep for an hour. Drink 1 cup sweetened with pure maple syrup 4 times daily on an empty stomach.

Supplements: Aqua-Vite from Great American Natural Products (see Appendix). (3 tablets twice daily with meals.)
Complete B-Complex (any brand) from a health food store. (3 tablets twice daily with meals.)
Vitamin C in the form of sodium ascorbate (25,000 mg. per day).
Calcium-Magnesium in the form of calcium gluconate (1,000 mg.) and magnesium sulfate (500 mg.).
Potassium (750–1,200 mg.) best taken in an 8 oz. glass of carrot juice (2/3) and mixed greens (1/3) daily with meals. Any dark, leafy greens (spinach, watercress, wheat grass, etc.) will do. Can be made at home with a juicer or obtained from some health food store juice bars.

The final part of this three-step program is rebuilding the body through sound nutrition. Evidence exists to show that a few prior heavy drug users experienced virtually *no* side-effects to speak of when suddenly and totally withdrawing from controlled substances. The major-league baseball star, Ron LeFlore, is a case in point. LeFlore began taking heroin when he was 15 and used it every single day—both snorting and injecting it—for nearly a year before being arrested and sent to prison. Much to his surprise, he experienced *no* withdrawal symptoms behind bars, even while spending time in solitary confinement. He attributes this lack of negative responses during withdrawal to his mother's good home-cooked meals, which consisted of many vegetable-meat stews, casseroles, soups, garden salads and whole-grain cereals and breads. A number of delicious recipes designed to promote good health and strength are scattered throughout this book and the reader is heartily encouraged to search some of them out as part of a very good nutrition program for recovering addicts. Also be sure to check the various entries under NOURISHMENT in the TABLE OF SYMPTOMS CONTENTS at the beginning of this encyclopedia.

Step III: Nourishing

Capsules: Slippery Elm Bark and Alfalfa Herb (3 of each per day with meals).
When taking them, drink only pineapple or papaya juice instead of water.

Tea:
- 1/2 bunch chopped, fresh parsley
- 1 handful cut, fresh watercress
- 1 handful cut, fresh spinach
- 1/2 cup fresh or dried nettle
- 1 small, *un*peeled parsnip
- 1 tbsp. each of wheat and barley
- 1 tbsp. cut, dried horsetail
- 1 tsp. each powdered kelp and Irish moss
- 1 tbsp. each yellow dock and burdock roots
- 2 tbsps. honeycomb (where available)

Simmer everything in 1 quart of spring or distilled water in a heavy stainless steel pot, covered, for several hours until the volume of liquid has been reduced to slightly less than half. Strain and return the liquid to the same pot, discarding the rest. While still very hot, stir in 4 tbsps. of blackstrap molasses. Then allow to cool. Take 1 tbsp. of this refined tonic five times daily with meals.

All three steps of this program need to be implemented simultaneously, but emphasis can shift first to cleansing for a couple of days and after this greater attention focused on relaxing and nourishing. Since each case is different, there will be obvious variability in which steps are emphasized the most. But the point to remember is that *all* three steps must run concurrent with each other when this program is in force.

Relieves Poison Ivy Rash

Goldenseal is a blessing in disguise for those unlucky enough to make an encounter with poison ivy at some point in their lives. An effective skin wash can be made by combining 1 tsp. of powdered root to a pint of hot water and dabbing this solution on the afflicted parts when cool. Also 2–3 capsules taken internally will expedite healing as well.

Reduces Insulin Dependency

A small number of diabetics I've known over the years have successfully managed to lower their insulin needs by taking 2 capsules of goldenseal root per day. One fellow in Toronto, Canada went from close to 30 cc of insulin to only needing injections of about half that amount each day, after taking the herb for about a month. CAUTION: Those with hypoglycemia should avoid taking the root internally, but can use it safely as a mouth wash and douche.

Incredible Sinus Relief

Changes in temperature, the arrival of Spring, the growth of pollen and the aftershocks of a cold all have one thing in common. They can cause your sinus cavities to swell like a water balloon and vibrate your entire skull to a heavy metal rock beat. What can be done about it, besides just gulping Dristans or squirting Neo-Synephrine up your nose?

Well, Dennis J. Partride, a long-time resident of coastal Florida, came up with one of the best remedies for relieving sinus miseries. He shared this with others in 1980. "I took the shaker of sea salt from the cupboard and rubbed 20 grains or so into my right hand, adding a pinch or two of goldenseal powder and enough unchlorinated water to form a liquid paste," he began. "I then proceeded to sniff this up my nose. The relief was felt almost immediately, because the herb was able to reach all of the mucous membranes. An ounce of the stuff usually lasts me a year and is far better than any drugstore sinus products I've tried," he concluded.

GOOSEBERRY (See under BERRIES.)

GOTU KOLA (*Centella asiatica, Hydrocotyle asiatica*)

Brief Description

This slender perennial is found throughout tropical regions of the world. Its nearly smooth surface and kidney-shaped or heart-shaped leaves accompanied by dark-purple flower petals makes for a somewhat exquisite plant.

But efforts to domesticate it have often failed, because its apparent obstinance requires human persecution in order to spread. Thus, when gotu kola is sprayed with herbicides, only the leaves die, while the root actually seems to thrive on these harmful chemicals. After one good spraying, the plant usually proliferates like crazy.

Improves Mental Retardation

Very few herbs in the plant kingdom have memory stimulating properties attributed to them, and even fewer still that can be clinically documented. Gotu Kola is probably the only herb thus far that has been scientifically tested and proven to definitely increase mental activity.

Dr. M. V. R. Appa Rao and his associates administered a 500 mg. tablet of powdered gotu kola daily to a group of 15 mentally retarded children at an institution in Madras, India. As reported by the *J. of Res. in Ind. Medicine* (1973), after a 3-month trial period on this herb, these youngsters experienced "increased powers of concentration and attention" moreso than did 15 other kids given a placebo. Dr. Appa Rao concluded that gotu kola "could be used for the routine treatment of mental retardation."

A gotu kola product under the Nature's Way label may be found at your local health food store. An average of 4 capsules per day is recommended for this.

Reduces Phlebitis, Varicose Veins

Edith Rosenbaum of Levittown, New York wrote to me some time ago about her experiences with gotu kola:

> I've been troubled with phlebitis in my legs for years. Also I've had some deep, ugly, purple varicose veins to go with it. Someone told me about this herb, gotu kola, helping them. So I figured I had nothing to lose by trying it for awhile.
>
> My sister, who gets around more than I do, got me some at a health food store in Manhattan. I started taking 2 capsules in the morning for the first couple of days, then increased that to 4 by the following week. I'd take them about 3 hours after eating.
>
> When I began noticing my phlebitis going down a little, I decided to up the dosage to 6 capsules a day, taking 2 in the morning, 2 at noon and 2 at night before going to bed.
>
> Some 6-1/2 weeks later, most of my varicose veins had shrunk back to a more normal size. And I didn't have so much pain in walking either. I could get around a lot easier, too. That's what gotu kola has done for me.

GOURD (See under PUMPKIN AND SQUASH.)

GRAINS
(See also BRANS, BREAD AND PASTA.)

Brief Description

BARLEY (*Hordeum vulgare*). Originated in western Asia, where it was one of the first grains to be cultivated. As human food, the larger, white-seeded variety of barley is pearled, or ground in a revolving drum until the hull and germ are removed. This reduces the grains to small, starchy balls which are then used to thicken soups. Pot, or hulled, barley is ground enough to remove only the husk.

BUCKWHEAT (*Fagopyrum vulgare*). Native to central Asia. Thought of as a cereal grain, but is really in a family of its own. Mainly used for making flour for pancakes. Groats, or kaska, are kernels with the hulls removed. They are eaten as breakfast food or as thickeners for soup, gravy and dressing.

BULGHUR (Parboiled cracked wheat. See under WHEAT.)

CORN (*Zea mays*). Native to the Americas. Commercial varieties are either yellow or white in color. Popcorn is distinguished by its small, hard kernels with tough outer covers, while flour corns have soft, starchy kernels. Other recognized types include dent, flint, sweed, pod and waxy corn. The basic products of refined or processed corn are starch, oil, syrup, hominy grits, cornmeal and flour.

Indian corn is noted for its unusual variety of colors. For instance, the Hopi of northern Arizona have at least 20 varieties, with multiple legends and religious beliefs being attached to each particular color. Considerable ceremony often attends the planting of corn by some southwestern Native American tribes.

MILLET (*Panicum milliaceum*). Native grain of the East Indies. Is a common name applied to a variety of cultivated grasses with small white or golden kernels. Among the most popular are foxtail and pearl millet. Since it lacks gluten, it's good for people who must avoid this protein.

OATS (*Avena sativa*). Developed from the wild grasses of eastern Europe and Asia. Today there are 3 general classes and nearly 100 varieties grown. They are equal to corn as a tissue builder. Steel cut oats are simply cracked oat kernels, while rolled oats have been flattened or rolled into thin flakes.

RICE (*Oryza sativa*). An ancient grain cultivated for over 4,000 years. Originated in southeast Asia. Each whole grain has an outside hull, a brownish-colored covering called bran and a finer, lighter-colored layer called polish which surrounds the kernel. Commercial varieties are classified on the basis of size and shape of the kernel—short-, medium- and long-grain. All have the same food value, but long-grain costs more since more kernels break during milling. Brown rice is simply rice that has not had the bran and polish removed.

RYE (*Secale cereale*). Developed from a wild variety still growing in the mountains of eastern Mediterranean countries. It's deficient in the glutinous proteins that give wheat dough the elasticity necessary for good leavening, so pure rye bread is heavy and compact by comparison.

TRITICALE (*Triticum secale*). A hybrid grain produced by cross-breeding wheat and rye. First bred in the 1930s by Swedish agronomists and has since become very popular in the U.S. and Canada.

WHEAT (*Triticum aestivum*). One of history's first cultivated grains in western Asia. Now covers more of the earth's surface than any other grain crop. For marketing purposes, five classes of wheat based on usage and habit of growth were established—hard red spring, soft red winter, hard red winter, durum and white. Generally, the harder translucent varieties are valued for the production of flours while durum is prized for the manufacture of macaroni, spaghetti and noodles.

WILD RICE (*Zizania aquatica*). Native to the Great Lakes region of the U.S. and Canada. Although used in the same way ordinary rice is, this really isn't a true "rice" as such. Wild rice has a gutsier, chewier, and somewhat smokier taste to it than conventional rice does.

Grain Roto-Rooters for Clogged Arteries

Certain grains such as barley and oats really help to clean out the arteries and valves around the heart that have become plugged up with layers of old fat buildup. And to a somewhat lesser extent, so do rye and wheat as well. All these grain fibers scrub away backlog deposits of grease that have accumulated over a lengthy period of time.

Cereal Grasses for Arthritis, Cancer and Ulcers

The green juice from young barley shoots possesses strong anti-inflammatory activity. A paper read at the 101st Annual Meeting of the Japan Pharmaceutical Society in April 1981, reported that the powdered juice significantly reduced arthritis and gastric ulcers in lab rodents. And research conducted by Dr. Chiu-Nan Lai at the M.D. Anderson Hospital & Tumor Institute in Houston, Texas shows that extracts of wheat sprouts can modify, even decrease, the formation of cancer of the esophagus, stomach, liver, breast and colon, if regularly used in the diet.

Two good sources exist for obtaining these cereal grasses in powdered form. Pines International of Lawrence, Kansas (see Appendix) provide both organically grown wheat grass and barley grass juices in tablets or bulk powder.

Grow Your Own Grain Sprouts

You can make your own grain sprouts by following these simple directions. Thoroughly wash 1/3 cup wheat berries, rye berries or brown rice. Place the grain kernels in a bowl and cover with enough water (about an inch) for grain to swell; then cover with lid. Let stand overnight in a cool place. Drain and rinse them.

Wash three 1-quart jars; place about 1/4 cup of the soaked grain kernels in each jar. Cover tops of jars with two layers of cheesecloth or nylon netting. Fasten the cheesecloth on each jar with two rubber bands or a screw-top canning-jar lid band.

Place the jars on their sides in a warm, dark place (68–75° F.). Once a day rinse the sprouts by pouring lukewarm water into the jars. Swirl to moisten all the grain kernels, then pour off the water. In 3–4 days, the grains should sprout, with the exception of brown rice which may take 5–6 days instead. Once grains have sprouted, keep them refrigerated until serving time. They should keep for up to a week, this way. Use in salads, sandwiches, soups or breads.

While most sprouts require a dark place, the cereal grains should be given a few hours of either artificial light or indirect sunlight after their initial sprouting to let them develop chlorophyll. A sprout length of 1–2 inches is generally good for this stage of growth. Green cereal sprouts make delicious, healthy drinks when juiced or blended with other vegetable juices like carrot or tomato, for instance.

Barley and Wheat for Body Building

Those in their 20s and 30s, who wish to develop finer physical physiques through strenuous exercise, should consider adding barley and wheat to their diets. Both grains contain growth promoting factors in their young shoots or sprouts. Interestingly enough, the ancient Roman gladiators were called *hordearii* or *barley men* because they consumed so much of this grain just before entering the amphitheaters to battle their opponents. Barley and wheat may be used in cooked breakfast cereals, breads, pancakes, soups, salads and delicious drinks to give increased strength and muscle expansion to those who work out regularly with weights.

Buckwheat for Appetite Control

If you're desperately trying to lose weight, but having a hard time doing it because you're unable to cope with the deadly "munchies," then may I strongly encourage you to start eating more buckwheat pancakes for breakfast. Just two medium-sized pancakes in the morning with a couple of pats of low-fat margarine and some pure maple syrup poured over them, will not only fill you up for the next 4–6 hours, but also prompt *lesser* food intake during your next meal.

In an informal study conducted by our Anthropological Research Center here in Salt Lake City several years ago, 11 overweight people were put on a 2-week program consisting of buckwheat pancakes, along with several other cereal grains. The buckwheat pancakes (2–3 medium-sized) were consumed every other morning and every other evening, with cooked oatmeal being eaten at alternate breakfasts and dinners. Subjects were permitted to eat whatever they wanted for lunch, no matter how sweet or fattening it was. For late night snacks, they were allowed as much shredded wheat and milk they desired, topped off with 2 tbsps. of a commercial brand of granola.

In this period of time, 7 of the 11 volunteers lost an average of 15 3/4 lbs., with 4 of the 7 losing in excess of 22 lbs. each. All 11 of them, however, noted *a substantial decrease* in the frequency of their snacks as well as in the volume of food actually consumed.

Bulghur Helps Diabetes

Clinical evidence shows that bulghur is one type of food diabetics can safely rely on to help lower their blood sugar levels.

Now there are two ways to make bulghur. One method calls for a cup of whole wheat grain to be boiled in a heavy, covered saucepan with 1 cup of water. After which the heat is reduced and the contents simmered for an hour. The second method calls for the same amount of wheat and water to be put into a small pot of some kind. This pot is then set on a rack in a larger pot which has water in it also. The water should come up almost to the level of the rack. Cover the larger pot and put on high heat for 15 mins. Reduce heat and steam until wheat absorbs the water (about 45 mins. longer). It can then be consumed either as a breakfast cereal or snack with goat's milk or else used wherever rice would ordinarily be called for.

All Parts of Corn Are Therapeutic

Perhaps no other grain, it can be said, has as many parts of it with therapeutic value as corn does. Consider this: the kernels, the cob, the cornsilk and the meal and starch made from the kernels all have medical significance to them.

When corn is frequently consumed in the diet, either fresh, canned or popped, cholesterol levels go down and bowel movements increase. Soft, boiled corn grits are good to eat every day in case of kidney problems, especially where kidney dysfunction is the cause of swollen legs resulting from lack of urination. Cornmeal made from the ground kernels makes a great facial, opening all of the pores and freeing them from dirt and oils. Just wash the face twice daily with cornmeal instead of soap. You'll find it doesn't even leave the skin as dry and flaky either.

And cornstarch makes a great dusting agent for relieving diaper rash and poison ivy itch, not to mention reducing insect bites and stings, as well as adding a large handful to a tub of lukewarm water to bathe chicken pox, measles, mumps and hives in. Besides this, taking a box along with you when traveling to a foreign country where the cleanliness of the food and water is in doubt, quickly stops diarrhea. Just add 1–2 level tsps. to a glass of cool water that's been previously boiled. This usually corrects the problem in a couple of hours.

Corncob tea is excellent for treating abdominal swelling, edema in the ankles and wrists and gout in general. Cover 2–3 fresh cobs from which the corn has already been removed or eaten with enough water to cover by 2 inches. Cook on low heat for about an hour, then strain and cool. Keep in the refrigerator, drinking 2–3 cups a day until problems subside, then reduce intake to only 1 cup per day.

Cornsilk tea is one of the finest remedies for weak or poorly functioning kidneys and kidneystones. It may be used fresh or dried. Steep 2 tsps. of cornsilk in 1 cup of boiling water for 20 minutes, strain, sweeten with honey and then drink 1/2 cup lukewarm every 3–4 hours. It is ideal to curb bedwetting habits when used with equal parts of catnip leaf and leaves, and valerian root.

Millet Useful for Celiac Disease

Celiac disease is an intestinal disorder caused by the intolerance of some individuals to gluten, a protein found in some cereal grains such as barley, rye and wheat. Symptoms of celiac disease are weight loss, diarrhea, gas, abdominal pain and anemia. Malnutrition usually accompanies this disorder because of the greatly reduced absorption of nutrients.

Besides rice and corn, millet is the only other cereal grain that can be safely consumed without a sufferer experiencing further health problems. The addition of cardamom and mace to these other grains makes their gluten more tolerable in those with this disorder.

Oats Lower Bad, Raise Good Cholesterol

In the old Western flicks the good guys usually wore the white hats, while the bad dudes were clothed in conventional black. With cholesterol it's high-density lipoproteins (HDL, the good guys) vs. low-density lipoproteins (LDL, the bad guys). HDL protects the heart from fatty deposits, while LDL on the other hand plugs arteries like crazy and contributes to general obesity.

Jim Anderson, M.D., a noted Kentucky researcher working out of the V.A. Hospital with the University of Kentucky College of Medicine in Lexington, has had considerable interest in plant fiber and its effects on cholesterol. His studies, along with recent 1987 research at Syracuse University in New York, both show that high-fiber, low-fat diets alone do not reduce cholesterol as much as when oat bran is added to both diets. Oats also raises HDL, thereby preventing heart attacks and hypertension.

Health food stores around the country carry oat bran in a ready-to-eat breakfast cereal marketed by Health Valley of Montebello, California (see Appendix). Or you can do as I've done for most of my 40+ years—eat a good helping of cooked Quaker Oats every morning. This is my typical breakfast, oatmeal and milk, with little or nothing else accompanying it. Seldom do I have sliced fruit on my cereal, fruit juice, or even toast. And I stopped consuming eggs a long time ago.

Now what effect has this had on my serum cholesterol levels? Well consider this: For someone who seldom exercises, for someone who is about 18 lbs. overweight, and for someone who is a heavy meat eater (mostly beef), my most recent medical checkup showed a mere 172 milligrams of cholesterol per deciliter of blood and a treadmill test that indicated a good, strong heart and relatively squeaky clean arteries. Anything under 200 mg/dl is considered by the American Heart Association to be good, with a reading in my range as "very good-to-excellent." Of course, the additional late hour snack of shredded wheat, granola and milk every night before retiring helps keep my cholesterol and triglyceride levels down too.

Oats Reduce Insulin Dependency

Dr. Anderson's work with many diabetic patients being placed on oats and other cereal grains has amply demonstrated a significant drop in the amount of insulin required each day. Patients thus placed on an oatmeal, Grape Nuts, and All Bran diet, have gone from an average of 26 units of insulin a day to only needing a mere 7.1 units a day. Truly, it can be said that oats and other grains are almost a "miracle food" for diabetics these days.

Kiss Skin Problems "Good-Bye"

With oatmeal as part of your regular skin care routine, you can just about kiss many common skin problems "good-bye." For instance, leading dermatologists now recommend Aveeno oatmeal baths for relieving psoriasis and contact dermatitis. Or bring 6 cups of cold water to a rolling boil. Then scatter in 10-1/2 tbsps. of old-fashioned rolled oats, reducing heat to a low setting and simmering for half an hour. Strain and use the water to bathe the face with morning and night. A good idea is to dip the edge of a wash-cloth in this oatmeal water and scrub the skin in a rotating motion.

Beauty salon expert Paul Neinast of Dallas recommends an oatmeal facial pack to get rid of cysts, blackheads and other unsightly blemishes, as well as excessively oily skin. Five to 6 tbsps. of freshly cooked oatmeal mixed into a paste with some honey and stiffly beaten egg whites and then applied all over the face, forehead and throat and left on the skin for half an hour before being washed off, will take away pimples and old, dead skin, leaving the surface much smoother and the complexion more rosy.

Oatmeal is also a real treat for hot, tired, aching feet, especially where corns and calluses are concerned. Just cook up a large pot of oatmeal, being sure to add only enough to give it kind of a soupy consistency. When still hot enough to tolerate, just stick both of your feet in a pan large enough to accomodate them and the runny cereal solution, and soak for up to an hour. This same oatmeal can be reused several more times before finally discarding, by just heating it up again on the stove.

Can Oats Stop Smoking?

A number of methods and products have been tried, including hypnosis and nicotine chewing gum, to help smokers kick the habit. But success has always remained somewhat marginal to say the least. Now comes a centuries old Ayurvedic remedy from India that could well prove to be a more workable solution to those looking for new ways to quit smoking.

The Oct. 15, 1971 issue of *Nature* reported an alcoholic extract of the fresh oat plant being used to diminish the craving for nicotine in a number of smokers with pretty good success. One and a half parts of the crushed whole plant picked just before harvest is put into 5 parts by volume of 90% ethyl alcohol. Kept at room temperature, it's frequently shaken for up to 3 days and then filtered into another clean container.

This alcoholic extract (1 milliliter) was then diluted to 5 milliliters and given in oral doses of 5 milliliters four times a day to a group of heavy cigarette smokers at Ruchill Hospital in Glasgow, Scotland. A second group of smokers were given a placebo intended to mimic the oat extract.

The first group taking this oat extract faithfully for nearly a month smoked an average of 19.5 cigarettes per day before the trial test began, but had dropped to an astonishing 5.7 cigarettes per day after the experiment ended. Whereas the non-oat group started out with 16.5 cigarettes per day and actually finished with a slight *increase* of 16.7 cigarettes smoked each day. Clearly, oats *do* help break the smoking habit when used as an extract in their fresh state! Old Amish Herbs of St. Petersburg, Florida (see Appendix) has a nice anti-smoking oat plant extract which might help to kick the habit. Between 7–10 drops 3–4 times daily *beneath* the tongue is recommended.

Rice Bran for Smooth Skin and Fractures

A chemist whom I met at the 28th Annual Meeting of the American Society of Pharmacognosy informed me that rice bran is used in his native country of India to keep skin smooth and to help bind fractures together so they can heal better. The bran is wrapped in cheesecloth and used in place of soap for daily washing of the face, neck, throat, arms and hands to keep them nice and smooth. For fractures, cold water is added to rice bran and the combination well mixed by hand with a wooden ladle until a smooth, thick paste forms. Some of this is then put into the palm of each hand and applied directly to the injured site. The hands are placed on either side of the fracture with the fingers spread apart. Gentle pressure is exerted in such a manner as to put the dislocation or fracture back together while the paste is still wet. This rice bran plaster is left on for several hours at a time, before a fresh one is needed. It helps to immobilize the injured bone. Equal parts of wheat flour and rice bran also make good plasters.

Rice Prevents Heart Disease

One of America's most successful diet programs, the Pritikin Diet, features generous quantities of cooked brown rice as one of the principal mainstays, along with steamed vegetables and baked potatoes. But can so much brown rice actually prevent coronary heart disease and help keep serum cholesterol levels down?

Well, the best evidence in support of this comes from the diet's originator, Nathan Pritikin himself. Prior to formulating his unique high-complex-carbohydrate, low-fat and low-cholesterol diet, Mr. Pritikin's serum cholesterol stood at an alarmingly dangerous 280 mg. per deciliter of blood in December 1955. About this time he was also experiencing some serious heart problems as well. *The New England Journal of Medicine* for July 4, 1985 published a summary of his serum cholesterol levels once he started on his now world-famous diet. In February 1958, he had 210 milligrams of cholesterol per deciliter of blood, in November 1985, it was down to 94 milligrams!

But even greater proof for the validity of his brown rice diet comes from a careful inspection of his heart at the time of his demise at the age of 69 in February 1985. An autopsy revealed Mr. Pritikin's heart to be virtually free of atherosclerosis with practically all of the arteries soft and clean.

Rice Water for Diarrhea

Donna Lee Ingram, R.N., who was a clinical nursing instructor at the University of Utah School of Nursing told me how she used an old wives' remedy to cure a bad case of diarrhea, even when the attending physician stood alongside of her snickering in disbelief.

Within hours after drinking from a polluted stream, a 63-year-old white male began to experience diarrhea which grew progressively worse by the afternoon of the following day. By the time he checked himself into the hospital a day later, his potassium count was dangerously low, which had produced heart fibrillations and some breathing difficulties as well. He was also pretty well dehydrated from his round-the-clock diarrhea.

"We first gave him an IV (intraveneous) potassium solution which brought his potassium count back up to normal again. He began to feel a little better after this, but the diarrhea problem persisted in spite of various antibiotics that we used on him.

"Now I remember my grandmother using flour and rice water to check diarrhea when we were kids. I mentioned this to the doctor on duty then, and he just laughed in my face, saying it was nothing but an unproven old wives' tale. Well, I went ahead anyway and got some rice from the kitchen and boiled up 1 cup of it in 3 cups of water, uncovered for 15 minutes on high heat. I then strained the water off and let it cool awhile before giving it to the patient. I gave the man a handful of flour first to swallow in small quantities, which he then washed down with sips of this rice water. Finally, I had him drink the rest of the rice water after all of the flour had been consumed.

"Within less than an hour, his heretofore uncontrolled diarrhea completely stopped, much to his own amazement, the doctor's complete surprise and my personal satisfaction!"

Rice Coffee and Tea Substitutes

In place of coffee or black and green teas, use these rice beverages instead. To make rice coffee, just put 10 tbsps. of raw rice into a slow oven on a cookie sheet and stir frequently with a ladle until it's well-browned, but not burned. Then pass through a coffee mill and store in an airtight container. When using, put the usual amount you would for coffee grounds in a coffee-pot or percolator and prepare as you would coffee. But allow the rice to steep in a warm place for at least 30 minutes before serving. Rice tea is made the same way, except that the browned grains remain whole instead of being passed through the mill. Rice coffee and tea are good for relieving the terrible pounding headaches accompanying an alcoholic hangover.

Rye Protects Against Chemicals

In the Soviet Union, rye and whole wheat breads are recommended often in the diets of factory workers exposed to some toxic chemical occupational environments. Clinical nutritionists and doctors there believe that both of these grains, especially rye bread, have profound neutralizing and eliminatory effects on such harmful chemicals. Those laboring under similar conditions here might give serious consideration to adding more rye to their diets.

How Wheat Prevents Cancer

Whole wheat accomplishes many of the same things which other grains do; namely, to increase bowel movements, reduce blood sugar and cholesterol levels and help prevent heart disease. It's also very useful for preventing cancer of the liver, small intestine and colon.

There are three possible ways that wheat may be able to do this. One is by actively binding cancer-causing compounds directly to grain fiber. Second is to reduce the length of time for a bowel movement, thereby limiting the potential damage cancer-causing agents could do. A third way is that wheat fiber seems to alter the microflora of the colon just enough so as to prevent chemical additives found in food from possibly producing tumors once it's consumed and thoroughly digested.

Relieves Rectal Itching

Wheat germ oil is the healing miracle for any kind of rectal or vaginal itching. It works far better than any known drug ointment does. Upon rising in the morning, bathe the rectum or vagina for several minutes with very hot water. Then apply wheat germ oil and leave for 3–5 minutes. After which you should wash the areas lightly with Aveeno or another brand of oatmeal soap. Rinse again in hot water and wash again.

Then mix together some concentrated vitamin C powder in a little water and apply to these areas, leaving on for just a minute before rinsing again. Thoroughly dry at once by using a heat lamp or hair dryer, concentrating on the sore areas. The drying is very important to the success of this treatment. Finally, apply some more oil and leave it on all day long. At night simply repeat the entire process again.

The Best Bread You'll Ever Eat

The following outstanding bread recipe is a composite of several different recipes from the isles of Corsica and Sardinia, and the Roman Empire some 1,800 years ago. You'll find it's probably the best bread you've ever eaten.

All-Grains Braided Loaves

Needed: 2 cups whole wheat flour; 1/2 cup rye flour; 1/2 cup buckwheat flour; 1/2 cup millet; 1/2 cup rolled oats; 1/4 cup each cooked and dried split peas and navy beans; 1/2 cup cornmeal; and 3-1/2 packages active dry yeast. In a mixing bowl combine *only* 1/2 cup whole wheat flour, together with other dry ingredients.

Needed: 5 cups of canned goat's milk; 2 tbsps. each of molasses, maple syrup and dark honey; 6 tbsps. butter; 2 tsp. salt. In a pan heat everything until lukewarm (115–120° F.), stirring constantly. Add to the dry ingredients above. Beat at low speed with an electric mixer for 1-1/2 minutes, scraping bowl frequently. Then switch to high speed and beat an additional 3 minutes.

Needed: 1-1/2 cups each chopped wheat berry and brown rice sprouts (see beginning of this section for instructions on making sprouts); 2 tbsps. each of toasted wheat germ, and bulghur and pot barley that's been previously cooked and allowed to cool. Using a ladle, stir in the sprouts, wheat germ, bulghur and barley, and as much remaining whole wheat flour as you can. Turn out onto lightly floured surface. Knead in enough of the remaining whole wheat flour to make a moderately stiff dough that's smooth and elastic (6–8 mins. total kneading time).

Next grease the inside of an electric slow cooker, turn the heat on low and let the pot warm. Then unplug it and put your dough inside, covering the top. Turn once. Let rise until double in size (between 45 mins. and an hour). Really works like a charm and is a virtual foolproof way to make sure the dough rises quickly.

Punch the dough down and divide into three separate portions. Cover with a cloth and let rest 10 mins. Roll each piece into a 10-inch rope. Braid the strands together, beginning in the middle and working toward each end. Pinch the ends together and tuck the sealed portion under the braid. Then place into oiled 8×4×2-in. loaf pans. (Grease them with olive oil or liquid lecithin from any health food store.) Cover and let them rise into braided beauties until nearly double. Make sure they are set in a warm enough place in order to nicely rise.

Bake them in a 375° F. oven for half an hour. Cover each loaf with aluminum foil the last 15 minutes, if necessary, to prevent over-browning. Remove from their pans to wire rack. Brush the tops lightly with melted butter to which has been added a tad of mace and cardamom. Allow to cool before eating. Makes three incredible-tasting loaves!

Cornbread Fit for a King

This is the perfect companion for your favorite bean dish. And comes from La Rene Gaunt's *Recipes to Lower Your Fat Thermostat* with the kind permission of the publishers (see Appendix).

Golden Cornbread

Needed: 1 cup whole wheat flour; 1 cup cornmeal; 4 tsp. baking powder; 2 tbsps. dark honey; 1 cup milk; 2 egg whites; 2 tbsps. olive oil; 1/4 tsp. seasalt. Combine flour, cornmeal, baking powder and honey. Add milk, egg whites, oil and seasalt. Mix well. Bake in a 9" square pan which has been covered with liquid lecithin from any local health food store, at 425° F. for 25 mins. Serves about 12.

Zesty Vegetable Rice Dish

Here's a dish that should really bring out the Nature lover in you with its unique "wilderness" appeal.

Wild Rice Delight

Needed: 1 cup uncooked wild rice; 1 tbsp. olive oil; 1/2 cup chopped Bermuda onion; 1/4 cup chopped green onion; 1/2 cup chopped green bell pepper (including seed center); 2 cups sliced zucchini; 3 small tomatoes, cut into eights; 1 crushed garlic clove; juice from 1/2 lemon and 1/2 lime; 2-1/2 cups boiling chicken broth.

Sauté rice in oil until golden brown, over low heat, about 7 mins. Spread in a greased, shallow, 2-1/2-qt. casserole pan. Layer onions, green pepper, zucchini and tomatoes over rice. Add garlic and citrus juices to broth. Pour over vegetables. Cover, and bake at 350° F. for 1 hour or until the liquid is absorbed and all the vegetables are tender.

Making Great Breakfast Cereals

To really liven up any cooked cereals, just add to them a little pure vanilla, some pure maple syrup, a dash of cardamom and any fruit you like, then top with a little half-and-half for a truly memorable breakfast treat!

Wilderness Cereal

Needed: 1/2 cup each of cracked wheat and wild rice; 2-1/2 cups boiling *spring* or Perrier water. Combine everything and cook in a covered saucepan for 35 mins., stirring frequently with a wooden ladle. In the last 10 minutes before the cereals are finished cooking, add 1/4 tsp. cardamom, 1/8 tsp. pumpkin pie spice, 1/8 tsp. pure vanilla flavor, and 1 tbsp. blackstrap molasses for an unforgettable taste! Serve hot with ice-cold canned or fresh goat's milk.

A Most Nourishing Tea

An extremely nourishing tea for infants, children, the elderly and anyone recuperating from a recent illness or surgery, can be made from three different wholesome grains.

In a heavy cast-iron skillet, *separately* roast 1/2 cup *each* of barley, buckwheat and wheat grains on medium heat for 12 minutes, making sure you *stir* each of them *continuously* with a wooden ladle. One small teaspoon of sesame seed oil may be used to lightly grease the bottom and sides of the frying pan so the grains won't stick. As each grain is done, remove it to a holding dish of some sort.

When all the grains have been thusly roasted, combine them together in a heavy stainless steel pot and add 1 gallon (16 cups) of spring or distilled water. Bring to a rapid boil, then reduce the heat to a lower setting and simmer, covered, for 25 minutes. Remove lid and stir in 1 tsp. pure vanilla and 1 tbsp. pure maple syrup. Cover again and steep until mildly warm. Strain and drink a cup several times throughout the day. A pinch of powdered cardamom may also be added when the vanilla and syrup are added, for extra flavor.

GRAPES AND RAISINS (*Vitis species*)

Brief Description

Grapes are readily identifiable as a fruit, with their trailing, climbing, tendril-clasping, wide-leaved vines and pale green to reddish purple fruit. Nearly half of this plant's innumerable grapes are native to North America. Many of our present species evolved from their cousins in the wild, such as the fox grape which kept the Lewis and Clark Expedition from near starvation. It's the ancestor of the now famous Concord grape. Apocryphal and ancient Jewish rabbinical sources all seem to suggest that the forbidden fruit consumed by Adam and Eve in the Garden of Eden was, in reality, a bunch of grapes and not the proverbial apple!

Wonderful Skin Moisturizers

Dallas-based Neinast Salon is the beauty mecca for that city's top media personalities, business executives, bankers, attorneys, doctors and real estate giants. The majority of patrons are men, who come to receive a variety of services.

Owner Paul Neinast has shared a number of his beauty secrets for the first time in a book like this. Earlier some of these were mentioned under citrus fruits. Here we deal with his wonderful skin moisturizers from grapes.

"I find that the green Thompson seedless kind make the best facial toner for dry, sensitive skin," he began. "Just cut the grapes in half and slowly squeeze the juice on the lips and beneath the eyelids. Also rub some of the juice around the corners of the mouth and eyes as well. It's great for getting rid of crow's feet and the tiny cracks around the edges of the mouth. Or these grape halves can be cut into a small "x" and crushed right on the skin and left there for 20 minutes or so. Or they can be mixed up in a blender and lightly rubbed all over the face, forehead, throat and neck and kept on for a little less than half an hour before removing.

"I also recommend champagne for tightening up loose skin and closing the pores with. Champagne costing between $5 and $7 a bottle is good enough to use. Just splash some on the skin like you would after-shave lotion or cologne and let the air dry it out. We've also used this a lot on women's skin with good results. The champagne works especially well on middle-aged to older women who have slightly sagging, drooping skin problems beneath the eyes and around their throats," he concluded.

Wine Reduces Heart Attacks

Wines made from a special kind of grape (*Vitis vinifera*) have been proven clinically to reduce the chances of getting a heart attack and even help to reduce high blood pressure, when taken in moderation. Doctors at the Kaiser-Permanente Medical Center in Oakland, California have surveyed the medical histories of over 200,000 patients and found that moderate alcohol users were 30% less likely to get heart attacks than nondrinking patients were.

Moderate alcohol intake increases good cholesterol (high-density lipoproteins) which, in turn, dramatically reduces the bad kind (low-density lipoproteins) that clogs arteries and eventually leads to heart attacks later on. Moderate intake of alcohol, especially white and red wines, should be about 2 fluid ounces or 1/4 cup per day for therapeutic benefits. Anything less or greater than this either won't work or can be harmful to health.

An effective concoction employed by some of the traditional *kanpō* doctors in Kyoto, Japan to relieve the chest pains accompanying angina calls for a raw egg to be mixed with 2/3 cups each of saké or wine and canned apple juice. This concoction is then brought to a boil and taken internally after it has cooled awhile but is still quite warm. An average of 3 cups per day for 3–4 days is taken.

Raisin Tea for Strong Immunity

Two Canadian microbiologists working with the Canadian Health and Welfare Agency in Ottawa, discovered that grape juice, red wines and raisin tea showed strong antiviral activity against poliovirus, herpes simplex virus and reovirus (an apparent cause of meningitis, mild fever and diarrhea).

Not everyone drinks wine and quite a few do not like too much grape juice on account of its tartness. But raisin tea is both a sweet and mild beverage that young and old alike can enjoy, while at the same time giving their immune systems a tremendous boost against future viral infections.

To make your own tea, just pour 3 cups of hot, boiling water over 1 cup of loosely packed raisins. Add 1-1/4 tsps. of blackstrap molasses, stir good, then cover and let set for an hour. Strain and refrigerate liquid. Drink 1 cup each day. The raisins may be saved and used a second time, before finding some other way to use them such as in a rice custard pudding, bread, cole slaw or carrot salad.

If you object to the chemical preparation of raisins, then just make your own. Wash a large bunch of grapes (any variety). Slice each grape lengthwise and remove the seeds, if there are any. Then arrange them in a single layer on flat cookie trays and slowly dry in a 165° F. oven with the oven door ajar until they are shriveled (somewhere between 13 and 21 hrs.).

An Aluminum-Free Baking Powder

Currently about 2 million Americans suffer from Alzheimer's disease, a form of senile dementia that afflicts mainly the elderly. A growing body of medical evidence links aluminum with this horribly progressive destruction of the brain, which causes severe memory loss, extreme personality changes and the inability to care for one's self. Aluminum is found in many things, ranging from deodorants, buffered aspirins and hemorrhoid preparations to baby food, baking powder, self-rising flour and cake mixes, processed cheese and nondairy creamers.

Your chances of getting Alzheimer's later in life can be drastically reduced by not using aluminum pots and pans, nor cooking acidic vegetables like tomatoes or cabbage in fluoridated tap water in any aluminum cookware. And also by using an aluminum-free baking powder in recipes which call for this item. Some food scientists have estimated that regular commercial baking powder may contain between 7–11% of pure aluminum in two forms, aluminum potassium sulfate and aluminum sodium sulfate, which can be injurious to human health over an extended period of time.

The simple recipe calls for mixing two parts of cream of tartar with one part of baking soda and cornstarch in a medium to large bowl. Blend thoroughly before storing in an air-tight container to prevent moisture from getting in. Cream of tartar (potassium bitartrate) is a natural byproduct of wine making, being a major part of the sediment left over. Arrowroot, the powdered starchy rhizome of *Maranta arundinacea,* may be substituted in place of cornstarch if you like. Arrowroot can be purchased in some larger health food or specialty food stores, while cream of tartar is found at most supermarkets as a rule.

GRAPEFRUIT (See under CITRUS.)

GREEN (SNAP or STRING) BEAN (*Phaseolus vulgaris*) (See also under BEANS.)

Brief Description

Green beans belong to the same *Phaseolus* species kidney, navy and lima beans do, except that they are picked while still green in their pods. These green beans were first introduced by Native Americans to early colonists and became an instant hit with them. Green beans are one of the "safest" vegetables to serve guests with finicky tastes and picky eating habits.

Acne Problems Vanish

The bane of every American teenager is the dreaded problem of acne. Now there is an effective remedy for alleviating much of this. All a teen needs to do is wash his or her face morning, noon and night with the pod tea of green beans.

For chronic acne, add 3 tbsps. of dried chamomile flowers to the pod tea after it's been removed from the stove. Cover and let it steep until the tea becomes cool, then strain and bottle. Wash the face every 3 hrs. if possible with the tea. A cup should also be drunk each day as well.

This same remedy works well for eczema, dermatitis, psoriasis, poison ivy rash, blackheads, herpes, cold sores and similar skin afflictions.

Cosmetic Aid

A simple decoction made of the flowers of green beans is great for softening the skin, preventing it from badly peeling during recovery from a nasty sunburn and can sometime hide freckles by making them paler in tone. Bring 1/2 qt. of water to a boil, remove from heat and add 2 handfuls of freshly snipped bean flowers. Cover and let steep 50 mins., then refrigerate, *leaving flowers in.*

Gently cleanse the face with this decoction or lay a wash cloth which has been soaked with the solution on the skin for about half an hour at a time. A tea made of stringbean pods and consumed daily is excellent for treating diabetes, claimed noted health authority Paavo Airola.

GUAR GUM (*Cyamopsis tetragonoloba* or *C. psoralioides*)

Brief Description

The guar plant is a small nitrogen-fixing annual that bears fruits known as pods containing 5–9 seeds per pod and can grow to nearly 6 feet in height. The part used is the endosperm of the seed. The endosperm constitutes 35–42% of the seed; it's separated from the other components of the seed (seed coat or hull and embryo or germ) during processing. The endosperm left is then ground to a fine powder, which is commercial guar gum. Major guar producers are India, Pakistan and the U.S.

Marvelous Weight Loss

A number of obese subjects at Salgren's Hospital in Göteborg, Sweden were put on a long-term treatment with daily intakes of guar-gum preparations, while still maintaining their normal dietary habits. In as little as 10 weeks their hunger cravings had been significantly reduced, their blood sugar and cholesterol levels lowered, and most of them had lost 10–15 lbs. of weight. An average of 4–6 capsules per day of Nature's Way guar gum from any health food store is recommended.

GUAVA (See TROPICAL FRUITS.)

H

HAWTHORN (See under BERRIES.)

HAZELNUT (See under NUTS.)

HICKORY NUT (See under NUTS.)

HOLLEYHOCK (See under ORNAMENTAL FLOWERS.)

HONEY AND OTHER BEE FOODS

Brief Description

It takes about 300 bees 3 weeks to gather one pound of honey for your table. Most of the honey made by the bees remains in the hive for their own consumption, but one out of every 3 lbs. is carefully removed by the beekeeper. Using a heated knife, the beekeeper loosens honey, beeswax and sections of honeycomb and collects them in a container. Law requires that honey be filtered or put through a nylon mesh. Honeycombs may be added later. FDA regulations prohibit additions of any sort. Honey is as pure as it is wholesome.

Honey keeps very well and never spoils. Honey is the ultimate preservative. So good in fact that wicked king Herod kept his murdered wife's (Mariamne) body perfectly preserved in a tub of the stuff for 7 years. And as late as 1943, the bodies of deceased Buddhist monks in Burma were still being preserved with honey until suitable funeral arrangements could be made months or even years later for them!

I've been to many countries and have sampled numerous kinds of honey. To me, the finest of them all has been Scottish heather honey—heavy and sweet and ecstatically fragrant. On the other hand, goldenrod honey yields a distinctly sassy sharpness to it. During my 1979 trip to the Soviet Union, I discovered the strong, macho qualities of very dark, heavy buckwheat honey, along with the almost dainty and angelic taste of beautiful white acacia honey. The lip-smacking honeys, though, come from fig blossoms and wild flowers found in and around the hills of Athens, Greece. They are undeniably the sweetest in the world.

Bee pollen is the male sexual grains of seed-bearing plants, which bees carry with them back to the hive. Pollen is comparable to spermatic cells in humans and animals. When bees enter the hive and brush it off, the substance falls to the bottom where it's later swept up by the beekeeper and sold to the health food industry for human consumption.

Propolis is a resinous substance, gathered by the bees, from the leaf buds or bark of trees (especially poplars). Bees use this stuff to seal any holes or cracks in the hive, to fix the comb of the roof and to protect the hive from outside contaminants.

When the honeycomb is constructed inside the hive, some of the cells are made to slightly larger dimensions. These are known as the royal cells. The eggs which are laid in these cells by the queen bee are designed to produce potential queens from the female grubs, which will be fed on royal jelly. This food is a sticky substance secreted by the glands near the mouth of the honeybee. It's a pearly-white, gluey kind of mass containing a high supply of protein and invert sugars like glucose and levulose.

Beeswax is the wax obtained from the honeycomb of the bee. After the honey is removed from the honeycombs the combs are washed rapidly and thoroughly with water. They are then melted with hot water or steam, strained and run into molds to cool and harden.

Great Wrinkle Remover

Honey adds softness and fresh beauty to the skin. Beekeepers' hands are often quite soft and wonderfully smooth during honey collection. Each day, splash warm water on your face and neck to open the pores, then apply a thin honey mask. The honey tends to soften and smooth away ugly, old wrinkles. Then just wash it off and finish with a dash of invigorating cold water to the face. Because of the composition of honey it causes the skin tissue to hold moisture. Dry skin cells plump up and wrinkles tend to smooth away.

By doing this often to the skin, you will notice a new glow of pink health returning to a heretofore "death warmed over" complexion. You may add dairy cream, whipped egg white, fresh lemon juice, apple cider vinegar or any fruit juice to your honey mask before applying it.

Undisturbed Sleep

Have a hard time hitting the hay at night? Then try an old Slavic remedy for your insomnia. It calls for a combination of 2 tbsps. of honey with the juice of a lemon and an orange. Mixed in half a glass of warm water, this beverage often provides the shortest route to Dreamland. The darker the honey, the better it works!

Allergy Relief

Sometimes the very things that give us the most misery, are also the very things that help us over these same discomforts. Hayfever and related pollen allergies may be corrected or at least minimized to a great extent by taking honey at least a month before pollen season starts.

The best course of treatment to follow in preparation for this is to take 1 tablespoonful of honey after each meal. Then every other day get a small, waxy piece of the actual honeycomb and chew on it for a couple of hours in between meals. The ideal preventative, of course, is to eat honey and chew some of the comb from your own area.

Having been plagued with hayfever myself for years, I can attest to the effectiveness of this remedy when *both* courses of action are followed. Although they've never actually cured my hayfever as such, I can testify that they have reduced the misery and aggravation of watery eyes and runny nose by at least 80% during the allergy season.

Drinking Honey Stops Diarrhea

Columbian Indians residing in the northwestern part of South America often drink a lot of bees' honey to stop diarrhea and cure dysentery with. Pediatricians at King Edward VIII Hospital in Durban, South Africa gave 169 infants and children afflicted with infantile gastroenteritis a strong liquid solution of honey to drink each day. This helped to reduce the incidence and recovery time from bacterial diarrhea.

In 8 oz. of water, 4 large tbsps. of honey should be thoroughly stirred in before drinking the same. It does not work, however, on nonbacterial diarrhea. Also those with diabetes should be careful about ingesting so much honey at one time.

Keeping Cool in Hot Weather

When bees are flying through the air in exceedingly hot weather, they will usually hold a droplet or two of nectar honey in the folds of their tongues in order to transfer heat from their heads to their thoraxes. This passive shifting of heat between both body parts produces a remarkable cooling effect.

Based on these recent entomological finds, we decided to conduct some informal experiments ourselves with human subjects on a hot July day, here at our Research Center in Salt Lake City.

We found that chewing a small piece of honeycomb and keeping it in the mouth for as long as possible during periods of strenuous physical activity in hot weather produced a drop in body temperature. Another method is to take a small amount of stiff, granulated honey, wrap it in some gauze and put it in the mouth to occasionally chew on and hold next to the cheek as one would with chewing tobacco. This serves the same purpose as the honeycomb would. In either case, it will keep the body a lot cooler.

Great Food for Dieters

Dieters, in particular, can benefit from the dual properties of honey. The sugars in honey are almost completely predigested and can be easily absorbed into the bloodstream. Dextrose is assimiliated very quickly, giving that "instant" boost of energy the body needs. On the other hand, levulose is absorbed much more slowly and maintains the sugar level for some time. Honey's double-action sugars quickly satisfy a craving for sweets and tend to maintain that sense of satisfaction for quite awhile. For dieters, this is an important thing to know about.

Wonderful Throat Remedy

For a sore throat, an old-fashioned home remedy may be just as effective as a shot of penicillin from the doctor would be. So says Dr. Neil Solomon, a nationally syndicated columnist, in one of his June 1987 medical columns. "Every time a person has a sore throat, he doesn't have to run to a doctor," the column began. This famous Maryland physician then added, "The American Academy of Otolaryngology—Head and Neck Surgery, recommends warm tea and honey for a sore throat."

You can make your own throat syrup too, if you like. Just peel some garlic cloves and put them in a jar. Add honey a little at a time over a couple of days until the jar is full. Set in a sunlit window until the garlic has turned somewhat opaque and all the garlic flavor has been transferred to the honey. This is a great remedy for relieving hoarseness, laryngitis or coughing. Take 1 tsp. every 3 hours as necessary. For a child, dilute each spoonful with a tiny bit of water. Bear in mind that garlic is decidedly hypoglycemic, so it should be used with care by those with known low blood sugar levels. An excellent honey-herb syrup is also available by mail from Great American Natural Products in St. Petersburg (see Appendix).

Sores and Shingles Healed Miraculously

Throughout this book, I've been very careful to use adjectives like "magical" or "miraculous" very sparingly, and only where I feel it's appropriate and deserving enough. Well, this is one of those few instances where it can be said that herpes lesions, bedsores and shingles are all miraculously healed within a very short time when honey is directly applied to them!

Either raw honey or the above garlic honey syrup can be applied two to three times daily as dressings with excellent results. Volume 62 of *The Chinese Medical Journal* for 1944 recommended mixing 80% honey with 20% Vaseline or Crisco shortening, to heal chronic leg ulcers, small burns and lupus erythematosus-like problems. The mixture was warmed and constantly stirred in order to make it easier to apply. The ointment was then applied in a thick layer to the afflicted areas and covered by sterilized gauze and bandages. When the infected sores showed much discharge of pus, the dressing was changed daily or every other day. When it was fairly clean and dry, the change was made every 2–3 days instead.

Of 50 cases of skin sores treated this way, there were 38 or 76% complete cures right off the bat, with another 10 or 20% showing considerable improvement or at least partial cures. Only 2 or 4% failed to respond to this honey dressing. Such an incredibly high cure rate does indeed suggest miraculous healing powers for one of Nature's simplest and most abundant remedies.

Cures Major Wounds

Major injuries should receive prompt medical attention as soon as possible. However, sometimes circumstances warrant improvising when emergency medical care isn't readily available. A Wyoming housewife living on an isolated cattle ranch reported to me an incident that shows the remarkable curing power of honey:

> One day while keeping myself busy in the kitchen, I sustained a very nasty laceration with a French knife on my left hand. The gash I judged to have been at least 2 inches in length and very deep into the muscles. Blood was spurting everywhere.
>
> My husband was out on the range at the time and our other car didn't run. I screamed for my teenage daughter to come and help me. When she hit the kitchen at a running pace, she almost fainted by the amount of blood I'd lost.
>
> I told her to fetch me the jar of honey we kept in our storeroom. When she did this and had removed the lid, I scooped several handfuls of honey with my good hand out of the wide-mouthed jar and generously covered my injured hand with it. Then I had my daughter wrap the whole thing up in gauze and tape it down good.
>
> The next day when my girl unwrapped the dressing, we noticed that much of the badly cut flesh had already started knitting itself together again. We decided to apply a second honey dressing. My husband returned that night and upon being informed of the accident, insisted that I go with him into Buford to our local hospital. But I decided to wait until the next day to see how it was doing.
>
> Imagine our surprise when the dressing was changed the next morning. Everything seemed to have come together of its own accord, almost as if the honey had acted like a glue of some sort to draw everything back like it used to be. We both decided to keep on using the honey dressing.
>
> No stitches were ever required and my hand mended nicely on its own, without even a trace of a scar. I mentioned this to our family doctor later on and he just scratched his head almost out of disbelief.

The ancient Egyptian physicians used a combination of honey and grease to treat major injuries suffered in work or battle. Their usual mixture was 1/3 honey 2/3 fat or butter. Some Harvard Medical School doctors tested this remedy out for themselves and found it to work quite well. The 1/3 honey was just enough to make a nice paste of smooth consistency; too much honey made it quite sticky. And because no bacteria of any kind can thrive in honey for very long, it makes a dandy antibiotic as well. A little garlic juice added to this honey/fat combination would seem to be the perfect cure for most major wounds, when other medical treatment isn't readily available.

Pollen Is an Energy Powerhouse

If you're dragging your feet these days and can't seem to get enough pep and energy, then you should probably be taking bee pollen. About 15% of pollen is lecithin, a fat-melting substance. Another 20% is top-of-the-line protein. The balance of the ingredients are energy-producing carbohydrates and vitamins and minerals that work on certain strength-giving glands of the body.

In some European countries, beekeepers who inhale the pollen while routinely working with their hives during honey gathering periods, demonstrate more vibrant health and physical activity than at other times of the year. No wonder, since weight for weight, bee pollen contains more complete protein than accepted sources like steak, eggs or cheese do.

A good quality bee pollen from Europe is sold in health food stores nationwide under the Nature's Way label. An average of 2 capsules per day is recommended for normal energy requirements. Caution should be exercised, however, by those with known pollen allergies before taking the stuff since adverse side-effects are possible.

Propolis Combats Infection

During an outbreak of influenza in Sarajevo, Yugoslavia several years back, Dr. Izet Osmanagic of the local university administered propolis to 88 students in a nursing college who were highly exposed to this epidemic. Another group of 182 students didn't take the substance. Of those who took propolis, only 7% became ill, while an amazing 63% of the nontakers came down with bad cases of the flu.

Dr. E. L. Ghisalberti of the Department of Organic Chemistry at the University of Western Australia has discovered that whenever propolis is administered along with penicillin or natural antibiotics such as garlic, propolis *increases* their effectiveness from as much as 10% to 100%. This helps to cut down drastically on the use of penicillin and potential drug side-effects from its frequent use. Propolis is available from any local health food store.

Royal Jelly as a Sexual Rejuvenant

An amazing study on the wonderful sexual rejuvenating properties of royal jelly was reported in Vol. 56 of the *Journal of the Egyptian*

Medical Association. Doctors in Cairo, Egypt administered royal jelly to a number of male patients known to be relatively sterile. Not only did the royal jelly increase their sperm count and make it more active, but also promoted growth of their genital organs as well. Ejaculations also seemed to be more frequent, too.

Royal jelly may be found at any local health food store. An average of 20 milligrams daily is recommended for infertility and poor sexual performance. An excellent combination of bee pollen, propolis and royal jelly is found in a unique food supplement called Aqua-Vite, available through Great American Products out of St. Petersburg, Florida (see Appendix).

The Ultimate Lip Balm

Many years ago when I was still in elementary school, we had a favorite reprimand for those who poked their noses into other people's business where they didn't belong—"Mind your own beeswax!" Although the saying has faded with time, yet the importance of beeswax as a lip balm hasn't.

Both yellow beeswax straight from the hive and the commercially bleached white beeswax are used extensively in lipsticks. If you have beekeepers in your immediate area, then I suggest you visit one of them sometime and purchase a little beeswax. It keeps well in a cool, dry place. Whenever you are out in the sun or wind too long, just carry some of this with you and rub a little bit over your lips every now and then. You'll find it keeps them nice and moist and soft.

HONEYDEW (See under MELONS.)

HOPS (*Humulus lupulus*)

Brief Description

The hop vine is a perennial climbing plant found wild in many places throughout the world. However it's mostly cultivated in the United States, West Germany and Yugoslavia for brewing beer. The bitter taste of beer is derived mostly from the humulone present in hops.

The vine has many angular, rough stems growing up to 20 feet in length from a branched rootstock. The leaves are rough, opposite, serrate and 3–5 lobed. Attractive yellowish-green flowers adorn the vine, with the male flowers arranged in hanging panicles and the female ones in catkins. The name hops generally pertains to the scaly, cone-like fruit that develops from the female flowers.

Kills Unfriendly Bacteria

Alcoholic extracts of hops in various dosage forms have been used clinically in treating numerous forms of leprosy, pulmonary tuberculosis and acute bacterial dysentery with varying degrees of success by doctors throughout the People's Republic of China. This could be due to a couple of antibiotic bitter acids, lupulon and humulon, occurring in the herb. Both kill Gram-positive and acid-fast bacteria such as strains of Staphylococcus, for instance. Staph infections are evident in suppurating wounds, runny sores, abscesses, boils and osteomyelitis (inflammation of bone marrow and adjacent bone and cartilage).

To make a strong extract, combine 1 1/2 cups of cut, fresh hop fruit with 2 1/4 cups of good-quality imported Russian vodka or an expensive brandy. Put into a bottle with a tight lid or cork. Shake daily, allowing the herbs to extract for about 2 weeks. Let the herbs settle and pour off the tincture, straining the liquid through a clean muslin cloth or fine filter paper. I recommend a piece of advice from an old European farm wife, if you expect a potent tincture: commence your extract during a full moon and strain off on a full moon in order that the drawing power of the waxing moon will help pull as many medicinal properties from the hops as possible.

Two tablespoonfuls each day taken orally on an empty stomach will help fight infection internally. The same amount may also be applied directly on bedsores caused by hospital-induced staph with some cotton. And clean strips of gauze may likewise be saturated in this tincture and then used to dress wounds with so they'll heal more rapidly.

Really Gets Rid of Dandruff

After the hair is scrubbed with a strong detergent and thoroughly rinsed with plain water, some of the above tincture may be rubbed into the scalp to help control dandruff. A quicker and easier way, though, is to rinse your hair good with a can of beer each day. Any brand will do just fine.

Calms Nervousness and Insomnia

Hops has been shown clinically to exert a strong sedative action on nervous patients and to help insomniacs get a good night's sleep.

Bring 2 pints of water to a boil. Add 1 heaping tbsp. each of hops and valerian root. Cover and reduce heat, simmering for 5 minutes. Remove and steep an additional 45 minutes. Sweeten with a little pure maple syrup and drink 1 1/2 cups at a time to help relax the body.

Keep in mind that since hops lose their sedative properties quickly when stored, they should always be used either as fresh as possible or pretty soon after they've been dried and cut up. An old favorite of country grandmothers used to be stuffing a cloth pillow case with hop flowers that had been sprinkled with a little alcohol to release their precious oils. Several elderly Amish women whom I've interviewed in the past solemnly swear on a proverbial stack of Bibles that they never missed a night's sleep and always enjoyed pleasant dreams when resting their heads on such an herb pillow as this.

Do Hops Contain Estrogens?

Estrogens are hormones which exert a variety of biological activities within the body. These include bone growth, preventing or stopping production of breast milk, suppressing ovulation, relieving cancer of the breast and prostate gland and stimulating sexual heat in women to permit intercourse with men.

Several studies cited in Vol. 11 of *Food & Cosmetics Toxicology* indicated an estrogenic activity in hops ranging from 20,000 to 300,000 I.U. (International Units) per 100 grams of herb. This is comparable to, or even higher than, the daily intake of estrogens by women taking certain oral contraceptive preparations. This may help to explain why some old herbalists have recommended hops tea for sexual stimulation.

HOREHOUND (*Marrubium vulgare*)

Brief Description

Horehound is a perennial found in waste places, in meadows and pastures and along railroad tracks and roadsides in coastal areas of the U.S., Canada, Great Britain, France and Germany. A tough, fibery rootstock sends up many bushy, square, downy stems. The leaves are somewhat distinctive, being wrinkled, rough on top and woolly-like underneath.

Real Congestion Buster

Nothing breaks up severe mucus congestion quite like horehound. In fact, I've found it to work a lot better than even coltsfoot, another congestion buster, does. One cup of warm horehound tea will instantly loosen impacted phlegm in the throat, lungs and sinuses like you wouldn't believe, and relieves a great deal of the misery attending a sinus headache.

To make the tea just bring 1 pint of hot water to a boil, then add 2 1/2 tsp. of the fresh or dried herb. Remove from heat, cover and steep 45 minutes. Drink while still lukewarm with a squeeze of lemon juice in it and sweetened with a touch of blackstrap molasses. Makes a real gutsy brew that will just about knock any cold unconscious.

Horehound candy makes a super remedy for sore throat and inflamed lungs due to cold, flu, allergies or smoking. Needed: 1 oz. fresh horehound or 1/4 cup dried; 1 1/2 cups water; 2 cups honey; 1 cup blackstrap molasses.

Boil water in small saucepan. Add horehound and simmer 10 mins. Allow to stand off heat for 5 mins., then strain liquid into large, heavy 5-qt. pot. Add honey and molasses to pot, mix and cook at medium heat until the temperature slowly reaches the hardcrack stage: 300–310° F. on a candy thermometer. Scum that forms can be scooped off and thrown away before the candy reaches the high temperature. Don't stir mixture while cooking even though it foams up. Pour into greased 9 × 13-inch pan and score into pieces before it sets but as it cools. Mixture will settle and harden as it cools. Refrigerate. Suck on a piece of this horehound candy to relieve nagging coughs.

HORSERADISH (*Armoracia lapathifolia*)

Brief Description

Horseradish is a perennial plant native to southeastern Europe and western Asia, and occasionally is found wild but usually is cultivated in other parts of the world. The long, white, cylindrical or tapering root produces a 2- to 3-foot-high stem in the second year.

The dried, powdered root found in many herb formulas today is practically worthless. The real benefits lay in the freshly dug root. When grated, however, the strong volatile oils are released, so it's necessary to cover the grated root with apple cider vinegar and refrigerate it in a glass jar with a tight-fitting lid. It will keep for at least 3 months this way or the entire root can be packed in damp sand and kept in a cool corner of your basement or garage. Keep sand moist.

Great Massaging Oil

A very stimulating massage oil to relieve muscular aches and pains and help break up chest congestion can be made by steeping a small amount of freshly grated root in some cold-pressed oil of your choice (wheat germ, sesame, olive).

Cosmetic Benefits

Horseradish vinegar lightens the tone of the skin and gets rid of freckles and blotches. Also makes a great hair rinse and really enlivens a dead scalp. Cover grated root with apple cider vinegar and permit to set on a sunny window sill for 10 days. Vinegar is then strained and stored in an airtight glass bottle.

When using on the skin, dilute with at least 50% water. Can be added to milk to bring more color to the face and to help relieve the itching of eczema. Soak 1 tbsp. freshly grated root in 1 cup of buttermilk for half an hour before straining. Dab on face and allow to remain for 15 minutes before rinsing with water. Refrigerate the rest for later use.

Warm Up Tea

During the winter time or when an older person experiences cold sensations in the hands, legs and feet due to poor circulation, a nice "warm up" tea can be taken to relieve some of this hypothermic feeling. Bring 1 quart of water to a boil. Add 1 tbsp. each grated ginger root and grated horseradish root. Cover and reduce heat, simmering for 10 minutes. Remove from heat, uncover and add 2 tbsps. each fresh or dried mustard greens and watercress. Cover and steep for an hour. Flavor with a pinch of powdered kelp and dash of lime juice. Drink 1 cup lukewarm every few hours.

Sauce Recipe

Here's a favorite horseradish sauce that's been in the Heinerman family for almost 200 years and was brought to America by my grandmother, Barbara Liebhardt Heinerman, from the old country (Temesvar, Hungary) at the turn of the century. It delivers full flavor and body, but without the unpleasant bite.

My Grandma's Basic Horseradish Sauce

Needed: 1/4 pint plain yogurt; 1/4 pint homemade mayonnaise (see recipe below); 2 1/2 tbsps. grated horseradish; 1/2 tbsp. each of lemon, lime and grapefruit juices. Mix everything together in blender or by hand. Goes great with fowl, fish and beef.

Good Homemade Mayonnaise

Needed: 1 cup sour cream; 1/4 cup plain yogurt; 3 tbsps. of pressed onion juice; 1/2 tsp. pure maple syrup; 1/4 tsp. ground ginger root; 1 tsp. dillweed; 1 tsp. each very finely minced French tarragon and chervil (both fresh). Mix everything in blender until a smooth and even consistency has been reached. Makes 1 1/2 cups.

HORSETAIL or SHAVE GRASS (*Equisetum arvense*)

Brief Description

This perennial plant is common to moist loamy or sandy soil all over North America and Eurasia. It is a strange-looking sort of plant with creeping, stringlike rootstock and roots at the nodes that produce numerous hollow stems, which are of two types. A fertile, flesh-colored stem grows first, reaching a height of 4–7 inches and bearing on top a conelike spike which contains spores; this stem quickly dies. A green, sterile stem grows up to 18 inches high and features whorls of small branches. In the dinosaur era, horsetails reached incredible heights of up to 40 feet or more and resembled skinny lodgepole pines, but lacking the green boughs. During the Middle Ages clumps of the plant were often used as scouring pads to clean iron cookware and pewter dishes due to a high silicon content.

Heals Fractures, Torn Ligaments

No other herb in the entire plant kingdom is so rich in silicon as is horsetail. This trace element really helps to bind protein molecules together in the blood vessels and connective tissues. Silicon is the material of which collagen is made. Collagen is the ''body glue'' that holds our skin and muscle tissues together. Silicon also promotes the growth and stability of the skeletal structure.

A few European clinical studies have determined that fractured bones heal much more quickly when horsetail is taken. The incidence of osteoporosis is, likewise, more greatly reduced when some horsetail is added to the diet. A few folk healers I'm aware of have recommended this herb to athletes who've suffered sprains, dislocated joints, pulled hamstrings or torn ligaments. Generally 3 tablets or capsules daily has been the rule-of-thumb until total healing has resulted of the injuries sustained.

An Internal Cosmetic

Horsetail is that kind of rare and unique cosmetic agent which beautifies from the inside out rather than just externally. It improves the texture and tone of hair, nails and skin, and greatly strengthens bones and teeth. Some even ascribe to this herb a certain hidden "youth factor."

A special type of horsetail, grown, harvested and processed in Europe, has become the favorite of many American consumers. This formula is marketed in local health food stores under the name of Alta Sil-X Silica and was developed by a Pasadena, California naturopathic/homeopathic physician, Dr. Richard Barmakian. His formula contains an extract more easily assimilated by the body without some of the harsh complications attending other horsetail products and found in the whole herb itself. An average of 2 tablets each day has been prescribed by him to a number of his patients for revitalizing their physical exteriors and rejuvenating their cellular interiors.

Reduces Bleeding, Good Diuretic

A tea made of horsetail helps to reduce minor bleeding. Half a cup internally every 45 minutes works well to stop bleeding in the urine and the stool. Some powder from an empty capsule or a crushed tablet can be sprinkled on a minor cut. Horsetail is a reliable diuretic for all urinary problems. In 1 pt. boiling water, add 2 tbsps. herb and steep for 30 mins. Drink 3 cups daily or 3 tbsps. every 1 1/2 hours. Dr. Barmakian's Alta Sil-X Silica from any local health food store or obtained directly from Alta Health Products (see Appendix) is just as effective, too.

I

IRIS (See ORNAMENTAL FLOWERS.)

J

JASMINE (Jasminum officinale)

Brief Description

This vinelike plant is indigenous to the warmer regions of the eastern hemisphere and is currently grown in some gardens throughout the southern United States. Some species of jasmine also appear as evergreen or deciduous shrubs. The vine leaves are usually opposite, dark green and pinnate. Both the vines and the shrubs produce extremely fragrant flowers which are of considerable value in the perfume industry.

The unique aroma has been described as being a "delicate, sweet odor so peculiar that it's without comparison one of the most distinct of all natural odors."

Overcomes Sexual Frigidity

In parts of China and India, the oil extracted from the flowers of jasmine has often been used to arouse erotic emotions in those who may experience frigidity during sexual engagements.

For those who can afford to purchase jasmine oil from specialty shops, they may find that massaging certain areas of the body with a few drops mixed in with some sweet almond oil should help to promote sexual stimulation. In India the abdomen and groin are those regions rubbed for this purpose.

It is also said that a few drops rubbed on the upper lip below the nostrils contributes to this heightened stimulation.

JUNIPER BERRY (See BERRIES.)

K

KAVA KAVA (*Piper methysticum*)

Brief Description

This tall, leafy shrub of the South Pacific has been used for many centuries among the islands of Oceania as a social beverage for many different occasions. The infusion prepared from the rhizome or stem of the plant is still used in many social ceremonies—to welcome visitors, commemorate marriages, births and deaths and to remove curses.

Polynesian Relaxant

A recently published study in the *Journal of Ethnopharmacology* reported that the pyrones in kava kava helped reduce anxiety and fatigue as well as relaxing twitching heart muscles and calming hysteria.

Other researchers who've worked with kava kava have described its effect upon the central nervous system as being "placidly tranquil." In a study with rats, they found that while this herb truly relaxed the rodents, yet in no way did it affect their overall mental or physical performances.

Hence kava kava can be taken on a regular basis without interrupting one's ability to work. In fact, it probably will help ease some of the stress that accompanies most jobs these days. The best brand of kava kava can be purchased in any health food store under the Nature's Way logo. An average of two capsules twice daily (late morning and late afternoon) on an empty stomach is recommended.

KELP (*Fucus vesiculosus*)

Brief Description

The common name of kelp applies to a broad range of seaweeds of many different species. But for those using herbs a lot, kelp probably refers to seaweeds of the brown algal order Laminariales which possess large, flat, leaf-like fronds. A class of brown algae called bladderwrack is generally used the most often for producing kelp products.

Iodine Content Controls Obesity

Kelp has many medicinal uses and claims attributed to it. One of the more popular is in controlling obesity. This role is attributed to the plant's iodine content which is believed to stimulate production of iodine-containing hormones that help keep you slim. Doctors recognize that the thyroid gland is the body's own pace-setter, either having our cellular engines merely poke along or else race at breakneck speed. When thyroid activity moves at a snail's pace, fat isn't burned rapidly enough and, therefore, accumulates in the body. However, when the thyroid accelerates faster, fat disappears more quickly before it can form deposits in body tissue somewhere.

Recommended intake of kelp tablets or capsules under the Nature's Way label from your local health food store for weight control is at least two per day with a meal. If you are on a sodium-restricted diet, you should monitor intake with care.

Great Seasoning

Kelp is an ideal substitute for table salt and black pepper and should be used wherever these other two seasonings are called for. It's a much healthier way to go with far less problems than either of the others is known to cause.

KIWIFRUIT

Brief Description

An egg-shaped fruit with a fuzzy brown outer skin and sweet, green flesh, the odd but appealing kiwi is a native of New Zealand, which leads the world in its production (some 1 billion kiwifruit was shipped to 30 nations in 1986 alone). The exotic interior represents a sunburst of neat white streaks radiating from a cream-colored core, past tiny black seeds and into the shimmering green flesh.

Sweet-tart in taste, it seems to be a succulent blend of strawberry, banana, melon and pineapple flavors all rolled into one. Incredibly delicious beyond compare!

Food for Hypertension

An average kiwifruit contains over 250 mg. of potassium. This high level of an important mineral for such a small fruit makes it an ideal food for hypertensive patients. And since it's a good diuretic, it will help to remove excess sodium buildup in the body. An average of 2–3 kiwifruits every other day are recommended for those suffering from high blood pressure.

A Delicious Digestive Aid

Certain fruits like papaya and pineapple contain important enzymes such as papain and bromelain which have proven to be of value in correcting digestive problems and in helping to heal up old sores and wounds. Kiwifruit also contains similar enzymes which have the same types of medical application to them. Eating 1 or 2 kiwifruits after a heavy meal will relieve the feeling of heartburn, which often accompanies indigestion.

KOHLRABI (See CABBAGE.)

KOLA NUT (*Cola acuminata*)

Brief Description

The dried seed or kola nut comes from evergreen trees with long, leathery leaves and growing up to 66 feet in height. They are native to western Africa, Indonesia and other tropical climates. The fruit consists of 4–5 leathery or woody pods each containing 1–4 seeds. The seeds are dried and their outer coats removed. Although not actually a nut as such, yet it's called that due to its hard consistency when dried, thus resembling a nut in appearance.

Eliminates Fatigue

In small doses kola nut produces a passing excitement on the central nervous system, increases blood pressure slightly, and elevates the strength of the heartbeat. This is due to the presence of 1.5–2% caffeine and lesser amounts of theobromine, both natural stimulants to the body. Mental activity is likewise increased due to the considerable amount of fructose occurring naturally in kola nut, which reaches the brain to nourish it.

A leading health magazine, *East West Journal,* did a survey of herbal energy stimulants currently available in the marketplace and concluded that one product called Super Energy had the highest amount of kola nut, making it extremely effective. An average of 2 capsules daily is the amount generally taken by thousands of consumers using this product from Great American of St. Petersburg (see Appendix).

Helps Drug Withdrawal

The *Journal of the American Medical Association* (Nov. 4, 1974) recommended kola nut for sustaining the body during symptoms experienced when withdrawing from alcohol, tobacco and drug addictions. The same company that manufacturers Super Energy also has another product called Kola Nut that's useful to take when quitting such bad social habits (see Appendix). Up to 4 capsules daily as needed in such cases.

Diet Coke as a Contraceptive

Kola nut occurs in all cola beverages, but in varying concentrations. Diet Coke appears to have an unusually high concentration of kola nut in it. Researchers at Harvard Medical School studied the effect of Diet Coke on sperm motility and reported their findings in a 1985 issue of the *New England Journal of Medicine*. They found that Diet Coke had the "most pronounced spermicidal action" of all the cola beverages. That is to say, Diet Coke killed all of the active sperm in the vagina when women used it as a douche immediately following sexual intercourse. Doctors speculate that it may have some as yet undiscovered value as a potential birth control agent in the near future.

KUMQUAT (See CITRUS FRUITS.)

L

LEEKS (See ONIONS.)

LEGUMES (See BEANS.)

LEMON (See CITRUS.)

LENTILS (See BEANS.)

LETTUCE (*Lactuca sativa*)

Brief Description

Iceberg lettuce is so common that it really doesn't require any kind of a physical description to speak of. To the ancient Egyptians, however, at least one kind of romaine-type lettuce that grew on the island of Kos off the Turkish coast, held sexual symbolism. The long, stiff leaves were thought to resemble a man's sexual organ and the milky juice from them the semen emitted during ejaculation.

Relieves Heartburn

While iceberg lettuce, for the most part, is very difficult to digest and not on my recommended list of foods that are good to eat, it, nevertheless, does possess at least one medicinal virtue. Any kind of lettuce is wonderful for treating acid indigestion and heartburn in place of antacids such as Tums.

In a blender whip up half of a cut lettuce leaf with 8–10 oz. of ice cold water until you have a nice semi-thick, green purée of near milkshake proportions. Drink slowly to relieve stomach upset. A little honey and a touch of vanilla may be added for flavoring, if desired.

Culinary Functions

Lettuce is generally used on sandwiches and forms the base for most tossed salads. It's also used to serve cottage cheese and fruit sections on as part of a meal appetizer or garnish. I prefer the romaine or darker kind of lettuce over the iceberg, just because it's a lot healthier for you. Be sure to wash any lettuce you use very thoroughly since it often contains more chemical sprays than most other vegetables do.

LICORICE ROOT (*Glycyrrhiza glabra*)

Licorice is a perennial plant found wild in southern and central Europe and parts of Asia, and cultivated in the U.S. and Canada to some extent. The woody rootstock is wrinkled and brown on the outside, yellow on the inside and tastes sweet.

Heals Peptic Ulcers

Certain constituents found in human saliva and licorice root have nearly identical actions in healing peptic and duodenal ulcers. More remarkable still is the fact that these several constituents bear an uncanny resemblance to each other when examined under a high-powered electron microscope. Two capsules daily of Nature's Way brand from any local health food store are good for this.

Treats Emotional Imbalances and Hysteria

My friend Michael Tierra, who is a Southern California practicing herbalist, really believes in the tranquilizing influence of licorice root on the nervous system. He often adds small amounts of licorice to balance many of his formulas, harmonize the action of the herbs in them and to avoid potential side-effects later on. He calls licorice root a "peace-maker" type of an herb.

In his book, *The Way of Herbs,* he recommends not only licorice, but also kava kava (a Polynesian herb from the South Pacific) and the usual calmatives such as hops, skullcap and valerian for hysteria and emotional-mental disturbances. Kava kava by itself and these other herbs in the HIGL and Ex-Stress Formulas are available from your local health food store under the Nature's Way label (see Appendix). An average of 2 capsules each on an empty stomach with an 8 oz. glass of water is recommended at a time.

Licorice root tea (1 cup daily) or capsules (3 daily) are also effective remedies for treating Parkinson's Disease with.

LIMES (See CITRUS.)

LOBELIA (*Lobelia inflata*)

Brief Description

A hairy annual or biennial herb with light-blue flowers, which grows about 2 1/2 feet high. The plant is native to North America and ranges from Labrador to Georgia and west to Arkansas.

Anti-Smoking Remedy

The lobeline salts found in lobelia are used as the active ingredient in several brands of smoking deterrent preparations with varying degrees of success. A decade ago in the mid-1970s and early 80s this herb was extremely popular with most of America's large herb companies, but today is hardly to be found anymore in their products due to FDA scare tactics. One company, though, out of Portland, Oregon, still sells a high-quality lobelia tincture, which those wishing to quit smoking should find extremely helpful. Six to eight drops at one time of Eclectic Institute's tincture (see Appendix), on the tip and just beneath the tongue whenever a craving for nicotine occurs, is suggested. A cup of the tea or 4 capsules of the powdered herb are sometimes used to induce vomiting.

Earache and Toothache Disappear

The same tincture mentioned above also seems to be good for relieving earache (6 drops), when dropped into the ear canal slightly warm. And is quite useful for reducing excruciating pain accompanying an infected tooth, when a small wad of cotton is soaked with the tincture and then applied directly to the afflicted area and kept there for awhile. The surrounding gums may also be rubbed with some of the tincture as well for further relief. Between 10–15 drops of the tincture, 2 capsules of the powdered herb or 1/2 cup of the tea slowly sipped allays whooping cough.

LOGANBERRY (See BERRIES.)

M

MACADAMIA (See NUTS.)

MACE (See under NUTMEG.)

MANGO (See TROPICAL FRUITS.)

MARIGOLD (See ORNAMENTAL FLOWERS.)

MARJORAM AND OREGANO (*Origanum majorana, O. vulgare*)

Brief Description

Sweet marjoram is a tender, bushy perennial herb with woolly-hairy leaves, which gets up to 1 1/2 feet in height. The herb is native to the Mediterranean countries, but is cultivated as an annual in colder climates. The dried flowering herb yields a faint sage-like odor and leaves a slightly minty aftertaste in the mouth.

Oregano, as such, is not just one or two well-defined species but rather any one of over 2 dozen known species that yield leaves or flowering tops having the flavor recognized as being oregano. European oregano is a hardy perennial herb with erect, more or less hairy, branching stems and hairy leaves. The herb can grow to over 2 feet tall, and is acrid and pungent with a strong sage-like aroma somewhat reminiscent of thyme.

Fevers, Cramps, Epilepsy

In my work entitled, *The Complete Book of Spices,* I discuss at some length a myriad of uses for both culinary herbs. When made into a tea and consumed warm to slightly cool, they help reduce fevers and relieve cramps, besides being good for bronchitis, childhood diseases such as measles and mumps, and irregular menstruation. And when Oil of Oregano (obtainable at some pharmaceutical houses) is applied to the neck, spine, throat, chest and temples of a person having a seizure and rubbed into the skin good, it will often help in bringing that individual out of his or her fit a lot sooner and with very little trauma.

To make a tea, simply bring 1 pint of water to a boil. Remove from the heat and add 1 level tsp. each of marjoram and oregano. Stir well, cover and let steep for 30 mins. or so. Strain and refrigerate, warming slightly on the stove only that amount to be consumed at any given time. Generally 1 cup two to three times daily is suggested.

Culinary Uses

Marjoram is used as a flavor ingredient in most food categories, including alcoholic (bitters, vermouths, beers, etc.) and nonalcoholic beverages, frozen dairy desserts, candy, baked goods, gelatins and puddings, meat and meat products, condiments and relishes and others. Sweet marjoram is also used in baked goods, meat and meat products, condiments and relishes, soups, snack foods, processed vegetables and others, with highest average maximum use level of about 1% in baked goods.

European oregano is extensively used as a major flavor ingredient in pizza. The more spicy Mexican oregano is widely used in Mexican dishes (chili, chili con carne, etc.); it's less preferred for use in pizza than the milder European type. Oregano is also widely used in other foods, including alcoholic beverages, baked goods, meat and meat products, condiments and relishes, milk products, processed vegetables, snack foods, fats and oils and others. Highest average maximum use level reported is about 0.3% in condiments and relishes and milk products.

MARSHMALLOW (*Althaea officinalis*)

Brief Description

Marshmallow is a perennial plant growing to a height of nearly 4 feet in some cases. It is both cultivated as well as found growing wild in damp and wet places everywhere. The rootstock is white and sweetish like unto a parsnip, but with considerable mucilage to it. The plant sends up several unbranched, woolly stems with serrate, pubescent leaves. The axillary flowers are about 2 inches in width and can be either light red to white or royal purple in color.

Formula for Healing Hernias

The late Utah herbalist, Dr. John R. Christopher, developed a special formula for helping knit together torn ligaments and herniated muscles. His formula consisted of marshmallow and comfrey roots, slippery elm and white oak barks, some mullein leaves and calendula flowers, along with lesser amounts of skullcap herb, black walnut hulls and a tiny amount of gravel root.

A particular lady in Orem, Utah, had a teenage son who accidentally sustained a hernia on the right side of his groin through the improper lifting of weights at his high school gymnasium. She told me that about 11 years ago she met Dr. Christopher at an herb lecture and explained the problem to him, saying that doctors were recommending surgery for her boy which she didn't want to go along with.

He told her about his special BF & C Formula, which she purchased from his family-owned herb company and gave her instructions on how to use it. She had her son take 4 capsules three times daily on an empty stomach with additional supplements of calcium, horsetail and zinc in unspecified amounts. Each time the boy took them, he would drink a full 8 oz. glass of papaya juice made from liquid concentrate. He also refrained from strenuous exercising as well. According to what the mother told me, her son's hernia healed within 2 1/2 months and a later physical examination and further X-rays by their family doctor confirmed this to, indeed, have been the case.

Nature's Way later obtained this BF & C Formula from Dr. Christopher and currently markets it to most health food outlets nationwide. The formula is good for sprains, too.

A Nice Wound-Healing Ointment

To make a marvelous ointment for helping heal facial sores, skin eruptions, leg ulcers and ugly-looking wounds a lot faster, lightly crush approximately 1 gallon each of fresh marshmallow leaves and elder flowers. Then scatter them around evenly in a large roast pan and add about 2 1/4 cups of melted lard or Crisco shortening and 1 1/2 lbs. of beeswax. Stir thoroughly with a wooden ladle and cover with a lid, simmering in a 150° F. oven until the herbs are fairly crisp, easily crumbling when touched. Strain mixture through a wire mesh strainer and continue stirring with a wooden ladle until entirely cold. Half a cup of glycerine or 2/3 cup powdered slippery elm can be added to help preserve ointment from rancidity later on. Put into clean jars while still relatively warm and allow to become somewhat firm. Seal with tight lids and store in cool, dry place until needed.

MELONS
CANTALOUPE (*Cucumis melo cantalupensis*)
CASABA (*Cucumis melo indorus*)
HONEYDEW (*Cucumis melo species*)
WATERMELON (*Citrullus vulgaris*)

Brief Description

CANTALOUPE. A variety of muskmelon having a warty rind and reddish-orange flesh.

CASABA. A variety of muskmelon or winter melon with a yellow rind. First introduced to Smryna in Asia Minor.

HONEYDEW. A sweet, smooth-skinned, white variety of muskmellon.

WATERMELON. Large oblong or roundish fruit of a vine of the cucumber family. It has a hard green or white rind, and a pink or red pulp with a copious sweet juice.

Some scientists who specialize in the evolution, migration and use of plants by indigenous cultures believe that these melons were brought to the western hemisphere around 2,000 B.C. by emigrants from central Iraq, who crossed the ocean in unique vessels.

Melons as Laxatives

Besides making good diuretics, these melons also help to correct constipation. Generally, a quarter or half a melon eaten by itself should induce a modest bowel movement several hours later.

Cure for Jaundice

An effective treatment for jaundice of the liver in some Caribbean countries calls for fresh green melons that are slightly unripe to be consumed along with some parsley tea on a regular basis. A handful of freshly chopped parsley steeped in 1 pint of hot water for 30 minutes, strained and drunk, makes a good tea.

Watermelon Remedies

The seeds of watermelon are universally acclaimed for their marvelous diuretic activity and soothing effect on bladder inflammation. Sometimes even the rind is dried and used the same way. In the Bahamas, freshly discarded seeds are pounded with a heavy object just enough to bruise them, after which they're boiled for about 45 mins. (6 tbsps. seeds to 1 qt. hot water) on low heat, then strained and the liquid drunk at least three times daily in 1-cup amounts each time. The same tea also is good for expelling some intestinal worms as well.

In some South American countries, the thick rind is bound around the forehead and temples to relieve excruciating migraine headaches. Or else the rind is mashed into a pulp and applied as a poultice directly over the liver or gall bladder to relieve pain and suffering in either of those organs.

A piece of watermelon consumed immediately after eating a meal of beans usually helps to relieve and reduce the embarrassment of intestinal gas which frequently occurs later on.

Great Cooler for Intense Heat

Nothing seems to quench thirst quite like fresh watermelon, especially if the flesh has been removed from the rind and mixed up in a blender with some crushed ice. My oh my, but does that ever feel good going down the hatch!

A most curious but seemingly effective remedy for poison ivy itch and rash was demonstrated to me one time back in the hills of Tennessee by some simple mountain folks. One of their youngins (as kids are often referred to back there) got into some ivy and came home a red mess. His folks fetched some fresh watermelon from their garden, split it open and methodically proceeded to rub down those afflicted parts of his body with the flesh and the rind itself. Next morning as my colleague and I got ready to leave, they brought the lad to us for inspection. And darned if the little tyke's rash wasn't in remission already by at least 70%!

But what has to be one of the most incredible yet highly successful treatments for major first-, second- and third-degree burns was witnessed by myself in the People's Republic of China in the Summer of 1980.

Fully ripened watermelon pulp and juice were placed in a clean glass jar, tightly sealed and allowed to stand at room temperature for 3–4 months. After which, the juice was filtered, having acquired a sour plum odor in the meantime.

I witnessed major burns first being washed with a cold normal salt solution or just with plain cold water. Then a piece of defatted or specially treated cotton was next dipped into the clear fermented watermelon juice and applied directly to the burned area. This dressing was changed several times each day.

My interpreter told me in response to a question I'd asked the doctors, that first- and second-degree burns generally took 8–9 days to heal and third-degree burns 17–21 days or less, as a rule.

MILK THISTLE (*Silybum marianum*)

Brief Description

Milk thistle is a robust annual or biennial, reaching a height of between 1 and 3 feet. The glabrous leaves have undulate margins and sharp spines, are brilliant dark green above and markedly streaked with white along the veins. The flower heads are a reddish-purple with bracts ending in sharp spines.

Milk thistle yields seeds that contain an important compound called silymarin, which holds enormous medical potential in the treatment of liver diseases.

Incredible Remedy for Most Liver Diseases

Nothing seems to work better in protecting the liver against harmful chemical poisoning and in treating certain liver diseases than milk thistle seed. Although the jury may still be out for a final verdict, the one which has been reached so far in the medical and scientific community is this: nothing works better as an antidote in the liver against harmful toxins than milk thistle seed!

Details of the evidence may be found in Craker and Simon's recent book, *Herbs, Spices and Medicinal Plants* (Oryx Press, 1986). Consider this, for instance—two groups of mice were given a dangerous compound found in a deadly species of mushroom. The untreated group died in 3 hours with massive internal bleeding around the liver, while the group treated with milk thistle seed survived very nicely.

In other test animals subjected to a variety of harmful chemicals that cause much damage to the liver, milk thistle seed has proven remarkable in not only protecting it against destruction if administered early enough, but has also prolonged the lives of some animals given the seed later on after some havoc had already been wreaked.

While extremely popular in Europe, milk thistle seed hasn't yet been adopted by the American herb industry to any great extent. One of the very few products in which it may be found here is Nature's Way Thisilyn available from most health food stores and nutrition counters. Three capsules daily seem to protect the liver against most toxins we unconsciously ingest on a daily basis from the food we eat, water we drink and air we breathe.

MILLET (See GRAINS.)

MINTS
PEPPERMINT (*Mentha piperita*)
SPEARMINT (*Mentha spicata*)

Brief Description

Both kinds of mints are closely related perennial aromatic herbs with runners by which they are propagated. The leaves of spearmint are sessile (no petioles), while those of peppermint are petioled. Both grow to about 1 yard high and are cultivated worldwide. Each species has numerous varieties that produce essential oils, which yield a menthol aroma and taste to varying degrees.

Relieves Migraines

Peppermint tea is excellent for relieving the pressure of migraine headaches. Bring 1 pint of water to a boil. Remove from heat, adding 2 tbsps. of fresh or dried mint leaves. Cover and steep for 50 minutes, then strain. Drink 1–2 cups of cool tea when a headache occurs. Also rubbing a little peppermint oil on either side of the temples and toward the back of the neck gives additional relief as well.

Calms Digestive Disorders

General nervousness and stomach disorders may be effectively treated by drinking several cups of lukewarm peppermint/spearmint tea sweetened with a little honey. This combination of equal parts of both mints is pleasantly soothing to the nervous system. The tea can be made according to the previous instructions given.

Digestive disorders of various kinds may be greatly relieved by taking a presteeped water extract in capsule form or powdered form as a tea. This European-made extract is only available under the Alta Health Products label from most health food stores or may be ordered directly from the manufacturer in Pasadena, California (see Appendix). Dr. Richard Barmakian, a renowned southern California naturopathic/homeopathic doctor, has included in his special formulation other herbs, besides peppermint, such as alder buckthorn, marigold flowers and marshmallow leaf.

Called Can-Gest, this pure herbal digestive extract helps to relieve heartburn, indigestion, abdominal cramps and other gastrointestinal discomforts. Some have reported no further need to rely on antacids once they've begun to use Can-Gest. Recommended intake suggested by Dr. Barmakian to many of his patients is between 1–3 capsules per meal as needed or 1/2 tsp. of the powder made into a tea.

Inhibits Herpes

Peppermint is strongly antiviral and may be used with good success in helping to inhibit the further progress of herpes virus. It works best in tea form, however, since the gelatin capsule tends to nullify its strong antiviral properties. Two cups of warm tea a day are suggested during those periods when the herpes virus is the most active. Dr. Barmakian suggests emptying the contents of about 3 capsules of Can-Gest into a cup of hot water sweetened with some honey, then sipping slowly when lukewarm.

MORNING GLORY (*Ipomoea purpurea*)

Brief Description

Although there are many kinds of morning glories, this particular species is quite common throughout the U.S. and Canada, often growing more as a nuisance weed in damp waste places or cultivated ground such as garden plots or farmers' fields. Its creeping, spreading vinelike stems can cover an area up to 7 feet in circumference. The leaves are usually alternate and the trumpet-shaped flowers, while of different hues, generally are white as a rule.

Flower Tincture for Sore Eyes

A tincture of morning glory blossoms is useful for getting rid of a headache and to relieve inflamed eyes. Combine 1 1/2 cups of finely snipped flowers in 2 cups of gin. Put in a jar with a tight-fitting lid, and set on a window sill for about two weeks. Be sure and shake the contents twice daily. Strain through several layers of cheesecloth or gauze.

Soak a clean cloth with some of this tincture, wring out the excess and apply to the forehead or over closed eyes for relief. A small hand towel may be applied over the cloth to prevent the rapid evaporation of the alcohol.

Antidote for Insect Bites

If perchance, you should be outdoors somewhere, and get bitten or stung by an insect such as a horsefly, mosquito or wasp, then just look around for some morning glory if you can. Pick a small number of the leaves, crush them with a smooth stone or hammer and then rub them on the afflicted site, retaining in place either by holding them there or else covering with a small, square piece of gauze and adhesive tape.

Bathing Sores and Wounds

In the Bahamas local practitioners skilled in folk medicine make a tea out of the leaves and flowers of morning glory. They use the resulting liquid for bathing herpes lesions, diabetic leg ulcers, gangrene, syphilitic sores and wounds. Bring 3 cups of water to a boil and add 1 cup of cut flowers and leaves. Cover, remove from the heat and steep for 45 minutes. Strain and use.

An Effective Poultice for Boils

Throughout Jamaica and Brazil, morning glory leaves are used as effective poultices for drawing the purulent matter out of serious abscesses and boils. The quickest way for making such a poultice is to throw a handful of picked and washed leaves in a food blender with 2 tablespoons of ice water, and purée. Apply this thick pulp directly to the boil or carbuncle previously lanced with a sewing needle that has been sterilized over an open flame. Cover with some gauze and secure with adhesive tape. Change every 45 minutes or so.

MULLEIN (*Verbascum thapsus*)

Brief Description

Mullein is aligned with snap dragon in the same family of *Scrophulariaceae*. Mullein flowers are stalkless with their sulphur-yellow corollas forming irregular cups an inch across, having five rounded petals enclosed in woolly calyxes. All manner of insects are attracted to this plant due to the easy accessibility of the nectar. By this means the plant is able to propagate itself elsewhere.

The unique leaves are large and numerous, 6–8 inches long and 2 1/2 inches wide, becoming smaller as they ascend towards the stem. Mullein can reach heights greater than the average man and prefers clearings, fields, pastures and waste places from the Atlantic to the Pacific. This herb is a common sight along many of our nation's highways and railroad tracks, but shouldn't be picked in these places due to frequent spraying with noxious chemical herbicides.

Cure for Asthma

A Beachy Amish woman from Goshen, Indiana (Amish who have electricity and cars) had spent large sums of money on various medications prescribed by her doctors for her asthma, but found little relief from most of them. Learning about the virtues of mullein from her minister, she gathered some from a river bank and made a tea out of it. This she did by steeping a handful of coarsely cut leaves and flowers in 1 quart boiling water for half an hour, then drinking 2 cups of the warm brew sweetened with some honey each and every day. In no time at all, her asthma was brought under control.

Medicine for the Heart

The French herbalist, Maurice Mességué, recommends mullein for palpitations, irregular heartbeat, angina and other coronary distress. Simmer 2 handfuls of coarsely cut leaves and flowers in 1 1/2 qts. boiling water for an hour, covered, until about 1 pint remains. Strain and add 3 tbsps. blackstrap molasses and 1/2 tsp. glycerine to give it longer shelf life. Take 1 tbsp. of this syrup twice daily in between meals, once in the morning and again in the evening; or more if pressure builds up in the heart.

Enema for Intestinal Infection

Mullein leaves were collected and tested by the Michigan State College of Agriculture and Applied Science in 1943–44 for possible antibacterial properties. Experiments showed that mullein extract inhibited growth of *Staphylococcus aureaus* and *E. coli*. The former bacteria causes boils, abscesses and wounds filled with purulent matter, while the latter genus of unfriendly microbes produces intestinal inflammation, peritonitis and inflammation of the urinary bladder.

To make an enema solution, steep 1 handful *each* of fresh cut leaves and flowers together in 1 1/2 qts. of boiling water for 40 minutes, covered. Then strain and use half of this amount, while still lukewarm for an enema. Follow the directions given under COFFEE for the proper way to administer an enema.

Treating Childhood Diseases

Mullein is one of the very best herbs that I know of to successfully treat a wide variety of childhood ailments, including tonsillitis, chickenpox, measles and mumps—especially when it's used in conjunction with catnip. Both herbs work well for pancreatitis, too.

A relatively delicious tea that can be made for sick children to drink calls for 1/2 handful *each* of dried or cut fresh mullein leaves and flowers, and dried or cut fresh herb to be steeped in 1 qt. of boiling water, covered and then set away from the heat for approximately 35 mins. or so. After this the solution is strained twice, once through a fine sieve and again through a piece of clean cloth. Then while still quite warm 2 tbsps. of dark honey, 1 tsp. of pure maple syrup and a couple of drops of pure vanilla should be mixed in to improve the flavor considerably. Give a sick child 1/2 cup of this *warm* throughout the day or every 3–4 hrs. *NO* dairy products, eggs, bread, meat, greasy foods, candy, soft drinks and so forth should be given to the child during his or her recuperation period.

A small enema may also be given as well at least once a day until the fever breaks and glandular inflammation begins to subside. In 1 pint of boiling water, steep 1/4 handful of dried or cut fresh mullein leaves, 1/4 handful of dried or cut catnip herb and 1 peeled, finely chopped garlic clove, covered, for 40 mins. or until lukewarm. Administer the enema to the child according to the foregoing instructions. Remember to tell the child to try to hold as much of the solution inside of the bowels as possible *before* relieving himself or herself on the toilet. And be sure to give the enema in very short spurts so the child can better retain the solution for a couple of minutes, else you might have a messy accident to clean up afterwards.

Nice Remedy for Skin Problems and Earache

Soak 2 handfuls of cut dried or fresh mullein flowers and leaves in 2 cups of olive oil or sweet almond oil for 8 days. Strain, bottle and store in cool place. Makes a very useful dressing for skin ulcers, wounds, sunburn, general burns and hemorrhoids. A few drops of this oil, slightly warmed and placed inside the ear canal, helps to relieve painful earache, when the ear is covered with a warm flannel afterwards.

(FIELD) MUSHROOM (*Agaricus campestris*)

Brief Description

Mushrooms are fungi that live in darkness, feeding off other organic matter. Lacking chlorophyll, they're unable to photosynthesize nourishment from sunlight. They have no roots, leaves, flowers or seeds. These mysterious characteristics have fascinated and tempted man since prehistoric times.

The ancient Roman emperor, Nero, poisoned his captain of the guards with deadly mushrooms. And almost 2,000 years earlier than this the Aryans, who swept into Afghanistan and India from the northwest, made a ceremonial drink from the fly agaric mushroom in order to experience religious hallucinations.

For the most part though, mushrooms are good to eat, especially when added to soups and salads. Since they are highly perishable, they should be stored in the refrigerator in a paper bag or an open basket, but never in plastic bags since they turn soggy. Cover them with a damp paper towel to keep them moist, because they dry out easily. Remember never to wash them as they'll lose their special texture. Just wipe them gently with a damp paper towel in order to clean them.

Mushroom Tea Is a Great Remedy

In midsummer 1987 I met a Dr. Yan Wu with the Institute of Botany at the Academia Sinica in Nankang (near Taipei), Taiwan, while both of us attended the annual meeting of the American Society of Pharmacognosy at the University of Rhode Island in Kingston.

Dr. Wu related the number of uses for mushroom tea in his country. The mushrooms used are those which grow on oak (*Cortinellis shiitake*). If used in dried form, several mushrooms are soaked for an hour until soft. If used fresh, however, they are then immediately cooked. The mushrooms are coarsely chopped into 1/4-inch pieces, put in 2 1/2 cups of boiling water with a pinch of kelp and simmered, covered, for 30 minutes on low heat until just 1 1/4 cups of tea is left.

Mushroom tea, he claimed, was effective in dissolving and getting rid of fat congestion in the body, stimulating kidney function, reducing fevers and relaxing tension.

A California physician, Lawrence Badgley, M.D., recommends shiitake mushrooms in the diets of those AIDS patients who visit his clinics often. Like figs, mushrooms contain the anti-cancer compound, benzaldehyde.

High in Zinc

Edible mushrooms are incredibly rich in the trace element zinc. Zinc is valuable in treating burns, wounds, and similar skin injuries, as well as helping the body to digest starchy foods. Zinc also regulates prostate gland function, encourages the growth and development of the reproductive organs, and helps in the metabolism of animal and plant proteins.

Culinary Use

Nothing is quite so good as homemade mushroom soup. It yields a body of flavor that commercially canned soups simply can't match.

Good Cream o' Mushroom Soup

The soup is prepared by washing and skinning 1/4 lb. of mushrooms and simmering the skins in 1/2 cup of water. The mushroom caps and stems should be chopped into small pieces and 2 cups of water added to the skins. The simmering should continue until the skins are tender.

Melt 2 tbsps. of butter, adding 2 tbsps. of whole wheat flour and 1 tsp. salt or kelp. Two cups of milk should gradually be added over low heat, stirring constantly with a wire whip until the soup eventually thickens. The chopped mushrooms are then added and sprinkled with chopped parsley before serving.

MUSTARD GREENS (See under CABBAGE.)

MYRRH (*Commiphora myrrha*)

Brief Description

Shrubs yielding myrrh gum grow upwards to 30 feet in height and are native to northeastern Africa and southwestern Asia, especially in and around the Red Sea. The part used is the exudation from natural cracks in the bark or from manmade incisions. The exudation is a pale-yellow liquid which soon hardens to form yellowish-red or reddish-brown tears or masses which are then collected.

Cures Breath, Gum Problems

In 1 pint of boiling water, steep 2 sprigs of coarsely chopped parsley, 3 whole spice cloves, 1 tsp. of powdered myrrh and 1/4 tsp. powdered goldenseal. Stir occasionally while cooling, and then pour the clear liquid part through a strainer and use as a mouth wash to help get rid of bad breath, or gargle to get rid of a sore throat.

Raymond Saunders of Detroit, Michigan wrote to me several years back about his own personal experience with myrrh for canker sores. They were caused by a certain food which he was allergic to. One day, while reading through the Bible, he came upon a verse mentioning myrrh. A thought immediately flashed into his mind, "This will help you with your mouth problems."

He bought a box of cotton swabs, then some Nature's Way brand myrrh gum at a local health food store. Going home, he emptied the contents of 2 capsules of the powdered gum onto the surface of a clean plate. Then he wet 2 cotton swabs under the tap before dipping them into the powder and applied them directly to the cold sores in his mouth.

Using this treatment twice each day, his condition completely cleared up in less than a week. This same remedy also works well for fever blisters that form on the lips. For curing gingivitis or inflammation of the gums, just dip your wet toothbrush in a little powdered myrrh and brush the gums every day until the problem disappears.

Because of its decided antibiotic effects, myrrh gum appears in certain formulas (Sinese, Herpese, Resist-All and Ginger-Up) used to treat allergies and infections. These are available from Great American Natural Products of Florida (see Appendix).

N

NASTURTIUM (See under ORNAMENTAL FLOWERS.)

NECTARINE (See under PEACH AND PEAR.)

(STINGING) NETTLE (*Urtica dioica)*

Brief Description

A perennial plant found all over the world. In America it grows in waste places and gardens and along roadsides, fences and walls in the states northward from Colorado, Missouri and South Carolina. The square, bristly stem grows from 2–7 feet high and bears pointed leaves which are downy underneath, and small, greenish flowers that grow in clusters from July to September.

Fantastic Hemostat

Nothing seems to stop profuse bleeding more quickly and effectively than stinging nettle! Because the evidence to be presented is so incredible, the source from which it has been obtained needs to be cited as well in order to make everything more believable.

Francis P. Porcher was a surgeon and physician in the Southern Confederacy. His book, *Resources of the Southern Fields and Forests,* was an important medical text during the Civil War. In it, he related how he and another doctor deliberately cut open and laid bare a major artery of an adult sheep. Then just by soaking some gauzelike material in a strong cold tea made of stinging nettle and applying the same directly to the open wound, he was able to stop all bleeding within just a matter of minutes. More remarkable yet, was the fact that when the pressed juice of the plant was added to fresh blood poured out into the palm of the hand, it immediately began coagulating.

To make a strong solution for your own personal needs, bring 1 quart of water to a boil. Remove from the heat and add a generous handful of *freshly* chopped stinging nettle plant. Cover and let steep for an hour, before straining. Always best to use when cold. Dried plant materials may be used, but don't work quite as well. Tea may be used internally for bleeding ulcers or externally as a wash or poultice to stop any major hemorrhaging.

Remarkable Hair Tonic for Baldness

Stinging nettle lotion seems to help hair grow again where baldness may now be present. The following two lotions should be used at the same time every morning after washing and rinsing the hair as you normally would do. The alcoholic portion to be used should be diluted by half as much of the infusion prior to rubbing into the scalp good with the fingertips. And when doing so, be sure to bend your head down low, massaging the lotion in from the nape of the neck upwards towards the front. Afterwards, allow the scalp to dry naturally without using a towel or hair dryer.

In 1 qt. or 4 cups of gin, put 2 handfuls of washed and chopped freshly picked stinging nettle, 3/4 handful of chopped fresh rosemary, 1 handful of chopped or cut fresh chamomile flowers and 2/3 handful of chopped fresh sage. Cover the fruit jar with a good, tight lid and let stand exposed to *indirect* (shaded) sunlight for 2 1/2 weeks, making sure you shake the contents of the bottle good twice each day. Strain and refrigerate in a clean fruit jar with a lid.

Bring 1 1/2 qts. of Perrier or other bottled mineral water to a boil, adding half each of a small, coarsely chopped rutabaga and unpeeled potato, and 1 diced stalk of celery. Cover with lid, reduce heat and simmer for 25 mins., then strain liquid into another pan, discarding the vegetables. Reheat to boiling point and add 1/2 handful of coarsely chopped, fresh stinging nettle, 1/2 handful of chopped, fresh garden sage, 1/4 tsp. grated horseradish root and juice from half of a lemon. Cover and remove from heat, allowing to steep for 50 minutes. When cool, strain and refrigerate in a clean fruit jar with a lid.

When using the alcoholic extract, just remember to dilute 1 part of it with 1/2 part of the infusion. If used regularly for several months, new hair growth should become fairly evident.

Fun Recipes for a More Slender Image

The late plant forager, Euell Gibbons, once wrote that "stinging nettle is very efficacious in removing unwanted pounds!" Those obese individuals who've written to me in the past desperate for advice on how to reduce and whom I've put on a semi-diet of stinging nettle have reported up to 32 1/4 lbs. in just three months or less!

Nettles should be collected in the early Spring when they are 4–8 inches high. As the plant matures, it becomes pretty tough and quite unpalatable. A pair of good leather gloves is recommended to protect the hands when handling the stuff. And heavy paper bags are preferable to plastic ones for carrying the nettle in.

After you've gathered enough nettle it should be washed in cold water. A pair of kitchen tongs will be of considerable help when removing the washed greens from the water. Allow them to drain on paper towels for a few minutes before refrigerating. They'll keep for up to a week.

Nettles freeze very well. Place the rinsed nettles in a large kettle. Pour boiling water over them to cover. After 5 mins. drain the water off, pack them into freezer containers and freeze. In the frozen state they'll keep for up to 9 months as a rule.

Nettle Greens, Georgia Style

Needed: 2 qts. stinging nettles; 3/4 cup stock from boiled chicken wings and chopped, cooked meat from those wings; 3 sliced green onions; 2 hard-boiled eggs and 1/4 tsp. lemon juice.

Snip greens into bite-size pieces. Put in pan with other ingredients except the eggs. Simmer on low heat for 20 minutes. Remove and serve, topped with sliced hard-boiled eggs. Season to taste with a little kelp, if needed.

Cream of Nettle Soup

Needed: 1 1/2 qts. nettle greens; 1/3 cup Perrier or other mineral water; 1/4 cup sesame seed oil; 1/4 cup whole wheat flour; 3 cups canned goat's milk.

Cook the nettles with water in covered saucepan over medium heat for 10 mins. Cool 15 mins., then purée in blender or food processor. In a saucepan, warm up the oil and stir in the flour, mixing both well. Then slowly add the goat's milk and cook until the mixture thickens over a low heat. Add the puréed nettles and heat thoroughly. Add some kelp to season. Serves 4.

Slenderizing Nettle Ale

This is a nice thirst-quenching ale that I've recommended highly to those seeking to lose weight. It's a healthier alternative to diet drinks and diet colas, not to mention helping shed unwanted pounds from around the thighs and hips in particular.

Needed: 4 qts. nettle greens; 2 gals. water; 2 thinly sliced lemons; 3 thinly sliced limes; 2 oz. grated fresh ginger root; 1/2 tsp. powdered nutmeg; 1/4 tsp. powdered mace; 2 cups light brown sugar; 1 cake of active yeast.

Boil the first 4 ingredients gently in a large open kettle or big pot for 50 mins. Strain through 4 layers of cheesecloth before adding sugar. Cool to lukewarm. Dissolve the yeast in 2 cups of this ale liquid, then stir in the remaining ale. Bottle in quart fruit jars or clean gallon jars with narrow spouts. Let stand for one week in a cool place. Refrigerate 15 hrs. before drinking.

NOTE: I'm deeply indebted to Darcy Williamson, author of *How to Prepare Common Wild Foods,* for her nettle recipes, which have been somewhat adapted to fit the needs of this book.

NUTMEG AND MACE (*Myristica fragrans*)

Brief Description

Nutmeg is the seed of the nutmeg tree, which is an evergreen with spreading branches and very dense foliage, reaching to a height of 66 feet or so. A native of the Molucca Islands of Indonesia, nutmeg is now cultivated in many tropical regions, but is produced commercially mainly in Indonesia and the island of Grenada in the West Indies.

The fruit of the nutmeg tree is fleshy like an apricot and about 2.4 inches in length. Upon ripening, it splits in half, exposing a bright-red, net-like aril wrapped around a dark reddish-brown and brittle shell within which lies a single seed. The net-like aril is mace, which on drying turns from red to yellowish or orange brown. The dried brown seed, after the shell is broken and discarded, is nutmeg.

Wonderful Stomach Tonic

Nutmeg and mace have been used for centuries to treat gas, indigestion, nausea, vomiting and other stomach as well as kidney problems. Mix thoroughly 1 1/2 tsps. of powdered slippery elm bark and dashes of powdered nutmeg and mace together with a little cold water in order to form a smooth paste that's not lumpy. Then bring a pint of half-and-half to the boiling point, removing immediately from the heat and quickly adding the powdered herb and spice paste. Keep stirring with a wooden ladle for about half a minute until the paste is thoroughly mixed in. Let it cool until lukewarm, before drinking 1/2 cup of it. Repeat this procedure three times daily, always drinking the mixture warm to help heal stomach problems.

Marijuana Substitute for Mental Disorders

In our present society, more and more people are turning to drugs and alcohol in order to escape reality and enter into a world of mental bliss and trance-like happiness. Especially is this so with high-school and college-age youth. Unfortunately for them, most of the psycho-active substances which they turn to are not only illegal to use, but also very bad for their personal health as well. In most cases, they become addicted in time to such things as marijuana, cocaine, "crack," LSD, heroin and alcohol.

Some medical doctors and psychiatrists who work with young people under such addictions have explored alternative possibilities for those of their patients who apparently still need some kind of mind-altering substance from time to time in order to help them better cope with reality, but which isn't addictive. Catnip is one of these, which is mentioned elsewhere in this book (see under CATNIP for details). Another, even more effective agent, is the food spice, nutmeg.

Both the *Journal of Neuropsychiatry* (March-April 1961) and the *New England Journal of Medicine* (August 22, 1963) have mentioned *only* 1 tbsp. of powdered nutmeg as being necessary to achieve somewhat "dream-like, floating and slightly euphoric" sensations. Such sensations of narcotic bliss have been equated with similar experiences produced by LSD, hashish, marijuana and alcohol.

One psychiatrist with the Department of Psychiatry at the University of Maryland School of Medicine in Baltimore subjected himself to an intake of nutmeg before recommending it to some of his own patients, in order to learn more about its hallucinogenic effects on the body. At 9 a.m. in the morning he took 1 tbsp. of the spice and drove to the university for his morning lectures. A particularly irritating problem had put him in a very angry mood. But, "by 10:30 a.m.," he said, "the anger was dispelled and I felt at peace with the world. I wandered out to a leisurely lunch with some friends and felt quite unconcerned about my work. This is unusual for me." Other feelings of detachment and isolation from reality reached a peak that ranged from between 6 to 24 hours and didn't completely disappear until some 36 hours later.

Prison convicts have often benefited from the use of nutmeg when other forms of illegal drugs were absolutely impossible to obtain. As with LSD, they usually lose all sense and meaning of time. Their personal guilts tend to disappear as they learn to be more forgiving and loving of themselves. Feelings of sensuality likewise increase, and it is not unusual for many male prisoners to experience near-constant erections for most of the 24 to 36 hours while under the influence of this incredible spice.

Another feature preferred by some psychiatrists who might recommend nutmeg to some of their patients on a very limited and controlled basis is that the user can wrench himself or herself back to reality any time they wish to; whereas, this isn't the case with either LSD, "crack," cocaine, heroin or marijuana. Also, the spice doesn't have any serious lingering side-effects once it wears off like the others seem to have. And nutmeg isn't addictive like the rest are.

Dramatically increased mental awareness, a closer communion with Nature and Infinity, a sense of drifting through time and space, deeper feelings of humility and peace and an attitude of being in control of what one wishes to experience, are some of the sensations which have been reported by college students, some nurses and a few doctors who have voluntarily tried nutmeg under carefully controlled conditions.

Certain physical discomforts are to be expected when under the influence of nutmeg, but nothing, it seems, that would be life-threatening. Bones and muscles in the body tend to ache, the eyes tend to hurt a little, the sinuses drain and limited diarrhea result from taking this spice. But some therapists and portions of their patients suffering from certain mental disorders seem to believe that these few inconveniences are worth putting up with in lieu of the greater therapeutic benefits to be derived from nutmeg.

Culinary Recipe

Besides eggnog, there are other creative dishes which call for the use of nutmeg and may be yet another way of obtaining this spice for mental pleasure without always having to ingest it straight.

Nutmeg-Baked Goldens

Pare and core 8 Golden Delicious apples 1/3 of the way down from the top. Place in a 13×9×2-in. baking pan. Combine 1 cup dark honey, 2/3 cup water, 1/4 cup lemon juice, 1/2 tsp. each grated lemon and lime peels, 1 tsp. nutmeg and 1 tsp. mace. Bring everything to a boil, then pour over and around the apples.

Bake, uncovered, at 350° F. 50–60 minutes or until apples are tender. Frequently baste with the liquid mixture in the pan every 10 minutes. Cool in the pan. When ready to serve, remove apples to serving dish. Add 1/4 cup boiling water to the pan to dilute the mixture in the pan, or simply use the nutmeg syrup in its full strength after heating up on the stove. Drizzle the mixture over the apples before topping with genuine vanilla ice cream. If desired, add rum or your favorite liqueur to softened ice cream and freeze for several hours or until sufficiently firm. Makes 8 delicious and invigorating servings!

NUTS

ACORN (*Quercus* species)
ALMOND (*Prunus amygdalus*)
BRAZIL (*Bertholletia excelsa*)
BUTTERNUT (*Juglans cinera*)
CASHEW (*Anacardium occidentale*)
CHESTNUT (*Castanea pumila*)
COCONUT (*Cocos nucifera*)
FILBERT (*Corylus avellana pontica, C. maxima*)
HAZELNUT (Synonym for filbert)
HICKORY (*Carya ovata*)
MACADAMIA (*Macadamia integrifolia, M. tenifolia*)
PEANUT (*Arachis hypogaea*)
PECAN (*Carya illinoensis*)
PINENUT (*Pinus* species)
PISTACHIO (*Pistacia vera*)
WALNUT (*Juglans nigra, J. regia*)

Brief Description

ACORN. Small nut-like fruits found on many species of oak with cup shapes resembling saucers. Acorns from red oak are bitter due to the tannin and must be processed before eating, while those of the white oak are sweet and edible raw.

ALMOND. Botanically classified as and related to fruits like peach and plum. The outer shell is leathery, but the seed inside the fruit, which can be either sweet or bitter, is the nut itself. Bitter almonds contain amygdalin or laetrile, and the oil contains mostly benzaldehyde, the same anti-cancer factor found in figs and mushrooms.

BRAZIL. This is one of the very few commercially available nuts which are never cultivated. It grows wild in the dense South American Amazon rain forest, the trees often towering up to 150 feet or higher. The nut is contained in a pod similar in shape to a coconut which holds 12–30 of them. When ripe these pods fall with such force they can bury themselves under the ground. Once removed from the pod the nuts are dried and put through a heavy brushing to remove their rough brown skin.

BUTTERNUT. The nut comes from the white walnut, a small tree with ash-gray bark, becoming separated into smooth ridges. The nut is found inside of a sticky, hairy husk, is thick and pointed and has very rough, obscure ridges on it.

CASHEW. This nut is the fruit of a tropical and subtropical evergreen, a species, interestingly enough, that's related to American poison ivy and poison sumac. The evergreen grows to about 40 feet tall and bears clusters of pear-shaped fruits called cashew apples. Below this fruit hangs the crescent-shaped cashew nut. The kernel has two shells, an outer one that's thin, flexible and somewhat leathery and an inner which is hard like most nuts and must be cracked open. Between both of these shells is a brown oil that's so toxic it has an extreme blistering effect on the skin. For this reason, the oil must be burned off before it can even be touched.

CHESTNUT. This is a magnificent tree growing almost to 100 feet with a very broad spread. Longfellow's poem to this effect—"Under the spreading chestnut tree, the village smithy stands. . ."—aptly describes its hugeness. Barely 100 years ago, vast forests stood in many parts of the eastern U.S.; but a severe blight at the turn of the century and over the next 40 years practically destroyed all of them. What remains today are crossbreeds of Japanese and Chinese species. The nuts grow 2–3 together in a spiney burr about the size of a baseball. When ripe the burr opens and the nuts are removed. This is the only nut usually served as a vegetable.

COCONUT. This is the fruit of the coconut palm, a very important economic product found throughout the tropics. Unopened coconuts keep at room temperature for 2 months. The white meat inside the shell can be eaten raw or fried. Or it can be grated and squeezed into a very rich, fatty "milk" of sorts.

FILBERT AND HAZELNUT. These brown-shelled nuts are actually fruits of the same bush that differ only in their shape. To tell the difference between them, hazelnuts are shorter and rounder than filberts. They have the sweetest meats of all the nuts and are mainly used in desserts and candies as a rule.

HICKORY. A tall, slender, straight tree belonging to the walnut clan. Also known as shagbark hickory. Stern schoolmasters of early America "taught readin', writin', and 'rithmetic, to the tune of the hick'ry stick," as the lines of one poem suggest. The outer husk of the nut is thick and woody, splitting to the bottom when the nut is ripe. The nut has prominent ridges, is quite sweet and edible.

MACADAMIA. Also called Queensland nut since it's native to Australia. The nut has a honey-brown shell that is extremely hard to crack open. The crisp, creamy-white nutmeat has a slightly sweet flavor to it.

PEANUT. Botanically classified as an underground pea of the legume (bean) family, peanut is also called ground nut or goober in the South. Native to Brazil, the peanut comes in two varieties—the small, round Spanish kind used for candy, butter and oil, and the larger, oval-shaped Virginia type which is generally used whole. About half of the entire U.S. peanut crop is made into peanut butter.

PECAN. It's believed that the pecan tree was distributed from its original home in the South by the Iroquois and other Native American tribes centuries ago, throughout the northern part of the U.S. When they made many canoe trips up and down the Illinois River and other tributaries, they deliberately planted the biggest and thinnest-shelled nuts at their main portages. The soft nutmeat is twin lobed and wrapped in thin, shiny, light-brown shells, and was a mainstay in many an Indian diet.

PINENUT. Comes from various pines (mostly the pinon). A very sweet-flavored, high-protein kind of a nut that varies in size (1/3–2–in.), shape (cylindrical to round) and color (white to pale yellow).

PISTACHIO. The tree is part of the poison sumac family and contains green nuts with ivory-beige shells that split open upon ripening. Those with red shells have been colored with vegetable dye, and those with white shells have been coated with salt.

WALNUT. There are two types, black and English. The former have a strong flavor, and their dark-brown shells are somewhat difficult to open. The latter or more popular kind are white on the inside and golden tan to amber on the outside. Their light-brown shells are easy to open. Black walnut is chiefly used for medicinal purposes by the American herb industry, while the English kind are consumed raw or cooked.

Acorns and Oak for Burns and Liver Problems

The Iroquois had a pretty nifty way for treating serious burns and rashes suffered by those unfortunate enough to have made contact with poison ivy and sumac. They would gather up a sufficient quantity of acorns, split them with a heavy stone or the blunt end of a tomahawk, then throw them into a large iron kettle full of boiling water.

After the mixture had boiled down to half of its original amount several hours later, it was strained and the strong tannic acid solution was saved for medicinal uses. Some of this healing water would then be applied to any severe burn or rash on the skin in the form of a poultice, as well as bathing the afflicted area often.

Today the same remedy can still be used with great success. Put two dozen or so cracked acorns in 1 1/2 gallons of hot water and boil down to half this amount, uncovered for a couple of hours. Then strain and store in sealed quart jars in a cool place until needed. Can this solution actually work in healing severe burns of any kind? Some medical doctors reading this might have their doubts, but clinical evidence suggests otherwise. The July 1926 issue of *Annals of Surgery* contained a lengthy and detailed report of some 17 pages by two Cleveland physicians who *successfully* treated extremely serious burns in children and adults with nothing but tannic acid. The before and after pictures speak for themselves. You too, in the confines of your own home, can do the very same thing for yourself and loved ones by using the above acorn solution or the following oak bark solution.

Simmer 2/3 cup of coarsely cut, dried oak bark in 1 qt. of boiling water, for 20 mins. on low heat. Then remove and steep an additional hour. Strain and drink 1 cup every other day for liver injury and to prevent hardening of the arteries. Or else use to wash and dress wounds and major burns when cold. Strips of clean gauze may be soaked in either solution to dress burns with and then changed every few hours.

Almonds for "Dish-Pan" Hands and Sore Lungs

Sweet almond oil is a super emollient for chapped, "dishpan" hands, diaper rash, herpes sores, shingles, psoriasis and lupus erythematosus. Just mix the juice of 1 lemon and lime with 4 tbsps. of oil and rub on thoroughly. Even helps to whiten or lighten dark skin somewhat.

"Almond Milk" is a very popular drink for throat and lung problems in Hong Kong and Canton, China. To prepare the drink, 10 parts of sweet almonds and 1 part of bitter almonds are soaked in water with a little rice. After both become tender enough, they are then ground into a paste by running them through a small food grinder or nut mill of some sort. The resulting milky mixture is strained to remove coarse particles and then diluted with a little more water and some honey before cooking on low heat until the consistency is somewhat syrupy.

A cup of the same is recommended 2–3 times daily to relieve hoarseness and the raspy or wheezing sounds common to heavy smokers and asthmatics. This is also good for scratchy, irritated throats and dry or hacking coughs.

Mental Energy from Brazil Nuts

All amino acids are valuable sources of energy, especially that needed for optimum brain function. Communication within the brain and between it and the rest of the central nervous system occurs through chemical "languages," called neurotransmitters. There are about 50 such languages; the amino acids, either as precursors or peptides, account for the majority of them.

Now Brazil nuts are one of the very few nuts or seeds that are so incredibly rich in both essential as well as nonessential amino acids. An Italian scientist who has studied the nut very carefully, calls it the "meat vegetable," because of its very high A, B-complex and C vitamin contents, not to mention the tremendous protein present as well.

Some university students in Sao Paulo will stir a teaspoonful or so of the meal into some juice and drink it for mental pep before taking their final exams. The meal can be purchased from some specialty food shops or else made by cracking open about 10 large nuts and running the meat through a nut mill.

Butternut for Intestinal Problems

Joseph Smith, Jr., a great American prophet, sometimes joked with his people (the Latter-Day Saints or Mormons) in a friendly way while sermonizing on topics touching human health. "If you have problems with your bowels," he was apt to say, "then take some strong physic or go gnaw down a butternut tree somewhere to get things movin' again."

Several of his closest confidants were themselves trained Thomsonian herb doctors, who often used butternut meal or tea mixed with some salt to correct the most stubborn constipation or eliminate parasites such as tapeworm. Two teaspoons of ground butternut mixed with a pinch of sea salt and stirred into hot oatmeal or several cracked butternuts simmered in a pint of boiling water with a tad of salt added, were two ways of taking this nut to give relief.

Cashews Make a Delicious Milk Substitute

Tired of milk or just can't drink it for some reason? Then try one of the most interesting and flavorful concoctions I devised some years ago for several adults and children who were allergic to real milk.

In a food blender, combine together at high speed for 4 minutes the following items: 1 cup of shelled, chopped raw cashew nuts, 1/2 cup unsweetened pineapple juice, 1 tbsp. *each* of honey and pure maple syrup, 1/4 cup chopped or crushed ice cubes, 2 3/4 cups spring or distilled water, pinch of powdered cardamon and 1/16 tsp. of pure vanilla flavoring.

After blending well, refrigerate in a closed container of some kind. This makes one of the sweetest, most delicious milk substitutes I know of. The above recipe yields about 4 cups and may be used on cooked or packaged cereals or just consumed straight by itself.

It's especially handy for those who are seeking to lose weight or are allergic to cow's milk in some way. In addition, this cashew "milk" furnishes a terrific protein drink for athletes and body builders.

Roasted Chestnuts for Bleeding Ulcers

A sure cure for bleeding ulcers is an old remedy I picked up some years back while lecturing among the Dunkard Brethren in North Carolina. This is an old-order religious group like unto the Amish, who advocate baptism by immersion; hence, their nickname "Dunkard."

One of their bearded ministers shared with me an effective treatment for all manner of stomach complaints. Roasted chestnuts are to be taken and run through a nut mill until rendered into a fine meal. After which about 2 tbsps. of the meal was combined in a wooden salad bowl with 1 tsp. of dark honey and 2 tsps. of pure maple syrup, and everything stirred good with a wooden ladle until a soft paste was formed. This was then served on a metal soup spoon and taken internally to stop intestinal bleeding and help heal ulcers.

I've had occasion to work with this unusual electuary myself from time to time and find it works well for the problems intended. It may also be used with satisfying results by women who experience excess menstruation.

Jock Itch and Cataracts Disappear with Coconut

An admirer of my work with herbs from Valleja, California, wrote to me about her own curiously devised remedy for getting rid of cataracts. "Take the fresh juice from an opened coconut and with an eye dropper apply as much as the eye can hold. Then apply hot wet cloths that have been wrung out over the eyes and lay down for 10 mins. One treatment is generally enough if done early on when they start to form," she claimed.

More remarkable still is an old Ayurvedic remedy for jock itch or vaginal infection, which I picked up from an old folk healer in Bombay. Dry an empty coconut shell in the sun for a week. Then break it into small pieces by smashing it good with a sledge hammer. Gather up the fragments and soak them in 1 qt. of vodka or Scotch for 11 days, shaking the solution twice daily. Strain, then bottle.

Bathe the groin area as often as needed to get rid of jock itch. Douche regularly to eliminate vaginitis. Soak feet in a pan of the stuff to stop athlete's foot. Or soak fingernails in the same to clear up any fungal infection that develops beneath them. Works relatively quick as a rule and seems to be quite effective in most instances.

Sweeten Your Breath with Filberts

The breath may be somewhat sweetened by chewing on a few filberts or hazelnuts for awhile. They work not so much because they're aromatic like peppermint would be, as they do by absorbing much of the bad breath like a sponge does water. They're quite expensive, but worth investing in for this purpose and to help stob a throbbing toothache by crushing several into some powder and sprinkling on top of a little peanut butter, before applying directly to the site of pain for relief.

Hickory Oil Makes a Tasty Condiment

Long before we came to have such condiments as catsup, mustard, pickles and mayonnaise, the Native Americans had devised their own tasty kinds from various nuts. The Cayuga (a tribe of the great Iroquois nation) used to crush the meats of the hickory, walnut, butternut and chestnut, then slowly boil them in water, making sure to skim off the oil which floated to the surface and saving it. This oil was boiled again by itself and lightly seasoned with a pinch of salt.

This condiment was later used with bread, potatoes, pumpkin, squash, buffalo jerky, roast venison and many other foods. The nut meats left after skimming off the oil were often seasoned and mixed with mashed potatoes or else added in with cornmeal to make an incredibly delicious bread. These same techniques ought to be used more often today as replacements for the stuff we put on our hamburgers, hot dogs and salads that are unhealthy and harmful to the body.

Macadamias for the Liver and Alcoholism

A snappy cocktail that seems to satisfy the urge to drink and to help rejuvenate the liver is made from macadamias (preferably raw), ripe tomatoes (or the canned juice), a squeeze of lemon juice, a pinch of cayenne and a thumbnail full of raw, grated ginger root. Combine 5 macadamias, 3 medium, very ripe tomatoes, 1/2 tsp. lemon juice, the pepper and ginger into a blender and mix well for 1 1/2 minutes, adding a little canned tomato juice, if necessary, to thin down a bit if it becomes too thick. Drink slowly by itself and E-N-J-O-Y! Beats the heck out of alcohol and tonifies a weak liver.

Peanut Butter for Hemophilia and Mouth Problems

A report appeared in *Nature* (194:980) for 1962, showing that peanuts have within them an unusual hemostatic factor, which can be of considerable benefit to hemophiliacs or those subject to chronic and prolonged hemorrhaging. Peanuts seem to have the ability to reduce this problem somewhat; wherefore, hemophiliacs are encouraged to eat more raw peanuts and to consume more peanut butter.

Peanut butter is also very good for helping to hold other medicaments in place within the mouth, when they're unable to be retained there of their own accord. For instance, when placing a crushed garlic clove by an aching tooth for relief, first put it on top of a small square piece of white bread covered with peanut butter before inserting. You'll find it stays in place a lot better.

Sores on the mouth or tongue are often difficult to treat with herbs, since they can't be retained for very long to do much good. But when a small slice of white bread covered with some peanut butter is sprinkled with either goldenseal root or white oak bark and then placed inside the mouth against the sores, better healing results can be shortly expected.

And a more convenient and pleasant way to take cayenne pepper so it doesn't burn the heck out of your gut is to mix a pinch of the spice with a little peanut butter and honey, before swallowing it whole. This is also a good way to persuade children to take bitter or burning herbs.

Pecans Relieve Migraines

As strange as it might seem, a small poultice made out of raw meats of pecans and English walnuts will relieve a headache! In a blender mix (well) 2 tbsps. each of both nut meats and a little water until a thick purée forms. Then spread on two squares of gauze and tape to either side of the temples while reclining. Remain this way for several hours or until the throbbing ceases.

An Apache Pinenut Beauty Mask

Back in the early 70s, I was introduced to a former runner-up in the Miss Arizona Beauty Pageant, who just happened to be Apache by birth. Later I accompanied her and some others to her home, where we met her folks. The girl's mother, a full-blooded Apache squaw herself, had one of the nicest complexions I had ever seen in a woman nearing the half-century mark of her life.

After chatting with them awhile, I gathered up enough courage to ask her outright what she did to make her skin look so young and beautiful. It was then that she explained to me about her nightly mask which she always put on before retiring.

Pinenuts, I came to find out, were her only secret ingredient. She would take a couple of handfuls and methodically chew up small portions of them very briefly in order to remove the shell, after which she spit them into a wooden bowl. Once this had been done she'd then run the nut meat through a small mill to make meal out of them.

Now pinenut meal is extremely greasy to say the least, but exceptionally wonderful to keep the skin from drying out. Before retiring each night she would mix some of this meal with a little goat's milk to make a soft paste, which was next rubbed on her face, forehead and throat. The rich amino acids from both the nut meal and the goat's milk had a chance to penetrate through the pores of her skin as she slept, and literally, rebeautify and enliven once more tired, old skin. By the time she awoke next morning and removed the mask with cold spring water, there was a supple youthfulness pretty enough to whistle at and draw the stares of many younger fellows.

A Nice Pistachio-Peanut Massage Oil

A good massage oil for dehydrated skin above the shoulders and for loose, flabby skin on the arms, buttocks and thighs, can be made by taking a handful of white, shelled pistachios which have been coarsely chopped and then simmering them in a quart of peanut oil on low heat for approximately an hour. After the oil has had time to cool down a bit to lukewarm, it should be strained before massaging well into the skin on these areas of the body.

Useful Walnut Remedies

Both kinds of walnut, especially the black, have a myriad of uses including the nut shell and tree leaves and bark. For one thing, the fat in English walnut kernels is a kind that the heart can easily handle without any problem.

An excellent herb tea for heart disease is made from the woody, interior walls of walnuts. Use the walls from 4–5 English nuts for each cup. Soak them overnight. Then boil them for 20 mins. the next morning. Take 3 cups a day. This tea really alleviates the pressure and the pain in the chest. Tea may be sweetened with honey.

The bark and leaves of English walnut make a darned good mouthwash for preventing and reducing cavities. Bring 1 qt. of water to a boil, then add a generous handful of well-pounded fresh bark. Cover, reducing heat, and simmer for 15 mins. Remove from heat, uncover and add 1 handful of finely cut leaves. Cover again and steep for 50 mins. Strain and store in the refrigerator. Gargle and flush the teeth with a cup of this mixture two to three times daily or after every meal.

Certain skin blemishes, ringworm and even warts just seem to disappear as if by magic, whenever *green* or immature black walnut is used externally. Just make a couple of incisions into its outer shell and rub the juice on whatever you want cleared up. At first there may be a slight burning sensation, but don't worry. At other times, the juice could turn the skin where it's applied a little brown, but this will eventually wear off. Practically all kinds of warts, dark, ugly age spots and ringworm have been successfully eliminated with this treatment.

The pericarp or ripened shell of the walnut is an effective remedy for fungal infection and to get rid of intestinal parasites as well. The best way in which to extract as much of the juglone (the active substance) as possible, is to use boiled cabbage juice which has just been strained.

Reboil about 1 qt. of the juice, adding the green, broken and bruised pericarps from 8 unripe walnuts. Cover, reduce heat to low, and simmer 15 mins. Remove from stove and steep an additional 25 mins. Strain and refrigerate. Take 3 cups daily in between meals to get rid of parasites and soak hands or feet, gargle and flush the mouth or else douche the vagina to remove any kind of persistent fungus.

The walnut meat itself is fantastic for dissolving and eliminating kidney and gallstones. Clinical reports published between 1957 and 1961 in the *Chinese Journal of Surgery* related how hundreds of patients young and old were cured of stones. In all cases, 2 1/4 cups of raw walnut meat were deep-fried in pure olive oil until crisp. The meat was then ground to a coarse powder and mixed with 2 1/4 tbsps. of dark honey to form a somewhat smooth paste. This paste was then given to each patient for two days, at the end of which most stones had partially dissolved, turned soft and been eliminated.

For excessive accumulation of phlegm in the lungs and persistent coughing in the throat, a combination of walnut and ginger seems to do the trick every single time! This is a very ancient Chinese remedy, which calls for the meat from 3 walnuts to be ground in a nut mill and 3 slices of fresh ginger root to be finely grated. Both are then combined with any kind of warm liquid or hot broth and slowly swallowed before retiring. By the next morning all symptoms of the coughing and phlegm will have disappeared for good. This remedy is especially handy for asthma, bronchitis and those who smoke a lot.

The teeth may be occasionally polished by emptying the contents of a capsule of powdered black walnut on a wet toothbrush. Black walnut powder also helps to remove plaque and yellow stains rather nicely. Use only occasionally, though, since frequent use might result in some loss of tooth enamel.

A tea made of walnut leaves is quite useful for drying up excessive milk flow once a child is past the nursing stage. Bring 2 cups of water to a boil. Remove from heat and add 3 tbsps. fresh-cut or dried, crumbled leaves and 1 tsp. chopped green outer shell which surrounds the actual walnut. Steep for an hour. Drink 2 cups each day.

Gray Hair Gone with Walnut

Gray can be easily removed from dark brown and black hair by dyeing them with walnut. A Texas grandmother explained to me once how she used to take 1 1/4 cups each of bruised walnut husks and coarsely chopped leaves and soak them both in a gallon of spring water (Perrier water may be substituted) for 24 hrs. After which she'd then pour the soak water into a large saucepan and boil until the liquid was reduced by half the original amount.

When it had sufficiently cooled, she'd then strain and add 1 1/8 tbsp. of either eau de Cologne or gin, bottle and store in her pantry cupboard. A small amount would then be put on the hair daily with a sponge, wherever there was gray until a darker color had resulted. The only drawback to this, she said, was that everything the dye touched, including her scalp, turned somewhat dark as well. But she felt that a little inconvenience was worth putting up with in order to regain a more youthful looking appearance.

Ellagic Acid for Paralysis and Cancer

According to the *Journal of Pharmaceutical Sciences* (Oct. 1968) and *Cancer Research* (May 1986), both black walnut and cashew nut shells contain a crystalline compound, which is of important therapeutic significance in treating muscular paralysis due to electrical shock, hypertension and skin cancer. Grapes, strawberries, black currants, raspberries and other nut shells also contain this valuable plant phenol as well.

In the first study, two groups of mice were subjected to mild electrocution. Seven out of the 17 receiving black walnut shell extract remained alive, while 14 out of 17 rodents without the benefit of ellagic acid, perished in the other group. And in the second study, mice fed this substance from the above berries and nuts, experienced 45% less tumors when exposed to a chemically induced skin cancer and a prolonging of onset of the tumors by up to 10 weeks, than did another group without ellagic acid. Therefore, it's strongly recommended that these nuts and berries be used in preferably liquid forms (berry juices and nut shell teas) when treating any of the aforementioned health problems.

Nut Meats for Stuffings

Consider the meats of fresh almonds, cashews, filberts, macadamias, peanuts, pecans and walnuts for use when making stuffings for roast poultry and fish, as well as for gravies and sauces. Nut meats really give them a dimension of culinary excitement, not to mention incredible, mouthwatering zest.

Homemade Nut Butters and Oils

You can make your own nut butters at home, either separately or several put together for a very interesting blend with an intriguing taste to it. Simply remove the meats from the shells of a couple of handfuls of any kind of nut and put them in a blender or food processor after mashing them first with a heavy object. Add 1 cup of cold water to begin with and turn on to "liquefy," continuing to add a little more water as needed until a somewhat thick, creamy consistency has been achieved. Remove with a rubber spatula and refrigerate. Nut butters like this taste great on pumpernickel, rye or cinnamon-raisin breads.

Hickory nut or black walnut butters of more runny consistency make very good sunburn lotions. Just follow the above same instructions with the exception of adding less nut meats and more water. They can then be rubbed directly onto a bad sunburn with good results.

To make nut oils, just remove the shells from 2–3 double handfuls of any kind of nut and then pound them good with a hammer or heavy flat iron. After this put them in 2 qts. of hot water and boil until their oils melt and float to the top. Skim this off and allow to cool. What results is a very good and rare cooking oil that may be used any number of ways to create some rather exotic-tasting dishes you won't forget!

O

OAK (See NUTS—ACORN)

OATS (See GRAINS)

OKRA (*Hibiscus esculentus*)

Brief Description

Okra is an annual herb with a tall, erect stem that grows 3–7 feet high and is covered with small hairs. The leaves are cordate, 3- to 5-lobed and coarsely toothed, while the large flowers are yellow with crimson centers to them. Okra pods are anywhere from 5 to 12 inches long, horn-like in appearance, green or creamy green in color and with ridges that are either smooth or hairy. The pods contain numerous seeds that are rounded, striate and hairy. The entire okra plant is aromatic emitting an ordor resembling cloves.

An unusual use for okra pods has been as blood plasma replacements. According to Volume Five of *The Wealth of India,* doctors used the mucilage in the pods as a blood volume expander in severely hemorrhaged mongrel dogs with good results. Further research some day may find this to be a useful agent in human blood transfusions

Effective Burn Dressing

For major burns of any kind, a very nice liquid dressing made out of slippery elm bark, white oak bark and okra can be effectively applied in serious cases where emergency medical facilities are not immediately available or economically affordable. The first thing to remember, though, when dealing with any critical situation like this is *TO REMAIN CALM*. Keep a cool head, let common sense prevail and follow the simple methods outlined here.

The afflicted area should be covered with or soaked in ice water (or preferably, clean snow) for some relief, until the dressing can be applied. In a stainless steel pot, bring 5 cups of *spring* or *distilled* water to a rolling boil. Reduce heat to a low setting and add 2 cups *each* of sliced okra and dried, cut slippery elm bark (*not* the powder), together with 1-1/4 cups of dried, cut white oak bark. In case the inside bark of slippery elm isn't available, the same amount of dried, cut comfrey root may be substituted instead. Cover and simmer mixture *for no more* than 45 minutes at the most. Mixture should be fairly thick and slimy by this time. Strain immediately while still hot, then again through several layers of muslin material.

For more rapid cooling, pour strained contents on a clean cookie sheet or layer pan covered with a clean piece of linen cloth of some sort. Set in the freezer for awhile to cool, but check it every so often to see that it doesn't become unduly stiff or frozen. Also setting the cookie sheet or layer pan on a table top and letting an electric fan blow cool air across the hot contents is yet another way of cooling it more quickly.

Before applying this cool mucilage combination to the injured skin, be sure that your hands are properly scrubbed and disinfected by soaking them in a small solution of Listerine Antiseptic Mouth Wash. Now there are basically two ways to apply this wonderfully healing herbal slime onto the burned skin. It may be lightly brushed on with a *sterile*, genuine camel hair brush with a fairly wide tip and then covered with gauze strips. Or else the gauze strips themselves may be first saturated with this herbal mucilage material and then laid onto the burned area by hand.

Five hours is about maximum before the dressing needs to be changed. Rapid healing will ensue and become evident in a day or so. The mucilage will not only reduce the pain and swelling of the severe inflammation, but the tannic acid present from the white oak bark should proliferate new cell growth and strongly discourage infectious bacteria from forming later on.

Poison Ivy and Psoriasis Relief

The foregoing treatment for major burns is also a handy remedy for relieving and promoting the healing of poison ivy rash and the misery of psoriasis. Follow the same basic instructions, except to omit the white oak bark. The solution should be strained while still hot, but may be cooled more slowly at room temperature. The mucilage can then be rubbed on the skin by hand and allowed to remain for several hours before repeating the treatment as often as may be necessary.

Okra Recipe

A former "P.M. Magazine" chef and famous Encinitas, California restaurateur, LaMont Burns, highlights a unique chicken gumbo in his recent book, *Down Home Southern Cooking* (Doubleday & Co., Inc., 1987) which has been reprinted here with the kind permission of his publisher.

Southern Chicken Gumbo

Needed: 1 (2-1/2 lb.) chicken; 3 tbsps. flour; 3 tbsps. butter; 1 tsp. brown sugar; 1/2 chopped, sweet red pepper; 4 cups cut okra; 1 large can tomatoes or 5–6 ripe, skinned tomatoes; 1 can corn or niblets or kernels cut from 3 ears of fresh corn; 2 sprigs chopped parsley; 2 snipped basil leaves.

Simmer chicken in water to cover for 1 hour. Remove chicken from stock and cool. Skin chicken and pick meat from bones. Cut chicken into bite-size pieces. Brown flour in butter, add vegetables, sugar and chicken stock. Simmer until tender and gumbo is thick. Add cooked and cut chicken and serve hot.

OLIVE (*Olea europaea*)

Brief Description

The olive tree is an evergreen, commonly found in all of the Mediterranean countries, but widely cultivated in tropical climates as well. The hard, yellow wood of the gnarled trunk is covered by gray-green bark. The branches extend upwards to 25 feet or more. The leathery leaves are dark green on top and have silvery scales underneath. The tree yields fragrant white flowers and an oblong or nearly round type of fruit called a drupe that becomes shiny black when ripe. Other kinds of drupes would be plums, cherries, apricots and peaches. The oil which is produced from the fruit is quite valuable, having worldwide appeal for its excellent cooking and baking properties.

Prevents Heart Disease and Cancer

Considerable attention has been focused in the past on the virtues of such polyunsaturated oils as corn oil, which are known to help reduce serum cholesterol in the blood. The problem with polyunsaturates, though, is that they tend also to lower "good" cholesterol (high-density lipoproteins or HDL) *and* seem to promote tumor development as well.

But lately a lot of favorable attention has been given monosaturated fats like olive oil, for instance. Not only can olive oil lower "bad" cholesterol (low-density lipoproteins or LDL) just as well as corn oil can, but it doesn't adversely affect the good HDL or promote cancer either. These are two definite advantages which olive oil seems to hold over many other kinds of cooking oils.

Epidemiological studies conducted in four European cities—Uppsala, Sweden; London, England; Geneva, Switzerland and Naples, Italy—found only the southern Italian population to have both very low incidence of coronary heart disease deaths and low serum concentrations of the harmful LDL. And this is due primarily to "the almost exclusive use of olive oil as the only visible fat" in their diets.

Furthermore, food availability data in 30 different countries was analyzed by computer in relation to death rates for cancers of the breast, prostate, ovary and colon. Mortality rates for all 4 cancers were related to total fat intake and animal fat intake, but not to vegetable fat consumption. Intake of milk, meat, animal protein and calories from animal sources were positively associated with cancer death rates. Especially interesting, however, was the fact that inhabitants of countries in which olive oil is a major source of fat in the diet tended to have more reduced risks of all 4 cancers, particularly of breast cancer. This data appeared in the December 1986 issue of *Cancer*.

Soothes and Heals Inflammation

Olive oil is terrific for ulcers and burns. To relieve heartburn, indigestion and ulcers brought on by stress, spicy food, alcohol, coffee and the like, just mix together 2 tbsps. of pure virgin olive oil with the white of one raw egg. Then take internally serveral times a day to experience rapid relief.

Severe burns on the surface of the skin can be effectively treated with just olive oil and egg whites, when nothing else is available. My own personal experience with this during a winter in the mid-1970's convinced me of its genuine healing effects. At that time we lived on a small farm in the central Utah community of Manti. I had put a can of granulated honey on the back of our coal-and-wood stove, which had a roaring fire going in it at the time. Worrying that the honey might get all over the stove and be hard to clean off, I immediately reacted before thinking and reached out with a couple of cooking gloves to remove the can. Just as I did so, a very hot geyser of honey spewed forth from the edge of the can, spraying the entire inside of my right forearm. I let out a considerable yelp of pain and dropped what I had on the floor.

Almost as if by sudden instinct. I ran outside and pushed my injured arm deep into a huge pile of snow to find temporary relief from the intense pain and burning. My father threw an old packing quilt over me so I could remain somewhat warm.

I stayed outside until I could no longer endure the cold. My father, meanwhile, prepared a simple remedy which his mother, Barbara Liebhardt Heinerman, had brought with her from Temesvár, Hungary (now part of Romania) many years ago.

It consisted of mixing 2 cups of virgin olive oil with the whites from 6 farm-fresh eggs that our chickens had laid the previous day. He then took an old basting brush from one of our kitchen drawers, sterilized it good under hot water and dried it thoroughly before using it to brush on the oil-egg white mixture with. After this, he lightly wrapped my injured arm from elbow to wrist with loose-fitting gauze.

This dressing remained on for about 16 hours until it was changed again the next day. Although it took awhile for the pain to decrease, healing was already evident by the following afternoon. Surprisingly no scars remained, except for one little 3/4 × 3/4-inch mark about 4 inches up from the wrist where the gauze had apparently become loose enough to expose the skin and probably cause some of the oil-egg white dressing to get wiped away on my blankets that night as I slept. In less than a week I was completely recovered and required no medical attention whatsoever.

Marvelous Degreaser

Olive oil makes one fantastic degreasing agent for getting other kinds of oil off the skin. An auto mechanic in Portsmouth, New Hampshire told me once that he never washed his hands in soap and water after working on customers' cars. "Heck no," he said, "I just pour some olive oil over them and rub it good into the greasy grime. Then I take some paper towels and wipe it all off. And if they're not clean yet, I just repeat the same process again until all of the grease has been removed. Then to remove the olive oil, I just run a little hot water over my hands and dry them with another paper towel."

Helps Tighten Loose Skin

For those who are bothered with loose, sagging skin around the face and throat areas or abdominal region due to recent loss of weight, an effective remedy used by Paul Neinast of Dallas in his famous beauty salon might just be worth trying. Neinast takes the yolks of two eggs and beats them good with 1/2 cup of olive oil. This then is brushed on the customer's face and throat and left there for 10 minutes. After which the stiffly beaten whites of both eggs are put over this, and the entire mask left for about half an hour. He claims that it really tightens up the skin good!

How to Get Rid of Gallstones

For the complete removal of gallstones, the following remedy seems to have worked for several thousand people across the U.S. and in Canada. Of this estimated number, I've personally interviewed about 125 within the last decade during my extensive lectures from coast-to-coast and in both countries. In every single instance, the treatment with some slight variations here and there always seems to have met with success. From these different variations, I've put together a relatively simple and pretty basic program that is 90% guaranteed to succeed in getting rid of stones.

The first step involves a two-day, mild-food fast and an easy internal cleansing that will help to prepare the body for the other steps later on. Only vegetables and fruits such as peaches, pears, soaked prunes (and the juice), figs and psyllium seeds should be consumed. In a food blender, combine 1 cup of carrot juice (either fresh or canned), 1 cup each of diced peach and pear halves (either fresh or canned with their respective syrups), about 5 pitted, soaked prunes *and* 1/4 cup bottled prune juice, 1 bunch of chopped parsley and 2 tbsps. powdered psyllium seeds from any local health food store. Liquefy good for 3–4 minutes. Makes a quart and can be refrigerated for several days. Drink 2 cups of this health juice cocktail every 4 hours during this two-day fast in which you should also be consuming plenty of soups and salads, but avoiding meat, bread, dairy products, coffee, soft drinks, condiments, (catsup, mustard, pickles, mayonnaise), deep-fried foods, sweets and the like.

The second step involves taking several good high enemas in order to cleanse the bowels adequately. This can be done in the evenings of both days. Coffee enemas are recommended and the complete instructions for administering them given under COFFEE.

Only on the third, fourth and even fifth day, if necessary, is the olive oil treatment to begin, continuing with your mild-food diet at the same time. *On an empty stomach* morning, noon and night, drink a well-stirred or well-shaken mixture consisting of 8 tbsps. of pure virgin olive oil, 3 tbsps. unsweetened grapefruit juice and 2 tsps. of apple cider vinegar, all of which is sweetened with 1 tbsp. pure maple syrup. Sometimes the response rate may be a little slower than usual, so the treatment may need to persist for a week or more. In such instances, a return to a more complete diet obviously is necessary for much needed strength and energy, but meat, animal fat and refined carbohydrate intakes should be modified as much as possible in order to assure the greatest recovery success possible.

Intakes of lecithin (2 tbsps. of granules) every 3 days seems to be a good preventative from having them form again later on. This program works well when a little patience, common sense and modest dietary sacrifices are employed with the serious intention of getting rid of gallstones once and for all.

Sure Cure for Earache

A friend of mine who lives in the orthodox Jewish section of Brooklyn, New York, Joel Bree, came up with an effectively simple solution for treating earaches and inner ear infections. This came about as the result of a necessity to find an alternative to the antibiotic drugs which the local pediatrician was giving his kids during the many visits made to his office for ear infections.

His simple remedy calls for olive oil (Eden brand), vitamin E oil in the capsule (Schiff brand) and garlic oil in the capsule (San Helios brand). "I've experimented with other kinds of vitamin E and garlic oil, but never found them to work as effectively as these do," he remarked to me during a mid-Summer '87 visit with him and his family.

First, get a small, clean glass container of some sort (an empty baby food jar is good for this). Then drop in it with an eye-dropper 13 drops of olive oil. Next, cut and squeeze the contents out of a single capsule of d-alpha tocopherol 400 I.U. vitamin E into the jar. Finally, cut and empty 1 garlic oil capsule so at least 7 drops are obtained. On account of the stiffness of the capsule itself, it may be necessary to squeeze rather hard to get the oil out.

Thoroughly mix all of these oils together by shaking the jar from side to side. Then set the jar in a soup bowl and pour some very warm water around it. Leave in the bowl for about 1 minute until comfortably warm. It's advisable to first test the temperature of the oil by dropping a little of it on your wrist so as not to burn the child's ear.

Then, with the head tilted sideways, drop equal amounts of the oil in each ear. Remove the excess by gently dabbing inside of the ear with a wad of cotton. But don't rub hard. It's also a good idea while dropping the oil into the ear to gently rub the hollow space directly beneath the ear lobe with the fingertips to permit more oil to enter the ear canal in order to reduce the pain and stop infection. This remedy is also good for ringing in the ear and water accumulation from swimming or taking a shower. However, Joel advises that this remedy shouldn't be used if there is a purulent discharge from the ear or if the eardrum has ruptured.

Relieve Pain in Teething Infants

When infant children begin their period of teething, oftentimes they are in varying degrees of pain. This seems to be most evident when they are fed with metal spoons, consequently a wooden one should be used instead. Another way of reducing their pain is to rub their sore, little gums with some pure virgin olive oil several times a day.

Dress Your Salads in Formal Attire

An infinite number of dressings for your favorite salads are in circulation these days. One which I'm particularly attracted to is a combination of several different recipes I've severely modified and borrowed from Frances Sheridan Goulart's excellent *The Whole Meal Salad Book* (Donald I. Fine, Inc., 1985), to whom I also express my gratitude for letting me use them.

Subtle Lime Liqueur Vinaigrette

Needed: 1 small crushed garlic clove; 1/2 tsp. kelp; 2-1/2 tbsps. lime juice; 1/4 cup unsweetened apple juice; 3 tbsps. of any fruit-flavored liqueur; 1/2 tsp. paprika; 1/8 tsp. thyme; 1/8 tsp. rosemary; 1/2 tsp. pure maple syrup; 2/3 cup pure, virgin olive oil.

Mash garlic and kelp to a paste in a small bowl using the back of a heavy spoon. Add the lime juice, liqueur, paprika, thyme, rosemary and maple syrup and blend thoroughly. Then gradually whisk in the olive oil and apple juice with a wire whip until the mixture is smooth and thick. Should make enough tuxedo-and-evening gown dressing for 4 whole meal salads.

ONION (See GARLIC AND ONION.)

ORANGE (See CITRUS.)

OREGANO (See MARJORAM.)

ORNAMENTAL FLOWERS

CHRYSANTHEMUM	(*Chrysanthemum* sp.)
DAFFODIL	(*Narcissus pseudo-narcissus*)
DAISY	(*Bellis perennis*)
DAY LILY	(*Hemerocallis fulva, H. flava*)
GERANIUM (GARDEN)	(*Perlargonium* sp.)
HOLLYHOCK	(*Althae rosa*)
IRIS (COMMON)	(*Iris Germanica*)
MARIGOLD	(*Tagetes erecta, T. patula*)
NASTURTIUM	(*Tropaeolum majus*)
PANSY	(*Viola tricolor hortensis*)
PEONY	(*Paeonia officinalis*)
PETUNIA	(*Petunia hybrida*)
ROSE	(*Rosa* sp.)
SNAP DRAGON	(*Antirrhinium majus*)
TULIP	(*Tulipa* sp.)
VIOLET	(*Viola cucullata, V. odorata*)

Brief Description

CHRYSANTHEMUM. An ornamental plant belonging to the aster family. The flowers are of various warm colors such as white, red or yellow, with dark green leaves; both of which taste somewhat like a mild cauliflower. The Japanese and Chinese have used both for centuries in their remedies and recipes.

DAFFODIL. There are several kinds. Some have a crimson or reddish-purple circle in the middle of the flower, while others have a yellow circle resembling a coronet or cup in the middle. The common daffodil gets about a foot high, with leaves that are long, narrow, grassy-looking and of a deep green. The single, large, yellow flower at the top of the stalk presses down a bit due to its weight.

DAISY. A low-growing European herb of the aster family which has small white or pink rays and yellow disks in its flowerheads. It grows to about 18 inches and has many broad leaves at its base with indented edges and finger-width size to them.

DAY LILY. This can be any plant of a genus of the lily family, which is characterized with long narrow basal leaves and showy yellow or tawny flowers in small clusters. Also any plant of a related genus (*Hosta*) bearing racemose white or violet flowers.

GERANIUM (GARDEN). A genus of South African plants, the species of which are widely cultivated in gardens everywhere on account of their very showy red or white flowers. There are also several kinds of scented geraniums as well, which some patients in the Soviet Union who suffer from hypertension and headaches sniff for 20 minutes every day in order to obtain relief.

HOLLYHOCK. A tall perennial Chinese herb belonging to the mallow family. This plant is cultivated in gardens as a biennial for its beautiful pastel flowers. Wee fairy folk were once thought to eat of its flowers a long time ago.

IRIS (COMMON). Cultivation has produced a great number of varieties, both among the bulbous or Spanish iris and the herbaceous or flag irises, which have fleshy, creeping rootstocks. The German or flag iris of modern American nurseries is a handsome plant with sword-like leaves of a bluish-green color that are narrow and flat. Flower stems are nearly 3 feet high with large, deep-blue or purplish-blue flowers that have an agreeable scent reminiscent of orange blossoms a little.

MARIGOLD. This can be any of several plants of the genus belonging to the aster family, especially African and French marigolds. A related species, marsh marigold, is known under the more familiar name of calendula for its marvelous skin-healing properties (see under CALENDULA also). All marigolds bear large yellow, orange or red terminal flower heads.

NASTURTIUM. This is an annual native to South America, but cultivated in gardens all over the world. The trailing or climbing stems grow 5–10 ft. long and bear small, almost round, radially veined leaves and are adorned with either red, orange or yellow flowers larger than the leaves themselves.

PANSY. An annual that's widely cultivated as a garden ornamental, but also occurs wild in fields and meadows and along the edges of forests in North America, northern Asia and Europe. The angular, soft, hollow stem bears alternate, ovate to lanceolate, toothed leaves. The solitary, axillary flowers may be yellow, blue violet or two-colored, the flowering time being from March to October.

PEONY. This is a perennial which grows wild in southern Europe and is cultivated elsewhere as a garden flower. The thick, knobby rootstock produces a green, juicy stem from 2–3 feet high. The leaves are ternate or bi-ternate, with large, ovate-lanceolate leaflets. The large, solitary, red or purplish-red flowers resemble roses and bloom from May to August. This "queen of all herbs" was highly prized by the ancient Greeks for its miraculous properties. But not until it eventually lost favor with herbalists in the 17th and 18th centuries, did it become a prize attraction of horticulturists.

PETUNIA. Any of a genus of tropical American herbs with funnel-shaped or tubular-spreading petals or corollas. The common garden petunia, as well as many forms and varieties, have all been derived from *P. axillaris* (with white flowers) and *P. violacea* (with violet flowers). Both are native to Argentina. Petunias belong to the same nightshade family (*Solanaceae*) that potatoes, tomatoes, tobacco and chili peppers do.

ROSE. There are over 100 species of rose in the genus *Rosa,* which consists of prickly shrubs found wild and widely cultivated in the temperate parts of the Northern Hemisphere. Their trailing, climbing or erect stems bear alternate, odd-pinnate leaves with familiar white to deep-red or, rarer still, black flowers that are single and five-petaled in wild species but mostly double in cultivated varieties. They yield fruit-like, fleshy hips rich in vitamin C.

SNAP DRAGON. Any garden plant of the genus having showy white, crimson, or yellow bilabiate flowers fancifully likened to the face of a roguish dragon. The nightshade family (*Solanaceae*) to which petunias belong is closely related to the snapdragon order (*Scrophulariales*) and is a connecting link between it and the phlox family (*Polemoniaceae*), which is confined primarily to the western U.S.

TULIP. The name applies not only to any plant of this genus, but also to its flower or bulb as well. Tulips have been so long in cultivation that the common garden types cannot really be traced to any existing wild species to speak of. Holland is still the center of tulip cultivation though bulbs for the market are now also raised in the U.S. Horticulturally, tulips are classed under two main divisions: early-flowering and May-flowering tulips.

VIOLET. Not only does this name apply to any plant, flower, or species of the genus, but also it pertains to actual colors resembling some violets. The common purple or hooded violet is common to the eastern U.S., and is the state flower of Illinois, Wisconsin, New Jersey and Rhode Island. Violets vary in hue from reddish-blue to blue-red, are of medium saturation and low to medium in brilliance of color.

'Mums for Hypertension, Angina and Bloodshot Eyes

Clinical evidence found in Chinese and Japanese pharmaceutical and medical journals show that chrysanthemum flowers are excellent for treating high blood pressure and its associated symptoms of headache, dizziness and insomnia. Snip enough mum flowers to equal 6 tbsps, then divide into 4 equal portions of 1-1/2 tbsps. each and set aside for use throughout the day. Beginning in the morning at 8 a.m. and every 4 hours thereafter, put 1 portion in a cup and pour hot, boiling water over the flowers and cover with a small saucer or piece of aluminum foil, allowing them to steep for 15 minutes before drinking. Repeat this same procedure 3 more times that day for up to one month. In one experiment where a total of 46 hypertension patients were thus treated, 35 of them showed fairly rapid improvement in their symptoms, with blood pressure returning to normal in less than a week. The remaining patients also showed varying degrees of symptom relief and dropping of blood pressure after 10–30 days treatment.

This same procedure twice daily in identical amounts brought considerable relief from very severe constricting chest pains in 80% of a group of 61 patients suffering from angina pectoris of the heart. In both applications, the infusions should be taken on any empty stomach preferably for maximum effectiveness.

Tired and bloodshot eyes due to excessive reading, close-range precision work, lack of sleep, air-borne allergies and related factors may be relieved with chrysanthemums. Steep approximately 2 tbsps. of whole flowers in boiling water for 5 mins. The liquid can be drunk as a stomach tonic. While the flower heads are still very warm and relatively free of excess liquid, they should be placed over the closed eyes while in a reclining position and kept there for 15 minutes. They are then to be replaced by other hot ones, but not so hot as to burn the skin. Continue this procedure for an hour before retiring to bed.

Daffodils for Boils and Tendonitis

The purulent matter occurring in herpes sores, leg ulcers, boils, carbuncles and nasty-looking wounds and abscesses can be effectively drawn out by applying a poultice of freshly grated daffodil bulbs and mashed chrysanthemum leaves, which both have been puréed together in a food blender. Turn the mixture out onto the wet side of a small clean linen cloth or white hand towel and then apply directly to the site, leaving there for about 45 mins. or so before changing again.

Put several chopped daffodil bulbs in a blender to purée. Then remove and mix with a little honey to form a rather stiff and sticky paste. Apply liberally to tendonitis, twisted ankle, dislocated shoulder, sprained elbow or injured kneecap for incredible relief from excruciating pain and soreness.

Please Do Use the Daisies for Gout and Ruptures

For the uninitiated, a past national best-seller, *Please Don't Eat the Daisies,* carried a somewhat clever prohibition against their use in its rather wry title. But here they're heartily recommended for gout, arthritis and inflammations of the liver and bladder. To 1 qt. of boiling water that's been removed from the heat, add a generous double-handful of cut daisy flowers and permit to steep *uncovered* for 1 hr. 10 mins. Sweeten with a little honey, after straining. Drink 3–4 cups a day, as needed.

The same decoction may also be used as an enema to help relieve various kinds of intestinal inflammations, such as colitis and diverticulitis, among others. Equally valuable, however, are the daisy's usefulness in helping to heal any kind of internal burstings, like hernias, or even to some extent, appendicitis—*but only when emergency medical care isn't readily available.* In such cases, 2 double-handfuls of daisies would be added to 1 qt. of boiling water and allowed to steep 1-1/2 hrs. uncovered, before drinking. About 5 cups per day, on the average, would be required in these instances.

Scalds and Burns Treated with Day Lilies

The root bulbs and leaves of day lilies are absolutely fantastic for sunburns, major burns and accidental scaldings by either hot liquid or grease of some kind. While the severe burn or scald is temporarily resting in very cold ice water, the coarsely chopped bulbs and cut leaves and flowers of 2 day lilies should be puréed in a food blender with a little crushed ice added to form a nice, thick paste. This is then carefully applied to the injured skin tissue and left for several hours until another change is required. It may be a good idea to add 1/2–1 tsp. of olive oil while blending the bulbs and leaves, since this will help to keep the poultice from drying out so fast. Also some wet pieces of muslin or linen cloth loosely laid over the poultice should help to retain moisture a lot longer.

Geraniums Make a Good Astringent

Garden geraniums make a good astringent both internally as well as externally in helping to check diarrhea and hemorrhaging. Bring 1/2 qt. water to a boil, adding 2 tbsps. grated or finely chopped root. Reduce heat and simmer *uncovered* for 7–10 mins. Then remove from the stove, adding 1/2 handful finely snipped leaves. Cover and let steep 40 mins. Strain, sweeten with honey to taste and drink 1 cup every 3-1/2 hrs. Or make a poultice of the strong decoction for external purposes.

This ornamental flower also makes a handy styptic for nicks and cuts encountered while shaving in the morning. Just take 1 geranium leaf and fold it over and over again both ways until you have a small, fat green square of material. Then pound this good with a hammer or rock until it's well-bruised. Apply to the cut or abrasion and hold in place with adhesive tape. Stops bleeding almost immediately. For smaller areas, use only 1/4 or 1/2 of one leaf instead.

Ulcers and Kidneystones Healed by Hollyhock

Peptic and duodenal ulcers seem to respond very well to a tea made from the leaves of hollyhock. Simply bring 1 qt. of water to a boil, then add 1-1/2 double-handfuls of freshly snipped hollyhock leaves. Remove from heat, cover with lid and let steep for 1 hr. Strain and drink 1 cup with every meal, sweetened with 1/2 tsp. of pure maple syrup.

A decoction made according to the foregoing instructions, with the exception of simmering on low heat for 5 mins. before removing and steeping for an hour, is very good for relieving the painful misery accompanying kidneystones. Two to three cups a day in between meals and on an empty stomach should also help to dissolve the stone as well. Another variation of this same remedy is to use only 1 double-handful of cut hollyhock leaves and 1/2 double-handful of cut, fresh catnip herb.

Edema and Bruises Disappear with Irises

Excessive accumulations of clear, watery fluid in any of the tissues or cavities of the body seem to disappear with a tincture of iris root. Grate enough fresh, clean iris root to equal 1 heaping tbsp. Add it to 1 pint of white wine, stirring good. Cap the bottle and let it set for 10 days in a cool, dry place, making sure you shake the contents twice daily. Strain, taking 2–3 tbsps. daily.

To remove black-and-blue marks just make a poultice of iris root and rose petals to lay on the bruises until they clear up. Clean a freshly dug iris root by washing it well under tap water. Then cut half of it into small pieces which can be puréed in a food processor or blender. If the root is too tough for this, then pound it with a hammer until well-mashed. Purée a handful of rose petals with a couple of tablespoonfuls of water and mix them in with the mashed root. Apply this entire poultice then to the injured skin, covering with a damp cloth or slightly wet towel. Leave in place for up to four hours. Repeat this process at least twice daily for a couple of days, at which time bruises should be gone.

Marigolds for Tetanus, V.D. and Constipation

In some parts of Central and South America, marigolds are extremely popular to *cure* tetanus or blood poisoning and to successfully treat venereal diseases such as syphilis and gonorrhea.

For tetanus just bathe the injured part frequently two or three times daily in separate hot and cold decoctions of marigolds. Bring 1 qt. of water to a boil, then reduce the heat and add 1-1/2 handfuls of finely chopped, cleaned roots. Cover and simmer for 10 minutes before removing from heat to steep another 45 mins. Strain and refrigerate this amount until it's ice cold. Next make another batch just like the first. Strain while still very hot and tolerable to the skin. Soak the afflicted part in the hot solution for 1 min. before switching to the ice cold one for another minute. Alternate this way for at least 1 hr. Repeat again 6 hrs. later. Use the same solution either as a wash or douche for treating venereal disease.

The ancient Aztecs of Pre-Columbian Mexico employed a tea made from marigolds for correcting chronic constipation. Aztec physicians would simmer a handful of chopped marigolds (flowers, stems and leaves) over a moderate fire in an earthenware vessel of some sort filled with a quart of boiling water for half an hour. When the brew was lukewarm, it was then strained through coarsely woven fabric of some kind and immediately given to the patient, several small bowlfuls at a time. This same brew was also used to relieve accumulations of serous fluid in the peritoneal cavity (ascites) and general fluid retention in other parts of the body, such as the legs, for instance. Aztec physicians also administered this brew while somewhat hot to induce sweating in their patients for the purposes of general body cleansing and ceremonial purification. According to *Science* for April 18, 1975, from which some of this information comes, better than 60% of the Aztec medicinal herbs evaluated by scientists proved to be as efficacious as the claims made for them from ancient native sources.

Nasturtium Is a Marvelous Expectorant

This winding ornamental really helps break up mucus congestion in the breathing passages and the lungs during colds and flus. A warm tea made of the flowers and leaves also acts as a disinfectant helping to kill unfriendly bacteria on contact, besides promoting the development of more white blood cells which fight infection inside the body.

The tea to be taken *isn't* made like your regular herb teas would be. Put a level double-handful of snipped nasturtium leaves and flowers into a food blender or processor. Then add enough hot *tap water* (*not* boiling) and liquefy to make a drink of smooth, somewhat runny consistency. Drink half of it and take the balance 3 hours later on an empty stomach, making sure both amounts are warm.

Pansies for the Heart and Skin

William Shakespeare referred to it in his plays as "heartsease," and several daily infusions while this plant's in bloom from March to October makes an excellent tonic for weak hearts. Certainly there is nothing wimpish about its lovely and gentle appearance when it comes to treating skin eruptions, particularly in children due to acne and contagious diseases like measles, mumps and chickenpox.

Steep about 3 slightly heaping tbsps. of plant snipped into small pieces in 1 pint of very hot (but *not* boiling) spring or Perrier water, covered, for 35 minutes. Strain and drink 2 cups daily while pleasantly lukewarm (*not* cool). Sores on the surface of the skin can also be frequently bathed with this solution as well.

Jaundice, Allergies and Peonies

An effectual remedy for jaundice, kidney and bladder problems is to make an alcoholic extract by steeping 2 tbsps. of fresh, minced rootstock in 1 pint of red wine for 9 days in a stoppered bottle, remembering to shake well twice daily. One tablespoon 4 times daily on an empty stomach helps the liver.

A decoction of the rootstock is also very useful in either preventing or else reducing the incidence of some allergies during those months in the Summer and early Fall when people are most prone to come down with them in some form or another. Bring 1-1/2 pints of water to a boil, then add 1-1/4 tbsps. finely chopped rootstock. Reduce heat and simmer 3 mins. before removing and letting steep, covered, for an additional 40 minutes. Drink warm in 1/2 cup portions throughout the day as needed, or every 4–5 hours, for relief and protection.

Under no circumstance should the flowers or above-ground plant be used internally, since they contain toxic substances that could make a person quite ill and uncomfortable.

A Good Night's Rest with Petunia Tea

A popular remedy for restlessness and insomnia which was introduced to me by a Costa Rican folk healer, calls for 1/2 cup of freshly snipped petunia petals and a few leaves to be *gently* brewed in 1-1/4 cups of hot (not boiling) water, *uncovered* for the space of 25 minutes. After which, it may be strained, sweetened with a touch of pure maple syrup and a drop of pure vanilla extract, then *slowly* drunk while pleasantly lukewarm.

Eating Disorders Corrected with Rose Tea

Lately several eating disorders, often associated with personality quirks, have been in the news a lot. One of them is anorexia nervosa, an extreme aversion to food. Its counterpart, on the other hand, is a sudden urge for a glorious pigout at the nearest buffet line. This morbid appetite seizure is called bulimia, and often alternates with periods of anorexia.

The best treatment I've ever found for both conditions is a regular infusion of rose petals, taken regularly about 6 times a day in 1-1/2-cup amounts. The best kind of roses to use for this are the red ones known as hybrid perpetuals. Bring 2 qts. of *pure spring* water to a rolling boil. Then remove the pot immediately from the heat and add 2 generous double-handfuls of *fresh* red rose petals, along with 2 tbsps. of *dried* chamomile flowers obtained from any local health food store. Cover with a good, *tight* lid and permit to steep for *only* 25 minutes *at the most!* Remove the lid and allow to set an additional 15 minutes until somewhat lukewarm. Strain, sweeten with a touch of pure maple syrup and drink according to the instructions previously given. Reserve the rest for later use in a cool, damp place, but *do not* refrigerate. Keeps up to 17 hours before a new batch must be made. Each time it's taken, the tea should be somewhat lukewarm in order to work the best.

Treat Sore Eyes to Snap Dragon

I'm really surprised that no American or Canadian herbalists have discovered the fantastic therapeutic powers of this unique and clever ornamental for all manner of eye disorders.

This book, in fact, may be the only recent herbal encyclopedia that *deliberately* omits eyebright altogether from its wonderful repertoire of plant medicinals. I have nothing against the herb personally. It's just that there's something *much better* for the eyes than this.

My Hungarian grandmother treated numerous eye disorders ranging from cataracts in the *early stages* and eye inflammations to conjunctivitis and you name it, with an eye wash made from snap dragon flowers, leaves and root (in other words, the *entire* plant)!

Bring 1 qt. of *distilled* water (very important to use *only this kind*) to a rolling boil. Add 1 heaping handful of carefully cleaned and coarsely chopped *fresh* root. Cover with a tight-fitting lid, reduce heat and simmer 15 mins. *exactly*. Remove promptly from the heat, uncover and add the cut and chopped contents of 1 small-to-medium snap dragon. Cover again and steep for an hour. Strain *twice*, bottle and refrigerate. Makes the best eye wash you've ever seen. Bathe eyes frequently with an eye cup as needed.

Tiptoe Through the Tulips for Pain

Certain kinds of pains seem to respond very well indeed to tulip bulbs, for some reason. An old Chinese pharmacist in Hanoi told me this while I was attending an international symposium on Oriental folk medicine and acupuncture in Taipei, Taiwan.

To relieve a terrible toothache or particularly painful insect bite or sting, simply crush a little bit of fresh tulip bulb and apply the mashed poultice to either for quick and effective relief. Fresh, crushed tulip leaves were also a very good poultice for running abscesses to help draw out the pus.

Violet Syrup Soothes Hacking Cough

For scratchy, irritated throats, raspy voice or hacking smoker's cough, nothing quite compares for comfort with a delicious syrup of violet flowers and leaves. It almost feels like liquid gold going down and leaves the throat and lungs with a silky feeling to them.

Add 5 cups of closely clipped violet flowers and 1 cup finely clipped leaves to either a stone crock earthenware or glazed china container (don't use *any* kind of metal or plastic). Over them pour 2-3/4 pints of boiling *distilled* water (or pure rain water) and cover with a tight-fitting lid. Steep for 24 hrs. before pouring off the liquid and straining it gently through several layers of clean muslin. It might be a good idea to shake the contents of the container several times during this 24-hour steeping period to slightly agitate things.

Transfer this liquid to a regular stainless-steel saucepan and warm up slowly on a low heat, making sure *it never boils!* At various intervals of the warming up stage, add portions of *lukewarm* honey in an amount equal to 4 cups total. Keep stirring with a wooden ladle until a syrupy consistency has been achieved. Bottle in clean fruit jars and store in a cool pantry. Use 1–2 tbsps. at a time as needed for throat and lung problems. Works like a charm every time!

Daffy and Daisy Duck Salad

Saturday morning TV cartoon fans would probably know that Daffy Duck is Bugs Bunny's crazy feathered friend, while Disney fans should recognize Daisy as Donald Duck's ageless heart-throb. Well a little of both, plus root and leaves from each respective ornamental, wind up in this rather comical treat.

Needed: 1 medium-size head of dark Romaine lettuce; washed and chopped into salad-size pieces; 1/2 head of shredded purple cabbage; 2 tsps. finely shredded fresh daffodil bulb; 1 tbsp. finely minced onion; 1 crushed garlic clove; 1/2 cup each chopped daffodil and daisy leaves; 1-1/4 cups finely snipped daffodil and daisy flowers; 2 cups coarsely chopped and boned cold duck; 1/4 cup chopped, shelled walnut meats; 1/4 cup finely chopped red apple (unpeeled); 1 pint plain yogurt; 7 pitted dates; 1/2 cup raisins and touches of sherry and pure vanilla mixed together.

First, rub a good-sized *wooden* salad bowl on the inside with the crushed garlic clove. Afterwards, add the lettuce, cabbage, ornamental leaves and flowers, walnuts, apple, raisins and duck. Mix everything very thoroughly. In a food blender combine yogurt, dates, daffodil bulb, onion, sherry and vanilla. Mix well. This is your dressing for what may appear to be a very daffy salad idea but with a daisy of a taste to it!

Scented Geranium Honey

Bruise fresh, scented geranium blossoms. Place them in layers on the bottom of a small saucepan. Pour room temperature honey into the pan and cook over low heat. Stir the mixture just until the honey is warm—about 2 minutes. High heat will damage the honey. Pour the mixture into sterilized jars and seal tightly. Store the jars at room temperature for about 1 week to allow flavors to blend. Rewarm the honey over low heat and strain the blossoms out. Recap or use immediately.

P

PANSY (See ORNAMENTAL PLANTS.)

PAPAYA (See TROPICAL FRUITS.)

PAPRIKA (See CAYENNE.)

PARSLEY (*Petroselinum crispum*)

Brief Description

Parsley is a non-hairy biennial or short-lived perennial with a much-branched stem. A thin, white, spindle-shaped root produces the erect, grooved, glabrous, angular stem that can reach a height of slightly over 2 feet. The plant is often cultivated as an annual for its foliage, especially in California, Germany, France, Belgium and Hungary. There are numerous varieties. Parts used are the ripe fruits (seeds), the above-ground herb and the leaves.

White or greenish-yellow flowers appear in compound umbels from June to August. Curiously enough, parsley is poisonous to most birds but is very good for animals, curing maladies such as foot-rot in sheeps and goats. The wild parsleys found throughout the British Isles are closely allied to the celeries and were used by the Anglo-Saxons in ancient times to mend skulls broken in combat.

Removing "Dragon Breath"

Ever smell a dog's breath or someone with acute halitosis? They're bad enough to gag you. But now there's a simple cure for both extremes. the next time you feed your dog, mix several sprigs of parsley in with a little raw chopped or ground beef, then combine that with the animal's regular dry chow. You'll be surprised how well this works! And as for human breath problems, simply dip a couple of sprigs in vinegar and thoroughly chew them slowly before swallowing. The purifying effect should remove offensive odors for at least 3–4 hours.

An Ignored Cancer Preventative

Unbeknownst to most people, a few sprigs of parsley pack a wallop so far as cancer goes. For one thing, they contain about as much vitamin A as 1/4 tsp. of cod-liver oil does. For another, they yield about two-thirds of the vitamin C that an *entire* orange does! Furthermore, parsley ranks higher than most vegetables in an important amino acid, histidine, which strongly inhibits tumor development within the body, according to *Mutation Research* (77:245–50). And vitamins A and C are now recognized as significant nutrients in the fight against cancer. Therefore, it seems we'd all be better off eating more parsley than just leaving it on our plates.

Yucatan Remedy for Kidney Problems

Throughout the Yucatan Peninsula of southeastern Mexico, a tea is made out of fresh parsley herb to treat kidney inflammation, inability to urinate, painful urination, kidneystones and edema. Bring 1 qt. water to a boil. Remove from heat and add 1 cup of coarsely chopped parsley. Cover and let steep 40 mins., then strain before drinking. Take 1 cup of warm tea 4 times daily with meals.

Overcomes Sexual Frigidity

This same parsley tea also manifests mildly aphrodisiac properties for couples experiencing sexual frigidity of any kind in their relationships. The same directions would be followed, except that 2 cups of chopped parsley are used with 1 qt. of water, steeping time is an hour and 2 cups of *very warm* tea are consumed by each partner at least 20 minutes before sexual activities begin.

Interestingly enough, parsley has been fed to sheep in Spain to bring them into heat in any season of the year. Some couples with whom I've spoken after they've tried the above remedy have reported to me somewhat increased stimulations in their sexual desires, although several wished that this herb worked more powerfully in this respect.

Clears Up Bruises

An old Romanian gypsy remedy called for several sprigs of parsley leaves to be crushed, then applied directly to any bruise on the skin and left there for awhile. Repeated applications would usually clear up any black-and-blue marks within a day or so.

Exciting Recipe

The following dish is part of a traditional Iranian New Year's feast that's both delicious as well as very, very tempting.

Parsley-Green Onion Rice with Fish

Needed: 3 cups uncooked rice; warm water; kelp; 2 bunches chopped green onions; 2 bunches chopped parsley; 3 lbs. fish fillets; sea salt as needed; pinch of turmeric; 2 tbsps. butter.

Rinse rice several times until water is clear; soak in warm water with salt added. Bring a large pot of water to boil (about 8 cups water). Drain water from soaked rice and add rice to boiling water. Boil about 10–15 mins. until rice is not crunchy but still quite firm. Stir occasionally to prevent grains from sticking together.

Drain rice in a strainer; add chopped onions and parsley. Pour some cold water over rice, parsley and onions. Cover the bottom of the pot with butter and some water. Sprinkle rice and these two vegetables into the pot a spoonful at a time, keeping them in the center of the pot so as not to touch the sides of the pot. Cover pot lid with paper or dish towel and place lid tightly on pot. Cook approximately 10 mins. over medium heat, then reduce heat to low. Allow rice to steam 30–40 mins.

Cut fish into serving pieces; sprinkle with sea salt, kelp and a bit of turmeric. In a skillet, brown fish, cooking until done on both sides in butter. Serve with rice.

PARSNIP (*Pastinaca sativa*)

Brief Description

Parsnips look like an anemic version of their cousin, the carrot. The parsnip's starchy root, however, is one of the most nourishing in the whole carrot family. This starch is converted to sugar whenever the root is exposed to the frost. Parsnip isn't a common vegetable anymore, even though most of us have heard of it. Americans usually serve parsnips glazed with brown sugar and fruit juice only on special holidays like Thanksgiving or Christmas. Refrigerated in a plastic bag, parsnips keep for nearly a month.

Fatigue Fighter and Cleanser

Imagine a food so highly concentrated with energy-giving properties that it is a remarkable internal cleansing agent as well. Such a one is parsnip, which is loaded with more food energy than most of our common vegetables except potatoes, yet is a relatively strong diuretic for helping to remove toxins from the body.

A diet of parsnips, either steamed or baked for lunch *and* dinner for at least a week, becomes an extremely valuable cleansing agent and even gets rid of some stones in the kidneys and bladder. And parsnips in the diet once a day or at least every other day is very useful for strengthening those who have hypoglycemia or are just recently recovering from serious illness or surgery or both.

Save the juice left from cooked parsnips and drink a glass morning and evening for up to 6 weeks in order to get rid of gallstones. This is an old remedy from Colonial America, which was introduced by the renowned 18th century religious reformer, the Reverend John Wesley.

Parsnip Perfections

For an unusual flavor, peel and slice or dice parsnips and boil them in a small amount of apple cider. Remove the parsnips when tender. Then boil the cider until it becomes syrupy and serve as a glaze. Add chopped parsley for color.

The next recipe comes from La Rene Gaunt's cook book, *Recipes to Lower Your Fat Thermostat,* and is reprinted here with the permission of her publisher (see Appendix).

Perfect Parsnip Patties

Needed: 6 cooked parsnips; 1/4 tsp. powdered cardamom; 1/4 tsp. powdered mace; 2 tbsps. whole wheat flour; 1/2 cup plain yogurt.

Wash, peel and quarter parsnips. Remove core and discard. Cook them in boiling water for 15 mins. until tender. Drain and mash. Use cooking water to adjust consistency. Season with spices. Whisk flour into yogurt. Stir into seasoned parsnips. Shape into 8 patties and brown slowly on a nonstick griddle or frying pan. Turn just once. They should have a crisp crust. Serves 5. Liquid lecithin from any local health food store can be used in place of oil for griddle or frying pan.

This last little recipe comes from Better Homes & Gardens' *Fresh Fruit and Vegetable Recipes*, which the author thanks them for letting him use here (see Appendix).

Potato-Parsnip Whip

Needed: 1-1/2 lbs. medium potatoes, peeled and quartered; 1 lb. or 5 medium parsnips, peeled and cut up; 2 tbsps. butter; some heated canned or fresh goat's milk.

Place potatoes and parsnips in a large saucepan, then add water to cover. Bring to boiling. Reduce heat and cook, covered, for 25 mins. or until tender. Drain well. Add butter, pinch of salt and kelp. Beat well with an electric mixer or mash with a potato masher. Gradually beat in enough warm milk (about 1/4 cup) to make light and fluffy. Makes 8 servings.

PASTA
(See also GRAINS.)

Brief Description

Pastas are basically high-starch, low-protein foods with small amounts of vitamin enrichment to them. Pasta can be divided into two main groups: noodles and macaroni. Noodles are characterized by the addition of eggs to flour. This increases the protein, but also increases the fat content as well. Yogurt may be substitued for eggs when making your own homemade noodles as the recipe below indicates.

The macaroni group includes spaghetti, lasagna, macaroni, shells and other macaroni shapes. These are usually enriched with vitamins or wheat germ. My suggestion is to use these products in small amounts with high nutrition foods. Fill out soups with a handful of whole wheat macaroni or noodles. Top whole wheat pasta with creamed chicken or tuna or a vegetable-tomato sauce.

The average American consumed 12 lbs. of pasta in 1985. Spaghetti leads the market share in pasta sales with 55%, followed by macaroni at 27%, egg noodles at 13%, lasagna and specialty shapes at 3% and all other kinds of pasta at a mere 2%.

Really Lowers Cholesterol

Most dieters have dismissed pasta as too fattening. Nothing could be further from the truth, however. In fact, clinical studies show that pasta is one of the best foods to help keep serum cholesterol levels low!

A team of international doctors from Minnesota and Italy worked together to study the diets and blood cholesterols of healthy Italian men in the age range of 40–55 years residing in Naples and their American counterparts residing in the Minneapolis-St. Paul area.

The great bulk of the Italian diet was bread, pasta and local vegetables, with meat, fish, milk, cheese and eggs being definite luxuries due to their costs. Some fruits and very small amounts of cheese were quite often consumed as well. Whereas the diet of the Minnesota businessmen was just the opposite, in that dairy products and meat were frequent meal favorites, along with sugary foods, potatoes, and greasy entrées. Some vegetables were consumed and fruits eaten occasionally. Refined bread and other white flour products were used more often than pastas were.

Cereal grains provided the Italians about 67% of all their calories with another mere 20% coming from fats. This probably explains why the Italians had 30 mg. of cholesterol *less* in 100 milliliters of blood, than did their American counterparts who obtained close to 50% of all their calories just from fats! And as a rule, Italians have considerably fewer heart attacks than Americans do, although many of them can be somewhat rotund and overweight. If anything, then, pasta can be a true life-saver so far as cholesterol goes and should be included in our diets more often.

Pasta Pieces

Homemade noodles and spaghetti taste great and are better for you than some of the store-bought pastas might be.

Whole Wheat Noodles and Spaghetti

Needed: 1-1/2 cups whole wheat flour; 1/4 tsp. seasalt; 1 cup plain yogurt. Mix flour and salt. Add enough yogurt to make a stiff dough. Knead the dough for about 3 minutes. Heavily flour the countertop. Press dough out with hands. Sprinkle more flour on top of dough and roll out with a floured rolling pin. *It is absolutely essential that the dough be very thin!* Let rest 5 minutes. Cut into 1/4″ slices for noodles and 1/8″ for spaghetti with a very sharp knife. Spread on wax paper and let dry until hard, about 3 hours. Cook by dropping noodles in boiling water or bouillon. Cook 10–15 mins. Serves 6. Note: These noodles make incredible chicken or turkey noodle soup!

Pasta Primavera

Needed: 1 tbsp. olive oil; 1 clove minced garlic; 1/2 chopped medium onion; 2 large chopped tomatoes; 1/2 tsp. oregano; 1/4 tsp. marjoram; 1/2 tsp. kelp; 1/2 cup white wine; 1 tbsp. olive oil; 2–3 cups favorite sliced vegetables (broccoli, carrots, zucchini, Summer squash, etc.); 1 pound hot, cooked pasta of your choice; some grated Parmesan cheese, if desired.

Heat 1 tbsp. olive oil in sauté pan. Add garlic and onion; cook until translucent. Stir in tomatoes, oregano, marjoram and pepper; sauté two minutes. Add wine; let simmer while preparing vegetables. In separate sauté pan, heat 1 tbsp. olive oil. Add vegetables and cook crisp tender. Add tomato-onion mixture and serve over hot, cooked pasta. Sprinkle with some grated Parmesan cheese, if desired.

PEACH, PEAR AND QUINCE

Brief Description

PEACH (*Prunus persica*). The many varieties of peaches are divided into two basic categories: "freestones," with soft, juicy flesh that separates readily from the stone, and "clingstones," with firmer flesh that adheres tightly to the stone. Clingstone varieties like the Red Haven are generally used for canning; freestones like the Rio Oso Gem are eaten fresh or frozen. Peaches originated in China several thousand years ago and were venerated as fruits of immorality.

PEAR (*Pyrus communis*). This is a delicate, aristocratic, temperate-zone fruit that exists in thousands of varieties—with new ones being constantly produced. Few fruits vary so greatly in color, texture, flavor, size and shape. Pears are also an exception to the usual rule that tree-ripened fruits are best—they are picked when full grown but still green, and attain their finest texture and flavor (soft on the inside but still firm on the outside) off the tree. America's most widely grown pear, the Bartlett, is bell-shaped, with yellow skin and a red blush when ripe. It's excellent for poaching, canning or eating raw in season, which is from July to mid-October.

QUINCE (*Cydonia cydonia*). These yellow, pear-shaped fruits originated somewhere in Asia Minor and have been cultivated for some four millenniums. In medieval times most Europeans ate them fresh as well as cooking and preserving them. Quinces were once thought to be a type of pear, and in fact pears are often grown on quince rootstock, but the two fruits simply cannot be hybridized. Until the late 18th century, marmalade was usually made from quinces: the word "marmalade," in fact, derives from *marmelo,* which is Portuguese for quince.

Towards Beautiful Complexion

Because of their extremely high moisture content and delicate mineral balance, peach, pear and quince make ideal beautifiers for a more wonderful complexion. Paul Neinast, who runs a famous beauty salon in Dallas, Texas, combines peach with papaya, banana and avocado in a blender until well puréed. This facial mask is then applied and left on 30 minutes, after which it is rinsed away with tepid water. Then he will saturate several cotton balls with any polyunsaturated oil (sunflower oil is good to use) and gently rub the skin in a circular motion. This keeps dryness out, moisture in and gives the skin more elasticity. The face may also be rubbed with a little juice from some freshly pressed green grapes before the oil is applied. This treatment appears to give the skin a much softer texture than it may have had before.

Also a morning cocktail consisting of these three fruits is a great way to help flush out the system of all the old debris which may have accumulated during the night. In a food blender, combine 1 fresh, pitted peach half, 1 fresh pear half and 1 whole quince. Do not peel any of them, but wash thoroughly before liquefying. Add just enough broken ice cubes and a small amount of cold spring or Perrier water to make a nice, refreshing beverage that's smooth but not too thick.

If someone is troubled with boils, carbuncles or similar festering sores that seem to refuse to heal, just have the individual mix together in a food blender about 4 fresh peach tree leaves, a couple of slices of raw, *un*peeled potato that are 1/16-in. thick and about 3-in. wide and 1-1/2 cups of extremely hot, boiling water. When a nice, warm purée has formed, pour onto a clean, thick cloth and hold on the boil for awhile. In the event nothing is drawn out, it may need to be lanced first with a sewing needle, which has been sterilized over a flame for 30 seconds, before the other warm poultice can then be applied with good success.

An old, but very reliable remedy for removing the inflammation and discoloration accompanying bumps, bruises and abrasions calls for 3–5 peach tree leaves to be first mashed by hand before simmering in about 2 cups of sweet condensed milk for some 25 minutes on low heat. After this the solution is allowed to steep by covering with a lid, then it is strained when cool. This handy lotion is applied to the injured area either by rubbing directly on the skin or else soaking a wad of cotton or gauze material in the solution and then holding it in place with some adhesive tape. By the way, this same lotion is also terrific for relieving intense sunburns as well.

You may want to gather a number of peach tree leaves during the Summer months when the fruit is ripe and preserve them by freezing for later use in the Winter time when they're no longer available. Now peach tree leaves have considerable enzyme activity which needs to be lessened before freezing, but *not* destroyed by boiling them in hot water. The best blanching method to use is to suspend them *over* boiling water and steam for about 10 minutes, before cooling *over* but *not* in, ice-cold water.

A large, somewhat deep pan with a good lid may be filled half full with water and brought to a rolling boil. Freshly picked and washed leaves can then be put into a large wire strainer (the kind often used for straining cooked spaghetti noodles with) and hung over the edges of the pan, making sure the bottom doesn't touch any hot water. The lid is put on and the pot kept on high heat, while the leaves steam for the allotted time. The same methods for cooling are next employed in another pot, which should be covered and placed in the freezer for just a couple of minutes to hasten the cooling process.

After this, the leaves should be carefully laid out on several thicknesses of paper toweling and covered with more paper toweling in order to completely drain them. Then they may be neatly stored in air-tight, plastic or glass containers in the freezer until needed later on.

Fresh peach tree leaves that are crushed and then mixed with a little sweet condensed milk are an effective lotion to help clear up poison ivy rash, shingles and the misery of psoriasis. An alternative to this would be for a handful of leaves to be added to 2 cups of hot, boiling water and then covered to steep for awhile before using.

Another highly effective skin lotion for burns and inflammation is to combine the fruits of all three (peach, pear and quince) in a food blender with enough shaved ice to make a thick, cooling purée, which is then spread on some clean muslin and laid on the surface of the skin. But no matter how you use them, they're great for a fantastic complexion!

Relieves Indigestion and Constipation

Peach tree leaves are sensational for digestive problems and constipation. A woman from Paris, Tennessee once wrote that she made a tea out of the leaves for her 15-month-old baby who was then suffering from intestinal gas. "He took right to the stuff," she said, "and it did the job I wanted it to." Furthermore, she, herself, drank several cups each day and found it to have marvelous laxative properties. The same tea also helps to relieve bladder inflammation in men.

Peach Syrup for Fevers and Congestion

An old reliable standby often employed by some Native American tribes and Black folks is a syrup prepared from peach kernel and peach bark to treat intermittent fevers, chronic bronchitis and asthma and the common cold and flu. Add about 2/3 cup *each* of pounded peach bark and dried, split peach kernels to 2 cups *each* of apple cider vinegar and pure *distilled* water. Cover and let stand in a warm place for 5 days, shaking several times each day. Then simmer gently on low heat until the contents are reduced to slightly over a pint of liquid. Half a cup of brandy or whiskey is then added to preserve it and the solution stored in a well-sealed fruit jar until needed. One tablespoonful of syrup at a time is given every 3–4 hours to reduce fevers and eliminate accumulated phlegm.

This syrup works quite well for intestinal parasites, too, in 2 tbsps. amounts 2–3 times daily. The hydrocyanic acid present is thought to be a good substitute for the drug, quinine, which is obtained from Peruvian bark. This syrup may also be used as drops to relieve a painful earache. CAUTION: *No more* than just a couple of tablespoons of this syrup should be taken at any given time, although the same amount can be spread over an entire day without any particular discomfort, if need be.

Fruit Tonic for Weak Constitutions

A very nice mucilage preparation can be made from pears and quinces as a soothing and strengthening tonic for delicate digestive systems, an aid for anemic conditions and speed recovery from serious illness or major surgery. Remove the inner cores from several ripe pears and quinces before cutting them up and inserting into a food blender with about 3 cups of carrot juice. Mix for several minutes on medium speed. Makes a delicious tonic drink when taken in the morning and evening in 8 oz.-glass portions. Chill before using.

Homemade Yeast

Back in early 19th century America, when baking yeast wasn't always available to make bread with, women often made their own. You can do the same, if you like, with peach leaves. Just take 3 handfuls of peach leaves and 3 medium-sized potatoes and boil them in 2 quarts of water until the spuds are done. Remove the leaves and discard them. Next peel the spuds and rub them up good with 1 pint of flour, adding enough cool water to make a paste with. Then pour on the hot peach leaf tea and scald the floured spuds for about 5 minutes. If you add to this a little old yeast, it will be ready for use in just 3 hours. Otherwise, if none is added, it will require standing a day and a night in a warm corner somewhere, covered with a cloth, before getting new yeast ready for use.

Making Good Fruit Jam and Jelly

Jam is nothing more than whole fruit, crushed or chopped, and combined with sugar, but will not hold its shape as resolutely as jelly does. Jelly, on the other hand, is a mixture of fruit juice and sugar that is clear and firm enough to hold its own shape very well.

The secret to making good preserves lies in properly blending 4 key ingredients: fruit, pectin, acid and sugar. The fruit gives the distinctive flavor and color. Pectin and acid are found in all fruits, but to varying degrees; combined with sugar, they cause the product to jell. Sugar also serves as a preserving agent, and, of course, adds its own sweet flavor.

For the health conscious crowd who may object to white sugar, brown sugar may be substituted instead, but will not give as clear a product as white sugar might, especially when it comes to jellies. Also 1/8 to 1/4 of the amount of sugar called for may be replaced with honey without seriously affecting the preserve.

Most fruits require adding high-pectin fruits such as apple, crab apples or grapes, or their juices; or adding instead commercial pectin such as Certo (a liquid) and Sure-Jell (a powder). The easiest way to make wild preserves is to use commercial pectin: cooking times are shorter and more predictable, and results are nearly always good.

Here is the basic procedure for making jelly. Crush the fruit and simmer it until the juices start to flow. Spoon the crushed fruit into a jelly bag. The best jelly bag I've ever seen was an old salt sack, whose heavy weave traps the pulp and seeds while letting the juices slowly drip through. About 5 layers of cheesecloth will also suffice very nicely as well.

After putting the fruit into the bag, be sure to collect all of the juice that runs or drips out. Then measure out the required amount of pectin called for on the recipe sheet found inside the box it comes in. Don't get greedy and go for large batches, but rather be content to stay with making smaller quantities which are easier to handle.

Put the juice in a pot, add the pectin, heat and stir in the honey/sugar. *Never* use iron, copper, aluminum or galvanized steel cookware when making jelly. *Always* stay with stainless steel, enamel or glass cookware. Boil, *stirring constantly*. Then administer the jelly test to see if it's ready to take off the stove. Dip your spoon in the boiling jelly stock, hold it above the heat to cool slightly and tip it sideways. If two drops form and then merge and slide off the spoon in a sheet, the jelly is done. If the liquid runs off like water, it needs to boil longer. As the late plant forager, Euell Gibbons, once wrote, "No amount of instruction can take the place of experience in performing this task well . . . (but) you will be surprised how quickly you master this art."

When your jelly passes this simple test and appears to be ready for the next step, remove it from the stove. Then skim off and discard the accumulated foam and ladle the jelly into sterilized half-pint Mason canning jars with two-piece lids (a metal band, and a metal cap with a rubber-like gasket surrounding the rim). These are a lot better to use than the more conventional recycled jars (baby food, mayonnaise, mustard, pickle and so forth).

After filling each jar, seal them good. Then submit all jars to a boiling-water bath for about 7 minutes, which helps to further sterilize the contents and tightens the lids more securely to the tops, thereby preventing potential contamination from occurring. Jellies and jams made thusly can be stored for up to 3 years in a cold, dry place. The metal ring portions of the lids should be removed after a year to prevent them from rusting. In the event, however, that mold should appear for some reason or another in your jelly and jam, under *no* circumstance eat them. Such molds can be highly toxic and have been known to produce cancer in lab animals. Discard such spoiled items at once!

Peach-Crab Apple Jelly

Use the ripe, red-colored fruit from the Japanese flowering crab apple, a common ornamental shrub, and exceedingly ripe Hailstone peaches, if possible. August is the best month for obtaining both fruits in a mature state of development. Cut them in halves and remove pits and seeds. Cover with spring or distilled water. Bring to a boil, simmering for 20 mins. Pour off juice; strain through coffee filter for clearer jelly. To 7 cups of juice, add 1 package commercial pectin. Bring to a complete rolling boil, stirring all the time. Boil for 1 min., then take off the stove. Skim foam and pour jelly into containers. Seal with 2-piece lids.

Peach-Pear-Apple Jam

Wash, peel and core about 4 2-1/2-in. diameter peaches and 5 Bartlett pears. Make sure both fruits are fully ripened. Crush the fruits good and measure 2 cups of this prepared mix into a large saucepan. Wash, peel and core 1 large apple; finely chop and add 1 cup to peaches and pears. Stir in 1/8 tsp. *each* of powdered cardamom and cinnamon. Mix 6 cups brown sugar and 1/2 cup honey with 1/3 cup bottled lime juice into the fruits and bring to a boil over high heat, stirring constantly. Then stir in 12 tbsps. (6 fl. oz.) of commercial liquid fruit pectin. Bring to a full rolling boil and boil hard for 1 min., stirring constantly. Remove from heat, skim foam, put into jars, and seal. (The author is indebted to Charlie Fergus for much of this information.)

PEANUTS (See NUTS.)

PEA (*Pisum sativum*)

Brief Description

Fresh garden peas are becoming extinct in U.S. markets because few customers want to shell them anymore. Instead they seem to prefer canned or frozen. Unfortunately, those that are available are often large, starchy and nearly tasteless. Besides garden or shell peas, there are two other edible-pod varieties: the small, flat, snow—or sugar—peas often used in Chinese cooking and the plumper sugar snap peas that can be eaten raw or cooked and shelled when mature. Peas were Thomas Jefferson's favorite vegetable and he grew them at Monticello.

Dissolves Blood Clots

Clinical studies conducted by doctors in Calcutta, India showed that peas have the ability to dissolve clumps of red blood cells that are destined to become clots eventually. This clot prevention property is due to the presence of special plant proteins called lectins. It is, therefore, suggested that peas be incorporated into the diet more often, especially in the diets of those more susceptible to clots due to poor circulation, thick blood and coronary heart disease.

Bathing Skin Eruptions

In some parts of Europe, children afflicted with measles, mumps or chickenpox are sponged with the water in which peas have been boiled. This apparently seems to keep them from itching so much and from forming permanent pit marks in the skin. A poultice made from dried peas, boiled until they are soft, is a wonderful remedy for boils and abscesses.

Safe, Gentle Laxative Soup

For an effective, yet easy to use laxative, turn to peas. Either fresh or dried peas, boiled as a vegetable or served as pea soup, really get the bowels working.

Garden Pea Soup

Needed: 1 tbsp. butter; 1 cup diced potatoes; 2 cups Perrier water; 1 cup distilled water; 1 cup freshly shelled green peas or frozen and thawed peas; 1 tbsp. chopped chives; kelp to taste.

Melt the butter in a 2-qt. soup pot and swirl the potatoes around in it. Add both kinds of water and simmer until the potatoes are soft, about 20 mins. Purée in a blender and return soup to the pot. Bring to a boil and put in the fresh green peas. Cook them until just tender—test by eating one—and stir in the chives before serving. Season with kelp. This recipe was adapted from *Eat Better, Live Better,* courtesy of Reader's Digest (see Appendix).

PECAN (See NUTS.)

PEONY (See ORNAMENTAL FLOWERS.)

PEPPERS (See CAYENNE.)

PERSIMMON (*Diospyros virginiana*)

Brief Description

Most of the persimmons grown for the U.S. market are an Oriental type—the tomato-shaped, bright-orange fruit known as "kaki." Many imagine them to be extremely sour, but in fact these fruits can be quite palatable—somewhat astringent, but rich and sweet. The key is ripeness: commercially grown persimmons are picked and marketed unripe because of their extreme perishability; they must be held at room temperature until quite soft for the flavor to develop.

Tea for Hangover, Seafood Poisoning

Raw persimmon when combined with a little horehound herb, are excellent for relieving the throbbing headaches accompanying an alcoholic hangover. Both the fruit and the herb are also good as an antidote in tea form to reduce the symptoms of poisoning encountered when eating any kind of spoiled seafood such as raw sushi or oysters, for instance.

Bring 1 pint of water to a boil. Add 1/2 cup of coarsely chopped, unpeeled, ripe persimmon and 1-1/2 tbsps. fresh or dried, coarsely cut horehound herb. Cover with a lid, remove from the heat and steep 40 minutes. Strain and drink the entire contents while still lukewarm for the above conditions.

Wonderful Astringent

Willie Lena, a Seminole town chief residing in Wewoka, Oklahoma, mentioned in 1983 that his tribe often made a tea of the fruit to stop diarrhea. Six near ripe persimmons were cut into sections and steeped in 3 cups of boiling water, covered, for 20 minutes before straining. Drink 2 cups in a 4-hour period for chronic diarrhea. The fresh juice of the fruit may also be taken, but the tea seems to work better.

Other Native Americans of the early 19th century employed persimmon juice for cleansing gangrenous leg ulcers and wounds, to stop bloody bowel discharges and to wash out an infant's mouth to cure thrush, a yeast infection caused by *Candida albicans*. The previously mentioned tea could also be used as a vaginal douche to eradicate this yeast infection as well.

The juice of one ripe persimmon mixed with 3-1/2 tbsps. of warm water makes an excellent gargle for sore throat brought on by the common cold and influenza. In Thailand the ripe fruits are valuable for getting rid of intestinal worms, particularly hookworms.

PETUNIA (See ORNAMENTAL FLOWERS.)

PINEAPPLE (See TROPICAL FRUITS.)

PISTACHIO (See NUTS.)

PLUMS AND PRUNES (*Prunus domestica*)

Brief Description

Plums are the most diverse and widely distributed of all stone fruits, with varieties suitable to almost any climatic condition; in fact, they are grown on every continent except Antarctica. Most commercially grown plums are descendants of either European or Japanese varieties. The European plums, oval or round in shape, include all the purple to black varieties (such as the El Dorado) as well as the smaller, greenish-yellow, richly flavored Green Gage. The small, bluish-black Damson is prized for jams and preserves. The larger, dark-purple Stanley is usually eaten as fresh fruit. The Japanese varieties are larger, with yellow to red skins and juicy flesh—like the crimson Santa Rosa. Native American varieties are seldom grown commercially, but they have been extensively hybridized with Japanese plums to increase their hardiness.

Prunes are the firm-fleshed variety of plums with a high enough sugar content to permit drying without fermentation around the pit.

Helps Heal Cold Sores

Irritating sores in the mouth like cold or canker sores may be effectively treated by taking 2 tbsps. of any fresh plum juice and swishing the same around inside for a couple of minutes before swallowing. Or for a particularly bad sore, soak a cotton wad with some fresh plum juice and then press against the sore and hold in place with either the tongue, jaw or a little bit of peanut butter smeared to one side.

An Undeniably Fine Laxative

Prunes have long had the reputation of being an outstanding laxative agent for constipated bowels. A therapeutic confection can be made by combining 5–6 pitted prunes, the same number of fresh figs, 1 tsp. of coriander seeds and a tablespoon or so of powdered psyllium seed in a food blender and puréeing until smooth and somewhat stiff in consistency. The amount of psyllium to be used can be adjusted according to the thickness desired for this confection. Portion off into equal tablespoonful amounts on individual pieces of cut wax paper before wrapping and refrigerating. These keep up to a month and several may be taken at one time for chronic constipation. Results usually appear within a couple of hours *or less.*

Very Moving Recipes

My appreciation goes to the folks at Better Homes & Gardens for letting me use this nifty little dessert found in their *Fresh Fruit & Vegetable Recipes* booklet (see Appendix).

Plums Poached in Wine

Needed: 1/3 cup brown sugar; 1/2 cup dry red wine; 1 tbsp. each lemon and lime juice; 2 whole cloves; 2 inches stick cinnamon; 8 pitted and quartered medium plums; some vanilla-flavored yogurt or plain yogurt to which a little real vanilla flavor has been added.

In a saucepan combine sugar and 1/2 cup water. Cook and stir till sugar dissolves. Stir in wine, citrus juices, cloves and stick cinnamon.

Gently stir plums into wine mixture. Bring wine mixture to boiling point. Reduce heat and simmer, covered, for 2 mins. Remove from heat, then remove cloves and stick cinnamon. Serve plums warm, spooning some of the wine mixture over plums. Top each serving with a dollop of yogurt. Serves 4.

Prune Whip

Soak 2 cups dried and softened prunes overnight in 1 qt. warm distilled water and then simmer on low heat the next day for 30 mins. Then mash 1 cup of these cooked and stoned prunes through a coarse sieve. Next beat 2 egg whites very stiff, adding 1/4 cup of sifted brown sugar and a pinch of seasalt afterwards. Fold the mashed prunes into the beaten whites. Bake in an oiled casserole 25 mins. in a slow oven (300° F.). Serve hot or cold with pure maple syrup.

POPPY SEED (See SEEDS.)

POMEGRANATE (*Punica granatum*)

Brief Description

The pomegranate grows wild as a shrub in its native southern Asia and in hot areas of the world. Under cultivation, it's trained as a tree to grow upwards to 20 feet in height, being grown in Asia, the Mediterranean region, South America and the southern states of the U.S. The slender, often spiny-tipped branches bear opposite, oblong or oval-lanceolate, shiny leaves about 1–2 inches long. One to five large, red or orange-red flowers grow together on the tips of the shoots. The brownish-yellow to red fruit, about the size of an orange, is a thick-skinned, several-celled, many-seeded berry; each seed is surrounded by red, acid pulp.

Seeds Expel Tapeworm

Dried pomegranate seeds have been used since time immemorial for getting rid of tapeworm, an incredibly long parasitic host which attaches itself to the intestinal walls of its host by means of spined or sucking structures. Constant hunger, large amount of food intake, yet persistent relative thinness are the most common symptoms.

Dry the seeds from 7–9 pomegranates either in the sun or else in a low-set oven on a cookie sheet for 7 hours. Then crush into powder with a hammer or other heavy object. Take 1 tbsp. of powdered seed in a 6 oz. glass of unsweetened pineapple juice 3–4 times daily on an *empty* stomach. If this is done in conjunction with a mild food fast, it might work quicker in getting the tapeworm out of the system.

POTATOES
WHITE POTATO (*Solanum tuberosum*)
SWEET POTATO (*Ipomea batatas*)
YAMS (*Dioscorea sativa, D. alata*)

Brief Description

White potatoes were first cultivated by South American Incan Indians in the high Andes, and later taken to England in 1586 by Sir Francis Drake. From there their cultivation spread to Ireland, continental Europe and finally, in 1719 to the American colonies.

Modern potatoes, the best of which are a far cry from the small, floury originals, fall into three general groups. New potatoes are the tender, thin-skinned ones usually harvested during late winter and early spring; they are used for boiling, creaming and potato salads. All-purpose potatoes like the Red Pontiac can be boiled, mashed, baked or fried. And the famous Idaho, or Russet, is a popular baking potato.

Yams and sweet potatoes are often confused. Both are edible tubers, but they are from different plant families. Yams probably originated in West Africa; whereas, sweet potatoes, like squash, are native New World vegetables. Sweet potatoes come in many varieties but are of two basic types: the dry fleshed, with rather mealy, pale-yellow flesh; and the moist fleshed, with deep-yellow to orange-red flesh (often incorrectly called a yam).

The common name (*D. sativa*) and the 10 months yam (*D. alata*) are both widely cultivated throughout the South Pacific and have been known to reach weights of up to 100 lbs. They can be baked, boiled, roasted and fried, or used raw in salads.

Potato Plaster for Relieving Pain and Inflammation

In 1987, I met a young pharmacy student from Nova Scotia, who had grown up in the potato country in nearby Maine. Over lunch one afternoon he shared with me some folk data passed on to his family by his late great-grandmother.

According to him, she made special potato plasters for reducing inflammations caused by contusions, sprains, burns, fractures, hemorrhoids, abscesses, appendicitis, arthritis, neuralgia and eczema.

To make her special plasters, she would peel and grate ordinary potatoes and mix half of them with an equal amount of green vegetable leaves (either cabbage, radish or spinach) which had been coarsely puréed in a food blender beforehand. To this wet mass was added about 10% white flour. Everything was then thoroughly mixed in a large pan by hand. Just enough ice-cold water (*never* warm) was slowly added to give the paste a wet, somewhat even and thick consistency without being runny or lumpy.

His grandma then applied this potato plaster directly to the skin. On top of it she would place a clean cloth and secure it in place with a lengthy swath of linen bandage fashioned from strips of old bedsheets. She would require that the person being treated stay in a reclining position during the time that this plaster remained on, which usually averaged about 3-1/2 hours.

Quite often the plaster would have dried out, so she would apply some warm water on the dry mass until it became moist again, permitting easier removal without much pain and discomfort to the patient. Once the plaster was off, the skin would then be rinsed with some warm water.

Sometimes, he said, she might rub a little olive oil on the area to be treated to prevent or reduce any chronic itching which might take place while the plaster was on the skin.

He noted that she also used the same potato plasters for drawing out purulent matter from boils, abscesses, infected acne, carbuncles, infected cysts and various types of tumors (benign, fibroid and even malignant). In a couple of instances, the women she treated for breast tumors, he observed, had most of the cancerous matter gathered towards the surface from further inside the body, thanks to her potato plasters. These women then had surgeries to remove these malignant accumulations, but, interestingly enough, the doctors didn't have to operate as much as they might have done had these women never been treated by her first of all.

Lose Weight Eating Potatoes

Potatoes by themselves are *not* fattening. It's the toppings that have earned for them the undeserved distinction of being fattening. Common sense tells you that a potato dripping with butter, sour cream or rich gravy is heavy in calories and bound to add more inches to the waistline. But a plain spud is no more fattening than eating a pear—the potato itself is 99.9% fat free, with a whole half pound of baked potato containing *less* than 250 calories!

Nutritionists at the Home Economics Dept. of Douglass College, New Brunswick, N.J. demonstrated the potato can be included in a reducing diet with good results. In a carefully controlled study, students who followed a food plan containing potatoes lost an average of 14 pounds in 8 weeks—an ideal amount to lose.

A Creole Grandmother's Remedies

A very old Creole lady by the name of Clothilde Rousseau, aged 86, gave me a number of very effective remedies for an assortment of health problems utilizing white potatoes.

"Back in the early 1930's I suffered from eye-strain. I washed one potato and then cut 6 slices the size of a quarter from it. These I laid on my eyes, 3 on either side, and tied a strip of cloth around my head to hold them in place. They were soothing and took away the pain and inflammation.

"For people who had neuralgia, I treated them by laying a baked potato against the side of their face or neck where it hurt them the most, and covered it with a towel to keep the heat in as long as possible. It worked everytime!

"For black-and-blue marks I found that potatoes worked a lot better than raw beefsteak ever did. I'd just make a simple poultice of grated raw potato and apply it to any bruises on the skin. After leaving it there for an hour or so the discoloration and tenderness usually had gone down quite a bit.

"When I was about 5 years old I suddenly came down with a bad case of gallstones. At first my momma thought it might be appendicitis 'cause it hurt my side so bad. But she consulted with an old Cajun healer who told her to peel some potatoes and make a broth of the peelings. This she did and gave me 4 to 5 cups a day for about a week. She usually checked my toilet waste and noticed that a number of the stones had started to come out. Pretty soon I was healed and never have been troubled with them since. I've used this same remedy myself on many others who've been bothered with the same problem over the years and never knew it to once fail them.

"Down through the years I've had folks referred to me who couldn't always handle our spicy food. In every instance, I'd have the person just take a small piece of raw potato no bigger than my thumb and chew on it good before swallowing it. Relief generally came to most in a minute or two. For those folks who had serious ulcers I'd have them drink a cup of raw potato juice in warm water first thing every morning.

"A lady who lived next door to me once came over screaming for help because her youngin' had just poured boiling water all over himself, scalding his skin pretty good. I went over there every day for nearly a month and applied lots of grated raw potato wherever he was burned. He managed to come out of it okay and never had any signs of scars that I know of.

"Potatoes have the greatest drawing power to them that I ever saw in a vegetable. I've used potato slices on infected sores to help draw out the pus and infection when nothing else seemed to work. I doubt you'll find anything that works better for abscesses and wounds than this. It really helps to get out the rotten stuff so they can heal faster."

Potatoes Reduce Heart Strokes

In Ireland men consume more than 170% more potatoes than their Irish-American counterparts do. Irish men ate 267 grams of starch daily (mostly from spuds), while second-generation Irish-Americans in Massachusetts consumed only 116 grams of starch daily (with only a small portion coming from potatoes). Statistics indicated that only 29% of all deaths in Ireland for the late 1960s in men aged 45–64 years were the result of ischemic heart disease (IHD), compared with a whopping 42% of all deaths for the same period in second-generation Bostonian men.

An analysis of fresh potatoes showed that they rank as the richest source of vitamin C out of a number of fresh vegetables examined. Researchers concluded that such vitamin C-rich foods offer some protection against coronary heart disease. A final study reported that large amounts of potato given in experimental diets significantly reduced serum cholesterol levels in man. And Dr. Elizabeth Barrett-Connor of the University of California at San Diego found that men and women out of a group of 859 between the ages of 50–79 years, with low-potassium diets were 3–5 times as likely to die after a stroke than those who had higher potassium diets. Among foods recommended to cut strokes significantly was "a small potato with 350 milligrams of potassium." Thus it would appear that potatoes are beneficial for the heart when consumed without fat and either baked or boiled.

Starch May Prevent Suicide

Suicide is often in the news these days, particularly among our young people. A San Diego State University history professor, Howard Kushner, is inclined to think that societies which consume significant carbohydrates have much lower incidence of suicide than those cultures which do not. In a paper published in the Summer 1985 issue of the *Journal of Interdisciplinary History,* Dr. Kushner postulates that potatoes and pasta could be keeping untold numbers of Irish and Italians from killing themselves; whereas, the Danes, Germans and Austrians, who consume less of these carbohydrates have higher suicide rates as a result.

Swedish and American experiments included extracting spinal fluid from 30 volunteers who had attempted suicide in order to determine the level of an important brain chemical called serotonin. A large number had significantly lower levels of serotonin than did a control group of normal individuals. Furthermore, those with less serotonin were more violence-prone too.

Now serotonin is a protein that transports messages to brain cells. It is produced in the body by the amino acid tryptophan, which must be supplied by diet. But tryptophan encounters stiff competition from other amino acids when it attempts to cross the barrier from the bloodstream into the brain. However, when some carbohydrates like potatoes or pasta are consumed, insulin is secreted and this then lowers the level of competing amino acids so that more tryptophan can get through. Once it reaches the area of the brain, then sufficient serotonin can be produced, which helps to lower depression and anxiety somewhat.

So it seems relatively safe to say that potatoes should figure frequently in the diets of those who may be experiencing mental and emotional instabilities of some sort as a reasonable precaution against potential suicide.

More Rapid and Frequent Bowel Movements

According to the Sept. 1977 *Irish Journal of Medical Science,* frequent consumption of *un*peeled spuds can do wonders for cleansing the intestines. Twenty-five of 48 volunteers maintained a daily intake of potatoes approximating to 2.2 lbs for a minimum of 10 weeks and maximum of 20 weeks. The average consumption was slightly under 2 lbs. and contained an estimated 1/7th of an ounce of crude fiber. A significant decrease in the length of time it took food to go through the intestinal tract and a reduction in colon-rectal pressures was evident. A significant increase in stool weights was also noted as well.

Yams Remove Heavy Metals from Body

Yams and sweet potatoes contain simple peptide substances called phytochelatins, that can bind heavy metals like cadmium, copper, mercury and lead, and thus participate in metal detoxification of body tissue. These metal-chelating compounds interact with the mineral sulphur to achieve this. In light of this it's interesting to note that doctors in the Soviet Union include potatoes, yams and cabbage (all sulphur-rich vegetables) in a special prophylactic diet for factory workers constantly exposed to toxic chemical occupational environments. When one considers that most of our big cities have a terrible smog problem, it only seems prudent for us to eat more of these three vegetables ourselves so that we don't accumulate and become ill from the heavy metals in the air we breathe each day.

Sweet potato and yam are also good for helping to remove any kind of foreign object accidentally swallowed by a small child or a mentally retarded adult (such as safety pins, needles, coins, tumb-tacks and the like). By feeding the individual some boiled, baked or steamed sweet potato or yam, it will help to coat the object and safely expel it from the body through the colon later on. Ripe, mashed bananas work just as well, I might add.

Cooking Creatively

The following recipes are simple and easy to prepare. They offer some "quickie" meals if served alone that are nutritious and good tasting as well.

O'Brien Potatoes

Start with Potatoes Lyonnaise, using sliced (1/8) or diced, medium-sized boiled potatoes, peeled, browned in melted butter, combined with sautéed onion and chopped parsley and seasoned to taste. When the Lyonnaise are ready, pop in 1/4 cup chopped green pepper, 1/4 cup chopped pimiento and 1/4 cup heavy cream. Cook the cream down over medium heat. Blend by shaking pan as the dish cooks. Serve in a hot dish.

Apricot Sweet Potato

Needed: 1 baked sweet potato; 4 chopped, dried apricot halves; 2 tsp. maple syrup; 1/2 tsp. lemon juice; 1/2 tsp. lime juice; 2 tbsp. applesauce; some toasted almonds to garnish (optional).

Cut about 1/3 off the top of the cooked potato. Scoop out pulp. Reserve shell and keep warm. Mix potato pulp with remaining ingredients. Stuff into the reserved potato shell. Serve hot.

PRICKLY ASH (*Zanthoxylum americanum*)

Brief Description

This tall shrub, or rarely a small tree, can reach heights of over 20 feet. It is characterized by thorny stems and branches and leaves that are hairy young, smooth when older with resinous dots on them and emitting the smell of lemon when crushed. The greenish flowers, in clusters on last year's wood, appear before the leaves. They are followed by reddish-brown, rough capsules containing black seed or seeds, the taste of which is spicy. Prickly ash is found from Canada to Virginia and Nebraska.

Great Relief from Paralysis and Pain

The 19th century plant authority, Charles F. Millspaugh, had a great deal to say about the wonderful virtues of prickly ash bark and berries in his book on *American Medicinal Plants*. For instance, while walking in the woods one day doing botanical research, his tooth began to ache. "But upon chewing the bark of prickly ash for relief," he recounted, "speedy mitigation of the pain followed!" A little dried bark ground into a powder and then sprinkled on an inch square piece of white bread coated with a little peanut butter to hold in place inside the mouth, or a wad of cotton soaked with some tincture and firmly held against the tooth, will relieve any kind of pain within minutes.

Millspaugh also praised its remarkable action upon inactive saliva glands, where the bark can promote full saliva flow within a very short time. Dr. Mary R. Leason, an elderly herbalist practitioner from Federal Way, Washington, wrote to me once how she effectively cured a friend of hers by the name of Fern Roemer, who had lost all salivary and taste functions due to the strong antibiotics given her while in the hospital. "I just fixed her up with some powdered prickly ash bark," Dr. Leason said, "which I had her put on her tongue every few hours. Pretty soon she was drooling all over the place and got back her taste buds again."

In his book, Millspaugh recited the success of various Cincinnati, Ohio physicians in the mid-19th century when they used tincture of prickly ash on their patients suffering peritonitis, distention of the bowels, severe abdominal inflammation and swelling, intense fevers like cholera, typhus and typhoid—and pneumonia.

Generally 1 tsp. of the tincture in 3/4 cup of water sweetened with a little honey was administered every hour and about 12 times these amounts (minus the honey) were given in the form of an enema too. "The action was prompt and permanent," Millspaugh wrote. "Prickly ash acted like electricity, so sudden and diffusive was its influence over the entire system. I consider the tincture of prickly ash berries and bark to be superior to any form of medication I know of."

Certain Native American tribes relied a lot on prickly ash for curing rheumatism, joint stiffness, muscle paralysis, lower back pain and other arthritic-like symptoms. The Algonquins, for example, made a tea by combining 2 cups of the fresh or dried bark with 2 qts. of hot water and simmering the same in a kettle or black iron pot over a low fire for an hour or so, uncovered, until the liquid had been reduced to half this amount. They would then drink freely of this brew in order to work up a good sweat, after which they would go and bathe in a nearby river or stream. This method never failed to bring them several hours of lasting relief from pain.

The Chippewa made the same kind of tea, which was used to bathe the legs and feet of sickly, weak children or the elderly in order to give them additional strength to walk and move about more freely. The fresh or dried cut bark was also steeped for several hours in hot bear grease (substitute lard for this) before rubbing on painful muscles and joints for incredible relief from pain. Cut or powdered prickly ash bark is available from Indiana Botanical Gardens in Hammond and a tincture of the berries from Eclectic Institute of Portland, Oregon (see Appendix).

Remedy for Sickle Cell Anemia

Sickle cell anemia is a disease occurring most frequently among Blacks throughout the world. Symptoms include those of anemia, leg ulcers, arthritic manifestations and acute attacks of pain, with the hemoglobin being quite abnormal. In his scientific reference work, *Medicinal Plants and Traditional Medicine in Africa,* Abayomi Sofowora, who is Professor of Pharmacognosy at the University of Ife in Ile-Ife, Nigeria, indicates that a water extract of the active principle from the powdered root of prickly ash "will revert sickle-cell anaemia." "Studies show that the extract of the root is not toxic orally," he adds. "It has reduced significantly the painful crisis of sickle-cell patients in a clinical trial carried out in Ibadan.'' Besides the root, however, the young leaves of prickly ash also are a very rich source of the anti-sickling acids, which stop the progress of this terrible disease.

Nigerian folk herbalists have consequently used strong tea extracts made of these young leaves of an African species of prickly ash for curing their patients who've been afflicted with sickle cell anemia. Usually a generous handful of leaves are added to a quart of boiling water and permitted to steep away from heat, covered, for 1-1/2 hours. The dosage generally administered to those in their care is approximately 3 cups daily in between meals as a rule.

Nature's Own Toothbrush

During my several trips to the African continent in the past, I've had the opportunity of observing and using the African version of a toothbrush. The root or slim stem of species of prickly ash are thoroughly chewed until they acquire brush-like ends. The fibrous end is then used to brush the teeth thoroughly. These chewing sticks, as they're called, are used frequently during the day.

When I tried them, they imparted a tingling, peppery taste to my tongue and left it and my gums kind of numb for awhile. But they sure helped to remove food particles from between my teeth and in those hard-to-get crevices. They worked better, I thought, than regular toothpaste, brushing and flossing did. My teeth and gums never felt stronger, cleaner or better than when I used these chewing sticks from prickly ash! If you have access to a prickly ash in your immediate vicinity, then I heartily encourage you to utilize its twigs for this very purpose. You may never want to go back to brushing with Crest or rinsing with Listerine after you've tried this method for awhile.

PRUNES (See PLUMS.)

PSYLLIUM (*Plantago ovata*)

Brief Description

A stemless or short-stemmed annual herb. Its leaves are in a rosette or alternate, clasping the stem strap-like, and average 3 to 10 inches in length and 1/4 to 1/2 inch in width. The flowers are white, minute, four-parted, in erect, ovoid or cylindrical spikes. The fruit is ovate with the top half separating when ripe, releasing smooth, dull ovate seeds that are either pinkish-gray-brown or pinkish-white with brown streaks on them. Each seed is encased in a thin, white, translucent husk which is odorless and tasteless. When soaked in water, the whole seeds expand considerably in size.

Obesity and Constipation Cured

Certain bulk laxatives such as Metamucil, Effersyllium and Syllamalt are all composed of the ground husks or seeds of psyllium in combination with sugar to make them taste pleasant. Clinical studies have shown that psyllium by itself is superior in its action to other known laxatives such as mineral oil, milk of magnesia, cascara sagrada, methylcellulose or phenolphthalein.

And various clinical experiments conducted in Italy have demonstrated the value of psyllium seed in obese and diabetic patients. In obese subjects, there was a noticeable decrease in serum cholesterol and a reduction of food intake as well. Diabetic patients benefited from a drop in their blood sugar levels. A Southern California group of medical doctors observed that psyllium helped relieve irritable bowel syndrome in many of their patients. An average of 3 capsules daily of a unique product called Fiber Cleanse is suggested for the above problems. The product may be obtained from any local health food store under the Nature's Way label.

PUMPKIN, SQUASH and GOURD
PUMPKIN *Cucurbita pepo*
SQUASH (Summer) *Cucurbita pepo*
SQUASH (Winter) *Cucurbita maxima*
SQUASH (Zucchini) *Cucurbita pepo*
GOURD (Bottle) *Lagenaria vulgaris*

Brief Description

Pumpkin is the fabled jack-o-lantern of Halloween tradition and that very same object which the headless horseman threw at a frightened and fleeing Ichabod Crane with great fury and deadly accuracy, in the immortal tale by Washington Irving. Pumpkin is a variety of winter squash recognized by its smooth, round shape and hard-ribbed, orange-colored rind. For cooking purposes, the small sugar pumpkins averaging 7 lbs. or so are best. But for scaring the wits out of young kids, varieties like the Big Max weighing 100 lbs. or more are hard to beat.

Squashes originated in the New World and were introduced to the conquistadores by early Native Americans, who in turn carried these food plants back to Europe with them later on. Squash is divided into two basic groups: the quick-growing, tender-skinned "summer" squashes, which are harvested immature; and the larger, slower growing, hard-shelled "winter" squashes, harvested when fully mature. Summer squashes like yellow crooknecks, pattypans and zucchini, are consumed whole. But winter squashes such as Hubbards, butternuts, acorns and sugar pumpkins have inedible skins which must first be removed after cooking them before they can be eaten. However they are usually tastier and more nutritious than the summer varieties are.

The name pumpkin goes back to the Greek word "pepōn," meaning ripe or mellow. In time the early French had it down to "poupon" and, having been nasalized into "poumpon," entered the King's English as "pompion," to which was later added the diminutive "-kin" ending. Squash, on the other hand, is derived soley from the Algonquin Indian word "askoot asquash," which translated means "eaten green."

There are many kinds of gourds, which serve a variety of uses ranging from domestic to ornamental. There are inedible varieties looking like waxy, warted apples, lemons and tangerines, all the fascinating produce of the same plant. During classical times and the Middle Ages a certain kind of edible gourd was known, probably one of the bottle gourds. These have woody rinds which are used as bottles, cooking and eating implements.

Cooling Effect on Inflammation

A number of remedies have already been given in this book for sunburn and burns in general. One of the quickest things I've ever found for immediate relief from the intense pain is to cover the burn with ice-cold mashed pumpkin, either freshly cooked or from the can, providing both have been refrigerated overnight. This handy remedy was first brought to my attention by an Indian woman named Sally "Big Thighs" Henderson, who resided on the Navajo Reservation in northern Arizona. That, by the way, is her honest-to-goodness name!

Tea for Any Kidney Problem

Among the Cherokee Indians, pumpkin and squash seeds were valuable for treating edema, gout, kidneystones, urinary burning and difficult urination. A handful of the seeds were crushed and then added to a quart of boiling water, covered, and simmered on low heat for about 20 minutes, then permitted to steep away from the heat for an additional half an hour. Several cups of the strained liquid were drunk each day as needed until the desired relief was obtained.

Leaves Reduce Sprains

A very useful application of the leaves of pumpkin, squash or gourd may be found in the treatment of sprains, bruises, torn ligaments and the like. Certain herbal practitioners in Jamaica, who also dabble in black magic and voodoo, will often utilize the fresh leaves for these purposes. The picked leaves are first pounded with a hammer or small round stone in order to macerate them a little, before being bound on a sprain or dislocation of some sort. They help to take the swelling down quite a bit and seem to hasten the healing process when other internal remedies for inflammation are used.

Recently several people have benefited from a variation of this same remedy that I've recommended to them for minor fractures, lower backache and tendonitis. First of all some special chamomile cream called CamoCare was gently rubbed on the injured areas, after which either a pumpkin or squash leaf poultice was then applied and left for several hours with very good results. The CamoCare cream is available from most health food stores or may be obtained from Abkit, Inc. of New York City (see Appendix).

Fevers and Diarrhea Go Away

Other very popular uses for the leaves is to reduce fevers and stop diarrhea.

Some Jamaican voodoo witchdoctors will make a tea from pumpkin or squash leaves or use equal parts of both. About 2 quarts of water are brought to a boil, after which a couple of double-handfuls of leaves are snipped into the pot with a pair of scissors or shears. The pot is then covered, removed from the flame and permitted to steep for about 35 minutes. A cup at a time is administered every couple of hours until the fever or diarrhea stops.

Keeping the Prostate in Great Shape

As men get older, body organs tend to wear out. One of the most frequent of these to break down is the prostate gland, which often requires surgery to correct. But now there is a much easier and safer way to keep this organ functioning like it should. A homemade syrup can be taken each day to assure a man past his prime that his prostate won't fail him later on in life.

First, shell and bruise with a hammer 6 tbsps. each of 6 ripe pumpkin and squash seeds. Then put them through a meat grinder so as to render finely ground. Next mix in equal parts of blackstrap molasses and dark honey or just enough of both to form a nice, thick syrup. Finally, flavor with a little powdered cardamom and cinnamon and the juice from half a lemon. Take one tablespoonful every morning before breakfast or at least three times a week for sure. This same syrup, I might add, is also another excellent way to take the seeds for expelling tapeworms and roundworms.

Migraines and Earaches Disappear

In certain parts of India and Europe the scraped pulp of fresh pumpkin or yellow and orange squash is applied to the forehead and temples as a cooling application to relieve intensely splitting headaches. And the same grated pulp is also applied to the sides of the face, neck and throat to relieve neuralgia or to draw out the purulent matter in ripe boils. This same pulp is likewise excellent for burns.

Throughout the Philippines, native practitioners will often squeeze the sap from fresh pumpkin stems into their patients' ears to help relieve earaches. A friend of mine tried this once when he got water into his inner ear after swimming. About an hour later he reported the misery had cleared up of its own accord.

Possible Cancer Preventative

A Symposium on Nutrition and Cancer was held at the University of Adelaide in Australia in November 1978. One of the featured speakers was Dr. Takeshi Hirayama of the National Cancer Research Institute in Tokyo, Japan. In his address, Dr. Hirayama revealed his research findings in his remarks on green-yellow vegetables. He consistently found *lower* risks of many kinds of cancer in those who frequently consumed pumpkin, squashes, carrots, broccoli and green bell peppers than in those who ate below average amounts of them. Highlights of his interesting paper were reported in the March 10, 1979 issue of *The Medical Journal of Australia.*

An Effective Cure for Tapeworms

Speaking from personal experience, I can attest to the wonderful benefits of either pumpkin or squash seeds for getting rid of tapeworm.

Even now I can recall having to chew very thoroughly each day for 5-1/2 days a cup of dried pumpkin seeds from the health food store when I was just 13 years old.

For several years prior to this, I had been eating voraciously, but never gained a single pound of weight. At first everyone thought it was just the "growing boy" syndrome, which every tall, lanky kid goes through during his teenage years. In time, however, several naturopathic doctors who examined me (my folks never believed in regular M.D.'s as such) confirmed that it was a severe case of tapeworm, which was robbing me of the proper nourishment I should have been getting from the tons of food I was shoveling down.

Well, they recommended the pumpkin seeds, which apparently worked quite good within just a short period of time. A succession of different bowel movements on my part discharged chunks and sections of what had been a pretty long parasitic worm attached to the walls of my intestine. Various estimates were made as to its overall length, ranging from 20 feet to well over 45 feet. For myself, however, I never bothered keeping track of these statistics. I was just glad to get the ordeal over with and back to a more normal diet. In the course of time I filled out very nicely. I would recommend grinding the seeds up into a powder and serving them 1/2 cup of powder at a time in 1-1/2 cups of apple sauce, or mixed in with some carrot juice in a food blender as a vegetable shake in order to make them more palatable. Some have even suggested making a tea out of the seeds, but I have never found this to work as effectively as taking the seeds straight.

A folk healer friend of mine from Merida on the Yucatan Peninsula shared with me some years back an old Mayan remedy for expelling intestinal worms of any kind that he had found never failed once in those of his patients to whom he had prescribed it in times past.

On an empty stomach 2 tbsps. of castor oil were first ingested. The next day 1/2 cup of shelled and powdered seeds of pumpkin or squash mixed with a little water were taken, followed by 1 cup of goat's milk. Then some two hours later, another 2 tbsps. of castor oil were ingested.

Helps Heal Scratches and Minor Wounds

The Zuni Indians of Arizona have long relied upon the seeds and flowers of pumpkin and squashes for healing cactus scratches and minor wounds. The dried seeds are first ground into a fine powder, after which freshly picked blossoms are gently crushed and added in. Just enough water is then mixed in with them to make a smooth, even paste, which is then applied directly on any kind of skin injuries with good results.

A Wealth of Recipes

Pumpkin and squashes make excellent soups, breads and pies not to mention tasty casseroles and vegetable side dishes as the following recipes prove.

Creamy Squash Soup

This delicious soup comes from Better Homes & Gardens' *Fresh Fruit & Vegetable Recipes* booklet through the courtesy of the publisher, Meredith Corp. (see Appendix).

Needed: 2 cups chopped, peeled potatoes; 2 cups chopped, peeled acorn squash; 1/2 cup chopped onion; 1-1/2 tsp. snipped fresh marjoram or 1/2 tsp. crushed, dried marjoram; 3/4 tsp. instant chicken bouillon granules; 1 minced clove garlic; 2 cups milk.

In a large saucepan combine spuds, squash, onion, marjoram, bouillon granules, garlic, 1 cup water and 1/8 tsp. pepper. Bring to boiling. Reduce heat and simmer, covered, about 20 mins. or until vegetables are tender. Transfer about half of the vegetable mixture to a blender container or food processor bowl. Cover and blend or process until smooth. Repeat with remaining vegetable mixture. Return all to saucepan. Stir in milk and heat through, but *do not* boil. Lightly season with a dash of cardamom just before serving. Makes 10 servings.

Willard Scott's Love Affair with Squash

America's favorite meteorologist, Willard Scott of NBC-TV's "Today" show, considers squash one of his favorite vegetables. This loveable and wacky weatherman is also pretty adept at cooking as well. According to Scott, one of the tastiest zucchini dishes he's ever tried is a sort of casserole, made with peppers, celery and cream. "You put that on crackers, and mmm, mm-mm," the forecaster rhapsodized.

Here is a slightly modified version of his scrumptious apple-squash bran muffins.

Needed: 1-1/2 cups All-Bran cereal; 1-1/2 to 1-2/3 cups canned goat milk; 1/3 cup corn oil; 1 large egg; 1-1/4 cups all-purpose flour; 1/2 cup brown sugar; 3 tsp. baking powder; 1/2 tsp. salt; 1 apple, peeled, cored and diced; 1/2 medium acorn squash, peeled, prebaked for 20 mins, and diced; 1-1/2 handfuls of raisins; 1/2 handful chopped, pitted dates; 1/2 handful finely chopped walnut meats; 1 tsp. ground cinnamon to taste.

Beat together cereal, milk, oil and egg with an electric mixer. In a separate bowl, mix flour, sugar, baking powder and salt. Add dry ingredients to bran mixture and stir until well-mixed. Then stir in apple, squash, raisins, dates, walnuts and cinnamon. Pour into greased muffin tins and bake at 400° F. almost half an hour or until the muffins have risen and are golden. Makes a dozen delicious muffins.

Mohican Pumpkin-Squash Bread

The Mohicans (also spelled Mohegan) were once a powerful North American Indian tribe residing in the state of Connecticut, who later became immortalized in James Fenimore Cooper's classic novel, *Last of the Mohicans.* Although they were unfortunately wiped out as a nation through the cruelty of the white man, several of their unique recipes still survive in old pioneer diaries and journals kept during that period. This is one of them, which has been slightly modified for 20th-century cooking methods.

Needed: 3/4 cups each of chopped, peeled banana squash and pumpkin; 1/4 cup olive oil; 1-1/2 cups all-purpose flour; 1 tsp. ground cinnamon; 1/2 tsp. baking soda; 1/2 tsp. cardamom; 1/4 tsp. ground cloves; 2 slightly beaten egg whites; 1/2 cup blackstrap molasses; 1/4 cup pure maple syrup; 1/4 cup brown sugar; 1/4 cup chopped, pitted dates; some liquid lecithin from any local health food store.

Put squash and pumpkin in a large saucepan, with about 2/3 inch of water. Cook, covered, for about 25 mins. or until sufficiently tender. Then drain. Place squash and pumpkin with olive oil in a food blender and mix until smooth and even in consistency. Then stir together the flour, cinnamon, baking soda, cardamom and cloves. In a medium mixing bowl stir together the egg whites, molasses, maple syrup, sugar and squash-pumpkin mixture. Then add flour mixture. Next fold in the dates. Thoroughly rub the insides of an 8x4x2-inch loaf pan with liquid lecithin. Transfer the batter to this prepared pan. Bake in a 350° oven for 50 mins. or until sufficiently done. Remove from the pan and cool thoroughly on a wire rack.

One loaf generally yields a little over a dozen servings.

R

RED RADISH (*Raphanus sativus*)
DAIKON RADISH (*Raphanus sativus longipinnatus*)

Brief Description

Radishes have been around since the days of Moses. The Egyptian pharoahs included them as standard rations, along with garlic, leeks, onions and cucumbers, for the several hundred thousand Hebrew slaves who constructed their mighty pyramids for them.

In the United States, the cherry-sized red radish is the most common variety sold, but radishes come in all shapes, sizes and colors, including an intriguing black one. Popular varieties besides the Scarlet Globe and Cherry Belle (both globular red radishes), are French Breakfast (an elongated, white-tipped red radish), White Icicle (long and mild tasting) and the favorite of all Japanese, the Daikon (a long, sharp-tasting white radish).

Helps in Digesting Starchy Foods

Throughout much of Europe, radishes are frequently consumed with bread and breakfast cereals. And the Japanese really like the daikon variety to accompany virtually all rich dishes. In both instances, we find that radishes seem to help in the digestion of starchy foods, such as grains, pastas, potatoes and the like. This is due, in part, to the presence of a special digestive enzyme called diastase, which occurs in the daikon radish in large amounts. So with those meals you're apt to consume that are loaded with starches, be sure to include some raw radishes as well for easier digestion.

Removing Hard Fat Deposits

Several years ago when I was in Tokyo attending an herbal medicine symposium, I had called to my attention an article in the *Asahi News* (Japan's largest circulated daily newspaper) by a Japanese colleague. This scientist friend of mine translated it into English for my benefit. The story dealt with a remedy employed by *kanpō* doctors in the eastern hills of Kyoto. These doctors, while practicing alternative folk medicine, were all regular M.D.s and had previously graduated from the prestigious Kyoto University School of Medicine.

The remedy employed for reducing and eliminating solidified deposits of hard fat imbedded in body tissue, consisted of a vegetable drink made with carrot and white daikon radish. Equal portions of grated carrot and daikon (1 tbsp. each) were added to 2 cups of water with 7 drops of soy sauce, 1 tsp. lemon juice and a pinch of kelp, and allowed to boil for 5 minutes. The broth was later strained and 1 cup prescribed twice daily, in the morning and again at night.

Stops Chronic Coughing and Raging Fevers

An old Chinese remedy calls for a handful of chopped, pithy roots from an old radish plant gone to seed to be boiled in a quart of water with a little pork for 40 mins. Several cups of this lukewarm broth are then drunk each day for relieving spasmodic coughing, reducing high fever and creating an appetite in those recuperating from recent illness.

Controls Diarrhea

Where diarrhea may persist and nothing else is readily available to stop it, some radishes will do the job effectively. In a food blender thoroughly mix together a handful of chopped red radishes, 1 cup of cold milk and 1/2 tsp. Kingsford cornstarch. Drink the entire amount slowly. This concoction should stop the runs in less than an hour. Repeat again in 4 hours, if needed.

Prevents Gallstones and Kidneystones

Good remedial management of existing stones in the gall bladder or kidneys, or to prevent their occurrence, entails making a daily drink in your food blender consisting of 2 chopped red radishes and 1/2 cup of red wine. This mixture may be taken twice a day for difficult urination too.

An old English remedy for stones has been used with very good success for several centuries now. The expressed juice of white daikon or black Spanish radishes is given in increasing doses from 1–2 cups daily. These 1–2 cupfuls are continued for 2–3 weeks. Then the dose is decreased until 1/2 cupfuls are taken 3 times weekly for nearly another month. The treatment may be repeated by taking 1 cupful at the beginning, then 1/2 daily and later 1/2 every other day.

Deodorant for Feet and Underarms

As a nutritious vegetable and wonderful medicinal, radishes also offer a third usefulness in the form of a toiletry for offensive body odor. But for this a juicer is needed. The juice from about 2 dozen radishes may either be put into an empty lotion bottle with a squirt top or else into a bottle with a hand-spray on it. About 1/4 tsp. of glycerine should also be added to the juice before bottling it to preserve it longer, unless you intend to refrigerate the same, in which case no glycerine is required.

After your morning shower or bath, pour some of this radish juice into the palm of your hand and rub under each armpit. Or else just spray some beneath each arm and on the soles of your feet and in between the toes, rubbing it in good to afford several hours' protection against odor. Radish juice is also useful for bruises, frostbite, insect bites, and stings and minor burns.

Quick Remedy for Burns and Scalds

Throughout this book a number of reliable remedies for treating serious burns and scalds are offered. (See Table of Contents for complete listing.) Many of them, however, take time to prepare.

A really fast remedy, though, calls for a handful of cleaned and chopped radishes to be put into a food blender with some crushed ice and thoroughly purèed until a nice, thick, even mixture is produced. This is then applied directly onto a burn or scald, covered loosely with clean muslin, and taped to hold in place. This brings almost immediate relief from pain and slows down infection considerably. To speed healing even more, add some zinc tablets and 1 tsp. of vitamin E oil while mixing the radishes and ice in your food blender.

Radishes for Cancer Treatment

Fresh radishes and radish seeds have been employed in the treatment of cancer around the world. Such success has been carefully documented in a variety of scientific publications. Lily M. Perry's *Medicinal Plants of East and Southeast Asia*, published by the Massachusetts Institute of

Technology Press in Cambridge, describes the use of the seeds made into a strong tea for reducing stomach cancer and their external application as a heated poultice for treating breast cancer in women.

Dr. Jonathan L. Hartwell, formerly of the National Cancer Institute in Bethesda, Maryland, carefully screened thousands of plants for potential anti-cancer activity. His comprehensive report appeared in different issues of the scientific journal, *Lloydia*. In the March 1969 number, Dr. Hartwell cited fomentations of radish juice in cooking oil as being useful for abdominal tumors, the entire plant itself cooked in wine and oil good for liver and spleen hardness and just the red radish itself boiled in red wine and honey for treating, as he described it, "cancer of the fleshy parts."

A thorough analysis of the possible anti-cancer constituents in daikon and red radish appeared in the September 1978 issue of *Agricultural & Biological Chemistry*. Among the many volatile sulphur components cited was methanethiol. This factor has an odor of rotten cabbage to it, also evolves from penicillin bread cultures and is used in the manufacturing of pesticides and fungicides due to its strong anti-bacterial properties. It's components such as this that make radishes very good for many different kinds of cancer. Certainly I'm not recommending that it alone be used, but am suggesting radishes be included with other sulphur-bearing vegetables and herbs like cabbage, kale, kohlrabi, Brussel sprouts, mustard greens, watercress, garlic and onion in a special dietary program to combat cancer nutritionally as well as medically.

Some Salad Ideas

The Japanese have over 100 different ways to cook with daikon radish. Raw, it can be grated and eaten with fish or meat. It's added to miso (fermented bean paste) soup. It's used to make flowers for a garnish, and is that stringy white stuff that's put with sashimi (raw fish) in Japanese restaurants. It can be shredded with carrots and dressed with a sweet vinaigrette for a salad. Or it can be cut into chunks and put in stews. A nice characteristic of daikon is that while it will get soft when cooked it won't dissolve.

Radishes go especially well in salads. Below are interesting salad ideas for the fussy gourmet and health enthusiast.

Radish-Cabbage Slaw with Sesame-Yogurt Dressing

Needed: 2 cups shredded cabbage (preferably a mixture of red and green cabbage); 1 cup grated carrot; 1 cup grated daikon radish;

2/3 cup grated red radish; 3/4 cup plain yogurt; 2 tsp. chopped fresh dill or 1 tsp. dried dill; 1 tsp. sesame seed oil; 1/4 cup toasted sesame seeds; 1-1/2 tbsps. tamari.

In a large bowl, combine the cabbage, carrot and both kinds of radish. Stir in the yogurt, dill, sesame oil, sesame seeds and tamari. Taste and add more tamari if desired.

Latin-Lover Salad

Needed: 1 head of romaine lettuce, torn into bite-sized chunks: 1 bunch of fresh, chopped coriander; 1 bunch of thinly sliced radishes and their leaves; 1 chopped green bell pepper (including its seeds); 2 peeled, pitted and sliced avocados; 2 sliced, ripe tomatoes; 1/2 lb. shelled, de-veined and boiled shrimp; 1/3 cup olive oil; 2 de-seeded limes, cut in half; kelp to taste.

Arrange the vegetables and shrimp in a large bowl, and drizzle with the olive oil. Squeeze on the lime juice, and add kelp. Toss lightly. Serves 4–6. NOTE: The last two recipes have been adapted from the elegant book, *Vegetables* by four San Francisco Bay Area writers and courtesy of the publisher, Chronicle Books (see Appendix).

RAISINS (See GRAPES and RAISINS.)

RASPBERRY (See BERRIES.)

CHINESE RHUBARB (*Rheum officinale*)

GARDEN RHUBARB (*Rheum rhaponticum*)

Brief Description

Species of rhubarb are denoted by their large and sturdy sizes and large leaves borne on thick petioles. These hardy perennials grow between 7 and 10 feet high, are native to southern Siberia, China and India, and widely cultivated elsewhere.

Chinese rhubarb is used more for medicinal purposes, while the garden variety is grown more for its edible stalks (petioles) and ornamental beauty.

Strengthens Tooth Enamel

Rhubarb is high in potassium and calcium with a lesser amount of phosphorus. These mineral salts, according to a Rochester, N.Y. dentist, occur in rhubarb juice and seem to coat tooth enamel with a thin protective film. Dr. Basil G. Bibby of the Eastman Dental Center believes that more frequent consumption of cooked rhubarb might be of some positive benefit in helping to reduce extensive decay.

Better still, a little bit of the expressed juice from fresh rhubarb stalks brushed on the teeth with a soft bristle brush or else rubbed on with some cotton balls every other day, should coat the enamel with these protective minerals.

Shows Anti-Tumor Value

Rhubarb has demonstrated some excellent tumor blocking abilities. For instance, the first supplement of Vol. 20 of *Pharmacology* related that two of the laxative compounds in rhubarb, rhein and emodin, also blocked Ehrlich and mammary tumors in mice by 75% at the relatively high dose of 50 mg. per kilogram of body weight per day.

A 1984 issue of *Journal of Ethnopharmacology* reported that rhein and emodin inhibited the growth of malignant melanoma at a daily dosage of 50 mg. per kilogram of body weight. The percentages of inhibition were 76% for rhein and 73% for emodin. In certain parts of mainland China, rhubarb juice and rhubarb tea are used in the treatment of some forms of cancer with good success. About 1/2 cup of juice twice daily obtained by putting fresh stalks through a mechanical juicer, are administered to patients. More often, though, tea is made by simmering 2 cups of finely chopped stalks in 1 quart of boiling water, covered, for up to an hour. Afterwards, the liquid is strained off and given to cancer victims in 1-cup amounts two to three times a day.

Relief for Psoriasis and Arthritis

The anthraquinones in rhubarb, besides exerting wonderful laxative action, also help to relieve the itchiness and pain accompanying psoriasis and arthritis. Combine 1 cup of chopped, slightly mashed rhubarb root,

1/2 cup of chopped, slightly mashed rhubarb stalk, 10 tbsps. of powdered wide Oregon grape root, and 8 crushed zinc tablets (50 mg. size) in 3 cups of quality gin or rum. Put in a tightly sealed bottle and shake twice daily for 15 days.

Then strain the tincture through clean muslin cloth and add 1-1/4 cups of cool cabbage juice. Thoroughly stir or shake up until both liquids are well mixed. The vegetable juice may be obtained by simmering half a head of chopped or shredded green cabbage in 1 qt. of boiling water until only half the amount (or 1 pt.) remains. Strain and cool before mixing with the alcoholic tincture. Then put in bottle with a tight lid.

One level teaspoon of this tincture should be taken five times a day on an empty stomach. Not only will this help bring relief to psoriasis and arthritis, but also it will work equally as well for eczema, herpes, acne vulgaris and hepatitis.

Great Laxative and Anti-Diarrheal

Two important compounds in Chinese rhubarb root, called sennosides E and F, exhibit the same identical properties on the bowels as do sennosides A and B, which occur in another well-known laxative herb, senna. And when used in large doses, it will quickly remedy even the most obstinate form of constipation. But strange to say, it's also an astringent and will stop diarrhea when used in small amounts.

As many as 4–6 capsules of powdered Chinese rhubarb root may be necessary for chronic constipation, but a mere 2–3 capsules should be all that is necessary for clearing up diarrhea. Or a tea can be made by bringing a pint of water to a boil and adding 1-1/2 tbsps. of cut, dried rootstock for constipation or just 1-2/3 tsps. of rootstock for diarrhea.

Reduce heat and simmer for 3 mins. before removing to steep, covered, for an additional half an hour. One cup at a time may be taken for constipation, but only 1/4–1/2 cup for diarrhea.

Heals Digestive Tract Diseases

Some interesting clinical studies conducted with Chinese rhubarb emerged from the Central Hospital of Luwan District in Shanghai in the early 1980s. In the first study, some 890 cases (79% male) of upper digestive tract bleeding (57% were duodenal ulcers complicated by hemorrhaging) were treated with rhubarb either in powder, tablets or syrup. These were administered in 1 tsp. equivalents three times a day until the bleeding ceased, usually averaging only two days with most. A 97% success rate was achieved.

A random comparison between this single use of rhubarb and the combined treatment of Western medicine and Chinese herbs was made in other patients experiencing the same type of difficulties. Furthermore, six different combinations of rhubarb were also tested. In all tests made, the single use of rhubarb took the shortest time to stop bleeding, reduce fevers and help patients towards quicker recovery than the others did. This action exhibited by rhubarb may be due to the presence of tannic acid, which constricts blood vessels.

In the next set of studies, 100 cases of acute inflammation of the pancreas (pancreatitis) and 10 cases of acute inflammation of the gall bladder (cholecystitis) were successfully treated with the equivalent of 4 tbsps. of a decoction of rhubarb between 5 and 10 times a day until full recovery was noticed in most of them. Related symptoms like abdominal pain, high fever and jaundice usually cleared up within 5 days or less. To make a decoction for any of these problems, simmer 2-1/2 tbsps. of cut, dried Chinese rhubarb root in 1-1/2 qts. or 6 cups of boiling water, covered, for 40 mins. or until about half (3 cups) of the liquid remains. Strain this and take as previously directed for any of the foregoing maladies.

Lowers Dangerous Cholesterol

A liquid solution of rhubarb root was fed orally to normal and hyperlipidemic rabbits. Those with the elevated levels of cholesterol, trigylcerides and lipoprotein experienced a significant *decrease* in all of these. Which suggests that a meal heavy in fats should be accompanied with a simple dessert of delicious cooked rhubarb to help control cholesterol.

Such can be made by washing and cutting into inch pieces about 7 cups (approximately 2 lbs.) of rhubarb. Cook in a double boiler with a little water and 1/4 tsp. sea salt until nearly tender. Then add 1-1/4 cups of dark honey and continue cooking another 40 mins. or until done. It may also be cooked in a covered casserole in the oven using 1/2 cup of water, but with the same amounts of salt and honey. Bake at 350° F. for 50 mins. A therapeutic dessert served with greasy or fatty foods should be about 1-1/2 cups of cooked rhubarb. Adding a little cardamom, 1/2 tsp. pure maple syrup and a touch of pure vanilla improves the flavor more for those who don't especially care for its puckering tartness.

RICE (See GRAINS.)

ROSEHIPS (See ORNAMENTAL FLOWERS.)

ROSEMARY (*Rosmarinus officinalis*)

Brief Description

This evergreen shrub originated in the Mediterranean area and is now widely cultivated elsewhere for its aromatic leaves. The many branches have an ash-colored, scaly bark and bear opposite, leathery thick leaves which are lustrous and dark green above and downy white underneath. They have a prominent vein in the middle and margins which are rolled down.

Effective Mouth Wash

Rosemary tea makes a wonderfully refreshing mouth wash for getting rid of bad breath. In 1 pint of boiling water removed from the heat, steep 3 tsp. of the dried flowering tops or leaves for half an hour, covered. Strain and refrigerate. Gargle and rinse mouth each morning or several times a day with some.

Remarkable Water Purifier

Certain of the aromatic spices like peppermint, rosemary, sage, savory and thyme, are believed to hold tremendous value in sterilizing water contaminated with unfriendly bacteria. Rob McCaleb, editor of the *HerbalGram,* speculates that if one were to boil suspected water and put in a little of any of these aromatics, that a person would have something pretty safe to drink without fear of coming down with diarrhea, cramps and fever due to a harmful microbe with a long Latin name to it. Any of these spices is especially handy to carry with you when traveling in Third World countries such as Mexico, where the conditions of cleanliness leave much to be desired.

Youthful Elixir

The famous French herbalist, Maurice Mességué, calls rosemary "the miracle herb that restores youth" to the physically decrepit and elderly. Some time in the 14th century Queen Elizabeth of Hungary fell in love with it when she was well into her 70s. She had been crippled with rheumatism and gout for a number of years, but rosemary gave her back her youth to such an extent that the King of Poland asked her to marry him!

The herb's tremendous diuretic action explains its effectiveness against rheumatism and gout, as well as kidneystones and the inability to urinate. Moreover it's a nice digestive, helping the liver to do its work by increasing the flow of bile into the intestines.

To make an elixir similar to that used by the Queen of Hungary for restoring some of your lost youth, lightly crush 2 handfuls of the flowering branches of fresh rosemary, then soak for 10 days in 2 cups of expensive brandy. Repeat the same process and measurements with fresh lavender. Place each solution of herbs in separate bottles with tight-fitting lids to them. Be sure and shake each one twice daily.

Strain each and store in a cool place until needed. The next part to making this elixir involves mixing together 3 parts tincture of rosemary with 1 part tincture of lavender. An older person should take 1 level tsp. of this a couple times each day on an empty stomach.

Soothing Liniment for Sore Muscles

An oil of rosemary can be made at home to rub on sore, aching muscles or sprained areas for soothing relief. Coarsely chop a double handful of fresh rosemary tops and leaves before soaking in 1 pint of olive oil in a well-sealed jar for a week. Strain and store oil in a cool, dry place. Since rosemary is a natural antioxidant and has been previously used to preserve cereal, luncheon meat and pizza in place of synthetic BHA and BHT, it should keep the oil from turning rancid.

Culinary Uses

Rosemary finds plenty of application in breadstuffs, some baked or cooked fruits, German cuisine that includes meat, cabbage and potatoes, meats like pork, fish and poultry, soups and stews. The flavor which this spice imparts is a refreshing pungency somewhat reminiscent of resinous pine.

RUTABAGA and TURNIP (*Brassica campestris rutabaga, B. campestris*)

Brief Description

Rutabaga is thought to have originated in Sweden somewhere during the Middle Ages. It is larger, coarser and more emphatically flavored than the turnip, of which it may be a mutant form. Rutabaga is more elongated than a turnip is and usually adorned with a slightly purple top. Most have yellow or orange flesh, but a few are white.

Throughout much of recorded history, turnip has occupied a lowly position on the gastronomic scale, being considered only as a food for peasants and livestock. Turnips come in many different varieties, but those grown here in America are generally the white-fleshed kind, with purple or green tops. This distinct-tasting vegetable goes well with braised beef or roast pork.

Reduces Cholesterol and Constipation

Both rutabaga and turnip are ideal for lowering serum cholesterol levels in the body, not to mention encouraging more frequent bowel movements. Half a cup of each, either cubed or sliced, or 1 cup of each mashed should be consumed at least once a week where the cholesterol count may be dangerously high or infrequent bowel movements persist.

A simple way to prepare either of them is to cut them into slices or cubes and boil in a small amount of water containing 1 tbsp. lemon juice and a sprinkle of kelp and melted butter, in a covered pot, for about 25 minutes.

Brooklyn Cure for the Common Cold

A health-minded friend of mine from Brooklyn, New York, Joel Bree, has developed what people in his neighborhood consider to be one of the very best remedies for treating the common cold and influenza, along with related symptoms such as high fever, swollen throat glands, ear infection and runny nose.

"The first time I made this soup my two-year-old daughter, Tziporah, ate about three bowls, which surprised all of us. She was better the next day and has never gone back on antibiotics ever since.

"I buy kosher chicken bottoms and put them in a pot with enough water to cover, leaving an inch above them. I cover with a lid and let this boil out until there's just a little over half of the liquid remaining. I also add a teaspoon of apple cider vinegar in order to leach or draw out all of the minerals in the meat.

"After the liquid has been boiled down to half the volume, I take the chicken out, but leave the broth in the pot. Next I peel and juice in my food extractor, 3 garlic cloves, a large red onion, 1 sweet potato that's been cleaned and with the *skin intact,* 1 *un*peeled zucchini or yellow crookneck squash, 3 *un*peeled carrots, 1 *un*peeled parsnip, 1 *un*peeled turnip, and 1 *un*peeled rutabaga. These juices are then added to the broth.

"After this, I return the pot to the stove and cook on a medium setting just long enough to where it starts to boil. At this point, I remove it from the heat so as not to destroy any valuable vitamins and enzymes. I find that this brief reheating helps to take away most of the starchy taste that would otherwise linger and make the blend taste unpleasant. I highly recommend this old family remedy to anyone seeking relief from the miseries of colds, flus and fevers."

Dentifrice and Deodorant

Eating a raw turnip once a week is a good way to clean the teeth and massage the gums at the same time. Frequently doing this on a consistent basis has been known to help reduce dental plaque and tartar somewhat.

A Japanese delegate told me that turnip juice was one of the "best things to use for getting rid of goaty armpits," as he so bluntly put it. He showed me a small bottle of turnip juice which he carried everywhere with him.

Being curious to see if it actually worked, I asked for and received some to use. First I washed both armpits good, then briskly rubbed 1 teaspoon of the juice beneath each of them. And although the temperature was in the high 90s and the humidity factor about 65%, yet there was *virtually no odor* to the perspiration. I recommend this over commercial deodorants, which contain harmful amounts of aluminum that may cause skin cancer in time. And unlike them, turnip juice won't prevent the sweat glands from doing their normal tasks, but *will* keep body odor from occurring for up to 10 hours as a rule.

Removing the Discoloration of Bruises

From the same Japanese friend, I learned that either a turnip or daikon radish were very effective to reduce the swelling and eliminate the discoloration accompanying nasty-looking black-and-blue marks. Just grate 1/3 of a turnip, apply it directly to the bruise and leave on for half an hour. Repeat the process several days in a row as necessary. This works like an ice pack in some ways to reduce pain and swelling.

Culinary Quickies

You can make a delicious and nourishing soup by adding 2 tbsp. of chopped chives to 3 cups of canned goat milk in a food blender, together with 2 cups of mashed turnips and 1 cup of mashed rutabaga.

Purée until smooth, then cook on low heat for 15 mins., garnishing with chopped parsley and a dash of paprika.

Turnip greens can be steamed for 25 mins. with a little lemon and lime juice and a dash of kelp and tad of butter added for flavor. Serve with hard-boiled egg on the side.

RYE (See GRAINS.)

S

SAFFLOWER (See SEEDS.)

SAGE (*Salvia officinalis*)

Brief Description

This perennial shrub grows wild in southern Europe and the Mediterranean area of the world, but is cultivated in many other places as a valued culinary spice. A strongly branched root system produces square, finely hairy stems which are woody at the base and bear oblong leaves. The floral leaves are ovate to ovate-lanceolate. The purple, blue or white flowers are two-lipped and grown in whorls.

Aid for Insect Bites

A quick little remedy for relieving itching and swelling accompanying insect bites, is to pick a few fresh sage leaves, then crush or chew them up a bit. Mix them with a little saliva to make a crude, wet poultice and apply directly to the afflicted areas and secure in place with a strip or two of adhesive tape.

Relief for Throat Problems

A tea made of the leaves of sage provides soothing, healing relief for sore throat, loss of voice and tonsillitis, as well as helping to remove mucus from congested lungs. Steep 2 tsp. dried or fresh leaves in 1-1/4 cups of boiling water for 35 mins. Strain, sweeten with honey if desired and take 1/2 cup every few hours as needed. Add 1/4 tsp. of fresh lime juice and gargle well before swallowing for raw, irritated throat.

Stops Milk Flow

More and more mothers seem to be returning to the natural art of breast-feeding their newborn infants, because they feel it is much better for their babies' overall health. When the nursing stage comes to a close, however, many aren't aware of how to properly stop their flow of extra, unneeded milk.

Two cups of warm sage tea daily for up to a week generally dried up the milk supply quite nicely. Bring 1 qt. of water to a boil and steep 8 tsp. dried or fresh sage leaves in it for 45 mins. covered. Strain, add honey and drink.

A Spice of Life Laxative

Many of today's herbal preparations sold in health food stores nation-wide, rely mostly on standard ingredients like cascara sagrada, senna or rhubarb root to get the job done. While all of these are excellent laxatives, they can be habit-forming and harsh in their actions if used too often by the elderly.

One particular herb product, however, is unique from the rest of the natural laxatives in this respect: it *does not contain any* of these traditional herbal laxatives. Rather, instead, it relies solely upon spices to get the job done. Any of us who've eaten Mexican or Chinese food or the traditional Thanksgiving dinner in which a lot of spices are used, may recall how soon we experienced a bowel movement shortly after such meals.

The key ingredients include sage, marjoram, oregano, rosemary and thyme leaves, along with turmeric and ginger roots, and cayenne pepper and kelp. These are further activated with pineapple enzymes, dried sour milk or yogurt bacterium (acidophilus) and a specially freeze-dried apple cider vinegar. Called Spice-Lax it's available only from Quest Vitamins in Canada (see Appendix). Generally 3 capsules at a time will effectively stimulate the bowels very soon.

Stops Profuse Sweating

Some people seem to have a real problem with excessive sweating. It has been said of such that they even perspire while standing still and thinking! The following ingredients made into an infusion usually begins to reduce sweating within two hours after drinking a couple of cups of this tea when cool, with the effects lasting up to several days. Bring 4 cups of water to a boil, then add 1 tsp. *each* of dried hops, dried stinging nettle, fresh-cut rose petals, fresh or dried strawberry leaves, fresh walnut leaves and 3 tsp. of dried sage leaves. Cover, remove from heat and steep for an hour. Strain and sweeten with honey if necessary.

A tincture of sage is also good for reducing perspiration. To make this tincture combine slightly more than 1/2 cup of powdered sage leaves with 1-1/4 cups of vodka or vermouth. Let stand for 2 weeks in a well-sealed bottle, shaking twice each day. Then strain and store in another bottle. Take 25 drops 3–4 times daily as needed.

Intense Itching Disappears

Any kind of intense itching, whether it be due to an allergic reaction to some unknown substance, general nervousness, psoriasis and eczema or coming in contact with poison ivy and sumach, may all be effectively relieved *and* healed with an old folk remedy from Nassau in the Bahamas.

A kindly old Black cook by the name of "Mistress Marshall," who lived to the decent age of 102, was known far and wide for her practice of "bush medicine" (as it was called in those parts) with a touch of black magic thrown in for good measure.

One of her favorite remedies for itching was to steep a handful of cut, fresh sage leaves, that had been lightly crushed first of all, in 1 pint of boiling water for about an hour. After this, the strained liquid was used to bathe the afflicted parts. Then while the skin was still wet with this solution, she would generously sprinkle *whole wheat* flour (*never* white) over the entire area and leave to dry. Relief came within 10 minutes as a rule and never failed once that I'm aware of.

"Voodoo" Memory Stimulant

This incredibly delightful lady, who charmed hundreds with her warm smile and winsome ways, made dozens of bottles of an effective "memory tawdy" for strengthening the mind and invigorating the powers of the brain more. Apparently the stuff worked, because she had a huge following of middle-aged to elderly people who testified of how well their memories improved when using her "tawdy" on a regular basis.

Her "secret" recipe calls for combining 2 cups of *fresh* sage leaves in an electric blender on *high speed for 5 minutes* with 4 cups of fine burgundy until they are thoroughly suspended in the alcohol. Store in a bottle with a cork and take 1 tsp. of this tonic in 2/3 cup of Perrier water every day.

Fantastic Liver Regeneration

Lest the reader misinterpret what we're talking about here, let me remind you that it's *regeneration,* as in "recreating or reproducing," and *not* rejuvenation or reinvigoration that we're to be dealing with! When one of the body's most important organs, the liver, breaks down or is partially removed through surgery, it has the remarkable ability to *regrow* or reproduce itself somewhat if the conditions are just right.

Now there are several spices and vegetables I'm very familiar with which will definitely assist the liver to do this very thing. They are sage and the freshly made juices of beets and tomatoes. Good clinical evidence exists to verify this. For instance, Vol. 3 of the Chinese medical journal, *Chung Hsi I Chih Ho Tsa Chih,* reported in 1983 that a team of doctors at the Shanxi Medical College removed the middle and left lobes of the livers in albino rats before giving them sage tea or just plain water to drink. Several days later when all rodents were cut open and carefully examined, it was observed that the control group on sage tea had begun to experience some liver regeneration over the other groups only on water. From this the scientists concluded that sage is valuable for liver regeneration. Another study which appeared in *The Tohuku Journal of Experimental Medicine* for 1953, noted that a marked increase in liver stimulation of adult male rabbits became evident soon after they were given fresh tomato juice to drink.

To make a useful health cocktail for liver regeneration, combine 1/2 cup of *fresh* sage tea in a food blender and mix well with 1/4 cup of *fresh* beet juice and 2/3 cup of *fresh* tomato juice. Drink this at least once or twice a day in between or with meals.

Inhibits Clots and Prevents Heart Problems

Recently published studies by a team of scientists from the Department of Microbiology and Chemotherapy at the Nippon Roche Research Center in Kamakura, Japan, indicates that powdered sage or sage tea helps to prevent blood clots from forming and is quite useful in the prevention and treatment of myocardial infarction and general coronary pains.

Darkening Gray Hair

You can make your own home-version of Grecian formula for taking away gray hair that's a lot safer to use because it's free of chemicals and only contains natural ingredients.

In a heavy ceramic mixing bowl put 2 heaping tbsps. of dried sage and the same amount again of either orange pekoe or black tea. Then fill the bowl or jar half full of boiling water. Cover with a small dinner plate or aluminum foil and place in a moderately warm (275° F.) oven or in a large pan of boiling water on top of the stove on a low setting for at least a couple of hours. Then remove, allow to cool, stir well and strain.

Now a small quantity of this infusion is to be rubbed into the roots of the hair 4–5 times a week. Pretty soon the grayness will start fading away as the hair becomes darker in color once more. Thereafter, this infusion ought to be used just once or twice weekly for maintenance purposes only. Many of those who've tried this for themselves have experienced moderate hair growth in bald places or at the very least, an overall improvement in the tone and texture of their hair. This infusion will keep longer if 3 tbsps. of either gin or rum are added to it.

Culinary Uses

Sage delivers a warm pungency to poultry and fish stuffings, soups, cheeses, dips, gravies, stews, poultry, wild game and stewed or baked vegetables like tomatoes, carrots and eggplant.

Sage and Fruit Stuffing for Poultry and Wild Fowl

This is an old Mormon pioneer recipe from Leah D. Widtsoe, wife of Apostle John A. Widtsoe, a deceased member of the Council of the Twelve Apostles of the Church of Jesus Christ of Latter-Day Saints. It goes well with domesticated poultry such as chicken and turkey or with wild fowl like Canadian goose and wood duck.

Needed: 6 cups of dried bread crumbs from a mixture of pumpernickel, rye, and whole wheat slices; 2-3/4 cups of hot pineapple juice; 1/4 cup olive oil; 1-1/2 tsp. sea salt; 1/2 tsp. kelp; 1 tsp. sage; 1/2 tsp. celery seed; 1/4 tsp. cardamom; 1/2 cup *each* finely minced celery and onion; 3 cups unpeeled, uncored, chopped raw apples; 1/2 cup shelled, chopped raw walnuts; 1/2 cup pitted, chopped dates; 3 finely chopped black mission figs; 1 cup soaked, pitted and chopped prunes and 1/2 cup raisins.

In a skillet, sautée the celery and onion in the olive oil on low heat, covered. On a large pan or mixing bowl, combine the rest of the above ingredients—crumbs, fruits, nuts and spices—with the hot juice. Mix well with hands or wooden ladle. Then turn in the sautéed celery, onion and oil and mix again. This should be enough dressing to adequately stuff a 5 lb. roasting chicken, a small turkey or goose.

ST. JOHNSWORT (*Hypericum perforatum*)

Brief Description

This shrubby perennial occurs in dry, gravelly soils, fields and sunny places throughout the world. A woody, branched root produced many round stems which put out runners from the base. The opposite, oblong to linear leaves are covered with transparent oil glands that look like holes. The yellow flowers have petals dotted with black along their margins.

Cancer Therapy

I remember some years ago, while lecturing in Athens, Georgia, of visiting with an old herb folk healer by the name of Bo "Big Swede" Erikson. He passed along some valuable instructions to make a fairly simple herb oil which he'd formulated for treating certain skin cancers and gangrene. The one skin cancer with which, he said, he always had the most success was basal cell carcinoma—the kind that forms on the forehead, face or nose of light-complexioned people. His key ingredient was St. Johnswort and his main method of preparation was exposing this herb to as much direct sunlight as possible.

"Big Swede" (as he preferred to be called) would first go out and collect some fresh St. Johnswort from nearby fields in his locale. These he would thoroughly macerate with a wooden mallet and then put about 2 handfuls of the crushed plant materials into a gallon jar filled about 1/3 full of olive oil, 1-1/2 pints of good white wine and 1 cup of gum turpentine. He would seal the jar with a loose-fitting lid and set it in the sun for 10 days.

After this, Big Swede would take a large pot used for canning fruit, and, before filling it 1/3 full of water, would place a large soup bowl *upside down* on the bottom. On top of this inverted bowl he would then put the gallon jar with *the lid left on very loosely,* so as not to build up pressure inside the jar. The pot would be set on the stove on medium heat and the water permitted to boil for an hour.

Following this procedure, the remaining liquid in the jar was then strained several times and put into another clean gallon jar. Into this second jar, an equal amount of more freshly macerated St. Johnswort leaves and flowers were put, but with *no more* oil, wine or turpentine added. This jar was also set in the sun, but only for 5 days instead. After which the entire preparation was set aside in some cool, dry place *without* being strained again until needed.

When treating basal cell carcinoma, he would transform some of this St. Johnswort oil into a simple salve. This was done by heating up 1 cup of the oil inside a pint jar which had been set inside a pot on an inverted dish, with the pot half full of boiling water. When the oil was hot enough he would then add 1–2 tbsps. of melted beeswax and frequently stir until it had been sufficiently dissolved enough to yield a salve-like consistency. A little gum benzoin or tincture of benzoin was also added to help preserve the salve (about 1/2 tsp. of tincture per pint of salve). His patients would then rub this salve on their skin and leave it exposed to the sun. He claimed to have better than a 75% success rate for this. His remedy was also used to treat burns, wounds, sores, bruises, eczema and psoriasis.

Help for Cerebrospinal Problems

St. Johnswort is one of the very few herbs for which there exists some documentation to show its value in treating certain conditions of the brain and spine. One of these is hydrocephalus, a condition marked by an excessive accumulation of fluid enlarging the cerebral ventricles, thinning the brain and causing a separation of cranial bones.

The Feb. 1981 Soviet medical journal, *Vrachebnoe Delo,* cited considerable relief from such intense head pressure in 150 patients who were given an herbal "cocktail" composed of St. Johnswort herb, Siberian ginseng root, peppermint leaves, birch buds and huckleberry or blueberry leaves. A similar brew can be made at home for such a condition. Bring 1 qt. of water to a boil. Add 2 tbsps. each of dried, coarsely cut Siberian ginseng root and 1-1/2 tbsps. of chopped buds from a birch tree. Cover, reduce heat and simmer for 5 mins. If only the powdered Siberian ginseng is present and birch buds are unavailable in your immediate vicinity, then proceed to this method instead. After the water boils, remove it from the heat and add 2-1/2 tbsps. dried St. Johnswort, 2 tbsps. mint leaves, 1 tbsp. blueberry leaves and the equivalent of 1 tsp. of powdered Siberian ginseng root. In place of birch buds, substitute 2-1/4 tsp. fresh, finely minced celery stalk. Stir all of these ingredients together, return pan to the heat and simmer for 7 mins. Then remove and steep an additional 25 minutes. Strain through a fine sieve, then strain again through a clean muslin cloth before drinking. Recommended amount is 1 cup three times daily on an empty stomach.

A tincture made from the flowering tops and fresh herb of St. Johnswort has outstanding benefits for various brain disturbances, among which is mental depression. Ten to 20 drops in a 6 oz. glass of spring or distilled water on a daily basis has been highly recommended by some naturopathic and homeopathic physicians in the past.

A prepared tincture may be obtained by mail-order from Eclectic

Institute (see Appendix) or you can prepare one of your own. Combine 10 tbsps. of powdered St. Johnswort, which can be obtained from Bio-Botanica of Happauge, New York (see Appendix), in 1-1/4 cups of vermouth. Let stand for 15 days, shaking twice each day; then strain through a fine cloth and bottle. Use as previously directed for mental problems.

For treating any kind of trauma to the nervous system, some of this same tincture may not only be given internally, but just as effectively rubbed on the spinal column, especially in cases of extreme shock or hysteria with reasonably good results. When the drops are given orally, they should be slowly placed beneath the front of the tongue or given sublingually for maximum penetration and benefit to the nerves.

Reduces Intestinal Swelling

A study published in number six of Vol. 18 of the Bulgarian journal, *Veterinary Sciences,* revealed that out of half a dozen anti-inflammatory herbs used on albino rats, only the freeze-dried extract of St. Johnswort was able to reduce intestinal swelling by nearly 70%. Three other herbal extracts, calendula (60%), German chamomile (55%) and plantain (38%) also suppressed inflammation to some extent. Therefore, it's suggested that those with intestinal inflammation of some kind take about 4 capsules a day of a product called Herbal Digestant, which contains a concentrate of St. Johnswort, along with calendula, chamomile, plantain, yarrow and comfrey.

This product is based on an old Russian folk remedy for the same purposes and is available from Quest Vitamins of Vancouver, B.C. (see Appendix). A second consideration is a tincture of St. Johnswort available from a naturopathic supply house, Eclectic Institute of Portland, Oregon (see Appendix). About 15 drops a day in 1/2 cup of warm water is recommended. Both products may also give some relief in colon cancer, but *won't* necessarily reverse it any.

SARSAPARILLA (*Smilax officinalis*)

Brief Description

This tropical American perennial plant produces a long, tuberous rootstock, from which grows a ground-trailing vine that climbs by means of tendrils coming in pairs from the petioles of the ovate, evergreen leaves. The small, greenish flowers grow in axillary umbels.

Treating Venereal Diseases

For venereal diseases such as syphilis and gonorrhea a sarsaparilla tea has been shown to be effective. Bring 1 qt. of water to a boil, adding 2 tbsps. each of sarsaparilla and yellow dock roots. Reduce heat and simmer, covered, for 5 mins. Remove cover and add 3-1/2 tsp. of dried thyme herb. Cover again and steep an additional hour.

Drink 1–3 cups daily as well as douching and/or washing the sexual organs with the same often. Both herbs may be found in any local health food store under the Select brand or else obtained either from Indiana Botanic Gardens or Bio-Botanica (see Appendix).

SAVORY (*Satureja hortensis*)

Brief Description

This annual herb grows wild in the Mediterranean area and is widely cultivated elsewhere in the world as a nice culinary spice. Its branching root produces a bushy, hairy stem which grows over a foot high, often taking on a purple hue as it matures. The small, oblong-linear leaves are sessile and usually have hairy margins to them. The pink or white, two-lipped flowers grow in whorl-like cymes. The entire plant is extremely aromatic.

An Aphrodisiac That Works

Savory has been considered an "herb of love" for centuries! The famous French herbalist, Maurice Mességué, has often used it in place of ginseng to help couples retrieve their married bliss. He advises them to sprinkle powdered savory on all their meat dishes. For impotent men and frigid women he advises them to run the base of their spine with a decoction of savory and fenugreek.

In 1 qt. boiling water, simmer 3-1/2 tbsps. fenugreek seed for 5 mins., covered. Remove from heat and add 2 handfuls of savory. Steep an additional 50 mins. Drink 2 cups before going to bed and apply to the bottom of the back as well.

SCHIZANDRA FRUIT (See YOHIMBINE)

SEEDS
POPPY (*Papaver somniferum*)
SAFFLOWER (*Carthamus tinctorius*)
SESAME (*Sesamum indicum*)
SUNFLOWER (*Helianthus annuus*)

Brief Description

Poppy seeds are grown in the temperate and subtropical regions of the world. In India, the seeds are mainly grown in the states of Madhya Pradesh, Uttar Pradesh and Rajasthan. The seeds are a good source of protein and oil, and have long been used in food preparations like curries, breads, sweets and confectionary. Ironically enough, this healthful food comes from the very same plant that the highly addictive, dangerously narcotic drug, opium, is derived. This illegal and destructive substance is obtained from the milky sap and the urn-shaped seed capsules or poppy heads.

The safflower is an annual plant native to the Mediterranean region and also cultivated in the U.S. and Europe. It's botanically related to lettuce, sunflower, artichoke, chicory and daisy. Safflower is a well-branched plant, varying in height from 1 to 4 feet with smooth white or light grey stems. The thistle-like inflorescence is made up of a dense mass of blossoms which might be white, yellow, orange or red. They are surrounded by numerous protective bracts formed by the prickly terminal leaves. The fruit or achenes are produced deep down inside the flower heads where they are safe from hungry birds. Each achene contains a single oblong seed, which, like the stems, is either white or light grey in color. Each seed contains between 24–36% of its own weight of an oil used extensively in cooking.

Sesame can be grown in tropical or less warmer climates such as the Southern U.S. It's a very attractive annual, reaching heights of between 2–6 feet, with heavy, glistening stems supporting variable leaves. Those near the base are broad, fleshy and tooth-edged while the upper ones are slender and smooth-edged. The flowers of sesame resemble those of the foxglove or digitalis plant. They are extremely beautiful, colored white with spots or a tinge of red, yellow or lavender. The flowers are always self-fertilizing and produce their seeds in inch-long keel-shaped pods or capsules. The tiny seeds are flat and oval with one end pointed, weighing no more than 1/10th of a grain each, and containing 50–60% of a fixed, semi-drying oil. A single pressing and filtration yields a clear pale-yellow oil without any definite taste, but highly edible. A much darker, inferior oil is also produced by two further pressings, under intense pressure from the heated residue, but needs refining and deodorizing to make it usable.

The state flower of Kansas, the sunflower, grows everywhere almost like a weed in many instances. The scientific name of the genus, *Helianthos,* comes from two Greek nouns—*helios* for "sun" and *anthus* for "flower." The showy yellow flowers are not only like a primitive reproduction of the sun, but they turn of their own accord toward this luminous celestial body's radiations. The annuals and perennials are upright and mostly rhizomatous. With up to a couple of dozen golden ray petals emanating from yellow and reddish purple to brown central disks where the seeds later mature, the often solitary terminal flowers become masses of gold in the summertime, from several to sometimes more than 15 feet high. The differing stems and leaves are mostly hairy. The numerous species all have neutral ray flowers and flat and fertile disk blossoms which also bear chaff. Sunflower seeds in the *H. annus* number about 650 to an ounce and contain about 50% of a semi-drying, pale yellow oil used in cooking and salad oils and in the making of margarine, cheese and other dairy products.

Seeds Inhibit Cancer

Recent epidemiologic evidence seems to suggest that plant seeds may lower the risk for developing certain types of cancer generally associated with too much meat and fat consumptions. At least that's the conclusion drawn by Dr. Walter Troll, professor of environmental medicine at the New York University School of Medicine and reported in the May 27, 1983 *Journal of the Am. Med. Assoc.* (*JAMA*).

Troll analyzed computer data from epidemiologic studies indicating that prostatic, breast and colon cancer rates are considerably lower in populations whose diet is rich in "seed foods." He found that certain enzymes, common to all seeds, when injected into lab mice previously inoculated with melanoma cells, prevented the development of cancers in the mice. In a similarly inoculated control group without benefit of these seed enzymes, tumors rapidly developed.

Dr. Troll told a reporter from *JAMA,* "A prudent diet would be one in which from 1/3 to 1/2 of all protein consumed is provided by seeds." The *New Eng. J. of Medicine* for Jan. 19, 1978 confirmed that frequent consumption of sunflower seed oil in Bulgaria, Romania and the Soviet Union resulted in lower mortalities from malignant tumors than elsewhere. So seeds are of definite benefit when it comes to preventing cancer!

Safflower Oil Prevents Heart Disease

Today's number-one killer disease in America is coronary heart disease. If you were to outline on graph paper the statistical increases of it in the last three decades alone, you would almost have a sharp vertical line shooting to the top, although slightly tilted to the right. Or, put another way, there have been *NO* decreases in heart disease for the past 30 years!

The use of hydrogenated cooking oils by the food industry is the cause. Way back in 1956, the respected medical journal, *The Lancet* (2:557), issued this dire warning: "The hydrogenation plants of our modern food industry may turn out to have contributed to the causation of a major disease!" How tragically prophetic they proved to be.

But in order to understand why this nation of ours has experienced such great leaps in heart disease, unparalleled to that of any other nation on earth, we need to briefly examine just what hydrogenation is all about.

First of all, the process of hydrogenation originated as a way of making low-cost soap from discarded animal fats. From there it eventually crept into the powerful food industry. Simply put, liquid oil or soft fat is purposely hardened at a high temperature and under intense pressure. Hydrogen is then bubbled through the oil in the presence of toxic metals like nickel, platinum or some other cancer-causing catalyst. The hydrogen atoms combine with the carbon atoms and the product becomes saturated or hardened.

Hydrogenation is generally done to cheap plant oils like palm and coconut or animal fats from which shortening and lard are made. After hydrogenation what you have is a bad-smelling and loathsome-looking grease that would be quite unacceptable to any normal human being. But the magical skills of clever food technologists are used to bleach, filter and deodorize this rank stuff with a myriad of chemicals into a pure, snowy white, odorless, tasteless, highly artificial fat.

So when you eat fried foods at your favorite fast food place, you are, in effect, laying the groundwork for coronary heart disease. Take it from an expert who knows what he's talking about. During those early years that I was getting my schooling as a medical anthropologist, I worked fulltime on the side for nearly 7 years in the restaurant business and almost 4 more years in the funeral business.

In my job at the funeral home, I occasionally witnessed autopsies whenever I had to pick up a corpse from the medical examiner's office. Several of those who were cut open had been individuals whom I'd previously known from my restaurant experiences. And I knew each of them had been *heavy* consumers of deep-fried food, which was recalled to mind when the doctor slicing them open let me take a look at their hearts out of curiosity. Sure enough, every one of them had hearts choked full and clogged up good with yellowish fat beyond belief. I can't begin to tell you what their livers and gall bladders looked like!

The best comparison I can make to eating anything deep-fried is if you were to pour a lot of motor oil *into your gas tank.* In no time at all, the valves would begin to stick, the carburetor would become clogged and the sparkplugs refuse to ignite properly. In short, the vehicle would no longer function. Much the same thing takes place inside the human body whenever any deep-fried food is consumed.

For the sake of your health and to prevent getting heart disease, you should cease and desist in eating such greasy fare. Instead, you ought to seriously consider eating only those foods which have been either fried or baked in safflower, sesame seed or sunflower seed oils. A recent Veterans Administration hospital dietary study showed that the average serum cholesterol was 17% higher on a diet rich in palm oil than on a diet containing equivalent amounts of a highly unsaturated safflower oil. This is by no means a trivial difference since a 10% drop in serum cholesterol would mean 24% less heart disease in the United States.

This is no joking matter! A report published in the February 1984 issue of the *American Journal of Clinical Nutrition,* for example, showed beyond a doubt that when hydrogenated fat was systematically fed to swine, it induced *far more* hardening of the arteries than swine fed other types of fat such as some of these seed oils.

Sesame and sunflower seed oils also play a valuable role as well in preventing coronary heart disease. Both oils contain a group of compounds called phytosterols, which researchers have found significantly lower blood serum cholesterol and do *not* build up any fatty plaque on the artery walls of the heart. In other words, a person could technically eat a lot of foods fried or baked with any of these three cooking oils and still have a relatively fat-free, squeaky clean heart.

Poor Blood Circulation to the Brain Improved

Years of dietary abuse, such as in frequently consuming foods cooked in or made with hydrogenated oils, can cause the blood to become somewhat thick and stagnant. Not only is overall circulation slowed down, but artery walls, especially those leading to the brain and heart, become narrower and occasionally clogged with clumps of thick blood and bacteria.

If you feel that your own state of blood is somewhat thick and sluggish and could possibly lead to cerebral vascular problems of some sort, then safflower oil may be just the thing for you. An intake of 1–2 tbsps. of the oil each day could very well improve a situation that's been going from bad to worse.

Difficult Wounds Healed

There are certain types of wounds which are very difficult to manage. These are wounds complicated with fractures and hard-to-heal surgical wounds, such as skin grafts or mediastinitis, a swelling of the tissue between the lungs that sometimes follows heart surgery.

Doctors in the Orthopedics Department of Tianjin Hospital in Tianjin, China and others at the Hospital Bichat in Paris used several different ingredients individually, which if combined together, appear to have a more diverse use. Of those substances employed by the Chinese physicians, only sesame seed oil (500 grams or 2-1/2 cups) and melted, filtered beeswax (90 grams or approximately 1/4 cup) added to the warmed oil, seem to have the most healing merits. I would, therefore, submit to the reader the following recipe for an effective wound remedy: 2-1/2 cups of sesame seed oil, 1/4 cup melted beeswax, 3/4–1-1/4 cups white sugar, 3 tbsps. powdered bonemeal and 2 tsps. crushed calcium supplement tablets in powdered form. Gently warm up the sesame seed oil on low heat, being careful that it doesn't smoke. Stir in the bonemeal and calcium powder. Then gradually add the sugar, stirring constantly with a wooden ladle or wire whip. Finally turn in the melted beeswax and keep stirring until there is an even, smooth consistency to the mixture, but not too stiff or lumpy. If so, add a little more heated sesame seed oil until the desired thickness has been achieved. Pack on and into wounds when completely cooled and change several times each day.

Sesame Oil for Ear and Eye Problems

Here are some folk uses for sesame seed oil that I learned from an Egyptian pharmaceutical student. Warm sesame seed oil is sometimes used as eardrops when the ear is plugged by excessive and hardened earwax. The oil, he assured me, would soften the wax, so that it can be washed out easier. The best way to warm the oil, he suggested, was to put a small amount in a glass jar (empty baby food jar, for example), then set it in a pan filled with about 2 inches of boiling water for no more than a minute or so.

For eye problems that involve the accumulation of water in the eye, such as glaucoma, myopia and trachoma, the finest sesame oil should be used. First of all, about half a cup of the oil needs to be cooked until it is rather hot. This can be accomplished in the same manner as the above oil is heated for use in the ear. Only in this case, about 2-1/2 inches of boiling water are put in the pan *and* a small plate put in the bottom in an inverted position. On top of this is placed the clean baby food jar containing the oil. The pan is returned to the stove and medium heat applied to keep the water boiling. When the oil is very hot to the touch, remove from the pan and strain through several layers of gauze. Allow to thoroughly cool until the oil is comfortably warm. This can be tested by simply dropping a little bit on the tip of the tongue. Then, using an eyedropper, put 3 drops of this oil into each eye just before retiring for the night.

Getting Rid of Dandruff and Headaches

This same Egyptian colleague of mine also shared with me another important remedy using sesame oil for scalp problems and headaches. Grate two fresh ginger roots on the smaller holes of a hand-held grater so as to obtain a finer pulp. Enclose this in enough double-layered gauze or cheesecloth and press hard enough to extract 1–2 tsps. of juice. This small bag of grated ginger can be placed between two small blocks of wood, set in a large flat pan, and a carpenter's bench clamp then put over the wood and slowly turned to get the necessary juice out.

The juice is then mixed with 3 tbsps. of sesame seed oil and 1/2 tsp. lemon juice. This sesame-ginger oil can then be rubbed with a wash cloth into the scalp by parting the hair with a comb every half an inch. This should be done 3 times a week to get rid of dandruff, seborrhea and keep hair from falling out. This same oil can be rubbed on the forehead with a piece of linen cloth to relieve a headache. It's also very good for relieving neuralgia and sciatica if rubbed directly on the sore areas.

Sesame Soup for Constipation

Noted research chemist and microbiologist, Albert Y. Leung, recalled that:

> By far the most common uses of sesame seeds in Chinese homes are as nutrients, tonics and laxatives. All three effects can be obtained from a drink (perhaps more appropriately called a soup) made from sesame seeds and rice.

To prepare this soup, 11 parts of sesame seeds are soaked in water, together with a small amount of rice. After the sesame seeds and rice are well soaked and become tender, they are ground to a paste by running them through a small food grinder or nut mill of some sort. The resulting milk mixture is strained to remove the coarse particles and then diluted with a little more water and some honey before cooking on low heat until the consistency is somewhat syrupy. Two cups of this delicious soup usually clear up the most obstinate form of constipation within an hour or so.

Paste for Spider Bites, Sores and Burns

An ancient 8th-century A.D. herbal from China gave an effective remedy for treating insect bites, especially painful spider and centipede bites, as well as minor burns and various types of skin sores. About 2–3 tbsps. of sesame seeds should be ground into a coarse powder and then made into a paste with the addition of a little water. This, in turn, is then applied to the afflicted area and left until the pain and swelling subsides somewhat. The seeds may be ground in a mortar with a pestle or finely crushed on a counter top with a heavy rolling pin or carefully pounded with the bottom of an empty Coke bottle or hammer.

In another herbal from 7 centuries later, sores on the head and face were treated just by chewing the raw sesame seeds for a couple of minutes and then applying the resulting wet mash to them. I've had occasion to try this only once on a small pimple on the side of my neck right by the collar line of my shirt which was irritating the heck out of me during my travels abroad. I secured some sesame seeds in one place on my trip, masticated them well and then applied this wet poultice to my neck and kept it in place with several extra-wide bandages from my shaving kit. I pretty much forgot all about it until the next morning, when I noticed after removing the Band-Aids that the redness and swelling had disappeared and the pimple itself was almost entirely gone.

Breaking the Smoking Habit

Back in 1980–81, a medical doctor by the name of John M. Douglass discovered an effective way to quit smoking while working long hours as an internist at the large, plush Sunset Kaiser-Permanente Medical Center near Hollywood. "It's a terrific tool with which to stop smoking," he admitted.

"They are an excellent substitute for smoking because the seeds have a comparable effect on those eating them to that of tobacco on smokers," he reasoned. According to him, this is the way they work: Tobacco releases stored sugar (glycogen) from the liver and this perks up one's brain. Sunflower seeds provide calories that give the same mental lift.

Tobacco has a sedative effect that tends to calm a person down. Sunflower seeds, too, stabilize the nerves because they contain oils that are calming and B-complex vitamins that help nourish the nervous system. Tobacco increases the output of adrenal gland hormones which reduces the allergic reaction of smokers. Sunflower seeds do the same. These allergic reactions can be a major problem to individuals attempting to stop smoking.

Dr. Douglass said that he had seen patients develop respiratory problems when they stopped smoking and he thought this was likely due to allergic reactions that had been kept in check by the anti-allergic effects of tobacco. "The sooner you start munching the sooner you will be an ex-smoker," he confided. "A few weeks can do the job. Only eat raw, shelled sunflower seeds. Stash several ounces of the seeds in your purse or pocket and every time you get the urge to light up, reach for a handful of seeds instead."

And if one gets tired of munching seeds all the time, then Dr. Douglass has accommodated the primal urge for variety in the form of sunflower wafers for smokers. This is how he told us to make them: Grind the seeds into fine meal. Moisten slightly to make a thick dough. Some people like to add raisins or miso (a salty paste made from soybeans). Pinch off small pieces and form them into half-dollar sized wafers. Put them on a screen and place on top of the refrigerator or some dry place for 3–4 days until the wafers are dry. "The resulting uncooked seed bread is filling, extremely nutritious and satisfying, and kills the taste for cigarettes just as raw sunflower seeds do," I remember Dr. Douglass saying.

Stops Ringing in the Ear (Tinnitus)

An old but effective Chinese remedy for reducing or removing altogether strange sounds and noises in the ear calls for drinking a decoction made out of the empty shells of sunflower seeds until the problem clears up. The seeds, themselves, are often added as well to the tea.

Bring 1-1/2 pints of water to a boil. Add 2 tbsps. *each* of crushed seeds and their empty shells. Cover, reduce heat and simmer for 15 minutes. Then remove from heat and steep an additional half an hour. Drink 1 cup of lukewarm tea, after straining, every 4–6 hours.

Putting Good Recipes to Seed

The following several recipes involve some of the different seeds covered in this section. You'll find them to be healthy, wholesome and delightful to eat.

Poppy Seed Rolls

Needed: 2 tbsps. active dry yeast; 1/2 cup lukewarm water; 6 tbsps. honey; 2-1/2 cups lukewarm buttermilk; 1 tbsp. tamari (an Oriental-style soy sauce available in some Oriental food shops and health food stores); 1-1/2 cups wheat germ; 6-1/2 cups whole wheat flour; 6 tbsps. sesame seed or safflower oil; some poppy seeds.

Dissolve the yeast in the water in a large bowl, and stir in the honey. When the yeast is bubbly, add the buttermilk, tamari, wheat germ and 2 cups of the flour. With a hand mixer on high speed, mix the wheat germ, flour and yeast mixture for 5 mins. Add 1/4 cup of the oil and the remaining wheat flour, 1 cup at a time, stirring after each addition. When the dough holds together, turn it out onto a floured surface and knead until smooth, adding only enough flour to keep the dough from sticking. Oil a large bowl or kettle, and turn the ball of dough around in the oil until it's coated. Cover the container and allow dough to rest in a warm place until doubled in bulk. Punch the dough down until it collapses, form again into a ball and cover, returning to a warm place. When the dough has doubled a second time, punch the air out again and turn the dough onto a floured surface.

Make small balls of dough, about 2 inches in diameter, and coat them with a little of the remaining 2 tbsps. of oil. Place the balls (12 should do) in the bottom of a lightly oiled, 8-inch, round cake pan. Sprinkle generously with poppy seeds and set aside to rise. When the rolls have risen almost double in bulk, place them in a preheated 400° F. oven. After 15 mins., turn the oven down to 350° F. and bake the rolls about 20 mins. longer, until they are browned and baked through. Remove from the oven and turn out on a cooling rack. The rolls will break apart easily for serving. Makes 1 dozen rolls.

Sesame-Rice Cereal

Needed: 3/4 cup raw brown rice; 1 cup powdered milk; 3-1/2 cups water; 1 tsp. salt; 2 tbsps. whole sesame seeds briefly ground in food blender to make a meal; 1/2 tbsp. Brewer's yeast; 1 tbsp. real vanilla flavor. Toast rice in dry pan over medium heat, stirring until browned. Grind in blender, then toast powder again briefly in dry pan, stirring constantly. Combine milk powder and water with wire whisk. Put in heavy pan, add salt and boil. Add rice powder, stirring constantly. Lower heat and simmer, covered, about 10 mins., or until cereal thickens. Toast sesame meal in dry pan over medium heat, stirring constantly for 1 min. or so and add along with yeast to cereal. Stir in sesame meal and yeast. Add vanilla flavor and stir again. Serve with canned or fresh goat's milk and dark honey. Serves about 5.

Lip-Smackin' Appetizer

One of the most delicious appetizers I believe I've ever tasted in my many trips abroad, was the *tahina* dish served to me in a small, out-of-the-way cafe in Doha, the capitol of the tiny Arab oil kingdom of Qatar in mid-Summer 1980. Tahina is an incredibly delicious paste made from the finely ground seeds of sesame. It can usually be obtained in certain gourmet food shops carrying Mideastern delicacies.

What I was served though was tahina mixed with a little dark red port wine and flavored with finely minced garlic and a hint of lime juice. With a saucer of this came chunks of dark rye bread, which I used for dunking purposes. My waiter also served me a glass of arrack (a rum-like alcohol) to go with my snack. So pleasing was this specially prepared tahina to my palate that I didn't even bother ordering dinner afterwards, but simply made a meal just of this simple and extremely tasty fare!

McSun Burgers

Here's a completely vegetarian burger that not even the people working beneath those golden arches of McRaunchydom could ever dream up. Preheat oven to 350° F. *Needed:* 1/2 cup grated raw carrots; 1/2 cup finely chopped celery; 2 tbsps. chopped onion; 1 tbsp. chopped parsley; 1 tbsp. chopped green pepper; 1 beaten egg; 1 tbsp. oil; 1/4 cup tomato juice; 1 cup ground sunflower seeds; 2 tbsps. wheat germ; 1/2 tsp. salt; 1/4 tsp. basil.

Combine ingredients and shape into patties. Arrange in an oiled, shallow baking dish. Bake in a moderate oven until brown on top; turn patties and bake until brown. Allow about 15 minutes of baking for each side. Serves 4. I'm indebted to Rodale Press for these recipes from their *Rodale Cookbook* and *Natural Healing Cookbook* (see Appendix).

SHEPHERD'S PURSE (*Capsella bursa-pastoris*)

Brief Description

This ubiquitous annual plant is found in fields and waste places and beside roads everywhere in the U.S. and Canada. Its erect, simple or branching stem grows from half a foot to a foot and a half tall; above it is a rosette of basal, gray-green, pinnatifid leaves. The small white flowers grow in terminal cymes, in many places blooming all year. The fruit can be flat, heart-shaped or triangular, notched pods.

Helps External Muscular Disorders

According to Maria Treben, one of Europe's greatest and most popular folk healers, it was revealed to her one night by divine inspiration that shepherd's purse was one of the finest remedies to use for all manner of muscular disorders.

Here is part of her recommendations on how to use this miraculous herb.

Pick some *fresh* shepherd's purse, enough to equal several handfuls. Finely chop and soak in 1 qt. of sour mash whiskey for two weeks. Keep it in the sun or near a warm stove or heater during this period. Be sure to shake well a couple of times each day. Using a 2-quart, Mason fruit jar or a glass, gallon, wide-mouthed jar is recommended for this.

This tincture is then thoroughly rubbed into the skin several times each day, especially on the soles of the feet, the backs of the upper calves and knees, the hips, the entire spinal column, the neck, the top of the head, the solar plexus near the belly button, the arms from the shoulders to the wrists and, last but not least, the palms and fingertips of the hands. The procedure of massaging with this herbal tincture should commence with the bottoms of the feet and follow the order just given, ending with the hands and fingertips later on.

An elderly lady from Vienna, Austria, who suffered from a prolapsed rectum, experienced continual pain from the navel to her hips. She came to Maria Treben who put her on 4 cups of Lady's Mantle tea daily. If unavailable, 4 cups of juniper berry tea may be effectively substituted with the same results. And when each cup of tea was consumed, Maria added 10 drops of her shepherd's purse tincture. She then instructed the woman's relatives how to administer to her the correct form of massage for this problem, which basically involves working from the feet towards the hips and buttocks in a kneading fashion, then from the neck to the small of the back in the same manner.

"My surprise was unimaginable," Maria states, "when the woman rang me after a time to tell me all her complaints were gone!" (See YARROW for more data on this.)

SESAME SEED (See SEEDS.)

SHAVE GRASS (See HORSETAIL.)

SKULLCAP (*Scutellaria lateriflora*)

Brief Description

This North American perennial grows in wet places throughout Canada and the northern and eastern U.S. as well as in other parts of the world, such as Southeast Asia, for instance. The fibrous, yellow rootstock produces a branching stem from 1–3 feet high, with opposite, ovate, serrate leaves that come to a point. The axillary, two-lipped flowers are pale purple or blue.

Soothes Nervous Spasms and Convulsions

Skullcap by itself or in conjunction with valerian root makes an ideal sedative for nervous muscle spasms, twitches and general convulsions. Three capsules of each herb should be taken every 4 hours for the worst cases, less, of course, for minor symptoms. Or 1-1/2 cups of warm tea every couple of hours or 1/2 cup as the case may be. In 1 pt. boiling water simmer 1 tbsp. cut, dried valerian root on low heat, covered, for 3 mins. Then add 2 tsp. of cut, dried skullcap herb, cover again, and simmer an additional 1-1/2 mins., before removing from heat entirely and steeping 40 mins. longer.

Lowers Cholesterol, Relieves Arthritis

Not all uses generally ascribed to medicinal herbs come from indigenous folk healers and makeshift herbalists. Nor is the full potential for some herbs to be found in the plethora of herb books currently inundating the health food market these days. Skullcap is a case in point to be more carefully studied by those who *think* they know something about this herb, but, in reality, may know very, very little.

Various Japanese scientists have been investigating the remarkable capabilities of this herb in regard to the heart and joint inflammation. As reported in various issues of *Chemical & Pharmaceutical Bulletin* (29:2308; 32:2724) skullcap inhibits the increase of serum cholesterol in the blood, increases the production of "good" cholesterol instead (high-density lipoproteins), inhibits fat cells from clumping so as not to cause hardening of the arteries and reduces muscle and joint swelling so common to rheumatoid arthritis.

Two to three capsules of Nature's Way skullcap from your local health food store after a heavy meal rich in fats is recommended, as well as 4 capsules once or twice daily for arthritic relief. Or 1–2 cups of tea may be taken instead, as needed for the same conditions.

SNAPDRAGON (See ORNAMENTAL PLANTS.)

SOYBEAN (See BEANS.)

SPINACH (*Spinacia oleracea*)

Brief Description

As a cultivated plant, spinach originated in or near Persia and later reached Spain by way of the invading Moors around 1100–1200 A.D. Spinach can be either smooth-leafed or, more commonly, of the crinkle-leafed "Savoy" type. It can also be round-seeded or prickly-seeded. The prickly seed varieties, once thought to be the hardiest, are often grown in the U.S.; whereas, the newer smooth-seeded kinds—thought by many to be superior in flavor—are more popular in Europe. Fresh, young, tender leaves are delicious in salads or can be steamed with a little water until tender. This is the vegetable of purported strength, which has been forever immortalized by that colorful cartoon character, Popeye the Sailor Man.

Potent Cancer Inhibitor

Recently spinach has been linked as a good food for helping to cut the risks of getting cancer. First there was Dr. Chiu-Nan Lai's study published in a 1980 issue of *Mutation Research* (77:248). In her report, Dr. Lai of the University of Texas System Cancer Center, M.D. Anderson Hospital and Tumor Institute in Houston, found that the high histidine content in spinach, along with cabbage, parsley, mustard green and broccoli, exhibited definite anti-mutagenic activities. That is to say these vegetables keep normal body cells from undergoing mutation, thereby becoming cancerous within a short time.

In August of that same year (1980), another report appeared in *Revista Brasilica de Biologia,* in which it was observed that extracts of spinach which had either been heated at 100° C. for 10 minutes or else freeze-dried, successfully inhibited Ehrlich tumor growth in 2-1/2-month-old male and female Swiss albino mice between 86–95% of the time. Then the November 13, 1986 issue of the *New England Journal of Medicine* linked the beta-carotene in dark-green leafy vegetables like spinach, kale and collards with reducing the risks of getting lung cancer. Based on such scientific evidence as this, it seems advisable to include this simple vegetable in our diets more often.

Anti-Diabetes Drink

For those with either diabetes mellitus (adults) or juvenile onset diabetes (young people), there is some nutritional benefit to be expected from spinach, since it contains manganese—a trace element important to those who are diabetics. Several handfuls of spinach should be well washed and pulled apart, leaf from leaf. Put these into a saucepan with a little kelp, 1 tbsp. *each* of lemon and lime juice and 1-1/2 cups of water. Simmer very slowly on very low heat for at least an hour. Then strain out all of the juice through several layers of cheesecloth. Take 1/2 cup before each meal by at least 30 minutes, twice daily.

Simple Recipes

Here is a couple of ways to prepare spinach without having to do a lot of work. They may be served as part of a meal or simple snacks by themselves.

Creamed Spinach

Needed: Approximately 1-1/2 cups raw spinach; 1 minced clove of garlic; 1/2 tsp. tamari (available from some Oriental food shops and health food stores); 2 tbsps. yogurt; 1/2 tsp. kelp; 1 tsp. lime juice; 1 tbsp. grated Parmesan cheese.

Wash the spinach, remove large stems and shake excess water from leaves. Reserve stems for making soup stock. Place spinach, along with garlic, kelp, tamari and lime juice in a large saucepan and steam in the small amount of water that clings to the leaves. When spinach is limp and has turned a deep green, remove from heat. Place spinach, drained if necessary, in a blender with yogurt and cheese. Process on low speed until spinach is puréed. Serves 2.

Cold Spinach Soup

Needed: 1-1/2 cups yogurt; 1 cup chopped spinach; 2 chopped scallions; 1/4 cup chopped parsley; 3/4 tsp. *each* lemon and lime juice; 1 tsp. tamari; 1/2 tsp. kelp; 1 mashed garlic clove; dash of paprika for garnish.

Put the yogurt in a blender and then slowly add the other ingredients, with the blender set on medium speed. Blend until reduced to soupy consistency. Some of the spinach will be totally pulverized, while much of it will still be in small bits. The combination of spinach, parsley and scallions give a real zing to this soup. If it's a bit too zingy for your taste buds, dilute the flavor with some more yogurt. Finally, garnish each bowl with a sprinkle of paprika. Other variations are to add 1/2 tsp. of fresh grated ginger root when blending everything up, or replace the paprika with a single cross-sectional slice of sweet red pepper instead.

SQUASH (See PUMPKIN, SQUASH, and GOURD.)

SQUAWVINE (*Mitchella repens*)

Brief Description

This perennial, evergreen herb is found around the bottom of trees and stumps in woodlands from Nova Scotia to Ontario and southward to Florida and Texas. Its creeping or trailing stems grow up to a foot long, rooting at various points, and bear opposite, orbicular-ovate leaves that are dark green and shining on top and are often streaked with white. The funnel-shaped white flowers grow in pairs and the fruit is a scarlet berry-like drupe up to 1/3 inch in diameter.

The Leading Herb for Pregnancy

A number of America's most famous herbalists concur that this herb is unexcelled in many ways for expectant mothers to take prior to delivery. Both the late Jethro Kloss and John R. Christopher regarded squawvine as the medicine par excellence to take during pregnancy in order to "make childbirth wonderfully easy." Michael Tierra, a practicing herbalist residing in Santa Cruz, California, recommends squawvine "to prevent miscarriages." And the late naturopathic doctor, John Lust, stated that "squawvine makes childbirth faster."

Cut squawvine herb is available from Indiana Botanic Gardens (see Appendix) to make a tea with. Steep 2-1/4 tsps. of dried herb in 2 cups of boiling water, covered, for half an hour. A pregnant woman should drink between 1–3 cups a day throughout the length of her pregnancy. A much stronger herbal extract is available from Bio-Botanica of Hauppauge, N.Y. (See Appendix). One tablespoon should be taken every morning on an empty stomach.

When making the tea, equal parts of red raspberry leaves and squawvine herb may be used together with excellent results.

Nice Eyewash for Infants, Elderly

Squawvine makes an excellent eyewash for newborn babies and elderly folks alike, when combined with other herbs. In 1 pint of boiling water, combine equal parts (1/2 handfuls) of cut, dried squawvine herb, raspberry leaves and strawberry leaves. Cover and steep for half an hour. Strain twice through fine sieve and cloth. Wash the eyes of infants and elderly adults frequently with this solution. It also makes a dandy vaginal injection for syphilis, gonorrhea and yeast infection.

Old Indian Remedy for Insomnia

The Menominee Indians of the Upper Great Lakes region made a tea out of the herb and leaves for insomnia in the 19th century. Steep a handful of cut, dried herb in 1-1/2 pints of boiling water, covered, for 45 minutes. Strain and drink lukewarm, about a cup and a half before retiring.

STRAWBERRY (See BERRIES.)

SUNFLOWER (See SEEDS.)

SWISS CHARD (See BEETS.)

SUMA (*Pfaffia paniculata*)

Brief Description

Suma (also called "Brazilian ginseng" or "Brazilian carrots") is a suffrutescent shrub growing prolifically in the Goias area south of the Amazon Basin in Brazil. Here much of the soil is very red, signifying large amounts of iron oxide and aluminum hydroxides but very little of other nutrients.

In this rocky, lateric soil, this member of the pig weed (amaranthacene) family grows. Its top part is rather fragile, but the below-ground rhizome is usually quite thick. Even with limited amounts of rainfall, suma has adapted quite nicely.

Women's Tonic

From what we know about the soil of the region in which it grows, we may assume that this herb is relatively high in iron. Additional research data from Japan indicates the presence of a number of natural sugars and several regular ginseng-related compounds.

In cases of anemia, fatigue and even premenstrual syndrome to some extent, it would appear that suma is very useful for women to take. One of the few companies that I'm aware of obtains their suma from this area of Brazil. Great attention is paid to the purity and integrity of the herb materials imported. Look for the best quality of suma bearing the Nature's Way logo in health food stores. An average of 2 capsules daily helps to supplement the diet with iron.

Possible Anti-Cancer Value

Some American herbalists have ascribed virtues to suma which cannot be substantiated in regular scientific literature. In addition to this, the actual ethno-botanical lore surrounding it is quite sparse. That is, there are virtually no officially recorded folk uses for it for any great length of time. One botanist, in fact, has told me in private that the folk uses attributed to it have all been of fairly recent vintage and, in his professional opinion, "were mostly created by a few Brazilian businessmen, to help sell more of the stuff." When I reported on this herb at a recent gathering of health food retailers in Philadelphia, a number of proprietors were quite surprised to hear this.

The only one not negatively affected was Ken Murdock of Nature's Way. When asked about my remarks later on, he replied, "It has always been our policy to support the truth, even if things don't always agree with our own views as manufacturers and distributors. We believe integrity is important when information on any herb is given."

Recent experiments in Japan with malignant melanoma cells in a culture medium, showed that certain naturally occurring constituents in suma manifest anti-tumor properties to them. These cancer-inhibiting compounds (pfaffic acid and pfaffosides) have been written up in volume 23 of *Phytochemistry* and Volume 102 (191149n) of *Chemical Abstracts*, among others.

Although not specifically recommended here for cancer per se, yet in an overall program of sound nutrition and good herbal supplementation, suma appears to have certain preventative value to it in regard to cancer. An average of 3 capsules daily is suggested.

T

TAMARIND (*Tamarindus indica*)

Brief Description

This is an evergreen tree which grows in tropical climates, reaching up to 80 feet or more with a shaggy, brownish-gray trunk that often is 25 feet in diameter. The alternate, even-pinnate leaves have from 20–40 small, opposite, oblong leaflets and the pale yellow flowers have petals with red veins, growing in racemes at the ends of the branches. The fruit is a cinnamon-colored oblong pod, from 3–8 inches long, with a thin, brittle shell enclosing a soft, brownish, aciduous pulp.

An Expeditious Laxative and Fever Coolant

The principal and widespread use of the ripe, sweet-sour, stringy pulp throughout the Americas and Caribbean is as a laxative. The ripe pulp contains between 10.86 and 15.23% of tartaric acid, the constituent frequently found in some baking powders that is believed to be responsible for stimulating bowel movements. Generally only one ripe fruit is needed for mild constipation problems.

In the West Indies, the ripe pulp from two fruits (minus their square, glossy, brown, hard seeds) is blended either by hand or mechanically with two cups of ice-cold water and 1 tsp. of white sugar (an equivalent amount of honey may be substituted instead). This, then, is administered to those who are burning up with fevers and within a relatively short time has cooled the body temperature down by several degrees.

Baking Powder Alternative

Towards the end of the section devoted to GRAPES AND RAISINS, an aluminum-free recipe is given for making baking powder. Those who have access to ripe tamarinds may want to substitute the two parts of cream of tartar with four parts of the fresh fruit juice. This should be done *only* at the time any baking is intended. Combine the one part each of baking soda and cornstarch first, then slowly stir in the tamarind juice, mixing everything thoroughly. Then add this to the rest of your recipe that calls for a specific amount of baking powder (which may be less than what you have to work with). This unusual type of homemade baking powder really gives breadstuffs an original and very unique flavor to say the least.

Jelly-Making in the Tropics

Throughout the Philippines the brownish pulp and seeds of ripe tamarinds are often made into balls of less than fist-size and sold in the public, open-air marketplaces under the local name of "tamarindo." A number of Filipino housewives will make jams, jellies, sweets and sherbet drinks from them, some of which I've tasted and found exceptionally delicious. This is because tamarind contains nearly 7% pectin, which is an important ingredient in making jellies and jams (see under PEACH, PEAR AND QUINCE for more details).

TANGERINE (See CITRUS.)

TAPIOCA (*Manihot esculenta*)

Brief Description

The commercial tapioca pearls commonly used in puddings comes from the starchy long, thick, tuberous roots of a half-woody shrub that grows anywhere from 3–12 feet high. These dark, brown, fat roots contain not only solid white starchy insides as potatoes do, but also considerable milky latex as well.

Poultice for Skin Eruptions

In Venezuela, Trinidad and elsewhere throughout the Americas, the dried, powdered starch of the root is used as a highly effective poultice on erysipelas, eczema, whitlows, boils, carbuncles, abscesses and herpes lesions. A similar poultice can be made by you at home for the same purposes. Combine 1 tbsp. of raw, peeled and grated potato with 2/3 tsp. of granulated, quick-cooking tapioca (*un*cooked however) in just a tiny bit of water to make a nice, even, sticky paste. Spread this on several layers of gauze cut into a small square. Affix this to the skin eruption and secure in place with adhesive tape. Change every day until purulent matter is drawn out of the sore, and healing ensues.

Helps Heal Stomach Ulcers and Colitis

In Sao Paulo, Brazil some doctors and local folk healers employ cooked tapioca for helping to heal peptic ulcers and colitis. Bring 1 cup of water to a boil, adding 2 tbsps. of Knox unflavored gelatin until thoroughly dissolved by vigorous stirring. Then add 4–6 average-sized ice cubes to the solution. When cool, slowly add this mixture to 8 stiffly beaten egg whites. Then add 1 cup pure maple syrup, a pinch of cardamom and 4 tbsps. of granulated, quick-cooking tapioca. Stir until the mixture becomes firm, then eat a dish of it. The rest may be refrigerated for consumption later on in the evening. This simple pudding, if consumed pretty regularly, has been known to engender healing of the entire intestinal tract within a short time.

Soothes Sore Breasts During Nursing

A common trend today among many women from all economic levels of society is to nurse their own infants, instead of bottle-feeding them ready-made preparations such as Similac, for instance. Usually women in the lower working and poverty classes who are used to having and feeding many children, such as Blacks and Mexicans, are seldom ever troubled with inflamed breasts and sore nipples. But middle- and upper-class mothers, many of whom are career-oriented, apparently seem to be more frequently afflicted with these conditions when nursing their own, some for the very first time as a matter of fact.

Now there is a useful remedy from Argentina for these very things. Mix some granulated, quick-cooking tapioca in milk, according to the instructions on the package or box. Be sure what you're making has the consistency of cooked cream-o'-wheat cereal. When it reaches this stage, ladle out with a wooden spoon onto several layers of gauze or a clean piece of muslin cloth. Then apply this poultice while still somewhat hot to one or both inflamed breasts, covering it with a bath or hand towel to retain the heat for as long as possible. Repeat as often as needed and change when it has become cold.

Enema for Infant Diarrhea

In Venezuela, a little granulated, quick-cooking tapioca (but *un*-cooked) is thoroughly dissolved in some water and employed as an enema in cases of diarrhea, especially in newborn infants. In the latter case, a bulb syringe would be used.

Delicious Pudding

This recipe can be made without orange juice by replacing the juice with a half cup of skim milk. Then add any fresh fruit in place of the orange segments. I'm indebted to the author and publishers of *Recipes to Lower Your Fat Thermostat* (see Appendix) for the use of this delicious pudding recipe.

Tapioca Pudding

Needed: 1½ cups skim milk; 1 tbsp. brown sugar; 3 tbsps. quick-cooking tapioca; 2 egg whites; ½ cup orange juice; ½ tsp. pure vanilla; either ½ cup diced orange segments or else ½ cup pitted and quartered dates. Combine milk, sugar and tapioca in a saucepan. Let stand 5 mins. Beat eggs till stiff. Set aside. Bring tapioca mixture to a boil over medium heat, stirring constantly. Add orange juice. Cool, stirring occasionally. Add vanilla. Fold in egg whites and diced orange segments or dates. Chill and serve. Makes about 6 servings. When dates are used, omit the sugar and orange segments. Add dates to boiling tapioca mixture *before* orange juice is added. Cook about 6 mins. Add orange juice and proceed as above.

TARRAGON (*Artemisia dracunculus*)

Brief Description

Tarragon is a green, glabrous perennial shrub found in sunny, dry areas in the western United States, southern Asia and Siberia. In Europe it is cultivated for its aromatic leaves that impart a licorice-anise flavor to sauces salads and vinegary foods. It grows about 2 feet high and has long, narrow leaves, which, unlike other members of its genus, are undivided. Tarragon is closely allied to wormwood and has long, fibrous roots spreading everywhere by runners and small flowers in round, yellow-black heads that are seldom fully opened.

Tea for Insomnia and Hyperactivity

An old French folk remedy for insomnia and hyperactivity that's been tried with pretty good success is tarragon tea. And though insomnia for me is extremely rare to say the least, I can testify to those very few times when the tea never failed to put me into dreamland in just a few minutes. Steep 1½ tsp. of the dried, cut herb in 1-3/4 cups boiling water, covered and away from the heat, for 40 minutes. Prepare about an hour before retiring, then strain and drink the tea while it's still lukewarm.

Improves Digestion, Promotes Appetite

The renowned French herbalist, Maurice Mességué, who once treated the likes of people such as Charles DeGaulle, King Farouk of Egypt and Pope John XXIII, said this about tarragon: "I prescribe the herb basically as a mild stimulant for the bowels and as a stomach aid. It can bring an appetite back to people in a very weak condition, to convalescents, nervous people, those suffering from anxiety and promote recovery from an episode of schizophrenia or nervous exhaustion following mental depression. It fights indigestion, air-swallowing and gassy distension, and is also useful in cases of gout, rheumatism, retention of urine, sluggish kidneys and bladder. It can regulate women's periods too."

Now the best way to take tarragon for digestive-related problems is in the form of a homemade vinegar, 1 tbsp. before each meal. To make tarragon vinegar, fill a wide-mouthed fruit jar with the freshly gathered leaves, picked just before the herb flowers, on a dry day. Pick the leaves off the stalks and dry a little on a flat cookie sheet lined with foil in a low-set oven (about 225° F.). Then place in the jar, cover with apple cider vinegar and ½ tsp. each freshly squeezed lemon and lime juices. Permit it to stand about 7 hours, then strain through about five layers of cheesecloth or a clean piece of flannel material into another jar with a tight-fitting ring lid to it. Store in a cool, dry pantry or cupboard.

Culinary Uses

The anise-flavored leaves and flowering tops are used to season salads, sauces, soups, stews, eggs, meat, fish and pickles. Leaves or essential oil are also used in the manufacture of tarragon vinegar, mustard, tartar sauce and liqueurs. Russian tarragon, a separate cultivar, is often confused with and sold as French tarragon. Except for being taller, the Russian variety looks similar to French tarragon but is considered far inferior to the French or true kind so far as taste goes.

TEA (See BLACK TEA.)

THYME (*Thymus vulgaris*)

Brief Description

Thyme is the general name for the many herbs of the *Thymus* species, all of which are small, perennial plants native to Europe and Asia. Common or garden thyme is considered the principal type and is utilized commercially for flowering and ornamental purposes. This low-growing, woody shrub has gray-green leaves and white, pink or purple flowers. Thyme is produced and collected in most European countries, including France, Spain, Portugal, Greece and the western U.S. The three principal varieties of thyme are English, French and German, and they differ in leaf shape, leaf color and essential oil composition.

A Natural Antibiotic

Europe's most renowned folk healer, the French herbalist Maurice Mességué, had this to say about thyme: "From my long years of experience as an herbalist, I can appreciate thyme because of its antiseptic qualities. It contains thymol and its smell destroys viruses and bacteria in the atmosphere as it destroys infectious germs in the body. I do not know any infection that cannot be mitigated if treated with this precious herb. It is an excellent weapon against epidemics and much cheaper than other means of controlling them. From boils to typhoid and whitlows to tuberculosis, it is excellent beyond compare!" This puts thyme in the same realm as garlic, both being "Nature's antibiotics" and replacements for penicillin and various sulfa drugs.

Mességué devised various preparations for using this wonderful natural antibiotic internally and externally. For gargling (sore throat), mouth wash (bad breath, tooth decay, cold sores) and drinking (common cold, influenza, fever, allergies) purposes, make a tea by steeping a dozen sprigs of fresh thyme in 1-3/4 pints of boiling water, covered and away from the heat for half an hour. Strain and drink 3–4 cups daily.

For external purposes, such as a hot compress on the chest to help break up lung congestion in cases of asthma, bronchitis, cold and flu or as a massage lotion for aching joints and muscles, put 1½ handfuls of fresh thyme in 2 pints of boiling water, covered and away from the heat, and steep for 40 minutes. Strain and use.

Footbaths, handbaths and a douche were also used by him for promoting better blood circulation, getting rid of nail fungus and athlete's foot, reducing a fever and treating *Candida albicans* or yeast infection of the vagina. One handful of fresh thyme is added to 1¼ pints of boiling water, covered and removed from the heat and permitted to steep about 25 minutes. Strain and soak hands and feet in this solution while still somewhat hot; douche with it when lukewarm, however.

Any of the above solutions may also be used to bathe wounds and burns, in the form of a compress on bumps and bruises and as a wash for sore eyes when moderately cool. This thyme eyewash is especially good for red eyes which have been irritated by the chlorinated water in public swimming pools. If fresh thyme isn't readily available, then the *cut,* dried herb may be used (2 tbsps. = 1 handful fresh herb).

Even the culinary form of ground thyme has some medicinal applications for various skin problems. Mix together 1 tsp. ground thyme, ½ tsp. lime juice, ½ tsp. onion juice with just enough honey to form a soft, sticky paste. Then apply directly on open, festering sores and boils of any kind and leave for 12 hours or so. Change again or wash away when showering or bathing and apply some new paste. Will help to heal them a lot faster, Mességué discovered.

A health liqueur for tonic and preventative purposes may be made by soaking 6 fresh or dried sprigs of thyme in 1½ cups of fine brandy for 5 days, shaking several times each day. Taking several teaspoonfuls of this throughout the day when you feel a cold or flu coming on, will not only help to prevent you from getting the "bug," but also lessen the seriousness of them should you come down with it. This same liqueur will tonify the stomach and stimulate the appetite a little, when a person doesn't especially feel like eating, but needs to for strength and sustenance.

Another interesting idea which Mességué came up with was prescribing an herbal toothpaste made out of thyme herb for people suffering with tooth and gum diseases. Soak 3 handfuls of fresh thyme, which has been lightly crushed with a rolling pin, in 1 cup of brandy for about 5 hours. A soft-to-medium bristled brush can then be dipped in this solution and the teeth cleaned with it each day. This solution is good for about 4–6 brushings or approximately 2 days use, before some more needs to be made.

Healing Salve for Facial Blemishes

A nice salve can be made at home for helping to heal cuts, bruises, acne, rash and so forth on the skin, especially in the area of the face, neck, throat and forehead. But its use also extends to burns, wounds and sores located elsewhere on the body as well.

The first part to preparing this salve is making the base for it. Ghee is used as an excellent base for many herbal salves and oils in India by Ayurvedic folk healers everywhere. This is nothing more than clarified butter, a delicious and fragrant oil that is semi-solid at room temperature. To make this ghee, melt 2 pounds of butter in a saucepan until it reaches a slow, rolling boil. Remove from the heat and carefully skim off the foam with a spoon. Return the pot to the heat and repeat this procedure twice more, removing as much of the foam as possible and discarding it. Allow the pan to cool a couple of minutes before removing the thin film that forms on top. Let the butter cool down somewhat, and then, while still liquid, pour through a fine-meshed tea strainer, but stop pouring when the heavier solids at the bottom of the pan move to the strainer. Collect the ghee in a glass bottle, cool completely and cover. The entire process takes less than half an hour to accomplish. Two pounds of butter yields about 2 cups of ghee. It can be stored without refrigeration for up to 6 months.

The next step involves reheating the ghee to just below the point where it will bubble without burning and smoking. Add 2 handfuls coarsely chopped and slightly crushed garden thyme to the pot. When the ghee is reheated, and during the gentle cooking of the thyme for an hour, the pot should always *remain covered.* After this, briefly uncover just long enough to strain through a coarse, wire sieve of some kind. Return to the stove and cover again to reheat for about 5 minutes. Then remove the lid and add between 1–2 tbsps. of melted beeswax and stir thoroughly. Also add about ½ tsp. of pure vanilla when putting the beeswax in. Finally, pour the entire contents from the pot into clean jars that aren't too deep (empty baby food jars will do). Allow to set up before screwing the lids on. Store in a cool, dry place.

Massage some of this salve into the skin each day after showering; and again in the evening before retiring for the night. I'm grateful to my friend, Michael Tierra, for the data on rendering butter into ghee and making a good, general salve.

Relieving Headaches and Cramps

The antiviral constituent, thymol, occurring in thyme is not only effective against combating unfriendly bacteria, but also helps to relax tense muscles and tight blood vessels. To help relieve migraine headaches or stomach cramps, just make a tea out of fresh or dried thyme, according to any of the previous directions given; and drink 1 cup of warm tea on an empty stomach before laying down for awhile. Also, soak a small cloth dish towel in some of the hot tea, wring out the excess liquid, then apply across the forehead and lay another dry hand or small bath towel over that to retain the heat longer. Change several times when it turns cold and continue the process for about an hour before getting up. Having the hot tea on a stool, table or small stand beside your bed or couch, will prevent you from having to get up every so often to change the compresses if you are alone and have no one else to assist you in this matter.

If fresh or dried, cut thyme is unavailable at the moment, you can effectively substitute some Listerine antiseptic in its place. Just bring a couple of cups of this commercial mouth wash almost to a boil or until quite hot. Remove from the heat to use *only* for compress purposes. *Under no circumstances* are you to drink this! A milder tea can be made *separately* by putting 1 tsp. ground thyme into 1½ cups of boiling water, covering and steeping for half an hour. Then drink slowly while still tolerably warm. The reason Listerine is recommended when thyme herb is readily available, is because this oral mouth wash contains a lot of thymol and eucalyptol from eucalyptus. Both of these constituents really help to relax the muscles when they are exposed to heat and then applied to the surface of the skin. In fact, these are some of the same constituents found in Mentholatum Deep-Heat Rub, which is used to relax sore, aching muscles.

Purifying Contaminated Water

Thyme is one of several aromatic herbs (peppermint, rosemary, sage and savory), which are handy to use in purifying water in countries such as Mexico, Spain, Portugal, Greece, Italy and, believe it or not, parts of the Soviet Union where the drinking waters are in serious question as to purity. Generally you will find some species of thyme in the public market places, which can then be used when boiling up water for drinking purposes later on. Figure about 1 good handful of cut thyme to 1 quart of water. Cover and boil, then reduce heat and simmer, covered, for 20 minutes. Strain and you now have safe drinking water that won't give you any more diarrhea and fever.

Culinary Virtues

Thyme is used for flavoring cheeses, soups, stews, stuffings, meats, fishes, dressings, sauces and honey. Thyme plants are especially attractive to bees and thyme honey is a taste treat all by itself.

Thyme Honey

If you don't have access to a beekeeper who has placed some of his hives near a large patch of thyme herb, then the second best thing to do is to make your own at home. Slightly crush a handful of freshly picked thyme herb *and* flowers (best gathered from June-August), then place them in layers on the bottom of a small saucepan. Pour room temperature honey into the pan and cook over low heat. Stir the mixture just until the honey is warm—about 4 minutes. High heat will wreck the honey.

Pour the mixture into sterilized jars and seal tightly. Empty Gerber baby food or Dijon mustard jars are good for this. Store the jars at room temperature for about 1 week to allow flavors to blend. Rewarm the honey over low heat and strain the thyme herb and flowers out. Recap or use immediately.

Brown Rice with Mushrooms and Thyme

Needed: 1 cup of spring or distilled water; 2 cups chicken stock; ½ tsp. sea salt; 1½ cups brown rice; ½ cup chopped onions; 1½ cups fresh, coarsely chopped mushrooms; 2 tbsps. butter and ½ tsp. thyme.

Bring water, stock and salt to a boil. Add rice slowly and return to boil. Turn down and simmer for 45 mins. Stir occasionally. While rice is cooking, chop onions and wash and chop mushrooms. Melt butter in large, heavy skillet. Sautée onions and mushrooms. Add cooked rice and mix well. Add thyme. Add a little bit of kelp and some more sea salt to taste. Makes 6–8 servings. I'm indebted to the folks at *Country Journal* (see Appendix) for the use of this recipe.

TOMATO (*Lycopersicon esculentum*)

Brief Description

The earliest tomatoes were harvested by the Incas of the Andes, but later carried to Europe by the Spanish conquistadores. These small, yellow fruits were about the size of today's cherry tomatoes. But fear and ignorance, to a certain extent, kept them from becoming very popular, especially in France and England. Even when reintroduced to America, they were still thought of as being poisonous, just like other members of the deadly nightshade group happen to be. The Creoles in New Orleans finally brought tomatoes into the kitchen in 1812, but another half a century had to pass before other sections of the country got up enough courage and curiosity to try them.

But even then the tomato's troubles weren't over. Botanically, they are really fruits, which confused many people because they are most often used like vegetables. Finally, it took, believe it or not, a ruling by the Supreme Court in 1893 to reclassify the tomato as an official vegetable, even though botanically speaking, it isn't and never will be!

Varieties of tomatoes available today include the large, all-purpose beefsteak types; the oval plum variety, used chiefly for cooking purposes; the small, tasty cherry tomato, often served in salads and the large, yellow or orange, low-acid tomatoes.

Looking for the Best Tomato

In the United States, more tomatoes are consumed than any other single fruit or vegetable. They far outdistance oranges, potatoes and lettuce, to say nothing of such popular staples as peas, carrots and bananas. But as the editors of *Reader's Digest* have noted, "Today's thick-skinned commercial tomatoes, usually picked green and 'ripened' with ethylene gas, have nothing to recommend them beyond the dubious values of the marketplace: ease of shipment and long shelf life."

"Such tomatoes are really only symbols of tomatoes," griped the food editor of the *Los Angeles Herald Examiner*. "They are tasteless, have a mealy texture, and a lower vitamin content than fully grown tomatoes that have ripened on the vine. To distinguish a vine-ripened tomato from a gas-ripened one (without tasting it), smell it. Gassed tomatoes are odorless, and vine-ripened ones have a telltale tomato fragrance about them."

As you've probably guessed it by now, the very best tomatoes to look for are the succulent, vine-ripened kind bought in season from local farms, outdoor produce stands, truck markets or simply grown in your own backyard. Nothing can compare with them in flavor and nutritional goodness!

Dried Tomato Prevents Diarrhea

Researchers at the Animal Nutrition Lab at Cornell University reported in the April 19, 1940 issue of *Science* that tomato pomace (dried residues from tomato juice) stabilized and gave form and consistency to the feces of dogs, foxes and minks when it was added to their diets. Before these improved mixtures, the looseness of these animals' stools almost bordered on diarrhea in many instances. But by adding to the diet a quantity of ground, dried tomato pomace (seeds, skin and minor pulp) equal to 5% of the wet ration, their feces assumed more solid and uniform consistency.

A similar preparation can be made at home to improve the form and consistency of your own stool. Choose firm, just-ripe tomatoes to work with. Wash and remove stems. Slice them into ½-in. thick slices with an even thickness throughout (not like the salad-sliced wedges, however). Place them on plastic trays, not metallic due to their high acid content, if you intend to dry them in a dehydrator for 2 hrs. at 155° F. and another 9 hrs. at 125° F. Or line a flat cookie sheet with foil and put them on if you intend to dry them in your oven instead for the same length of time at the identical temperatures just cited.

By the time they're done, they will be very thin and crisp. Check around the peel for any remaining moisture beads. When cool, store in airtight containers. Four to five slices equals a fresh tomato, depending on the size, of course. You can also put the dried slices in the blender and make a nice tomato powder. Figure about a dozen dried slices for enough tomato powder to stir in 2/3 cup of cool water to drink for mild diarrhea. This amount can be increased, as needed.

For a really effective anti-diarrheal preparation combine equal parts of dried tomato powder with dried apple powder, having rendered them into this state by way of your food blender. Figure 2 level tbsps. (one of each) in 1¼ cups of warm water to take care of the problem nicely.

To make dried apples, cut *un*peeled apples into slices or rings about ¼-in. thick. Pretreat them by dipping slices in lime juice before drying. Dry at 155° F. for 2 hrs., then at 125° F. for about 3 hours more in your dehydrator or oven. Test for dryness by removing a slice, allowing it to cool, then cutting it in half. No moisture beads should appear when squeezed. Pieces that aren't quite dry tend to feel cooler, as well as moist. Remove the slices as they dry, allow them to cool, then store in airtight containers.

Dried tomato slices can also be topped with a slice of slightly melted cheese for a tasty snack or used in soup. Apple and tomato slices may be rehydrated for culinary purposes by covering them with boiling water and steeping for 20 mins. in a pan with a lid on top.

Vine-Ripened Tomatoes for Hypertension

Clinical evidence cited earlier in this work indicates that potassium has a very positive influence upon the kidneys, whereby high blood pressure can be substantially reduced in many instances. Now just one jumbo tomato approximately 3 inches in diameter and weighing some 7 ounces contains nearly 450 milligrams of potassium. Imagine then if two such good-sized tomatoes were consumed every other day in the form of a delicious vegetable cocktail, just how much potassium the body would be getting.

But wait, there's more: if 1 tsp. *each* of ground tarragon, paprika, ground turmeric, ground basil and 1 tbsp. of lemon juice, along with 2/3 cup of spring or distilled water were added with the two ripe tomatoes and thoroughly blended, you would have a zesty, lip-smacking beverage that would contain almost 1,200 milligrams of straight potassium *and only* about 15 mg. of sodium. This is an incredible ratio of 80:1 and *potent* therapy for helping to bring hypertension under control!

Turning Sunburn into a Nice Tan

Paul Neinast, owner and operator of Dallas' leading beauty salon, came up with a nifty idea several years ago for turning a relatively painful sunburn into a modestly decent tan. He takes peeled tomato slices, soaks them awhile in buttermilk, then applies them directly to the skin. They not only help to relieve the pain, but also close up the pores and turn the burn into some kind of a tan. Another way he has used them is to make a purée out of *thinly* peeled tomatoes with a little bit of buttermilk added, but not enough to make it too runny. This, then, is spread over sunburned skin to give a more even and slightly darker tan.

Heals Festering Wounds and Sores

In Papua, New Guinea some Stone Age tribes still rely on the pounded leaves of wild tomato plants in the form of poultices as a means of helping to heal old wounds and sores. A couple from Rhode Island shared similar minor experiences of their own with me in this regard. He had a badly festering forefinger that kept oozing out a lot of pus and blood. So he took a slice of fresh tomato and wrapped it around the finger, holding the same in place with some adhesive tape. He changed this a couple of times a day and within 2–3 days the infection had all cleared up.

His wife, on the other hand, had been trying out some new high heels recently purchased at an expensive department store in downtown Providence. But they were too small for her and kept pinching her big toe. Soon an excruciating pain developed. She just put a slice of tomato over it, then some gauze and finally taped it down. *In less than a day*, the pain had entirely gone! Such is the power of tomatoes.

Building Strength in Place of Fatigue

One of the common symptoms seen so frequently in hypoglycemics or those who have low blood sugar is their constant fatigue and apparent lack of energy. Well it seems that tomatoes can play a vital role in rebuilding their strength. Doctors at Tohoku University in Sendai, Japan reported that fresh tomato juice was extremely effective in accelerating the glycogen (blood sugar) formation in normal rabbits by further stimulation of the liver.

Nor should it come as any surprise either that the next most important constituent of the tomato are various naturally-occurring sugars, which account for some 50% of the total dry matter. Ripe tomatoes are especially high in glucose and particularly fructose. Interestingly enough, when tomatoes are grown in the shade, their sugar contents are drastically reduced.

Furthermore, for those who are athletically active in any way, they may find powdered tomato seeds worth taking as an ideal protein supplement. The amino acid profile of tomato seed protein, says the *CRC Critical Rev. in Fd. Science & Nutrition* for Nov. 1981 is "similar to that of sunflower and soybean." Anyone fortunate enough to live near a cannery or soup factory can probably get all the free tomato seeds that their hearts desire.

The Health of the Liver

In the Soviet Union, many doctors prescribe tomatoes in the diets of factory workers exposed to toxic chemical occupational environments. One chief reason for this may be due to the fact that tomatoes contain two very important detoxifying trace elements; namely, chlorine and sulphur.

Natural chlorine helps to stimulate the liver in its function as a filter for body wastes and further assists this major organ in its efforts to remove toxic waste products from the system. Sulphur helps to protect the liver from cirrhosis and other debilitating conditions. In 100 grams of raw, edible tomato (2-2/3 in. diam. and 3½ oz. wt.) there are 51 mg. of chlorine and 11 mg. of sulphur.

Limited clinical evidence also suggests that fresh juice from vine-ripened tomatoes can actually help the liver to regenerate or reproduce a part of itself if another portion has been destroyed or surgically removed. Thus we can see that tomatoes definitely help promote the health and well-being of one of the body's most important organs. "A tomato a day, keeps the liver in good stay!"

A tomato is also good to consume when eating too much animal fat in the form of butter, cheese, eggs, pork, beef and many deep-fried foods. The tomato will usually help to dissolve this fat, thereby preventing hardening of the arteries.

Challenging Recipes

The following culinary uses for tomatoes should challenge your imagination and definitely tantalize your palate for sure.

Early New England Tomato Catsup

"The best sort of catsup is made from tomatoes," observed a very serious Mrs. Child in her 1832 *American Frugal Housewife,* as if to imply almost that catsup can be made from other types of vegetables as well. "The vegetables should be squeezed up in the hand, salt put to them, and set by for 24 hours. After being passed through a sieve, cloves, allspice, pepper, mace, garlic and whole mustard-seed should be added. It should be boiled down one-third and bottled after it is cool. No liquid is necessary, as the tomatoes are very juicy. A good deal of salt and spice is necessary to keep the catsup well. It is delicious with roast meat; and a cupful adds much to the richness of soup and chowder. The garlic should be taken out before it is bottled." Anyway that's pretty much how they made catsup in Boston in those days.

Tomato Fettucini

Needed: 7 oz. (approximately 3/4 cup) tomato pasta; 6 tbsps. raw, chopped shallot bulbs; 8 slices of dried tomato (see this same section under "preventing diarrhea"); 1 tbsp. olive oil; 1 tbsp. melted butter; 4 tbsps. white wine; 10 olives; 2 slices of goat cheese; and pinches of basil, rosemary, sage, tarragon and parsley. Sautée shallots with butter and oil. Add sun-dried tomatoes, olives and white wine. Reduce slightly and add herbs. Toss with tomato pasta and goat cheese.

Tomato Leather

A popular snack and much less expensive to make at home is tomato leather. Before you begin make sure the tomatoes are clean, with any bruises or spoiled areas removed. Cut them into ½-in. chunks and leave the peel on. Purée the fruit in a blender until no large chunks remain. You can then add 1 tsp. lime juice per cup of tomato purée to help prevent it from darkening any.

Place the puréed fruit on lightly oiled plastic dehydrator sheets or foil-covered and lightly greased cookie sheets. Spread the purée out as evenly as possible, less than ¼-in. thick. Dry the fruit leather at 135° F. for 6–8 hours in a dehydrator or low-set oven until leathery and no longer sticky to the touch. Peel the leather off the trays or sheet pans and cut into serving size pieces. Place on clean plastic wrap, rolling the slices along with the plastic wrap, jelly-roll fashion to keep the tomatoes from sticking to themselves. Store the slices in a plastic bag in a cool, dark place. This same process can be used for different kinds of fruit as well; some, like bananas, pears, pineapples, watermelon and oranges, would need to be peeled, however, while others would not.

Enchilada Casserole with Tomato Sauce

The author is indebted to La Rene Gaunt and the publishers of her book, *Recipes to Lower Your Fat Thermostat* for letting him use their "out of this world" Mexican meal treat. (See Appendix for more information on how to get their cook book.)

Needed: 1 chopped onion; 1 minced garlic clove; 1 chopped green bell pepper; ½ cup sliced mushrooms; 1 recipe basic tomato sauce (see below); 1 tsp. chili powder; 1½ cups cooked pinto beans; ½ cup yogurt; 1 cup cottage cheese; 8 corn tortillas; ½ cup grated Mozzarella cheese.

Sautée onion, garlic, green pepper and mushrooms until onions are transparent. Add tomato sauce, chili powder and beans. Heat through. Stir yogurt and cottage cheese together. In a 1½-qt. casserole dish rubbed with liquid lecithin (available from any local health food store), put a layer of tortillas, a layer of sauce, a sprinkle of Mozzarella cheese and a layer of yogurt mixture. Repeat until all ingredients are used, ending with a layer of sauce. Top with yogurt mixture. Bake at 350° F. for 15–20 minutes. Serve hot. Makes 8 servings.

Basic Tomato Sauce

This sauce has a wide range of uses. It can be poured over spaghetti, stuffed cabbage, stuffed green peppers, cooked rice and so forth.

Needed: 1 cup diced onion; 2 minced garlic cloves; 1 28-oz. can stewed tomatoes; 3 tbsp. tomato paste; ½ tbsp. kelp; ½ tsp. oregano; ½ tsp. basil; 1 diced green bell pepper (including the seed center); ½ cup mushrooms.

Tomato Versatility

One of the tomato's great virtues is its versatility. You can stew them using no water at all by dicing them and stirring over low heat. You can broil them under moderate heat for about 10 minutes, creating fresh taste sensations through judicious applications of toppings, or bake halves in a preheated 425° F. oven for 10–15 mins. Here are a few ideas for toppings, from the kitchen of the California Fresh Tomato Advisory Board: (A) Bread crumbs seasoned with a pinch of basil, sage, thyme or lemon thyme; (B) grated Parmesan or cheddar cheese; (C) chopped green onions or chives and butter; (D) blue cheese crumbled in sour cream; (E) chopped smoked salmon in softened cream cheese.

Finally you can stuff your tomatoes, but be careful of the ripeness and consistency. Leave them unpeeled, cut out the stem and core, then, starting at the center of the uncut end, divide into quarters, three-fourths of the way down. Pull apart gently and fill with tuna, chicken or vegetable salad, cottage cheese or avocados chunked or mashed. Or try a real treat by precooking chopped onion, cracked wheat, tomato pulp, chopped mint and raisins in olive oil, then stuff tomatoes with this mixture. They are then baked in a 350° F. oven for 30 minutes. This last version of Tomatoes a la Greque is an international favorite with gourmets.

TROPICAL FRUITS

GUAVA (*Psidium guajava*)
MANGO (*Mangifera indica*)
PAPAYA (*Carica papaya*)
PINEAPPLE (*Ananas comosus*)

Brief Description

GUAVA. Guavas are small, thin-skinned tropical fruits. They are often processed into jellies, jams and preserves, but they can also be consumed fresh. The fruits are round to pear-shaped, usually less than 3 inches in diameter, with green or bright-yellow skins; some have a reddish blush. Ripe guavas have a musky, pungent odor. They contain small, hard seeds that may irritate the throat, but some of the newer varieties are relatively free from seeds. Guavas are sensitive to frost, which explains why the majority of them grown in this country are found only in California and Florida.

MANGO. These are the most luscious of all tropical fruits. However when they aren't of good quality, the flesh can be disagreeably fibrous, with a flavor of turpentine. These highly perishable fruits also vary greatly in size—anywhere from 6 oz. to 4–5 lbs.—and shape: they can be round, oval, pear or kidney shaped, or even long and thin. The tough skin is usually dull green, with red and yellow areas that broaden as the fruit ripens. Some people have an allergic skin reaction to the fluid beneath the peel and must wear protective gloves when peeling the fruit. India still produces 80% of the world's crop of mangoes.

PAPAYA. A native of the Caribbean, the papaya now grows abundantly throughout tropical America. The fruit is usually pear-sized and has a central cavity filled with edible, pea-sized black seeds; the sweet, juicy flesh is rather bland, with a slight muskiness and a melonlike texture. Unripe papayas can be baked or boiled as vegetables, and the leaves, if attached, are often cooked as greens. Like mangoes, papayas also secrete a fluid that usually causes an allergic skin reaction in some people, thereby necessitating the wearing of rubber gloves while peeling the fruit.

PINEAPPLE. These plump, heavy fruits with fresh, green crown-leaves, emit a fragrant aroma and have a very slight separation of the eyes or pips. Though the shell turns yellow as the fruit matures, pineapples do not ripen after harvest as some are inclined to think is the case. Columbus encountered the first pineapples on his second voyage to the New World on the tiny island of Guadeloupe. These fruits were not introduced to Hawaii until 1790 and it took until the early part of the 20th century for Hawaiian plantations to dominate the world market in this delicious fruit.

Guava Juice for Congestion

The Negritos of the Philippines have used ripe guava as a tonic for strengthening weak hearts. Among the Choco Indians of Panama, ripe guavas are consumed to overcome congestion of the lungs and throat. Fresh juice can be made by thoroughly mixing one coarsely chopped, ripe mango in 1 cup of crushed ice and 2/3 cup of ice water. Sip slowly. Or 1 cup of canned mango juice may be taken at least 3 times a week for helping improve the heart. Those bothered with asthma, bronchitis and hayfever would benefit from drinking ½ cup of *lukewarm,* canned mango juice with ¼ tsp. of lime juice and 4 drops of pure vanilla stirred in, twice a day during bouts with serious respiratory congestion. Drinking this just before retiring will enable an asthmatic to rest better without choking up so much during the night.

Guava Leaf Extract for Seizures

In parts of the West Indies, an alcoholic extract is made from the pounded leaves of guava plants for treating epileptic seizures and convulsions. The tincture is also rubbed into the spines of young children and young adults, besides being given internally.

If guava plants are available near you, then pick about 10 leaves, crush them lightly and snip into inch-square pieces. Put them into the bottom of a quart glass Mason fruit jar and cover with 1 cup of vodka and 1 cup of gin. Cap and permit the herbs to steep in this solution for 15 days, remembering to shake the jar twice daily. Then strain through a fine wire sieve and put in a clean pint jar with a ring lid. Store in a cool, dry place until needed.

Two teaspoonfuls of this alcoholic extract may be taken by young to middle-aged adults suffering from seizures and convulsions (half this amount for children under the age of 15). Some of the tincture should also be rubbed on the spine each day from the base of the neck to the tailbone.

Mango and Hypertension

On the island of Curacao, many residents drink a decoction of the semi-dried leaves for high blood pressure. Pick 1½ large or 2 medium-sized leaves and dry halfway on a piece of clean cloth for only one day. While still somewhat moist, snip with shears into inch-size pieces and place in 1 quart of boiling water. Cover, remove from the stove and steep for an hour. Strain and drink 2 cups a day, three days in succession, as they do in Curacao. Then go for several days without the tea, before repeating the process all over again. This sedative action to the leaves may be due, in part, to eremophilene, which also occurs in the herbal tranquilizer, valerian.

A Proven Anti-Diabetic Remedy

A group of tannins called anthocyanidins are found in mango leaves. For over 20 years, according to a back volume of the French journal, *Plantes Médicinales et Phytothérapie* (11:143–51 Suppl.), some European physicians have been using a watery extract (tea) of mango leaves to treat not only diabetes, but also blood vessel problems and eye complaints related to this disease. They help to slow down the progress of diabetic angiopathy (disease of the blood vessels due to diabetes). In fact, the definite improvement observed in diabetes is due primarily to the healing influence of these leafy compounds on the blood vessels in and around the pancreas.

Excellent results have also been obtained with a tea made from mango leaves in the treatment of diabetic retinopathy. This is a noninflammatory degenerative disease of the retina occurring in those who've had diabetes for many years. The condition is marked by small hemorrhage dots and very tiny enlargements of blood vessels within the retina itself, as well as sharply defined waxy exuded matter.

Make a tea according to the instructions previously given for hypertension. Drink 1 cup each day to which has been added 2 tbsps. of either guava, mango or papaya juice. This remedy in the same amount is also ideal for strengthening fragile blood vessels, treating purpura (hemorrhage spots in the skin) and varicose veins, and in the prevention of bleeding accidents through the use of anticoagulant drugs.

Gastrointestinal Problems Relieved

Ripe mango, papaya and pineapple are all extremely useful for any disturbances of the G.I. tract. In the Philippines, ripe mangoes are employed to settle nervous and upset stomach and to stimulate the bowels in times of constipation. Papaya contains the remarkable digestive enzyme, papain, just the same as pineapple contains its own unique enzyme, bromelain.

Those who have had difficulty digesting certain starchy foods, (breads, cereals, and potatoes) or meats (beef, pork, chicken) have sometimes accompanied their meals with an 8 oz. glass of either mango, papaya or pineapple juice. Any one of these can bring quick relief to the heartburn common to rapid eating and poor chewing habits, and heavy meals.

It may be interesting to note here that the proteolytic enzyme from papaya (papain) is employed a lot in the tenderizing of tough meat fibers by such food outlets as Sizzler, which is known for serving steaks at relatively cheap prices. They can afford to do this in most instances simply because they purchase lower grades of beef carcass—standard (young steers), commercial (mostly old cows) and utility (tough, old bulls)—which are then saturated with papain for certain lengths of time in order to make them seem more tender. Also, those who like to drink beer may find it interesting to know that papain is extensively used in stabilizing and chill-proofing beer. Which just goes to show that a fruit like papaya with an enzyme in it good for the healing of stomach ulcers, likewise has diverse applications in the giant food and beverage industries.

Papain for Insect Stings and Deadly Snakebites

A retired school nurse by the name of LaFonse Webber, who resided for years in Houston, Texas until her recent death, shared the following information with me during one of many lecture trips I've made to that city in the past.

> When I worked as a school nurse, both in the junior highs and local high schools here years ago, I always used to keep a bottle of Adolph's meat tenderizer in my desk for treating bee, wasp and hornet stings, and also mosquito and horsefly bites that the kids would get during the Spring and early Fall. I never knew any case to fail when I used the stuff on them.
>
> The way I used to apply Adolph's was to mix a little of the tenderizer in ¼–½ tsp. of water, which I'd then soak up with a cotton ball. This I'd place on the kid's sting or bite and have him or her hold it in place until some of the pain had subsided. I figure it took about 20 minutes for the tenderizer to soak into the skin where it could do some good.
>
> One time a big, heavy built kid in one of the high schools here in Houston happened to step on a couple of honeybees feeding on some dandelions, while he was training on the grass. Boy! Did he ever holler. He was still moaning and groaning when his coach brought him limping to my office. For a guy with so much muscle and size to him, he sure didn't have much courage. Anyway, I mixed 2 tbsps. of Adolph's in a pint of warm water, which I then put into a small square pan and had the kid soak the bottom of his foot in this for awhile. In less than 15 minutes the pain went away and in another half hour or so half of the swelling had gone down too.

Jim Nelson, M.D., an allergist in Fort Wayne, Indiana, told the *Intermountain Reporter* (a publication of the U.S. Forest Service regional office in Ogden, Utah) once that the best way to treat a bee sting was first to "scrape off the stinger, then apply a paste of meat tenderizer and water (¼ tsp. in 1–2 tsp. water) to destroy the venom." This also works well for insect bites too. And in Australia a similar method is used with meat tenderizer to treat jelly-fish and man-o'-war stings.

Now it is interesting to note that the proteolytic enzyme in papaya, called papain, is far more effective in the hydrolysis of protein substrates than related proteases such as trypsin and pepsin, are. Which helps to show its extreme importance in the successful treatment of poisonous snakebites from the likes of cobras, black mambas and other deadly species. The *Journal of the American Medical Association* for Dec. 22, 1975 pointed out that trypsin and similar enzymes like papain help to degrade the venom protein molecules injected into the blood stream.

In experimental animals, if a dose of trypsin followed injection of venom in less than 15 minutes, all animals survived. If the enzyme was injected 50 minutes after the snakebite, at least 50% of animals survived. Since the papain from papaya is superior to trypsin in this respect, it only stands to reason that it should be taken orally when an individual is accidentally bitten by a poisonous snake here in America; such as a rattlesnake or copperhead, for instance. Papaya tablets are available from some health food stores. Between 5 of them and about 1 level teaspoonful of Adolph's meat tenderizer dissolved in a cup of warm water, there should be enough papain ingested to begin neutralizing quite a bit of any such snake venom. First swallow the tablets one by one, then take small gulps of the warm water and meat tenderizer solution.

Pineapple and Sports Injuries

Dwight McKee, M.D., a New England physician, has recommended the digestive enzyme bromelain, and raw pineapple in which it's found, for acute cases of tendonitis. "Sometimes just a day of eating nothing but raw pineapple will clear it up," he observed.

Another health practitioner, Dr. Robert W. Downs, a noted chiropractor who writes often for *Bestways* magazine, also believes very much in the therapeutic potentials of bromelain. "It's going to be used by more and more doctors for younger individuals engaged in heavy athletics—such as jogging, running and weight lifting—because it speeds up the healing process," he stated. "There have been studies suggesting that people who are damaging their tissues with athletics (especially the weekend athlete) can reduce the inflammation and speed the healing dramatically by the use of bromelain. In the future," he predicted, "I look for quality bromelain products to be one of the major supplements recommended for sports injuries."

One of the contestants in the Iron Man Triathlon held yearly in Hawaii with whom I spoke, confided that he ate nothing but raw, ripe pineapple and drank only pineapple juice several days before competition began in order to greatly minimize the pain and inflammation expected from such a grueling test of physical strength and human endurance.

Bromelain Thins the Blood

For those with thick blood and poor circulation, the rat poison compound called warfarin has usually been the standard drug prescribed for them by their physicians. But warfarin, coumadin and related medications are toxic and can produce nasty side-effects in the course of time. Now scientists have discovered that the bromelain in ripe pineapple and pineapple juice can also thin the blood and prevent blood clots from forming, not to mention helping increase circulation more.

One cup of pineapple juice daily or the inner ripe flesh of half a raw, ripe pineapple are recommended in place of harmful drugs for the above conditions. However, it should be noted that hemophiliacs and others with bleeding problems should avoid this fruit, since it is liable to only aggravate their situations more.

Pineapple Juice and Dental Surgery

The removal of impacted wisdom teeth from teenagers is a fairly common dental procedure in many parts of the country. But this type of operation is not without its drawbacks; namely, extreme swelling, black and blue marks and considerable pain. But pineapple can change all of that in no time before and after surgery.

Prior to the operation, the patient should eat at least one can of pineapple chunks packed in its own juice for 15 days and drink one 6 oz. glass of unsweetened pineapple juice each day during this period as well. Following the operation, the patient should begin drinking two 8 oz. glasses of pineapple juice each day, one glass fresh and the other glass canned juice. Along with this should be taken one 50 mg. tablet of zinc, up to 3,500 mg. of vitamin C tablets, a couple of strong B-complex tablets and about 750 mg. of bioflavonoids (unless they are included with the vitamin C supplement to be used). Ice packs may also be applied externally to the jaw as well.

The results will be nothing short of amazing. Swelling will be extremely minimal, pain will be practically nonexistent as such and there will be no black-and-blue marks. If fresh pineapple is readily available, then it should be the obvious first choice no doubt. By way of interest, the crushed leaves and petioles of mango are used in parts of Mexico to scrub the teeth with. This cleans them, hardens the gums and relieves pyorrhea.

Getting Rid of Warts and Corns

Papaya and pineapple are very useful in getting rid of warts and corns. In Jamaica the milky latex of the green papaya fruit is slowly dripped onto warts several times each day for a week or less. This gummy residue shrivels them up and they soon fall off of their own accord. A slice of pineapple rubbed gently on a wart will remove it, but several applications are necessary before success results.

As a corn cure the pineapple is nearly always successful. Cut off a small, inch-square piece of the peel and bind it on the corn with *wide* adhesive tape, making sure that the inner side of the peel faces the corn. Leave it on all night and in the morning soak the foot in hot water. The corn will be easily removed. Some stubborn cases, however, may require 4–5 applications, but it nearly always works!

Eliminating Intestinal Worms

Both papaya and pineapple are excellent for removing intestinal parasites such as roundworm, hookworm and the like. The gummy, milk sap in the unripe papaya as well as the little black seeds destroy such parasites by digesting them. If you're not up to eating some of the green, bitter fruit, then why not chew and swallow a piece of the leaf or a tablespoonful of the seeds after each meal? The seeds have a pungent taste to them, not unlike that of watercress or radishes.

In Venezuela and Colombia, coarsely cut, ripe, unpeeled pineapple fruit is steeped in 1 quart of boiling water for up to 3 hours. This can be accomplished by first putting the cut chunks of unpeeled fruit in a 2-qt. fruit jar and then pouring the hot water over them. Seal with a ring-type of lid while steeping this way. Strain the infusion and drink up to 4 cups a day in between meals and on an empty stomach in order to expel greater numbers of intestinal parasites.

Relieving an Aching Back

At one point or another in their lives, 8 of every 10 people on earth it's estimated, will suffer from this universal affliction. In the U.S. alone, as many as 75 million Americans have back problems. Of these 5 million are partly disabled, and 2 million are unable to work at all. Beyond the personal grief, back pain exacts a staggering social cost. In the U.S. 93 million workdays are lost each year because of back problems. Americans spent about $5 billion a year for tests and treatment by a dizzying array of back specialists, including orthopedists, osteopaths, physical therapists and chiropractors, to say nothing of self-styled gurus who promote every manner of cure imaginable.

Besides complicated back surgery which can be very risky and only moderately successful, there is another alternative—the injection of an enzyme called chymopapain from ripe papayas. Developed in the early 1960s by orthopedist Lyman Smith of Elgin, Illinois, the treatment is designed to dissolve a ruptured disc's gelatinous pulp and eliminate the need for an operation.

The chymopapain is injected while the patient is under a light general anesthetic. Fluoroscopy is used to help guide the needles to the proper location. Two milliliters of fluid are inserted into the disc and allowed to remain for 4 mins., after which the needles and fluid are removed.

The fluid becomes cloudy, because during that 4 minutes, the enzyme has already begun dissolving the disc. Usually pain is alleviated within 48 hours and all symptoms are gone by six weeks.

A University of Wisconsin (Madison) study found that 83 of 114 patients who had received chymopapain for herniated discs had little or no back pain 3–6 years after the treatment. Now-a-days, though, because of FDA skepticism and a lot of "bad press," chymopapain is mostly used by Canadian physicians. Mark Brown, M.D., who was with the University of Miami School of Medicine in 1980, commented that 90% of his patients referred to Toronto doctors, came back feeling just fine and "didn't need anything else" to help them.

In 1983, some 70,000 treatments of chymopapain were given in the U.S. But as of 1986 this figure had been drastically cut to the paltry sum of only 15,000. A couple of years ago, Smith Laboratories, one of the makers of the drug, sent a form letter to over 22,000 surgeons warning them of several of its possible side-effects. Among them are transverse myelitis (inflammation of the spinal cord) which can lead to muscle paralysis and analeptic shock.

Still, though, chymopapain remains an effective therapy for relieving back pain where surgery can and ought to be avoided. Using several herbs will help to reduce the risks associated with it. Just prior to and for sometime thereafter, an individual receiving chymopapain from his or her attending physician here or in Canada, should be drinking several cups of yarrow-chamomile tea each day *and* rubbing the spinal column with some CamoCare Cream from Abkit of New York (see Appendix). A good peppermint oil from any local health food store is likewise recommended for the spine too, rubbing a little in each day. To make the tea, bring 1 qt. of water to a boil. Remove from the heat and add 1½ tbsps. of cut, dried yarrow and 1½ tbsps. of cut, dried chamomile. Stir a little before covering with a lid. Steep for 50 minutes before straining.

Cosmetic Applications

Paul Neinast employs papaya and pineapple in his expensive and renowned Dallas beauty salon. He prepares a papaya facial mask by puréeing a little bit of the peeled, ripe fruit (minus seed) in a food blender. He claims that this "really helps to lift blackheads off the skin." And he finds that rubbing a chunk of peeled ripe pineapple segment over the skin not only neutralizes fatty acids, but also wipes up any greasy film which might be on the surface.

For a really youthful, smoother complexion, try using a formula that includes green papaya concentrate, sunflower seed oil and blackstrap molasses. Take one green papaya, if available in your area somewhere, and cut it up into 2-inch chunks. Put them and the milky latex in a food blender and purée until thick and even. Then add approximately 2 tbsps. of sunflower oil and 2–3 tbsps. of molasses and whip again until smooth. The consistency should just be thick enough to adequately spread on the face, forehead, throat and neck each night without being runny or messy. A couple of tablespoons of whipping cream and 4 egg whites should also be added at the very last, but only blended for about 15 seconds and no longer.

Those who've had occasion to use this wonderful remedy report that it seems to work great on acne vulgaris and dried, old, scaly skin. There appears to be a rapid turnover of epidermal (surface) skin cells, which leads to a much younger, baby-soft type of skin for many. Some have even claimed that the papain present in this formula has actually lightened dark patches in their skin or nearly faded away existing freckles. But documented proof is wanting on these assertions, so they must be taken for just what they are—untested claims—until more solid evidence can be forthcoming in the near future.

Healing Wounds and Sores

The papain in papaya, because of its incredible ability to digest dead tissue without affecting the surrounding live tissue, has gained for itself the reputation of being a "biological scalpel."

This reminds me of an episode which occurred about a decade ago in a London hospital. A young doctor recently assigned to the medical staff from South Africa, was treating a male patient with a lingering infection from abdominal surgery. Antibiotics had proved virtually useless.

Remembering an old folk remedy, this physician purchased all of the ripe papayas at a local market. He instructed the nurses to slice some of the fruit in strips and judiciously place them over the patient's wound, leaving them there for about 5 hours before replacing with fresh ones. Needless to say the infection cleared up in a day or so and the patient was discharged shortly thereafter.

Cold sores around the lips and inside the mouth, cracked and furred tongue and inflamed tonsils can all be readily cleared up by sucking and chewing on several papaya tablets a couple of times each day until healed. In Brazil a piece of the fresh leaf is chewed for oral sores or else just tied onto a wound or external sore with good success.

Treating Inner Ear Infection

A really good oil for curing inner ear infection can be made by soaking 4–6 crushed, powdered papaya tablets and two peeled, finely minced garlic cloves in 1 pint of virgin olive oil for 10 days. This can then be strained through several layers of gauze and rebottled in a dark, well-sealed container and stored in a cool, dry place until needed.

For a child under the age of 12, use about 2–3 drops; while teenagers and adults should be given up to 6 drops in whichever ear canal is infected. Do this once a day and repeat as often as needed until the infection clears up. It seems to work well in most cases.

Bathing Rashes

Some Indians of the Amazon Basin in Brazil boil the rind of ripe pineapple with rosemary, then frequently wash skin rashes and hemorrhoids with the concentrated decoction. In a quart of boiling water, simmer the cut up rind of one pineapple with 1 tbsp. of dried rosemary, uncovered, for the space of 35 minutes. Besides washing eczema, dermatitis, psoriasis, jock itch and diaper and poison ivy rashes with it, several cotton balls can also be saturated in this solution, the excess liquid squeezed out and then inserted into the rectum on hemorrhoids. Fresh pineapple or powdered guava leaves can be put on ringworm with good results.

Preventing Nausea

For those experiencing nausea while flying or traveling on a ship or train, or for pregnant women with morning sickness, an 8 oz. glass of canned pineapple or papaya juice diluted from concentrate may be just the ticket for ending their unsettling discomforts.

Dealing with Foot Fungus

One of the niftiest ways to cope with athlete's foot or fungus around the fingernails is just to soak the hands and feet in some canned pineapple each day for about an hour. Wipe dry and sprinkle with a little Kingsford cornstarch. Rub this all over the feet and in between the toes, as well as on the hands and fingers.

Stimulating Milk in Dry Breasts

An effective way of promoting mammary secretion in more or less dry breasts, appeared in the *Ceylon Medical Journal* (26:105). Coarsely chop one green papaya and add it to 2 cups of boiling apple cider vingar and 1 cup of water. Cover and simmer the same on low heat for half an hour. Remove and steep for an additional 15 minutes. Strain and take internally in 1 tbsp. doses five times a day or as needed.

A solid extract of the fruit of somewhat glutinous consistency can also be taken in place of the liquid extract. Thoroughly blend together one semi-ripe papaya cut into sections with seeds included and only enough water to make a thick purée. Use an electric blender for making this. A nursing mother should eat about 1 cup of this per day.

An alcoholic tincture can also be topically applied to the breasts if preferred. In a Mason quart fruit jar, soak half of a finely chopped green papaya and 4 finely chopped leaves in 2 cups of Jamaican rum for 10 days, being sure to shake the container a couple of times each day. Strain and take 1 tsp. three times daily, or as required.

There will be an abundant stimulation of milk production in most normal breasts. And even in the virgin breast a transient, limpid fluid will soon be evident.

Cooking in Paradise

Tropical fruits add certain distinctive flavors to otherwise dull dishes and really help to liven up so-so meals. Additionally they shorten both the cooking time and digestion of some foods, as recalled by noted research chemist, Albert Y. Leung:

> It is common knowledge among peoples of the tropics that cooking meat with a piece of green papaya or wrapped in papaya leaf will make it tender faster.

Guava Fruit Slaw

Needed: 3 cups shredded cabbage; 1 peeled and sectioned orange; 1 cup halved, seedless red grapes; ½ cup sliced celery; one 8 oz. carton orange yogurt; 1 small guava, chopped and with seeds removed. In a large salad bowl combine cabbage, orange sections, grapes and celery. For dressing stir together yogurt and guava. Spread dressing over cabbage mixture. Cover and chill. Just before serving, toss salad gently. Serve on cabbage-lined plates, if desired. Makes 10 servings.

Mango Ice

Needed: 1 medium, very ripe mango; 2 tbsps. sugar; 1 egg white; 1 tbsp. sugar. Peel mango and cut flesh from seed. Cut mango into chunks. In a blender combine mango pieces and the 2 tbsps. sugar; cover and blend till nearly smooth. Set aside.

In a small mixer bowl beat egg white and the 1 tbsp. sugar with an electric mixer on medium speed till stiff peaks form. Lighten mango mixture by stirring in some of the egg white mixture. Fold mango mixture into remaining egg white mixture. Pour into an 8×4×2-in. loaf pan. Cover surface with clear plastic wrap. Freeze about 3 hours or till firm. Scoop mixture with a small ice cream scoop or melon baller into dessert dishes. Makes 4 servings.

Both the guava fruit slaw and the mango ice recipes may be found in Better Homes & Gardens' *Fresh Fruit and Vegetable Recipes* and *Eating Healthy Cook Book,* which may be obtained from your local book store or directly from the publisher (see Appendix). I'm grateful to the publisher for their use here.

Baked Papaya Custard

This recipe is one of the favorites of restaurateur and chef, LaMont Burns of Encinitas, California, and may be found in his book, *Down Home Southern Cooking* (see Appendix). I'm grateful to his publisher, Doubleday & Co., Inc., for its use here.

Needed: 4 cups papaya pulp; 1 cup shredded coconut meat; 1 orange (pulp, juice and grated rind); 4 eggs; 4 cups milk; 1 cup sugar. Preheat oven to 350° F. Arrange papaya, coconut and orange in baking dish. Make a custard by beating together the eggs, milk and sugar. Pour over the papaya. Insert knife in center of custard. If it comes out clean, it is done. If any of the milk clings to knife, bake longer. Serves 4–6.

Pineapple-Almond Turkey Salad

Needed: 1 pineapple; 2 cups cooked, diced turkey (or chicken); ½ cup Italian dressing; 1 tbsp. soy sauce; ½ cup toasted, slivered almonds; 1 chopped green onion (including stem); 2 thinly sliced celery ribs; ½ cup seedless grapes.

Cut pineapple into halves or quarters, lengthwise. Remove fruit, leaving a half-inch of shell. Drain shells on paper towels. Cut fruit into small chunks. Set aside 1 cupful for salad. Refrigerate remaining fruit to use in another recipe. Combine turkey, dressing, soy sauce, almonds, onion, celery, the reserved pineapple and grapes. Toss gently to combine, making sure all ingredients are coated with dressing. Divide equally among pineapple shells. Chill for 1 hour. Serves 4.

Tropical Fruit Cocktail for Getting Well

A rather health-minded friend of mine who lives in the Jewish section of Brooklyn, has come up with a simple combination of fruit juices for getting well. Joel Bree insists that "this stuff is great for getting you or the kids well again after your family has been hit pretty hard with the flu."

First, take two medium oranges and ream the juice out of them by hand on a glass juicer. Next peel close to the skin one medium-sized, ripe pineapple, and scrub but do *not* peel one ripe papaya. Run these through a juice extractor. Then mix these two juices with the hand-reamed orange juice and refrigerate. It keeps about two days before some more needs to be made. Drink this in the morning and early afternoon as much as you want.

"Then wash but do *not* peel two large red apples. Cut them up and run through the extractor, core, seeds, skin and all. Do the same with an equal volume of black grapes, seeds and all. Mix the two together good. Drink this from midafternoon on into the evening as much as you want. I think anyone will agree after trying this regimen that these different juices really help to flush poisons out of the body, while giving you some badly needed energy and bounce at the same time.

TULIPS (See ORNAMENTAL PLANTS)

TURMERIC (*Curcuma longa* or *C. domestica*)

Brief Description

A perennial herb of the ginger family with a thick rhizome from which arise large, oblong and long-petioled leaves. Turmeric grows to almost a yard high and is extensively cultivated in India, China, Indonesia, Jamaica, Haiti, Philippines and other tropical countries. The part used is the cured (boiled, cleaned and sun-dried) and polished rhizome. India is the major producer of turmeric. This spice is the major ingredient of curry powder and is also used in prepared mustard.

Paste for Skin Ailments

In Samoa, natives have used the powdered rhizome to treat skin ulcers, heal the navel of newborn children, get rid of pimples and relieve the pain and itching of dermatitis, eczema and psoriasis. In some cases, such as with diaper rash, the powdered rhizome is just sprinkled into the hand and then rubbed on the baby's skin. In other instances, however, some turmeric is mixed with a little coconut oil and gently applied to more severe inflammations.

In India and China, a little powdered turmeric is mixed with the juice from half a squeezed lime and a little water to make a smooth, even paste, which then is put directly onto herpes lesions, leprosy sores, measles, mumps, chickenpox and so forth with excellent results. Several crushed zinc tablets (50 mg. each) may also be added if desired. The same paste works well for snakebites insect stings and ringworm, too.

Curing Ear and Eye Discharges

Among some Ayurvedic practitioners in India, it still is a common custom to use a piece of clean cloth soaked in turmeric solution for wiping away discharges of acute conjunctivitis and ophthalmia. And a little powdered turmeric is sometimes mixed with an equal amount of baking soda and then a tiny portion put into the outer ear to help dry up any fluid discharges.

Stops Bleeding During Pregnancy

According to the *Philippine Journal of Nursing* (50:95), a decoction of turmeric followed by 3 glasses of water is very helpful for alleviating any bleeding experienced during pregnancy. And when combined with eggplant seems to be even more beneficial for this and healing wounds. Early pregnancy bleeding usually denotes threatened abortion and should, therefore, be taken quite seriously.

This remedy may be adapted for American households. In 1 pint of boiling water, simmer 1 cup of diced eggplant on low heat for 45 minutes, covered. Strain into another pan and add ½ tsp. of powdered turmeric. Cover again and steep until this liquid becomes lukewarm. Strain through several layers of gauze and drink 1 cup at that time. Repeat this process each day for as long as needed to stop bleeding.

Relieving Sprains, Fractures and Arthritis

Turmeric has manifested remarkable anti-inflammatory properties by inhibiting induced edema and subacute arthritis in rats and mice. These positive results are comparable to the same effects achieved by popular anti-inflammatory drugs like hydrocortisone acetate and phenylbutazone. Two half teaspoonfuls taken morning and evening in juice can help somewhat.

Additional relief may be obtained for this disease, contusions, sprains and fractures by mixing together 2 tbsps. turmeric with 1 tbsp. lime juice and just enough boiling water to make a nice, smooth, warm paste. This can then be applied directly to the area of swelling and pain, and then covered with some plastic food wrap to retain the heat and moisture longer. The consistency of the paste should be similar to that of creamy peanut butter so that it can be spread on the skin easily.

Counteracts Liver Fat

Turmeric is good at lowering serum cholesterol levels and preventing fatty accumulations in and around the liver. Rats fed on diets containing 10% fat colored with turmeric, showed virtually no fat buildup around the liver as did other rodents on the same diet but without the benefit of this spice. It works twice as good when combined with some cooked eggplant. Mix 3/4 tsp. turmeric with 2 tbsps. cooked, mashed eggplant and 1½ tbsps. boiling water until smooth. This can then be spread on a piece of rye or whole wheat bread and eaten following a meal of fatty foods to protect the liver.

Turmeric appears to be of definite value in the treatment of certain forms of cancer. Not so much from a curative aspect as from arresting the further progress of them, *if* it's taken in the *early* stages of cancer development. For instance, the *Journal of Ethnopharmacology* (7:95–109) for 1983 noted that several constituents in this spice have proven to be very active against cervical cancer, but *only in the early stages.*

These same active components (curcumol and curdione) displayed strong cytotoxic effects against Dalton's lymphoma cells *in the beginning* stages of development. This research was conducted in India, according to *Cancer Letters* (29:197–202) for 1985. And *Nutrition & Cancer* for July-Sept. 1986 stated that powdered turmeric is able to prevent cell mutations from occurring when certain types of aggravating food are consumed. Scientists working at the Tata Memorial Cancer Research Institute in Bombay, India discovered that turmeric helps to offset the mutagenicity of hot chili peppers and related dietary mutagens. Which seems to suggest that whenever anything this hot or spicy is consumed, some turmeric ought to be taken along with it as a good preventative measure.

Inhibits Gas

In another Indian experiment, some rats were fed a particular diet intended to produce intestinal gas. But when turmeric was added later on, further gas production ceased altogether, this being due to the yellow-orange pigment present called curcumin. It's advisable to take ½-1 tsp. of turmeric in a cup of warm water to help relieve heartburn and indigestion discomforts.

Increasing Shelf Life of Food

Recent studies from Japan have confirmed that spices can increase shelf life of oils and fats. Turmeric and ginger, among other spices, showed significant anti-oxidant activity when they were added to olive, soybean or sesame oils. Interesting applications of turmeric have been found in extending the refrigerated storage life of seafoods. Since turmeric is used popularly with most fish preparations, the effect of a dip treatment in turmeric, or turmeric with salt, each at 5% level for 15–30 minutes was studied by one group of scientists.

Control shrimp only had a shelf life of 13 days, developing black spots and fishy decomposition odor. But by dipping the shrimp in a turmeric plus salt dip solution, the shelf life increased another week. And when a combination of spice-salt dip plus irradiation was employed, shelf life increased to 42 days.

Colorful Dishes

Turmeric really adds color to otherwise dull-looking dishes. Plain rice can suddenly take on a nice golden hue when a dash of this spice is added in the final cooking process.

Making Your Own Curry Powder

Needed: 1 tbsp. ground coriander seeds; ½ tsp. ground mustard seeds; ½ tsp. ground cumin seeds; ½ tsp. ground turmeric; ¼ tsp. ground ginger; ¼ tsp. cayenne pepper. Combine all ingredients in a bowl and mix thoroughly. Transfer to an airtight jar and store in a cool place. Curry powder often accompanies fish, lamb, poultry, some salads, lentil soup, stews, and a number of other Far Eastern dishes.

Curries in Asia vary, but often contain onion, garlic, salt and usually a souring agent such as tamarind, lime, unripe mango or other sour fruit as well as other flavors derived from mustard, coconut, lemon grass, and so forth. Using any of these with your curry powder will definitely accent the taste of any meal prepared.

TURNIP (See RUTABAGA.)

UVA URSI (*Arctostaphylos uva-ursi*)

Brief Description

Uva ursi or bearberry is a small, evergreen shrub found in the northern U.S. and in Europe, especially in dry, sandy or gravelly soils. A single long, fibrous main root sends out several prostrate or buried stems from which grow erect, branching stems 4–6 inches high. The bark is dark brown or slightly reddish. The small leathery obovate to spatulate leaves are rounded at the apex, ½-1 inch long, and slightly rolled down at the edges. Fall is the best time to pick the leaves.

Remedies Bladder Inflammation

Uva ursi is remarkable for reducing accumulations of uric acid in the body. The herb also relieves the extreme pain accompanying kidney and bladder stones and inflammation of the bladder itself. This is best accomplished by soaking a handful of fresh leaves in enough brandy to cover for one week, after which 1 tbsp. of these leaves, chopped or cut, are then simmered in 1 cup of boiling water for 20 minutes. Then before drinking when lukewarm, add a teaspoon of the brandy solution in which the leaves had been soaked to each cup of tea consumed.

V

VALERIAN (*Valeriana officinalis*)

Brief Description

Common valerian is a perennial plant, about 2–4 feet high, which has escaped from cultivation to inhabit roadsides and thickets from New England south to New Jersey and west to Ohio. It is also very common all over Europe. The yellow-brown, tuberous rootstock produces a hollow, angular, furrowed stem with deeply dissected leaves each bearing 7–10 pairs of lance-shaped leaflets. The resulting smell of the dried, powdered rootstock is reminiscent of dirty socks or unwashed underwear.

Various constituents within the root account for the peculiar smell and the strong sedative properties. The butyl isovalerate present has been used in a synthetic, fermented egg product to attract coyotes and repel deer, while eremophilene has also been detected in ripe African mangoes. The valepotriates exert strong tranquilizing actions on the central nervous system.

Nature's Tranquilizer

Various Russian clinical journals indicate that valerian root has been successfully used throughout the Soviet Union for treating hysteria, high blood pressure, backache and occasional migraine headaches. Sometimes the tea, made by steeping 1½ tbsps. of dried root in 1 pint of boiling water for 30 mins., was administered 1–2 cups daily. On other occasions, 2 tablets were prescribed twice or three times daily. The same amount also applies for taking capsules of this root by consumers in America. Valerian may be obtained from local health food stores under the Nature's Way label.

It is the valepotriates within valerian root which exert a profound sedative effect upon the central nervous system. Once the root is ingested, these compounds attach themselves to individual receptor sites within portions of the brain, spine, and nervous system, where they help to remove stress and tension.

VANILLA (*Vanilla planifolia*)

Brief Description

Liquid vanilla flavoring is obtained from the fully grown but unripe pods or beans found on large green-stemmed perennial herbaceous vines growing wild and extensively cultivated throughout the tropics (Mexico, Malagasy Republic, Comoros Islands, Tahiti, Indonesia, Seychelles, Tanzania and Uganda, among others). Pollination is all done artificially, except in Mexico where it's partly performed artificially and partly by certain hummingbirds and butterflies not found anywhere else in the world. Because of the high price of vanilla and the low cost of vanillin, vanilla extracts have been extensively adulterated. Vanillin is the major flavor component with over 150 other aroma chemicals being present as well.

Sexual Stimulant

In various Central and South American countries such as Mexico, Argentina and Venezuela an alcoholic extract of the dried pods is taken for increasing amorous desires. Generally 4–6 pods are steeped in 2 cups of tequila or imported cognac for 21 days in a well-stoppered flask or glass container of some kind. The bottle is shaken several times each day during this period of time. The tincture is then taken in doses of 10–20 drops 2–3 times a day, usually at night.

Calms Hysteria

Pure vanilla flavor fluid extract may be used to help calm hysteria and related emotional traumas. The best manner for successfully accomplishing this is to soak one or two cotton balls completely with the vanilla extract, lightly squeezing out any unnecessary excess fluid before placing them beneath the tongue, one on either side of that vertical fold which elevates the tongue as needed.

By positioning each cotton ball thusly, it permits the vanilla to slowly penetrate the smallest of the salivary glands called the sublingual gland. The vanilla then travels through the tiny blood vessels which empty into the sublingual and submental arteries. These last two arteries, in turn, hook up directly with the much larger internal jugular vein and the external and internal carotid arteries. Now the internal jugular vein and the internal carotid artery both supply blood directly to the brain, which suggests that this is the route by which vanilla travels in order to reach that part of the brain responsive to its calming effects in episodes of hysteria.

VIOLET (See ORNAMENTAL FLOWERS.)

VITAMIN SUPPLEMENTS

Clinical nutritionists generally agree that the majority of our vitamins, minerals, amino acids, and enzymes ought to come from a well-balanced diet that includes items from each of the four major food groups. However, this isn't always practical, which necessitates the use of food supplements occasionally.

From a number of health practitioners I've spoken with here and in Canada, they all felt that one of the very best line of supplements they've recommended without any hesitation was manufactured by a Vancouver, Canada vitamin company called Quest Vitamin Supplies Ltd. Among some of their favorite supplements made by this firm are a superb amino acid complex, a nice 25,000 I.U. beta carotene, a strong citrus bioflavonoid (1000 mg.), an effective mega-capsule antioxidant formula, organic germanium, two super once-a-day and super-stress multi-vitamin formulas, a vitamin A and D formula and mega B-complex and C that are both time-released (see Appendix).

W

WALNUT (See NUTS.)

WATERCRESS (*Nasturtium officinale*)

Brief Description

Watercress is a perennial plant which thrives in clear, cold water and is found in ditches and streams everywhere. It's cultivated for its leaves, which are principally used as salad greens or garnishes. Connected to a creeping rootstock, the hollow, branching stem, 1–2 feet in length, generally extends with its leaves above the water. The smooth, somewhat fleshy, dark green leaves are odd-pinnate with 1–4 pairs of small, oblong or roundish leaflets.

Healing Mouth Sores

One of the most popular remedies among Chinese residing in Hong Kong and Canton, China is a special watercress soup used to treat canker sores on the tongue or lips, blisters in the mouth, swollen gums, bad teeth and foul breath. There is no specific amounts called for, but generally for one person, about ½ lb. each of cut watercress and chopped carrots are cooked in 2 qts. of water. The liquid is boiled down slowly to 1/3 or ¼ of the original fluid volume and then the soup is consumed with the vegetables intact. It's also good for hot flashes when consumed cold.

Relieves Headaches

Watercress forms the basis of an excellent remedy for headaches brought on by some kind of sickness or general nervousness. A handful of watercress, having been first washed thoroughly, is then put into a clean quart fruit jar and 2 cups of boiling apple cider vinegar added. After the solution becomes cold several hours later, it is strained and rebottled for use later on. When the headache occurs, a clean handkerchief should be dipped in the vinegar, wrung out and laid over the eyebrows and forehead. A wash cloth may also be used in place of a hanky.

Soothes Skin Ailments

An old and effective cure for eczema and dermatitis consisted of an infusion of watercress. A large panful should be thoroughly washed and put into a stainless steel saucepan that has just enough cold water added to cover the cress with. Bring this to a boil, then reduce heat and simmer slowly until quite tender. Strain through muslin cloth or several layers of gauze material and refrigerate.

The afflicted part should be bathed with this infusion often. It's better to use a piece of soft linen for this purpose. This infusion is excellent for roughness of the skin due to frequent exposure to the wind, sun and cold weather.

Diuretic and Expectorant

Watercress tea or juice is valuable for eliminating accumulated fluids in body tissue such as in gout and for clearing mucus congestion from the lungs. To make the tea steep 1 tbsp. chopped fresh cress in 1 cup boiling water for 20 minutes, then strain and drink. Fresh juice can be easily obtained from an electric juicer, but should be combined with some carrot or tomato juice before drinking.

Watercress Soup

Needed: 1 qt. chicken stock; 1 tbsp. honey; ½ tbsp. blackstrap molasses; pinch of kelp; 1 bunch watercress; water to cover stems; pinch of cardamon.

Heat stock and season with honey, molasses, kelp and cardamom. Before untying the bunch of purchased watercress, cut off stems. Wash stems and boil for about 10 minutes. Drain and add the cooking water to the stock. Cooked stems by themselves can be eaten when seasoned with a little tamari soy sauce.

Wash tops of watercress (flowers) and add to boiling stock just before serving. Boil soup 3 minutes, no longer, as you don't want to lose the emerald green color. Be sure to cook uncovered after you add the watercress or it will darken. Yields 4 cups.

WHITE OAK (See NUTS-ACORN)

WILD OREGON GRAPE (*Berberis vulgaris* or *Mahonia aquifolium*)

Brief Description

This is an evergreen shrub found in mountain areas on wooded slopes below 7,000 feet from British Columbia to Utah, southward to Oregon and California. Although native to North America, it was introduced to Europe as a cultivated plant and has become naturalized. Its irregular, knotty rootstock has a brownish bark with yellow wood underneath. This yellow pigment is the antibiotic alkaloid, berberine—the same constituent found in goldenseal root. Its branched stems have 10 or more spiny, sessile leaflets adorning them. (NOTE: See GOLDENSEAL for more data on berberine.)

Inhibits Spinal Meningitis

One pharmaceutical study published a decade and a half ago demonstrated that berberine was even more potent against that species of bacteria (*Neisseria meningitidis*) which causes meningitis in the spine and brain than the antibiotic drug, chloramphenicol. Berberine also kills on contact a species of staph which infects stitches and other skin wounds, as well as *E. coli* and other infectious bacteria. Two to three capsules daily on an empty stomach is recommended. Or 1 cup of tea made by simmering 2 tbsps. of the rootstock in 1 pint of water for 7 minutes, then steeping for another 25 minutes, before straining and drinking. Infected wounds and herpes lesions can also be either dusted with the powder from some empty capsules or else frequently bathed with the tea.

Counteracts Scorpion Stings and Snakebites

The Ramah Navajo of northern Arizona use a strong solution of wild Oregon grape rootstock tea internally and compresses externally on the immediate site of injury to counteract the deadly effects of poisonous scorpion stings and deadly rattlesnake bites. The same tea has also been given immediately on an empty or evacuated stomach to those who've been bitten by a rabid animal or bat in 1-cup amounts 5–6 times daily until cured.

WINE (See GRAPES AND RAISINS)

WORMWOOD (*Artemisia absinthium*)

Brief Description

Wormwood is a shrubby perennial herb with grayish-white stems covered with fine silky hairs, and growing from 1–3 feet tall. The leaves are silky, hairy and glandular with small, resinous particles and yellowish-green in color. The plant emits an aromatic odor and yields a spicy, somewhat bitter taste. It's native to Europe, northern Africa and western Asia, but now extensively cultivated.

Parts used are the leaves and flowering tops (fresh and dried), harvested just before or during flowering. Wormwood has been used in the manufacture of vermouth. Sweet wormwood, another species (*A. annua*) is often grown as an ornamental, but contains an essential oil that has strong antifungal and antibacterial activities.

Overpowering Relief for Pain

The team of Simon, Chadwick and Craker in their *Herbs—An Indexed Bibliography* (1971–1980) mention that "wormwood has been used as a pain reliever for women during labor and against tumors and cancers." An alcoholic tincture of the same applied externally often has a profound effect in relieving the soreness of aching muscles, the hurt accompanying swollen, arthritic joints, and the terrific pain felt with a bad sprain, dislocated shoulder/knee or fractured bone.

The following episode was related by the eldest son of the Mormon prophet, Joseph Smith, Jr. The prophet's son was a teenager residing in Nauvoo, Illinois at the time he had this experience with wormwood.

> Our carriage had stopped by the roadside for lunch and to rest the horses. Upon getting back into my seat after the brief interval, I thoughtlessly put my hand around one of the carriage posts, and as the driver closed the door, two of my fingers were pretty badly crushed.
>
> The wounds bled freely and Mother (Emma Smith) bound them up with some cloths from her bag, and we traveled on. My fingers

> became very painful, and after awhile we stopped at a farmhouse. Mother unwrapped them, soaking the temporary dressing off with warm water and rewrapped them with fresh cloths. Taking from her trunk a little bottle of whiskey and wormwood, she turned the tips of my fingers upward, and poured the liquid upon them, into the dressings—at which, for the first time in my life I promptly fainted! It seemed as if she had poured the strong medicine directly upon my heart, so sharply it stung and so quick was its circulatory effect.
>
> When I returned to consciousness I was lying on a lounge against the wall and Mother was bathing my face most solicitously. I soon recovered and we proceeded on our journey, reaching home in good time and without further mishap.

To make an effective tincture for relieving excruciating pain, combine 1½ cups of finely cut herb or else 8 tbsps. of the powdered herb in 2 cups of Jim Beam Whiskey. Shake the jar daily, allowing the wormwood to extract for 11 days. Let the herbs settle and then pour off the tincture, straining out the powder through a fine cloth or paper coffee filter. Rebottle and seal with a tight lid until needed. Store in a cool, dry place. When using this tincture to relieve external pain, remember that because of its *strong potency* a little bit goes a long way! Wormwood oil used externally can relieve pain, too.

Destroys Intestinal Parasites

The wisdom of the ancients often holds up under modern scientific testing. A case in point has to do with a certain passage written in the *Zhou Hou Bei Ji Fang* (*A Handbook of Prescriptions for Emergencies*) by an herbalist named Ge Hong who lived to be 110 years old (231–341 A.D.): "Take a handful of sweet wormwood, soak it in a Sheng (about 1 liter) of water, squeeze out the juice and drink it all for malaria."

Now a researcher from the Institute of Chinese Materia Medica of the China Academy of Traditional Chinese Medicine, who had been perusing ancient medical texts in search of new antimalarial drugs, decided to find out if soaking this wormwood had been done to avoid the loss of antimalarial properties by boiling or brewing it instead. She and her colleagues not only proved this to be a fact, but also were able to actually test the herb on humans afflicted with the malaria parasites. The clinical results turned out to be very good.

Just recently chemists from the Division of Experimental Therapeutics, part of the Walter Reed Army Institute of Research in Washington, D.C., have begun to conduct their own lengthy investigations into sweet wormwood's ability to reduce fevers by killing intestinal parasites causing them.

The previously mentioned tincture may be used here for internal purposes. Using an eye-dropper, put 10 drops of tincture in with 1 tsp. of dark honey or blackstrap molasses. Mix good before eating. The honey or molasses helps to alleviate the bitter taste of the tincture.

Insect Repellant

Crush a handful of fresh wormwood leaves into a soggy pulp, then mix in with some apple cider vinegar. Next put a small amount of this wet mixture in a 6-inch square piece of gauze. Draw up the end corners together and tie at the top. Then rub the skin thoroughly with this to keep horseflies, mosquitoes and gnats away from you while outdoors. The same mixture can also be rubbed directly onto household pets to keep flies, fleas and ticks away from them.

Remedy for Jaundice and Hepatitis

A study published in a recent issue of *Planta Medica* (37:81–85) points out that species of wormwood have been employed on a clinical basis for the treatment of hepatitis and to protect the liver from lesions produced by the ingestion of harmful chemicals. Another journal (*Chem. Pharm. Bulletin* 31:352) noted that wormwood is an important remedy for treatment of jaundice and inflammation of the gallbladder (cholecystitis). A tea might prove useful in these instances. Bring 2 cups of water to a boil. Remove from the heat and add 4 tsp. leaves or tops. Cover and steep until slightly lukewarm. Drink in ½-cup amounts morning, noon and night on an empty stomach. Sweeten with a little pure maple syrup to allay some of the bitterness. Or take 2 capsules of the powder twice daily for these problems, but on an intermittent basis. Remember that *wormwood is an herbal drug,* as are goldenseal root, chaparral and some of the other medicinal herbs cited in this text. And *they should be used with care only when needed,* and not taken indiscriminately.

Y

YARROW (*Achillea millefolium*)

Brief Description

Yarrow is a perennial herb found the world over in waste places, fields, pastures, meadows and along railroad embankments and highways where it should never be picked on account of the chemical spraying that's routinely done to keep the weeds down. The simple stem bears aromatic bipinnately parted and dissected leaves, giving a lacy appearance. The plant can grow up to a yard high, yielding pretty flower heads with white rays and yellow (turning to brown) disks in them. The light brown, creeping rootstock produces a round, smooth, pithy stem that branches near the top.

Extremely Useful for Inflammation

One of the most remarkable studies I've ever run across concerns yarrow's great ability to reduce tissue and joint inflammation in everything from wounds and edema to gout and arthritis.

The report which appeared in the August 1969 *Journal of Pharmaceutical Sciences*, explained in clear detail that a number of closely related protein-carbohydrate complexes or glycoproteins within the yarrow plant usually accumulate at the site of inflammation and remain there while injured tissue is being repaired. In one experiment a number of Swiss-Webster female mice were injected with a substance designed to induce swelling in their left foot pads. Later half of the group were injected with yarrow fractions, which reduced inflammation by 35% as compared with the untreated group.

Yarrow can be utilized in a variety of ways to reduce all manner of inflammation very nicely. One is a two-fold approach, incorporating the tea internally and a chamomile hand cream externally. Both the dried herb and the CamoCare Pain-Relieving Cream (see Appendix) may be obtained from local health food stores. Bring 2 cups of water to a boil and add 3 tbsp. of the dried yarrow. Cover, reduce heat and simmer 4 minutes. Remove and steep for 20 minutes. Drink 1 cup several times daily when cool. At the same time rub some CamoCare Pain-Relieving Cream on the external points of inflammation. Both seem to work well for this purpose.

Dennis Carman, who works for the Correlation Dept. of the LDS Church in Salt Lake City, related the following true incident to me sometime back:

> About 12 years ago, myself and some other adults took a number of 'problem youth' from various Mormon wards on a weekend camping trip in a remote part of Yellowstone Park. One teenage boy happened to be scouring a nearby meadow for some dead firewood. In the process of pulling back on a dry limb jutting up from a fallen tree, he accidentally fell against another protruding piece of sharp wood, causing it to go into the side of his leg quite a ways.
>
> We realized soon enough while attending to his injuries just how ill-prepared for this trip in terms of adequate first aid needs we really were. One adult picked a handful of yarrow and crushed it between two stones, then applied this poultice directly to the kid's wound. It was then bound up with adhesive tape. A couple of days later we were able to get the youngster to a hospital, where a doctor looked at his leg. In his opinion, nothing seemed wrong with the leg and so he released the boy immediately. We attributed this remarkable healing to yarrow.

Heals Sore Nipples, Chapped Hands, Stops Bleeding

Yarrow tea and chamomile hand cream may also be utilized effectively in the treatment of sore nipples, chapped hands, cracked lips, weathered skin, herpes sores, hives, hemmorhoids and minor bleeding.

Yarrow for Female Needs

Maria Treben, a renowned West German folk healer and popular herbalist, recounted her own experiences with yarrow some time ago for the benefit of a large audience:

> I cannot recommend yarrow enough for women. They could be spared many troubles if they just took yarrow tea from time to time! Be it a young girl with irregular menstruation or an older woman during menopause or already past it, for everyone young and old, it

is of importance to drink a cup of yarrow tea from time to time. It is very beneficial for the reproductive organs of women.

To make the tea, pour 4¼ cups of boiling water over 1½ heaping tbsps. of yarrow, cover and steep for awhile. The tea should be taken regularly. Or 100 grams (about 2 cups) of yarrow may be steeped in cold water overnight. The next day bring it to a boil, then add to just enough bath water in which the body can recline to soak the area of the kidneys.

Cataracts and Glaucoma Cured

Maria Treben insists that glaucoma is not an eye disorder, but rather a definite malfunction of the kidneys instead. A tea should be made, she observes, from equal parts of stinging nettle, yarrow, calendula and horsetail, and 2–3 cups consumed each day. Bring 1 qt. of water to a boil, add these herbs, cover and simmer for 7 minutes; then remove and steep another 45 minutes. Strain and sweeten with honey before drinking.

For cataracts, she advises brushing some Swedish Bitters across the eyelids frequently. There are various types of this herbal compound under different names at some but not all health food stores. An alternative to this that is just as effective calls for rubbing a little aloe gel obtained from a *fresh plant leaf* with an equal small amount of juicy latex gathered from a *fresh milkweed plant,* between your wet thumb and index finger until well mixed. This mixture is then gently brushed over the closed eyelids towards the corners of the eye, but *never* under any circumstances to be rubbed into the eyes direct! Although applied in this manner, they seem to be reasonably beneficial in helping cataracts and spots on the cornea to gradually disappear. Of course, as with anything, this may work better for some than for others.

YELLOW DOCK (*Rumex crispus*)

Brief Description

Yellow dock is a perennial plant considered by some to be a troublesome weed in many fields and waste places throughout Europe, the U.S. and southern Canada. Its spindle-shaped, yellow taproot sends up a smooth, rather slender stem, 1–3 feet high. Lanceolate to oblong-lanceolate in shape, the pointed light green leaves have predominantly wavy margins. The lower leaves are larger and longer-petioled than the upper are. The numerous pale green, drooping flowers are loosely whorled in panicled racemes. The seed is a pointed, three-angled and heart-shaped kind of nut.

The Ultimate Purifier

What more can be said about this wonderful herb that hasn't been stated already with other cleansing herbs scattered throughout this book? Suffice it to say, this remarkable herb root is a dandy blood purifier for just about any kind of eruptive disease that may come to mind.

To make a useful decoction of the same, just bring 1 qt. of water to a boil. Reduce the heat and add 1 cup of chopped, fresh or dried root, cover and simmer for 12 minutes. Remove and steep 1½ more hours. Strain, sweeten with honey and drink up to 4 cups a day, especially during a *short*-weekend, *mild*-food fast in which much of your nourishment is derived only from liquids.

Many different kinds of skin afflictions may also be judiciously bathed with this same tea, when it's cool, to relieve some of the itching and inflammation. Equal parts of this root and sage make a great tea to drink while using a sauna or sitting in a jacuzzi (those with hypertension, however, should avoid excess heat like this).

A cup of warm tea improves digestion when consuming a particularly heavy meal or rich foods. Yellow dock tea also stimulates the liver and colon as well.

Comforts Emphysema

Yellow dock syrup is a nice, little remedy for relieving upper respiratory problems, especially emphysema it seems. A half-pound of the root is boiled in a pint of *distilled* water until the liquid is reduced to a mere cupful. Strain and discard the spent root, and to the liquid add ½ cup dark honey, ½ cup blackstrap molasses and 1 tbsp. pure maple syrup, then a dash of genuine vanilla flavor. Mix everything together by hand until you have an even syrup. Take 1 tsp. at a time for bronchitis, asthma and the like to stop tickling sensations in the throat or lungs.

Strengthens Eyes in Night Blindness

The late plant forager, Euell Gibbons, asserted that "yellow dock greens are richer in vitamin A than carrots are." He believed that by eating many helpings of these greens, one could definitely improve his or her night vision, particularly if it had become somewhat dim with age.

Gibbons' Greens

Gibbons stated that the best time for collecting dock greens was either in the early Spring or the late Winter just after the first or second frost had come. A real treat for him was to combine equal parts of fresh dock greens and watercress in a little water and cook for about 15 minutes. Then the greens were drained, chopped and seasoned with kelp, butter, minced raw Bermuda onion, some crumbled crisp bacon, thin slices of a hard-cooked egg and a dash of lime juice (something I've added for good measure).

"This will make a hearty supper dish that I would enjoy for taste alone," he once confessed, "even if it weren't fairly bulging with all those healthful vitamins and minerals. A little apple cider vinegar, he believed, also adds zest to dock greens.

Because dock is a large plant and grows in great patches, one gathering can furnish many meals. Cook dock alone or mix it with other Spring greens. It doesn't cook down much, so it's particularly good for canning—just follow standard directions for canning greens. It also freezes well. Enclose it, after blanching in boiling water for a couple of minutes, in plastic bags, then wrap it again in freezer paper to keep it from turning dark in your freezer later on.

YOHIMBINE (*Corynanthe yohimbe*)

SCHIZANDRA FRUIT (*Schizandra chenensis*)

GINKGO (*Ginkgo biloba*)

Brief Descriptions

These three are included together because of their remarkable sexual rejuvenating properties, particularly when used in conjunction with each other.

Yohimbine is the popularized name of a real tongue-twisting chemical known officially as 17 alpha-hydroxyyohimban-16 alpha-carboxylic acid methylester. Yet it has clinically verified aphrodisiac effects to it and is obtained from the bark of an African evergreen by the same name and growing in Cameroon, West Africa.

Schizandra is an aromatic, woody vine with alternate, petiolate and oblong-obovoid leaves. The flowers adorning it may be either pink or white. The nourishing fruit is a collection of berry-like, ripened carpels in a short, spike-like, drooping head that's fleshy but not splitting open when ripened.

Ginkgo happens to be the only living representative left of a once vast order of tall, resinous trees widely distributed throughout the Mesozoic Era. The drupe-like fruit yields yellow seeds when it matures and acquires a rather foul-smelling odor to it. The outer fleshy portion of the fruit provokes a very warm sensation to the skin when brought in contact with it. The leaves also are used as well.

Both schizandra and ginko are very popular in Chinese folk medicine for a *wide variety* of health complaints, especially sexual frigidity.

Ultimate Sexual Rejuvenaters

During a 1984 stopover visit I made in Singapore on my way to Indonesia, I had the good fortune of being introduced to an old Chinese herb doctor by the name of Hsü Ching-tso. Through an acquaintance who spoke both languages fairly well, I was able to obtain a very old sexual rejuvenating formula which had been in this man's family for at least 17 generations.

What had attracted me to this old gent were the wide number of claims I had heard from many others (especially men) concerning the amazing effectiveness of his simple formula. I learned that his only three ingredients were yohimbine bark, dried schizandra berries, and ginkgo leaves and seeds.

Now I already knew about the medical success of yohimbine as reported in the August, 1984 issue of *Science.* Therein scientists from Stanford University discovered to their astonishment that when impotent male rats were given yohimbine, they went absolutely wild and mounted female rodents up to 45 times in less than 15 minutes—about twice as often as they normally would. Even when castrated rats were given a shot of the stuff, they climbed longingly on females.

And I also was aware of the in-depth study on yohimbine published in Volume 35 of *Pharmacological Reviews* concerning its fantastic erection-promoting ability when sexual desires were present in men, but when their penile veins weren't up to much contracting.

So the old fellow's inclusion of one-third yohimbine bark in his powerful sexual stimulant obviously made sense. I also knew about the warm, sexual energies attributed to schizandra berries by ancient Chinese herbalists. But I couldn't for the life of me figure out why he included one-third ginkgo leaves and seeds along with his other one-third schizandra fruit. It was explained to me by this patient, old fellow that ginkgo helped to increase the vital "life energies" passing through the brain. He said it wasn't enough to lift a man's copulating organ—holding up a drooping, bony finger that quickly became firm and elevated as he spoke—but it was also necessary to raise his *mental* powers of sex as well. This, he believed, is what ginkgo essentially accomplished with the mind, while the other two ingredients worked on the reproductive organs themselves.

He made and sold this concoction in tablet form, instructing those who purchased the same to take 6–8 tablets at a time at least 30 minutes before sexual activities commenced. In recommending this same formula to different men here in the states who were unable to buy it directly from him, I soon found that an alcoholic tincture of the yohimbine worked better than when taken in capsule form with the other two ingredients.

Mix 6 ounces of powdered yohimbine bark with ¾ of a pint of brandy. Shake daily, allowing the mixture to set for about 12 days. Strain and bottle. Then when taking approximately 5 capsules of Nature's Way Ginkgold and Nature's Way Schizandra Fruit with adequate water, follow taking these capsules by squirting about a dozen drops of mixture beneath the tongue and allowing it to enter the bloodstream sublingually. All of these herbs may be obtained at most local health food stores or nutrition centers.

YUCCA (*Yucca* species)

Brief Description

This acclaimed "Guardian of the Desert" stands silently silhouetted against an azure-blue sky, its many sharp, lance-like leaves assuming a defensive position of sorts against all manner of unwanted intruders. And as in the imagination of the naturalist's mind, so too does this ubiquitous plant perform similar service when it comes to protecting our health. Yuccas can be either tall trees ranging in heights from 15 to 60 feet as it were (Mojave yucca and the Joshua tree), or much humbler looking specimens averaging no more than a couple of yards in height.

Potential Cancer Remedy

A team of scientists working at the AMC Cancer Research Center and Hospital in Lakewood, Colorado several years ago, isolated a strong anti-tumor factor from *fresh* yucca flowers, which disappears when the flower wilts or dries. In mice with B16 melanoma, a crude extract of yucca flowers caused a 50–100% increase in their lifespan, as mentioned in *Growth* (42:213–23) for 1978.

Similar findings were also confirmed by Dr. Kanematsu Sugiura of the prestigious Sloan-Kettering Cancer Research Institute in New York City. There the partially purified extract of yucca flowers inhibited almost completely both sarcoma 180 and Ehrlich carcinoma. Also Dr. Jonathan L. Hartwell, formerly with the Cancer Chemotherapy National Service Center, reported in the scientific press that extracts of certain yucca flowers *strongly* inhibited Lewis lung mouse tumor and the Friend virus leukemia in mice by some 70%. This data appeared in a back issue (1968) of *Oncology* (22:57), a well-respected cancer research journal.

What all of this means then to those of us interested in finding natural solutions to the problems of cancer, is that the fresh blossoms or flowers of different yucca species may be picked and *immediately* be included in a carrot-mixed greens juice concoction whipped up in a food blender. Not that yucca alone will do the job, but it's merely another good weapon in the natural arsenal to be used in combating this dreaded disease.

Arthritis Under Attack

During the mid-1970s Drs. Bernard A. Bellew and Robert Bingham conducted studies with 101 arthritic patients, giving half yucca tablets and the other half lookalike placebos. Of the 50 receiving an average of 4 yucca tablets daily, 61% reported feeling less pain, stiffness and swelling in their arthritis than did those on the placebo. These tests were conducted at the National Arthritis Medical Clinic in Desert Hot Springs, California, and later published in *Journal of Applied Nutrition* (Fall 1975). Four capsules of Nature's Way yucca from any local health food store twice daily on an empty stomach is suggested.

Z

ZUCCHINI (See PUMPKIN, SQUASH AND GOURD.)

(See PUMPKIN, SQUASH AND GOURD.)

****

With the zucchini comes the close of this informative work. Of all the some two dozen odd books on health, nutrition and herbs that I've penned over the years, I believe that this project has been the most exciting, challenging and grandest undertaking I've ever attempted. Yet for me, it's also probably been the most personally satisfying because of the enormous amount of self-care data presented for the very first time on such a wide range of illnesses under one cover.

Nothing that I'm currently aware of even comes close to it. And I'm stating this more as an observed fact of truth than as a self-administered pat on the back.

Finally, let it be said that although we may never have the pleasure of meeting each other in this life, yet hopefully, some day you, the reader, and I, the author, will be able to meet together in another dimension where time stands still, peace abounds, love surrounds, health is for all and there are no more tomorrows—only an eternal period where the soul may finally rest and the spirit can be of good cheer!

Appendix

I. Herbal Products

ABKIT, Inc.
1375 N. Mountain Springs Pkwy
Springville, UT 84663
1-800-944-4365
- CamoCare Hand Cream
- CamoCare Pain-Relieving Cream
- CamoCare Throat Spray/Breath Freshener

Altra Health Products, Inc.
300 Main St.
Idaho City, ID 83631
1-800-423-4155
- Altra-Sil-X-Silica
- Can-Gest

Bio-Botanica, Inc.
75 Commerce Dr.
Happauge, NY 11788
1-800-645-5720
- St. Johnswort (Powdered)
- Sarsaparilla Root
- Yellow Dock Root

Great American Natural Products, Inc.
4121 16th Street North
St. Petersburg, FL 33703
1-800-323-4372
- Aqua-Vite
- Ginger-Up
- Herb Oil
- Herpes
- Kola Nut
- Herbalmune
- Sinese
- Super Energy

Health Valley Foods
700 Union St.
Montebello, CA 90640
1-213-724-2211
- Oat Bran Cereal

Indiana Botanic Gardens
POB 5
Hammond, IN 46325
1-219-947-4040

- Birch Bark
- Blue Cohosh
- Blessed Thistle
- Chaparral
- Cleavers
- Prickly Ash Bark
- Sarsaparilla Root
- Yellow Dock Root

Nature's Way Products, Inc.
1375 N. Mountain Springs Pkwy
Springville, UT 84663
1-800-962-8873

- Alfa-Max
- AKN Formula
- Bee Pollen
- BF & C Formula
- Black Cohosh
- Blessed Thistle
- Burdock Root
- Cranberry Fruit
- Efamol Evening Primrose Oil
- Ex-Stress Formula
- Fenugreek-Thyme Formula
- Fiber Cleanse
- Garlicon
- Ginkgold
- Gaur Gum
- Herbal Up
- HIGL Formula
- ImmunAid Formula
- Kava-Kava
- Kelp
- Marshmallow Root
- Milk Thistle Seed
- Myrrh
- Naturalax 3 Formula
- Rose Hips
- Schizandra Fruit
- Siberian Ginseng
- Slippery Elm
- Suma
- Valerian
- Yucca

Nu-World, Inc.
612 6th Ave. NW
Naperville, IL 60567
1-312-369-6819

- Amaranth

Old Amish Herbs
4121 16th St. N.
St. Petersburg, FL 33703
1-800-323-4372

- Cabbage Compound
- Calendula Dairy Salve
- Carrot Concoction
- Cohosh Two
- Concentrated Canberry Fomula
- Country Health Syrup
- FarmLax
- Fig Paste
- Night Nip
- Old Fashioned Rose Hips
- Super C
- Thistle Milk

Pines International, Inc.
1992 E. 1400 Rd
Lawrence, KS 66044
1-785-841-6016

- Beet Powder
- Wheat Grass (Tablet, Powdered, and Bulk)

Quest Vitamin Supplies
312-8495 Ontario Street
Vancouver, B. C.
CANADA V5X 3E8
1-877-265-2615

(NOTE: Although located in Canada, their excellent line of products are also available in the U. S. Write or call them for specific details.)

Amino Complex
Beta-Carotene
Citrus Bioflavonoids
Herbal Digestant (Q37 Formula)
Mega (Antioxidant) Capsules
Organic Germanium
Spice-Lax (Q-36 Formula)
Super Once-a-Day Vitamins
Super Stress
Vitamin A and D Formula
(Vitamin) Mega B-100: Timed Release
Vitamin C: Timed Release

II. Customized Herb Formulating

Many of today's excellent herbal formulas sold in health food stores and nutrition centers across the country are manufactured in mass quantities for public consumption. This obviously helps to keep the cost down, thereby making them more affordable for the average consumer.

However, in certain instances, herb formulas customized to particular health needs is more desirable, though not always economical. But some people, especially health practitioners, who may need specific formulas tailored to their patients' individual conditions, prefer this method of formulating over those which are manufactured in mass quantities.

For expert formulating and customized blending, please contact:

Custom-Made Formulas
P. O. Box 1623
Salt Lake City, UT 84110-1623

III. Additional Books By Dr. John Heinerman

Natural Remedies From Around The World
1-882330-88-9

Heinerman's Encyclopedia Of Anti-Aging Remedies
978-1-882330-95-9

Nature's Seven Wonder Medicines
1-882330-87-0

Natural Cures For Your Dog & Cat
1-882330-91-9

Donald I. Fine, Inc.
128 East 36th Street
New York, NY 10016
F. S. Goulart, *The Whole Meal Salad Book*

Doubleday & Co., Inc.
245 Park Avenue
New York, NY 10017
L. Burns, *Down Home Southern Cooking*

McGraw Hill Book Co.
1221 Avenue of the Americas
New York, NY 10020
J. D. Kirschmann, *Nutrition Almanac Cookbook*

Meredith Corp.
Locust at 17th
Des Moines, IA 50336
Better Homes & Gardens Eating Healthy Cookbook
Better Homes & Gardens Fresh Fruit & Vegetable Recipes
Better Homes & Gardens Cooking with Whole Grains

Paradise Farms
POB 436
Summerland, CA 93067
Guide to Cooking with Edible Flowers

Reader's Digest Assoc., Inc.
Pleasantville, NY 10570
Eat Better, Live Better

Rodale Press Book Division
Emmaus, PA 18049
Rodale Cookbook
M. Bricklin, S. Claessens, *Natural Healing Cookbook*

Simon & Schuster
1230 Avenue of the Americas
New York, NY 10020
M. Tierra, *The Way of Herbs*

St. Martin's Press
175 5th Avenue
New York, NY 10010
M. Kushi and A. Jack, *Diet for a Strong Heart*

Trado-Medic Books
102 Normal Avenue
Buffalo, NY 14213
J. Duke, *Culinary Herbs*

Vitality House International
3707 North Canyon Road/8-C
Provo, UT 84604
L. Gaunt, *Recipes to Lower Your Fat Thermostat*

Workman Publishing
New York, NY
B. J. Tatum, *Billy Joe Tatum's Wild Foods Cookbook and Field Guide*

IV. Miscellaneous

Regenerating Your Immune System with Foods and Herbs

A 12-hour audio cassette program (eight tapes) based entirely on a week-long symposium presented to several hundred participants in Salt Lake City in mid-January, 1988. The lengthy workshop was taught by Dr. John Heinerman. Considerable material was given and fully documented from the appropriate medical/scientific references. It is the first such lecture series of its kind taught by Dr. Heinerman to ever be recorded. The complete package retails for $39.95.

Mobiltape Co., Inc.
West Avenue Stanford
Bldg. 250, Suite 70
Valencia, CA. 91355

Controlling Immune Diseases Naturally

A 2-hour video cassette made of a special workshop given by Dr. John Heinerman at a major health convention in San Francisco at the end of April, 1988. A number of major immune diseases including AIDS, cancer, chronic fatigue syndrome (also known as mononucleosis or EBV), common cold, herpes, influenza, multiple sclerosis, staph infection, venereal disease and the like were covered in some detail. Simple step-by-step instructions for their effective management and treatment were included. Close to a hundred health-care professionals and some interested lay people were in attendance. NOTE: The information given on this video is considerably different from that contained in the cassette tape series cited above. The video retails for $29.95.

Anthropological Research Center
P. O. Box 11471
Salt Lake City, UT 84147
(801-521-8824)

Index

A

B

R

S

Y

Z